ROUTLEDGE LIBRARY EDITIONS:
DEVELOPMENT

TRADE AND DEVELOPING COUNTRIES

TRADE AND DEVELOPING COUNTRIES

KATHRYN MORTON

and

PETER TULLOCH

Volume 50

Routledge
Taylor & Francis Group
LONDON AND NEW YORK

First published in 1977

This edition first published in 2011
by Routledge
2 Park Square, Milton Park, Abingdon, Oxon, OX14 4RN

Simultaneously published in the USA and Canada
by Routledge
711 Third Avenue, New York, NY 10017

Routledge is an imprint of the Taylor & Francis Group, an informa business

First issued in paperback 2013

British Library Cataloguing in Publication Data
A catalogue record for this book is available from the British Library

ISBN 13: 978-0-415-58414-2 (Set)
eISBN 13: 978-0-203-84035-1 (Set)
ISBN 13: 978-0-415-59382-3 (Volume 50)
ISBN 13: 978-0-415-85173-2 (Volume 50 pbk)
eISBN 13: 978-0-203-83839-6 (Volume 50)

Publisher's Note

The publisher has gone to great lengths to ensure the quality of this reprint but points out that some imperfections in the original copies may be apparent.

Disclaimer

The publisher has made every effort to trace copyright holders and welcomes correspondence from those they have been unable to contact.

TRADE AND DEVELOPING COUNTRIES

KATHRYN MORTON and PETER TULLOCH

CROOM HELM LONDON

in association with

THE OVERSEAS DEVELOPMENT INSTITUTE

Croom Helm Ltd
2-10 St John's Road, London SW11

ISBN 0-85664-303-3

CONTENTS

ACKNOWLEDGEMENTS

In preparing this book, we have benefited from the help, advice and encouragement of a large number of people and to all of these we offer our thanks. We should like to give particular thanks to the members of the consultative committee, convened by ODI under the chairmanship of Robert Wood, who read and commented on our drafts; and to our former colleagues at ODI who provided help and support throughout the book's gestation. We alone, however, are responsible for any errors of fact remaining in the book and for the opinions expressed therein.

Finance for the preparation of this book was provided by Grindlays Bank Limited and the Ministry of Overseas Development, to whom we wish to record our thanks.

TRADE AND DEVELOPING COUNTRIES

1 TRADE AND DEVELOPMENT

INTRODUCTION

In this first chapter, we aim to do two things. The first is to look at some of the conflicting views on the role of trade in development, and consider the range of policy choices which follow from them for developing countries. The second is to provide a general picture of the developing countries' position in world trade at present as a background to the more detailed discussions in later chapters.

First, however, we must define our terms. What do we mean by 'development'? And what is a 'developing country'?

No precise definition of 'development' exists and there are many, sometimes conflicting, views of what is meant by the term. When we talk of 'development' here we refer to the economic aspects of a process of economic, social, political, and cultural change in a given society, i.e. *economic* development. Such development is not the same as economic growth – that is, an increase in total national income wealth – nor does economic development necessarily entail economic growth in any given period. Economic development involves structural changes: changes in patterns of employment and economic activity, changes in institutions and attitudes. That such changes are in some sense for the better is implicit in the word 'development'. In relation to developing countries, there is at least some broad agreement that for economic change to be 'for the better' – and hence to be regarded as 'development' – it should involve, besides an increase in national income, an increase in the material living standards of the majority of their people:

> The purpose of development is to raise the standard of living of the masses of the people in the poor countries as rapidly as is feasible – to provide secure jobs, adequate nutrition and health, clean water at hand, cheap transport, education for the children. The test of any (development) strategy is the extent to which it helps or hinders in meeting the basic needs of the majority of the people.[1]

We use this view of the development process in developing countries as a working definition of development.

An exact definition of a 'developing country' is equally difficult to reach. In practice, we have generally defined as 'developing' those countries so classified by such organisations as the United Nations, although we recognise that all the countries conventionally labelled as 'developing', 'under-developed', 'poor' or – as preferred here – 'less developed' are neither accurately nor uniquely described by such epithets. Nonetheless, despite their diversity, taken as a group they do tend to be differentiated in socio-economic terms from so-called developed countries.

Generally, the official lists of developing countries include all those countries in South and Central America including the Caribbean, all in Africa, bar South Africa, all in Asia, including the Middle East but bar Japan, and all in Oceania, bar New Zealand and Australia. Mainly for political reasons, some Communist countries in these regions – in particular China – are occasionally excluded from official lists although, aside from their chosen development strategy, they share many characteristics with other so-called 'developing countries'. In addition to the countries noted above, certain European countries – Malta, Cyprus, Greece, Spain, Portugal, Turkey, Yugoslavia, and Romania – are variously included in or excluded from official lists.

In historical terms, the most important shared characteristic of the so-called developing countries is that, while the 'developed' countries of the West underwent a process of widespread capitalist industrialisation, they did not. That is not to say they were untouched by the development of Western capitalism (or that such industrialisation is the necessary object of development). Virtually all present-day developing countries have been – some still are – colonies of Western industrial states while those that were not colonised tended to have similar economic, political, and cultural links with industrial countries to those developed under colonialism. These links have had and continue to have a major influence on the pattern of economic, political, and social activity in developing countries: for instance, the predominance of raw materials in their total output and exports, the predominance of their trade with developed countries, in particular with ex-colonial powers, and their reliance on Western capital and technology.

Viewed in the context of the world economy, the most salient characteristic of developing countries taken together is their relative poverty. More than 70 per cent of the world's population lives in developing countries. Yet developing country inhabitants consume less than 20 per cent of the world's output. Their average income per head is some $240 as compared with roughly $2,900 in developed countries.

There are, of course, many differences among developing countries, and the distinction between those called developing and those called developed is blurred at the edges. Some developing countries, for instance in the Middle East and Latin America, are nearly as rich as, or richer than, developed countries in terms of average incomes per head, while others like Chad and Ethiopia are extremely poor. Some, like India and Brazil, have developed sophisticated industrial sectors, and others, like Hong Kong and South Korea, earn most of their foreign exchange through the export of manufactured goods, while others, like the Gambia and Sudan, still rely almost exclusively on primary product exports. Some, like Taiwan and Brazil, have experienced rapid economic growth while others, like Niger and Senegal, have experienced scarcely any. Virtually all so-called developing countries, however, are differentiated from developed countries by the existence of widespread poverty – indicated, for instance, by high levels of illiteracy, malnutrition, and disease – within their borders. This in turn reflects the lack of economic development or its unevenness: the internal disparities in income, wealth, and productivity are marked in comparison with developed countries (in general, but note the North-South problem of Italy).

The role of international trade in the development process is a subject of controversy, and is an important issue in the debate between outward-looking and inward-looking, autarkic, strategies of development. A traditional Western view, based on classical economic theory and the experience of major industrial countries, is that international trade brings gains to a nation – whether rich or poor – that cannot be had in its absence, and that it can act as an important stimulus to growth. Some observers, while not contradicting this view, have agreed that such gains are unlikely to be significant among less developed countries (ldcs), *because* they are less developed and lack the responsiveness to the market opportunities and dynamic influences of international trade found in developed market economies, Others have argued that the market opportunities open to ldcs limit the possibility of gains from international trade. They point to the slow growth of export earnings from many primary commodities, the risks attendant in ldcs' current degree of specialisation in such exports, and the difficulties of obtaining access to overseas markets for a more diversified range of export products.

Such arguments, as we shall see, do not apply to all ldcs. Nor do they suggest that developing countries should seek to reduce their involvement in international trade in order to further development. Rather they suggest that the choice between an inward-looking or outward-looking development strategy should, so far as international trade is concerned, depend on the market opportunities, production capabilities, and prospects of the individual ldc. A more radical view suggests that international trade, or more specifically trade between rich and poor countries, is actually harmful to ldcs' development prospects. The unequal exchange thesis, for instance, suggests that such trade is carried out at the expense of poor countries. More usually, however, the view is supported by arguments relating to the adverse social, economic, and political repercussions on development which can result from poor countries' general involvement in the international economic system. The conclusion drawn from these sorts of arguments is that development will be best furthered by a strategy which increases the self-reliance of individual ldcs or groups of ldcs and reduces their economic links, including trade links, with developed countries. We examine some of these arguments below, beginning with a brief examination of the conventional case for international trade.

THE CASE FOR TRADE

Few, if any, countries can produce all the goods they need. Most, therefore, need to trade with others. Those which can come nearest to self-sufficiency are likely to be either very simple, subsistence economies, or at the other extreme to be countries which are very well endowed with the resources of manpower, land, skills, and capital which are needed to produce goods. In the first category might come Ethiopia (in a good crop year); in the second the United States and China.

Most ldcs certainly do not produce all the goods they need to develop and diversify their economies. They may need more food than they can produce to feed a rapidly growing population. If they want to develop industries or increase the productivity of agriculture, capital goods and raw materials, or new strains of seeds and fertilisers, may have to be imported. Clearly, these imports have to be paid for. Foreign investment and foreign aid can help. But they are unlikely to be enough. For many reasons – lack of skilled manpower, lack of 'infrastructure', small scale of domestic markets – foreign investors are unlikely to be very interested in ldcs, except where raw material resources exist or as a pre-emptive bid to keep competitors out (see Chapter 6). Foreign aid has historically been only a small part of the external resources ldcs have been able to use. So ldcs must, largely, depend on their own export earnings to acquire the means for raising production and incomes.

Stating the situation in this way, however, gives no guide as to how far a particular country should or can rely on foreign trade to provide the goods it needs. The decision to engage in international trade depends not only on the existence of needs that cannot be satisfied by domestic production but also on the possibility of exchanging domestically produced goods for foreign goods. If this possibility exists, the question then is how far a country should develop its own production capacity in response to the opportunities for buying and selling goods overseas: should it keep international trade to a minimum, should it aim to reduce or eliminate its need for imports, or should it aim to trade more, to specialise in production for overseas markets? Theories of international trade point to reasons why even a country which can produce all it needs domestically can benefit from participating in international trade and from specialising in response to the international market. The benefits postulated are of two kinds: direct, or static, gains and indirect, or dynamic, gains. The first bring once-and-for-all benefits to the trading nation, the second generate benefits over time as a result of the stimulus to increased productivity and economic growth resulting from international trade.

Direct Gains

Differences between countries, as between individuals, result in both absolute and relative differences in their productive efficiency. As long as there are relative differences between countries in the efficiency with which any set of goods is produced, it can be shown that there will be direct gains from international trade even if one country is absolutely more efficient than another at producing all goods. The potential for such gains can be seen in the following simple example, involving two countries, A and B, and two products, cloth and wheat.

Country A is more efficient than B (i.e. uses less productive resources) at producing both cloth and wheat. However, while it costs the same in terms of productive resources to produce one unit of cloth or one unit of wheat in country A, in country B twice as many productive resources go into the production of a unit of wheat as into a unit of cloth. Country A is therefore relatively more efficient, or has a comparative advantage, in producing wheat, while country B has a comparative but not absolute advantage in producing cloth. This being so, there is scope for both countries to benefit from international trade and specialisation so long as country A can exchange one unit of its wheat for more than one unit of cloth and B can obtain more than half a unit of A's wheat for a unit of its cloth. In other words, they can gain so long as the terms of exchange allow them each to end up with a combination of cloth and wheat which is greater than that which they could produce domestically. It will then pay each country to specialise in production for export. By transferring resources out of cloth production into wheat for export, A will be able to obtain more cloth from B than it could have produced by leaving the resources where they were. Similarly specialisation in cloth production by country B will enable it to obtain more wheat from A than it would have produced domestically.

In theory, then, specialisation – the resource re-allocation brought about by international trade – permits a country to enjoy a higher level of income and consumption than would be possible without trade. This gain is static in the sense that, once resources have been re-allocated, no further gains will ensue: there is no change in the country's production possibilities. The gains are not costless: international trade will make some people within a nation better off but will also impose costs on others. Thus, for instance, in the wheat exporting country, wheat producers and cloth consumers will gain but cloth producers and wheat consumers will suffer some losses since the domestic price of cloth will fall and that of wheat will rise. On balance, however, specialisation will increase the total national income. The extent of the gains and of specialisation will depend on the terms of exchange and the scope for resource re-allocation.

Comparative advantage theory assumes the full employment of productive resources. Other gains of a static type may ensue if access to the international market permits a country to use idle or under-employed resources to produce export goods in exchange for imports. In this case, international trade is said to provide a 'vent for surplus'. The initial opening-up of some developing countries to international trade is thought to have resulted in gains of this sort, since previously under-employed or idle land and labour resources were brought into production.

Indirect Gains

The productivity theory of trade postulates additional, dynamic, gains from trade. The wider markets and the scope for specialisation provided by trade permit countries to realise, from producing on a large scale, gains which could not be obtained with the production levels required to meet the needs of the domestic market alone. These two factors may have the further effect of encouraging technological innovation and raising workers' skills. Trade may also, by increasing the range of goods that can be purchased, stimulate new wants and so create new areas of production or higher productivity. In these ways, trade should not only bring a static gain but also act as a stimulus to growth.

LIMITS TO LDCS' OPPORTUNITIES FOR, AND GAINS FROM INTERNATIONAL TRADE

Much of the debate on the role of international trade has, in fact, arisen from the apparent failure of such trade to act as an 'engine of growth' in many – but by no means all – developing countries. The initial expansion of the export sector in ldcs often failed to stimulate widespread growth and development – and indeed it has been argued that its overall impact may have been harmful to ldcs – with the result that in a large number of ldcs, the export sector was an 'enclave of development' amid the largely traditional, subsistence economy. The continued unevenness of development in many developing countries has also been attributed to the indirect effects of participation in international trade on the domestic economy, for example on patterns of consumption, on savings and investment, and on the choice of technology. Leaving aside these indirect effects, the ability of ldcs to exploit their comparative advantage in international trade is limited by the imperfections of the market mechanisms within their economies: resources do not move freely between uses in response to internal or external supply and demand. This ability is further limited by external restrictions on the opportunity to trade. Meanwhile, the poor demand prospects for many primary products, which form the basis of most ldcs' export earnings, limit the ability of at least some ldcs to import the various inputs which are needed if they are to exploit new areas of comparative advantage, and benefit from trade and specialisation.

Enclave Development

A number of reasons are advanced to explain why the opening up of ldcs to the world economy frequently failed to generate widespread growth and development – why, in other words, the gains from specialisation tended to be of a limited and often static nature. The key factors are generally stated to be, first, the existence in ldcs of a ready supply of cheap labour – previously idle or unemployed – which could be absorbed by the export sector without significant effect on the rest of the economy. Second, the distribution of the gains from trade was such that a significant proportion accrued to foreigners in the form of profits and was not available to act as a stimulus to the local economy. Third, the gains accruing to local wage-earners tended to be diverted to the purchase of imports rather than local produce. Some writers, notably Gunnar Myrdal,[2] have suggested that the displacement effect of this switch to imports may, in some cases, have exacerbated internal income inequalities in ldcs by depressing incomes outside the export sector. It is probable, however, that some benefits accrued to the rest of the economy with the increase in wage employment in the export sector as a result of increased demand for locally produced food. Moreover, it must be observed that population growth is probably a more important factor in explaining any reduction in incomes in the rural sector.[3] Finally, the type of export industries set up were not such as to result in many links between the export sector and the traditional or rural sector (domestic producers were not significantly involved as suppliers to the industry or as processors of its output) and a spread of skills and production techniques to other sectors of the economy.

These sorts of factor tend – as indeed does the notion of export enclaves – to apply mainly to the kind of capital-intensive export development that occurred with foreign investment in mines and plantations. While the latter types of industry dominated the export sectors of most ldcs, there were important exceptions: for instance cocoa exports from Ghana and rice exports from Burma and Thailand were produced by peasant farmers, although they were generally exported by foreign trading firms. Here the failure of export expansion to generate widespread development tends to be explained by the failure of specialisation in export production to be accompanied by any radical changes in production techniques. Peasant farmers, it is argued, were able to respond to the new overseas market opportunities simply by increasing their use of land and labour resources which were previously not fully employed.[4] Thus, as with enclave export development, the gains from trade were largely of a static nature.

Export Bias

It has often been argued that the early expansion of exports left ldcs with a degree of export dependence – commonly measured by the proportion of exports in total output – which makes them extremely vulnerable to external fluctuations in supply and demand. Thus continued participation in world trade may be harmful to ldcs to the extent that they can neither control nor easily adjust to such fluctuations, and that instability has an adverse effect on investment and hence growth. The notion that ldcs are generally more export dependent than developed countries or that their exports, by value or volume, are especially unstable has, however, been widely questioned.[5] So too has the notion that export instability is harmful to economic growth.[6] Moreover, the conclusion that ldcs should reduce their participation in world trade as a result is only one of several alternatives, including the adoption of policies to cushion the effects of export instability, and the diversification of exports to reduce dependence on export products which are particularly prone to fluctuations in demand or supply.

While, as a generalisation, the notion of export bias falls down, it is nonetheless true that their present pattern of export specialisation has left a significant number of ldcs more vulnerable than developed countries to the changing fortunes of their exports, by virtue of the importance of exports to their national economies and their dependence on only one or two primary product exports for most of their export earnings. Moreover, while export instability may not be significantly associated with poor economic growth (taken as a crude proxy for development), a slow growth of export earnings is so associated. To the extent that ldcs' major export products face poor demand prospects, they may rightly complain that early specialisation has left their economies with a bias towards the wrong sorts of export. If this bias means that the growth of export earnings is insufficient to keep pace with import demand, it does not necessarily follow that the country should attempt to reduce its import requirements by, for instance, a programme of import substitution. An alternative response would be to seek out new areas of comparative advantage, entering into the production of different exports with better demand prospects.

Export Pessimism

According to some, however, ldcs' opportunities for participating in international trade are so limited that their main hope for development lies in an import substituting, inward-looking strategy. It is argued that prospects for the kind of export in which ldcs have a comparative advantage are poor, either because of slow-growing international demand or because of trade restrictions imposed by importing countries. Hence the export sector cannot be expected to be the source of increased employment opportunities or of income which could be used to generate such opportunities.

Poor market prospects are said to exist for various reasons. Food or food-related products (e.g. coffee, tea, spices) exported by ldcs face slow-growing demand since, in general, food consumption grows more slowly than personal incomes. Exports of many processed agricultural goods and of labour-intensive manufactures – in which ldcs often have a clear comparative advantage *vis-à-vis* developed countries – are subject to various tariff and other restrictions imposed by such countries to protect their relatively uncompetitive domestic industries. These restrictions, it is argued, may be expected to continue to inhibit the growth of exports from ldcs. Meanwhile even raw materials, for which demand is generally more buoyant, face competition from synthetic substitutes, while technological changes in developed countries have generally acted to reduce the importance of raw material inputs in a given product – and this trend is expected to continue.

Although there is undoubtedly some truth in this gloomy outlook, it is far from being fully supported by ldcs' past experience. While ldcs' export earnings have certainly grown more slowly than those of developed countries, this generalisation does not apply equally to all ldcs or all ldcs' export products.[7] Manufactured exports to developed countries from ldcs have, for instance, grown rapidly despite an increasing number of trade restrictions on imports of 'sensitive' products. Meanwhile the experience and prospects for certain primary product exports from ldcs, for example, do not accord with the export pessimists' view. Thus, while ldc manufactures exporters, such as Hong Kong and Taiwan, have tended to experience the fastest export growth rates over the last decade, other, mainly primary product exporters, for instance Zambia and Malawi, have also done almost as well if not better than developed countries. It may well be true that all ldcs could not have expected to do as well as these developing countries: that the latter's export performance was to some extent made possible by the relatively poor performance of other ldcs. But while there is no doubt that trade barriers and sluggish demand can and do limit ldcs' opportunities to gain from trade, it is also true that the domestic policies of developing countries have affected their ability to exploit the opportunities for trade.

Import Substitution

In talking of import substitution, it is important to distinguish between the import substitution which occurs 'naturally' in the course of economic growth and development and that which forms the object of government policy. 'Natural' import substitution takes place as domestic incomes rise and the range of products which can be produced competitively for the domestic market increases: thus, goods that were previously imported because domestic demand was too small to support competitive local production are gradually replaced or supplemented by locally produced goods. The case for a deliberate policy of import substitution rests on two types of argument. First, it is argued that 'natural' import substitution – the process of developing and diversifying the domestic production structure – is likely to be inhibited by the initial inability of domestic producers to compete with established foreign suppliers. Not only will domestic producers have to solve the internal problems, e.g. of management, of entering into new fields of production, but also they may be hampered by the backwardness of supporting services and industries, e.g. banking, insurance, transport, communications, power, in the local economy. It is therefore argued that some form of protection, for instance import controls or tariffs, must be given to domestic producers in ldcs to allow them to establish new industries and overcome their disadvantage *vis-à-vis* foreign suppliers. This sort of argument may be used not only in the case of import competing industries; it may also be applied to new export-orientated industries which have to compete with established suppliers elsewhere. Import substitution or protectionist policies in this context form part of a broad development strategy.

The second type of argument for import substitution is that of the export pessimists. Given that the limitations on export earnings are such as to hold back the growth of those imports needed for development, there are grounds for attempting to replace 'non-essential' imports through import substitution. Most import substitution policies in ldcs have, in fact, been adopted for this sort of reason.

While for a variety of reasons a policy of import substitution may seem easier than export promotion,[8] even if export opportunities exist, such a policy may give rise to a number of problems – and in many ldcs has done so. There is a real danger that the protection afforded to import-competing industries will be too great and, rather than giving them the necessary breathing space to become established, will become a necessary condition for their operation, which in international terms is costly and inefficient. At the same time, the protection afforded to certain industries leads to distortions in the price system which tend to discourage those industries which are not protected – often in the agricultural and export sectors. Even if import substitution reduces the import bill, it often does so at high cost to the domestic economy. Meanwhile, the development of high-cost, protected industries and the discouragement to export industries limit the possibilities for subsequent export-orientated development. This is particularly important given the frequently observed tendency for import substitution possibilities to be exhausted before any balance has been achieved between the import requirements of development and foreign exchange availability. At this point, attempts to solve payments problems by cutting back imports become even more difficult since imports have been pared down to 'essentials'. A final problem which should be mentioned is the tendency for import substitution to involve import replication, resulting in the growth of capital-intensive consumer goods industries, yielding few employment opportunities and catering to the needs of the élite. Such a pattern of import substitution is not a necessary consequence of import substituting policies, however, and even if a more desirable pattern were encouraged, for instance one involving a concentration on developing agriculture to meet domestic food needs, the other pitfalls of protectionism would remain.

Lack of Technological Dynamism

If the export pessimists' view of ldcs' market opportunities were correct, then their present and likely pattern of export specialisation would be unlikely to yield them significant gains. An alternative argument resulting in a similar conclusion is based on the proposition that the rates of technological progress in the kind of complex and advanced manufacturing export industries in developed countries exceed those prevailing in ldcs' primary product and simple manufacturing export industries. This argument does not imply that poor countries are impoverished by trade relations with developed countries but suggests that economic growth in developing countries will be inhibited so long as they continue to specialise in 'undynamic' export industries. In order to change their current pattern of specialisation and to establish new 'dynamic' industries, however, a period of protection from external competition will almost certainly be required.

According to this argument, different rates of technological progress and hence productivity growth increase the income gap between rich countries and poor countries. International trade could allow ldcs to share the gains from the more rapid technological progress of developed countries in the form of lower prices or better quality imports. However, it is argued that the fruits of technical progress tend to be distributed to the producers in the form of higher incomes, rather than to the consumers in the form of lower prices. Hence ldc importers are unable to benefit from such progress in rich countries, although they may continue to exchange the same volume of exports for the same – or a slightly greater – volume of imports. Indeed, as long as the rate of growth of productivity in developed countries is faster than in developing countries, and the gains accruing to developed country producers increase faster than the rate of productivity increase in ldcs, ldcs will 'lose' by their trade with rich countries, in the sense that the output of ldcs' productive resources will be able to command a progressively smaller share of the output of developed countries' productive resources.

Why the fruits of technological progress should tend to accrue to producers rather than consumers is discussed below, in the context of the Prebisch thesis. The argument that some industries exhibit technological dynamism more than others and that the types of export industries in ldcs are undynamic relative to those in developed countries is not wholly acceptable. Rates of technical progress may vary by industry but they clearly also vary according to the country of location: primary producing industries, for instance, in developed countries, have exhibited very rapid technical progress. Indeed, a more credible basis for the argument stated above is that technological dynamism depends not simply on the type of industry but on a complex of factors which prevail in developed, but not in developing, countries (even so, note for instance the technological dynamism of the rubber industry in Malaysia). Thus if developing countries are to match the growth of developed countries, they must create internally the conditions for technical progress.

Deteriorating Terms of Trade

For somewhat different reasons, it has often been argued that ldcs' present pattern of exports – the predominance of primary product exports to developed countries in their total exports – does and will actually result in progressive losses to ldcs. Over time, not only do their productive resources command less of those of rich countries but their goods are exchanged for progressively smaller volumes of rich countries' exports. In other words, proponents of this view suggest that ldcs specialising in primary product exports to rich countries suffer a progressive deterioration in their commodity terms of trade. Although this view, initially put forward by Prebisch and Singer,[9] has been criticised on empirical and theoretical grounds, it still commands support, especially among developing countries.

The explanation for the purported deterioration in ldcs' terms of trade with developed countries rests on the existence of forces acting on international demand and supply in such a way as to result in a transfer of the fruits of technical progress to developed countries – the Centre – and away from developing countries – the Periphery. Strong trades union activity in the Centre ensures that workers, not consumers, benefit from improvements in productivity: wages are increased rather than prices reduced. Meanwhile, the ready availability of labour in the Periphery countries weakens the ability of workers there to benefit from increases in productivity, which tend therefore to result in lower prices rather than higher wages. Thus ldcs' import prices tend to stay the same while their export prices drop, and developed countries benefit from the fruits of technical progress occurring in both the Centre and the Periphery. Prebisch ties in this process of change in the relative prices of developed and developing countries' exports with the cyclical fluctuations in production in rich countries. One theoretical challenge to this explanation questions why the change in the relative prices of the two sets of exports brought about by differences in labour power should not result in a change in the demand for ldcs' exports relative to developed countries' exports such as to prevent any progressive deterioration in ldcs' terms of trade. This is answered in terms of differences in the responsiveness of the Centre's demand for primary products and that of the Periphery's demand for manufactured goods. And the stress that is frequently placed on the sluggish trend in demand for primary products relative to manufactures suggests that more militancy among ldc workers would not alter the relative price movements unless accompanied by restrictions on primary product output and reductions in employment.

However convincing the Prebisch-Singer thesis may be in theory, the main criticism of it arises from the absence of any clear evidence that the phenomenon it purports to explain actually exists. According to their hypothesis the commodity terms of trade for ldcs' trade with developed countries, or for trade in primary commodities relative to manufactures, should show a long-term deterioration. The factual evidence indicates that there have been long periods during which these terms of trade have deteriorated, but that these periods have been punctuated by sharp improvements – as in the early 1950s with the Korean War boom and again in 1972-4. The problem is therefore one of deciding whether the latter are interruptions in a downward trend, and reference must be made to movements in the terms of trade over a longer period. But this poses two more problems. On the one hand, the longer the period, the scantier the statistical evidence. On the other hand, the longer the period, the greater the difficulties of making meaningful comparisons between the terms of trade at the beginning of the period and those at the end (the relative price movements recorded in terms of trade over a period of time tend to reflect changes in the quality and composition of the goods traded, which confuses the issue at stake). Consequently the most that can be said with conviction is that the evidence is insufficient to support any particular hypothesis about the nature of the long-term trend. At the same time, there are a number of factors besides those referred to by Singer and Prebisch which could help to explain the various periods during which the terms of trade deteriorated. Thus, for instance, the deterioration in the latter part of the nineteenth century has been attributed largely to reductions in freight charges for primary commodities, while an alternative explanation for the deterioration in the 1950s and the 1960s is that the growth of ldcs' supply of primary commodities had outstripped demand.

Unequal Exchange

A somewhat similar thesis to that of Prebisch and Singer has been advanced by Arghiri Emmanuel.[10] He, however, attaches little importance to demand factors in explaining the supposed deterioration in the terms of trade of ldcs relative to developed countries. His argument rests rather on factors leading to a widening gap between the supply prices of goods produced in developing countries and those produced in developed countries.

Emmanuel's argument proceeds as follows. The price of goods produced in any country is determined mainly by the level of wages in that country. Wage levels do not simply reflect the productivity of workers (but see below) but depend also on institutional factors – such as the power of trade unions – which are peculiar to each country. Given that labour does not move freely between countries, he argues, these international differences in wage rates are unlikely to be removed: wage rates in developing countries, for instance, will remain low so long as there is a relative abundance of unorganised labour, and in developed countries they will remain high so long as labour is organised and relatively scarce. Capital, on the other hand, is relatively mobile internationally and profit rates in different countries tend to be equalised as a result. The prices of goods produced in the different countries, therefore, will reflect the wage differentials between countries, and high-wage countries will benefit from the lower wages in poor countries by being able to purchase goods at lower prices than if these goods were produced internally. Low-wage countries, conversely, will lose in that they will pay higher prices for goods produced in high-wage countries than if they were produced internally. The quantities of factors used in production of goods in ldcs will be traded for smaller quantities from developed countries even if there is no difference in the relative productivity of production factors. This unequal exchange, he argues, will tend to be cumulative in that the surplus for investment will be low in developing countries, and low wages will limit the incentives for technological improvements and the range of investment opportunities.

So long as low-wage countries are unable to redress the balance of exchange either by raising wage rates, or profits, or by subjecting goods exported to high-wage countries to an export tax, Emmanuel concludes, they will lose – and are likely to lose progressively – by trading with rich countries. It follows, then, that for an individual ldc, a policy of seeking to reduce its trade with rich countries and either increasing its trade with other low-wage countries or increasing its self-reliance, or both, is the only possible way of avoiding unequal exchange and retaining the benefits of its low-cost production.

Emmanuel's thesis is a fundamental challenge to much of 'standard' trade and economic theory. As we noted above, the empirical evidence does not support the notion that the terms of trade between rich and poor countries are deteriorating. This in itself does not remove the possibility that unequal exchange occurs as hypothesised by Emmanuel. There are, however, two major reasons why this is to be doubted. First, it is by no means evident that the differences in wage rates between developed and developing countries do not reflect differences in labour productivity: differences in wages and in productivity rates in different countries tend to be closely related – and indeed the low wages in developing countries relative to those in developed countries are often associated with even lower levels of productivity relative to developed countries.[11] Secondly, as Emmanuel acknowledges,[12] where countries trade in the same product, or a substitute for that product, any differences in wages will, under conditions of free trade and competition and profit equalisation, correspond to differences in productivity. Yet the list of traded products which are specific to developing countries is short – even the so-called 'tropical' products often compete with substitutes produced in developed countries. Thus, it is reasonable to conclude that, even if Emmanuel's thesis of unequal exchange due to institutional differences in wage rates between countries were accepted, the extent to which trade between rich and poor countries results in such an unequal exchange is limited.

Technological Dependence

From different starting points, others have reached similar conclusions to those of Emmanuel about the undesirability of continuing trade relations between rich and poor countries. This conclusion, in particular, is drawn from arguments relating to trade and the technological dependence of developing countries. The main thesis is that patterns of production, consumption, and income distribution in ldcs are distorted by their dependence, engendered by rich-poor trade, on technologies imported from and evolved in developed countries.[13] This thesis makes two important assumptions: first, that particular products are always produced in particular ways; second, that changes in products, and in consumer tastes, tend to be irreversible. In other words, it assumes that the technology needed to produce fixed-wheel bicycles or black and white televisions is necessarily different from that needed to produce free-wheel cycles or colour TVs, and that once consumers have accepted the advantages of new products, they do not return to more 'primitive' products. Hence, developing countries which plan to export products which are in demand in the West have to use techniques of production – generally evolved in Western conditions of capital abundance and labour shortage – which are not suited to their own 'mix' of factors of production. These assumptions would be radically wrong if different, but equally efficient, production techniques for a given product were separately developed in labour-abundant and capital-abundant countries. But, since the developed countries are the source of most research and development on new products, this does not often happen.

From these assumptions, a number of consequences are said to follow. If ldcs import consumer goods from rich countries, as most do, patterns of consumption which imitate those of the rich countries will be built up. If ldcs then seek to produce the same goods domestically instead of importing them, they will have to use capital-intensive techniques since these are the only ones available. The same will happen if ldcs try to develop industries to export goods to rich countries. These industries will create relatively little employment and tend to increase inequalities within ldcs. And even if, in accordance with ldcs' comparative advantage, labour-intensive products are chosen as export industries, the speed of technical change and the evolution of consumers' tastes in rich countries will, it is argued, eventually force ldcs to adopt capital-intensive techniques to produce goods desired by rich-country consumers.

On the export side, there would appear to be only two ways out of this trap compatible with continued trade with developed countries. First, ldcs can exploit their comparative advantage in labour-intensive production by exporting processes rather than products: that is, by specialising in those *stages* of production which, for one reason or another, remain labour-intensive. Second, ldcs can export those labour-intensive handicraft products which are valued by rich consumers precisely because they are 'primitive' and not mass-produced. Neither of these ways out, however, alters the supposed problems arising from ldcs' imports from Western countries, and it has been observed that the growth of export processing may make only a limited and risky contribution to ldcs' development.

It is difficult, however, to accept the thesis in its entirety. While doubtless technological dependence is a factor contributing to the kinds of distortion in ldcs' development noted above, the assumptions in relation to trade and technology are questionable. Consumer tastes in rich countries are not always irreversible – less evenly hand-woven cloth may be preferred to machine-woven cloth if it costs half the price. Moreover, as this last example suggests, not all available production techniques are capital-intensive, nor, as the growth of developed country investment in export processing in ldcs suggests, is it inevitable that future technological developments by rich countries will lead to more capital-intensive production techniques. The existence of a range of techniques for the production of a given product is notable in the agricultural sector, but can also be found elsewhere, for instance, fashion shirts may be made by labour-intensive as well as capital-intensive techniques. Once the assumptions in relation to consumer tastes and technology are relaxed – and therefore it can be allowed that import substitution need not necessarily entail import replication based on a given production technique – the consequences of trade relations with developed countries look less grim. Nonetheless, it has to be added that, so long as ldcs are technologically dependent on the West, the production techniques employed in their developing industries are likely to result in some distortions in ldcs' pattern of development.

Dominance and Dependence

The notion that ldcs are technologically dependent on developed countries has been further generalised in the dominance-dependence thesis.[14] According to its proponents, trade is just one part of a network of relations in which rich countries dominate poor countries. This dominance-dependence network extends beyond economic relations – arising from investment aid and trade flows between rich and poor countries – to include socio-cultural relations: the dominance of Western culture and society being seen in various ways, for instance, in the educational systems developed in poor countries. This external dependence, it is argued, inhibits autonomous development or, indeed, any development in the real sense of widespread growth in material welfare. The mechanism whereby the dominance-dependence relationship actually impedes genuine development is not precisely formulated. Implicitly or explicitly, however, ldcs' failure to overcome internal obstacles to development, for instance low agricultural productivity and the existence of gross internal income inequalities, is attributed to the inequality of international relations.

Without attempting to list all the aspects said to characterise the ldcs' dependence, it is worth pointing to a few which have been stressed. The dominance-dependence thesis begins by pointing to the process whereby colonial – or colonial-type – relations with metropolitan countries gave rise to a small wage-earning and salaried élite in developing countries. This local élite tended to adopt the patterns of consumption and behaviour of the metropolis and to become divorced socially and economically – except as buyers of food – from their own people. Elements from this élite assumed power at 'independence'. The pattern of production which they sought to develop after independence followed their own westernised consumption patterns. Hence efforts were focused on import-substitution of an imitative, capital-intensive, and often inefficient nature with the object of producing consumer goods for the relatively wealthy élite. These new industries created few new employment opportunities and probably destroyed others in the 'informal sector' of ldcs. Foreign capital, according to this thesis, has played a fundamental role in creating patterns of dependence – being involved in both the initial development of export industries and the subsequent 'independent' industrialisation programmes.

The dominance-dependence thesis tends to ascribe the relative backwardness and internal polarisation of ldcs to their involvement in the international capitalist economy. That the latter is of major importance in explaining ldcs' present situation is clear, although the pattern of development usually described in the dominance-dependence thesis is more relevant to the experience of some ldcs, e.g. in Latin America, than others, e.g. in Africa. What is less clear is precisely how participation in the international economy impedes ldcs' development or how withdrawal from it – as suggested by the thesis – would improve ldcs' development chances. In respect of trade between rich and poor countries, for instance, it is not clear how such trade necessarily impedes development – unless the various arguments about unequal exchange and technological dependence are accepted – or why a more egalitarian development policy would preclude such trade. And even supposing that all or most economic relations between rich and poor countries produced tendencies towards uneven, inegalitarian, and dependent development, it has to be recognised that independent, autarkic development, if politically feasible, is scarcely compatible with the present economic position of many ldcs, given the paucity of their resources. Some trade, at least, with developed countries would seem necessary unless the baby of economic development (including economic growth as one element) is to be thrown out with the bathwater of socio-economic inequality.

CONCLUSION: AN ESCAPE ROUTE THROUGH TRADE AMONG DEVELOPING COUNTRIES?

The basic logic of the case for trade suggests that a development strategy which has self-reliance as one of its main objects and is designed to reduce participation in international trade is likely to be more costly than one which permits some international division of labour. Indeed, the narrowness of most ldcs' internal markets and their limited range of productive resources would inevitably impose severe constraints on their development possibilities if they attempted an autarkic strategy. In this sense, the choice between an outward-looking or inward-looking development strategy is unreal for most ldcs.

The arguments outlined above, however, suggest that there are a number of limits to ldcs' potential gains from trade. Mostly these limits are said to derive from the relative underdevelopment of ldcs' economies and from the predominance of primary products in their total exports and the predominance of developed countries among their trading partners. Some arguments suggest the possibility of individual action by ldcs or multilateral action by ldcs and/or developed countries as a means of reducing the problems of international trade (for instance, economic intervention by individual ldc governments to limit the otherwise inhibiting effects of external competition on the establishment of new industries; the formation of trading cartels along OPEC lines; trade liberalisation to improve ldcs' access to Western markets; the development of technologies appropriate to production conditions in ldcs). These possibilities are discussed in later chapters. Others suggest that trade relations, *inter alia,* with the West are so harmful that they should be avoided, in the interests of creating societies with a fair division of labour and income. Our main conclusion in relation to this sort of argument is that there are no necessary or universal grounds for ldcs to avoid trade relations with the West. Such trade links may have helped to bring about and to reinforce tendencies towards socio-economic inequality within ldcs, but it seems unlikely that the severance of these links would remove the various obstacles, including the internal power relations within ldcs, to a more evenly spread development, or that their continuance will automatically prevent the latter.

Nonetheless, the various arguments relating to the limitations on the gains that may be expected from rich-poor trade, the difficulties of multilateral solutions to ldcs' trade problems, and the likely costs of individual autarkic solutions, raise the question of the possibility of developing trade *among* ldcs. On the face of it, such a development would appear to be an attractive solution, especially if one accepts the more radical arguments against rich-poor trade. If ldcs open up their markets to each other, the scope for import substitution and the possibility of reducing undesirable Western influences on patterns of consumption and production would be increased.

We discuss some of the moves that have been made towards greater economic and trade co-operation among ldcs in Chapter 8. There is no doubt that some success is being achieved in the alteration of 'traditional' patterns of trade. But it would be wrong to suggest that the development of trade among ldcs provides an easy alternative to rich-poor trade. Many ldcs have attempted to develop their individual economies behind high, protective trade barriers. The reduction of these barriers to permit increased trade with other ldcs, and the re-allocation of resources to accommodate that trade and to permit a shift away from trade dependence on the West is a slow and costly business – in both economic and political terms.

STATISTICAL BACKGROUND

This section is designed to provide a statistical overview of ldcs' position in world trade as a prelude to the more detailed discussions in later chapters. We look at the changes in the volume, composition, and direction of world trade and, in particular, at the changes in, and current state of, ldcs' trade relations with the rest of the world. Each subsection below is intended as a brief commentary on the statistical material presented in the different tables.

World exports, 1953-74 (Table 1.1)

There was a more than ten-fold increase in the total value of world trade during the period 1953 to 1974. Up to 1970, the expansion of world trade largely reflected an increase in the volume rather than the prices of goods traded internationally. But during the early seventies, it was the increase in the prices of exports which accounted for the major part of the increase in the value of world trade.

During the period from 1953 to 1970, the most rapid growth in international trade was in goods traded among the developed capitalist countries (North America, Western Europe, Japan, Australia, New Zealand, and South Africa). The value of their exports in 1970 was some 4½ times what it had been in 1953, and developed countries' share of world trade had risen from 63 per cent to nearly 72 per cent. The trade of member countries of the EEC, in particular, grew extremely fast in this period. These countries had, by 1970, achieved completely free trade amongst themselves, a substantial measure of protection for their internal production and trade in agricultural products, and a degree of free trade with other European and Mediterranean countries. The share of developing countries in world trade fell, over the same period, from 27 per cent to 17.7 per cent. This drop reflected both the relatively slow growth in the volume of their exports and a deterioration – following the favourable effects of the Korean War boom in the early fifties – in the prices of their export commodities relative to the prices of manufactured exports from developed countries.

After 1970, the aggregate picture changed considerably, as a result

Table 1.1. World Exports, 1953-74 and 1975

	1953		1960		1970		1973		1974		1975	
	$m fob	%	$m fob	%	$m fob	%	$m fob	%	$m fob	%	$m fob	%
Total exports of which:	78,300	(100.0)	128,660	(100.0)	313,100	(100.0)	577,490	(100.0)	838,890	(100.0)	879,120	(100.0)
Developed market economies[1]	49,300	(63.0)	85,950	(66.8)	224,290	(71.6)	407,810	(70.6)	544,250	(64.8)	579,920	(66.0)
Centrally planned economies	7,900	(10.1)	15,260	(11.9)	33,360	(10.7)	57,890	(10.0)	71,990	(8.6)	86,800	(9.9)
Developing countries	21,000	(27.0)	27,450	(21.3)	55,450	(17.7)	111,790	(19.3)	222,650	(26.5)	212,400	(24.1)
OPEC	n.a.		n.a.		17,250	(5.5)	43,440	(7.5)	123,920	(14.8)	113,940	(13.0)

[1] including Australia, New Zealand and South Africa.
Source: GATT, *International Trade,* 1965 and 1975-6

of three things: a rapid inflation of most commodity prices between 1972 and early 1974, fuelled by boom conditions in the West on the one hand and by widespread crop failures on the other; the beginning of serious domestic price inflation within the Western countries after 1970; and finally the four-fold increase in oil prices imposed by the member states of the Organisation of Petroleum Exporting Countries (OPEC) at the end of 1973.[15]

Shares in World Exports after 1970 (Table 1.2)

The events of the early seventies brought substantial shifts in the shares of different groups of countries in world trade. Data drawn from International Monetary Fund statistics[16] show that the share of developed countries dropped while that of developing countries rose markedly.

Distinguishing between different groups of developing countries, it can be seen that the main factor in ldcs' greater share of world trade in 1974 was the vast increase in the export earnings of the oil exporting states. In 1970-2, the latter accounted for 7.3 per cent of world trade and just over a third of ldcs' total exports, which in turn accounted for some 20 per cent of the value of world exports. In 1973, both oil and non-oil exporting ldcs' share of world exports increased with the rise in commodity prices. However, by 1974, non-oil exporting ldcs' share of world trade had fallen below the 1970-2 level, from 13.1 per cent to 12.6 per cent, while that of oil exporting ldcs had increased to almost 18 per cent, with their exports accounting for nearly 58 per cent of all ldcs' exports.

The only groups of developing countries other than the oil producers which increased their share of world trade between 1973 and 1974 were Latin American and Caribbean states (including a number of important meat and sugar producers, as well as exporters of minerals whose world price levels remained high) and the members of the Association of South East Asian Nations (ASEAN), in particular Singapore with its rapidly growing manufacturing sector.

Developing Countries' Trade Balances (Table 1.3)

In Table 1.3, ldcs' imports are set alongside their exports to provide a summary picture of their external trade balance in the seventies. For some years now, ldcs have tended to import more than they export – frequently for development reasons – and have financed their trade deficit with grants, loans, and investment funds from abroad. The only group of ldcs that has been able to maintain a consistent trade surplus

Table 1.2. World Exports[1] 1970-2 (Annual Average), 1973, 1974 and 1975

Exports from[2]	1970-2 $m	% of world	1973 $m	% of world	1974 $m	% of world	1975 $m	% of world
Developed market economies (inc. Australia, New Zealand, S. Africa	236,246	72.5	371,660	70.6	497,131	63.6	570,859	71.8
Developing countries – total	66,520	20.4	118,473	22.5	244,016	31.2	218,171	27.4
Oil producing countries	23,767	7.3	45,200	8.6	138,900	17.8	114,932	14.4
Argentina, Brazil, Mexico	6,617	2.0	12,099	2.3	15,513	2.0	14,583	1.8
Other Latin America and Caribbean (exc. oil producers)	6,775	2.1	9,446	1.8	15,769	2.0	16,994	2.2
European ldcs	2,687	0.8	4,440	0.8	5,779	0.7	5,789	0.7
Middle East and N. Africa (exc. oil producers)	3,516	1.0	4,912	0.9	7,459	1.0	8,469	1.1
Other Africa (exc. oil producers)	6,958	2.1	10,143	1.9	13,527	1.7	11,091	1.4
ASEAN member states[3]	6,727	2.1	13,125	2.5	22,273	2.9	20,788	2.6
Hong Kong, Taiwan, S. Korea	6,235	1.9	12,685	2.4	15,939	2.0	16,392	2.1
India, Bangladesh, Pakistan, Sri Lanka	3,275	1.0	4,623	0.9	5,857	0.8	6,233	0.8
Other Asian ldcs	685	0.2	512	0.1	681	0.1	672	0.1
Developing countries (exc. oil producers)	42,753	13.1	70,540	13.4	98,279	12.6	103,239	13.0
World total	325,900		526,200		781,900		795,100	

1 Excluding Socialist countries.

2 For definitions of country groupings, see Note, p.49.

3 Including Indonesia. (Excluding Indonesia, ASEAN members' share of world exports was 1.64% in 1970-2, 1.91% in 1973 and 1.94% in 1974.)

Sources: International Monetary Fund, *International Financial Statistics,* to November 1976; *Direction of Trade.*

Table 1.3. Developing Countries: Trade Balance, 1970-2 (Annual Average), 1973, 1974 and 1975

Exports from/ imports to	Exports (fob) 1970-2	1973	1974	1975	Imports (cif) 1970-2	1973	1974	1975	Balance 1970-2	1973	1974	1975
						$m						
Developing countries – total	66,250	115,740	237,179	211,038	69,734	108,058	173,614	207,250	–3,214	+7,682	+63,565	+3,788
Oil producing countries	23,767	45,200	138,900	114,932	13,100	21,900	35,800	58,418	+10,667	+23,300	+103,100	+56,514
Argentina, Brazil, Mexico	6,617	12,099	15,513	14,583	8,201	13,386	24,236	24,086	–1,584	–1,287	–8,723	–9,503
Other Latin America/Caribbean[2]	6,775	9,446	15,769	16,994	8,364	11,571	19,200	24,553	–1,589	–2,125	–3,431	–7,559
European ldcs	2,687	4,440	5,779	5,789	4,805	7,558	12,614	13,119	–2,118	–3,118	–6,835	–7,330
Middle East/N. Africa[2]	3,516	4,912	7,459	8,469	6,154	9,813	16,210	20,041	–2,638	–4,901	–8,761	–11,572
Other Africa[2]	6,958	10,413	13,527	11,091	7,677	10,166	14,283	13,823	–719	+247	–756	–2,732
ASEAN members[3]	6,727	13,125	22,273	20,788	8,268	14,197	22,814	23,595	–1,541	–1,072	–541	–2,807
Hong Kong, Taiwan, S. Korea	6,235	12,685	15,939	16,392	7,654	13,712	20,595	19,956	–1,419	–1,027	–4,656	–3,564
India, Bangladesh, Pakistan, Sri Lanka	3,275	4,623	5,857	6,233	4,080	5,486	8,551	10,264	–805	–863	–2,694	–4,031
Other Asian ldcs	685	512	681	672	799	1,505	2,349	1,516	–114	–993	–1,668	–844
Developing countries exc. oil producers	42,753	70,540	98,279	90,016	56,634	86,158	137,814	148,832	–13,881	–15,618	–39,535	–52,816

1 For definitions of country groupings, see Note, p.49.

2 Excluding oil producing countries.

3 Including Indonesia.

Source: As for Table 1.2.

has been the oil producing states (see Chapter 7). With the oil price rise, the different trade positions of the oil and non-oil exporting ldcs have been accentuated. Whereas in 1970-2 oil exporting states had a surplus of $10.6 billion and other ldcs had a deficit of $13.9 billion, in 1974 the surplus of the oil states had risen to $103 billion while the deficit of other ldcs had risen to nearly $40 billion – with the result that some ldcs had deficits equivalent to or greater than their annual export earnings. In 1975 the oil states' surplus declined by 45 per cent, to $57 billion; other ldcs' deficits grew by one-third, to $53 billion. This partly reflects the increase in prices of manufactures imported from the West.

The vastly increased deficits of the non-oil producing ldcs mean that problems of finance, short and long term, assume vastly greater importance than in the past. The oil states themselves are doing a great deal to cover the deficits of certain oil importing ldcs.[17] But many ldcs need to find new ways of covering their trade deficits – hence the urgency that lies behind talk of a 'new international economic order' discussed in Chapter 3, Chapter 7 and Chapter 9.

Composition and Direction of ldcs' Trade (Table 1.4)

This two-part table shows the most important product groups exported and imported by developing countries, and their destinations and origins by broad categories of countries over the period 1960-74.

There has been relatively little change in the direction of ldcs' trade in aggregate. The Western developed countries (including Japan and Australasia) are still the most important market for ldcs' exports and the major suppliers of their imports. Some three-quarters of ldcs' exports go to the developed market economies, as against one-fifth to other developing countries and around 5 per cent to the Socialist states of Eastern Europe and Asia. The share of ldcs' imports coming from developed capitalist countries is smaller, about 69 per cent, while the Socialist economies are a more important source of imports than destination for exports, with some 7 per cent of world exports to ldcs.

Since 1960, however, the product structure of ldcs' exports has changed considerably. The single most important change is the increase in the share of fuel exports in the total, from 28 per cent in 1960 to 60 per cent in 1974. If fuel exports are excluded from ldcs' total exports, the other important change – namely the increase in manufactures relative to primary product exports – becomes more apparent. In 1960, manufactures accounted for 19 per cent of total ldc exports excluding fuel; by 1970, they accounted for 37 per cent

Table 1.4: Composition and Direction of ldcs' Trade

(a) Exports from developing countries

Product groups	Exports to	Developed market economies[1] 1960	1970	1973	1974	1975	Centrally planned economies 1960	1970	1973	1974	Developing countries 1960	1970	1973	1974	World total[2] 1960	1970	1973	1974	1975
Food	$m	5,885	10,580	16,790	21,290	22,100	349	1,370	2,160	3,260	1,460	2,330	4,170	6,390	8,070	14,450	23,330	31,270	
	% of world total	21.5	19.5	15.0	9.6	10.4	1.3	2.5	1.9	1.5	5.3	4.2	3.7	2.9	29.5	26.1	20.9	14.0	
Agricultural raw materials	$m		3,350	6,050	6,630	5,400		840	1,220	1,510		1,060	2,230	2,750		5,330	9,660	11,080	
	% of world total		6.0	5.4	3.0	2.5		1.5	1.1	0.7		1.9	2.0	1.2		9.6	8.6	5.0	
Ores and minerals	$m	5,595	2,750	4,000	5,820	4,000	775	260	350	600	1,100	160	430	590	7,640	3,180	4,880	7,150	
	% of world total	20.5	5.0	3.6	2.6	1.9	2.8	0.5	0.3	0.3	4.0	0.3	0.4	0.3	27.9	5.7	4.4	3.2	
Fuels	$m	4,840	13,780	34,920	103,140	96,800	2	50	490	980	2,260	3,730	8,740	25,960	7,650	18,090	44,990	132,640	
	% of world total	17.7	24.9	31.2	46.3	45.6	0.0	0.1	0.4	0.4	8.3	6.7	7.8	11.7	28.0	32.6	40.2	59.6	
Total primary products	$m	16,320	30,460	61,760	136,880	128,300	1,126	2,520	4,220	6,350	4,820	7,280	15,570	35,690	23,360	41,050	82,860	182,140	(172,400)
	% of world total	59.7	54.9	55.2	61.5	60.4	4.1	4.5	3.8	2.8	17.6	13.1	13.9	16.0	85.4	74.0	74.1	81.8	(81.2)
Metals	$m	n.a.	3,490	4,200	6,760	4,200	n.a.	120	140	330	n.a.	510	990	1,340	n.a.	4,140	5,310	8,470	
	% of world total		6.2	3.7	3.0	2.0		0.2	0.1	0.1		0.9	0.9	0.6		7.4	4.7	3.8	
Chemicals	$m	167	410	880	1,880	1,700	9	50	70	130	105	450	950	1,490	290	930	1,960	3,620	
	% of world total	0.6	0.7	0.8	0.8	0.8	0.0	0.1	0.1	0.1	0.3	0.8	0.8	0.7	1.0	1.7	1.8	1.6	
Vehicles & engineering products	$m		850	2,920	4,290	4,350		20	40	40		800	1,960	3,080		1,710	5,130	7,610	
	% of world total		1.5	2.6	1.9	2.0		0.0	0.0	0.0		1.4	1.8	1.4		3.1	4.6	3.4	
Textiles and clothing	$m	2,390	1,980	5,450	6,440	6,500	88	260	390	560	1,035	950	1,850	2,210	3,550	3,330	8,040	9,730	
	% of world total	8.7	3.6	4.9	2.9	3.1	0.3	0.5	0.3	0.3	3.8	1.7	1.7	1.0	13.0	6.0	7.2	4.4	
Other manufactures	$m		2,580	5,770	6,280	6,100		90	180	180		960	1,630	2,260		3,700	7,790	9,020	
	% of world total		4.7	5.2	2.8	2.9		0.2	0.2	0.1		1.7	1.5	1.0		6.7	7.0	4.1	
Total manufactures	$m	2,557	9,310	19,320	25,650	22,850	94	540	820	1,240	1,140	3,670	7,350	10,380	3,840	13,810	28,230	38,450	(37,600)
	% of world total	9.3	16.8	17.3	11.5	10.8	0.3	1.0	0.7	0.6	4.2	6.6	6.5	4.7	14.0	24.9	25.3	17.2	(17.7)
Total exports	$m	19,040	39,970	81,100	163,900	152,550	1,220	3,150	5,100	7,650	6,010	11,090	23,350	46,450	27,350	55,450	111,800	222,650	(212,400)
	% of world total	69.6	72.1	72.5	73.6	71.8	4.5	5.7	4.6	3.4	22.0	20.0	20.8	20.9	100.0	100.0	100.0	100.0	(100.0)

Table 1.4: Composition and Direction of ldcs' Trade (cont.)

(b) Exports to developing countries

Product groups	Exports to	Developed market economies[1] 1960	1970	1973	1974	1975	Centrally planned economies 1960	1970	1973	1974	Developing countries 1960	1970	1973	1974	World total[2] 1960	1970	1973	1974	1975
Food	$m	2,700	4,640	9,250	13,220	14,250	236	760	1,390	2,410	1,460	2,330	4,170	6,390	4,660	8,250	15,810	24,090	
	% of world total	9.4	8.1	8.9	7.8	7.3	0.8	1.3	1.3	1.4	0.5	4.1	4.0	3.8	16.4	14.3	15.2	14.3	
Agricultural raw materials	$m	889	1,030	1,960	2,830	2,860	98	240	460	680	1,100	1,060	2,230	2,750	2,140	2,450	4,880	6,590	
	% of world total	3.1	1.8	1.9	1.7	1.5	0.3	0.4	0.4	0.4	3.9	1.8	2.1	1.6	7.6	4.3	4.7	3.9	
Ores and minerals	$m		300	520	810	900		20	50	80		160	430	590		490	1,070	1,630	
	% of world total		0.5	0.5	0.5	0.5		0.0	0.0	0.0		0.3	0.4	0.3		0.9	1.0	1.0	
Fuels	$m	516	590	790	1,580	1,800	93	190	320	790	2,260	3,730	8,740	25,960	2,900	4,570	9,930	28,420	
	% of world total	1.8	1.0	0.8	0.9	0.9	0.3	0.3	0.3	0.5	8.0	6.5	8.4	15.2	10.2	7.9	9.6	16.9	
Total primary products	$m	4,105	6,560	12,520	18,440	19,550	427	1,210	2,220	3,960	4,820	7,280	15,570	35,690	9,700	15,760	31,690	60,730	(61,200)
	% of world total	14.4	11.4	12.0	10.9	10.1	1.5	2.1	2.1	2.3	17.0	12.6	15.0	21.1	34.1	27.4	30.5	36.0	(31.5)
Metals	$m	n.a.	3,270	6,050	12,520	12,700	n.a.	280	480	700	n.a.	510	990	1,340	n.a.	4,200	7,780	14,990	
	% of world total		5.7	5.8	7.4	6.5		0.5	0.5	0.4		0.9	1.0	0.8		7.3	7.5	8.9	
Chemicals	$m	1,987	4,440	7,750	13,120	13,400	70	200	370	600	105	450	950	1,490	2,200	5,180	9,240	15,420	
	% of world total	7.0	7.7	7.5	7.8	6.8	0.3	0.4	0.4	0.4	0.4	0.8	0.9	0.9	7.7	9.0	8.9	9.1	
Vehicles & engineering products	$m		17,370	29,560	43,650	62,150		1,700	2,310	2,800		800	1,960	3,080		20,210	34,420	50,020	
	% of world total		30.2	28.4	25.9	32.0		3.0	2.2	1.7		1.4	1.9	1.8		35.1	33.1	29.7	
Textiles and clothing	$m	14,132	2,410	3,780	4,780	4,850	732	350	670	710	1,035	950	1,850	2,210	16,100	3,730	6,340	7,730	
	% of world total	49.7	4.2	3.6	2.8	2.5	2.6	0.6	0.6	0.4	3.6	1.7	1.8	1.3	56.6	6.5	6.1	4.5	
Other manufactures	$m		4,570	7,300	10,490	12,250		530	720	1,240		960	1,630	2,260		6,190	9,870	14,400	
	% of world total		7.9	7.0	6.2	6.3		0.9	0.7	0.7		1.7	1.6	1.3		10.8	9.5	8.5	
Total manufactures	$m	16,119	32,060	54,440	84,560	105,350	802	3,060	4,580	6,050	1,140	3,670	7,350	10,380	18,300	39,510	67,650	102,560	(126,100)
	% of world total	56.7	55.7	52.3	50.1	54.2	2.8	55.3	4.4	3.6	4.0	6.4	7.0	6.2	64.4	68.6	65.1	60.8	(64.9)
Total exports	$m	20,580	39,930	69,100	106,400	129,500	1,230	5,140	8,800	11,500	6,010	11,090	23,350	46,450	28,440	57,600	103,950	168,650	(194,400)
	% of world total	72.4	69.3	66.5	63.1	66.6	4.3	8.9	8.5	6.8	21.1	19.3	22.5	27.5			100.0	100.0	(100.0)

1 Excluding Australia, S. Africa, New Zealand.
2 Including Australia, S. Africa, New Zealand.

Source: GATT, *International Trade:* UN *Monthly Bulletin of Statistics,* March 1964.

and by 1974 – despite the general rise in primary commodity prices – they accounted for 42 per cent. The share of primary product exports in total non-fuel exports by ldcs in turn fell from 80 per cent in 1960 to 54 per cent in 1974.[18] The factors behind this shift in export composition are examined in Chapters 3 and 4, on competing and non-competing primary commodities, and Chapters 5 and 6, on manufactures exports and the role played in their development by foreign investment in ldcs.

Compared with their exports, imports into ldcs have shown little change in structure over the period. Manufactured goods, in particular engineering products, continue to dominate their imports, reflecting their development efforts and their continued reliance on external sources for industrial goods.

Direction of Ldcs' Trade Flows (Tables 1.5 and 1.6)

These tables go into greater detail about the destinations and sources of developing countries' exports and imports. They set out estimated export and import figures, and annual growth rates, over the ten-year period between 1960-2 and 1970-2, for all ldcs, including and excluding the oil producers, and ten separate groups of developing countries. The same groups of ldcs, plus the major developed capitalist countries and the Socialist states, are taken as destinations and sources.

Among developed countries, the European Economic Community (EEC) stands out as ldcs' most important trading partner, followed by North America (USA and Canada) and then by Japan. Within the EEC, the United Kingdom is an important trading partner for ldcs: over the decade, however, the United Kingdom's share of EEC imports from and exports to ldcs has fallen. In aggregate, the EEC's trade balance with ldcs' was in deficit in both periods, but its trade balance with non-oil developing countries was in surplus, growing from $1 billion in 1960-2 to $4 billion in 1970-2. This underlines the fact that the oil producing states are the most important source of ldc exports to the EEC. On the whole, however, the EEC's trade relations with ldcs are not markedly biased towards any one geographical region. North America's trade, on the other hand, is more concentrated geographically with Latin American countries, the region's most important trading partners. Hong Kong, Taiwan, and South Korea, taken together, have, however, significantly increased both their exports to and imports from North America with the result that in 1970-2 they accounted for 20 per cent of ldcs' exports to North America and 11 per cent of ldcs' imports from North America, as

Table 1.5: Exports from Developing Countries to Selected Areas and World Totals: 1970-2 (Annual Averages) and 1974

(a) $m.

Exports from:	Year	All ldcs inc. oil producers	All ldcs exc. oil producers	Oil producing states	Argentina, Brazil, Mexico	Other LA and Caribbean[1]	European ldcs	Middle East and N. Africa[1]	Other African states[1]	ASEAN states[2]	Hong Kong, Taiwan, S. Korea	India, Bangladesh, Pakistan, Sri Lanka	Other Asian ldcs
Exports to:													
North America	1960-2	6,495	4,432	2,063	1,159	1,487	112	95	444	711	202	363	31
	1970-2	13,225	9,820	3,405	2,159	2,204	214	228	704	1,270	2,698	486	39
	1974	44,452	24,893	19,559	5,631	7,073	493	638	1,528	4,534	5,626	787	39
EEC (9)	1960-2	11,650	7,220	4,430	1,098	1,137	424	717	2,098	774	174	754	187
	1970-2	22,968	12,197	10,501	2,050	2,005	1,196	1,279	3,059	1,012	969	686	114
	1974	67,486	25,850	41,636	4,246	3,299	2,004	3,018	6,376	2,633	2,677	1,340	162
United Kingdom	1960-2	3,982	2,469	1,513	271	373	105	167	631	294	120	520	45
	1970-2	5,207	2,960	2,247	306	442	222	204	756	261	385	367	30
	1974	13,358	5,252	8,106	660	759	258	486	1,160	418	838	566	40
EFTA	1960-2	879	627	252	126	108	73	67	172	44	13	18	10
	1970-2	2,177	1,554	623	275	281	267	141	353	50	130	45	15
	1974	6,214	3,275	2,939	554	492	459	332	784	163	355	96	33
Australia, New Zealand	1960-2	808	466	342	17	10	–	17	124	167	34	131	15
South Africa	1970-2	809	551	258	39	11	3	36	56	50	179	98	4
	1974	3,121	2,044	1,077	154	37	9	96	99	624	734	207	3
Japan	1960-2	1,717	1,135	584	129	146	3	31	55	502	118	111	98
	1970-2	7,093	3,992	3,101	382	677	19	144	473	1,593	780	360	121
	1974	28,005	9,856	18,149	1,040	922	68	295	902	6,878	2,642	596	61
Total developed market economies	1960-2	21,989	14,092	7,897	2,581	2,922	642	968	2,911	2,228	541	1,387	341
	1970-2	47,553	28,954	18,599	5,160	5,355	1,770	1,954	4,786	4,116	4,767	1,690	297
	1974	149,098	65,738	83,360	11,625	11,823	3,033	4,379	9,689	14,652	12,034	3,026	300
Centrally planned economies	1960-2	1,689	1,577	112	141	261	207	298	54	219	18	192	250
	1970-2	3,101	2,908	193	212	149	824	638	231	196	16	631	26
	1974	6,777	5,994	783	781	453	1,751	1,089	383	660	81	782	45
Oil producing states	1960-2	1,368	583	785	38	44	32	88	45	150	62	89	39
	1970-2	2,421	1,215	1,206	110	53	73	263	95	106	290	216	11
	1974	6,219	4,325	1,894	695	153	271	569	239	712	850	643	41
Argentina, Brazil, Mexico	1960-2	567	295	272	123	80	15	2	7	42	1	17	9
	1970-2	1,138	736	402	390	236	12	31	17	12	19	18	2
	1974	5,400	2,294	3,106	901	882	37	172	101	116	52	32	0
Other LA/Caribbean[1]	1960-2	596	388	208	135	169	3	18	2	17	12	33	0
	1970-2	1,675	1,137	538	436	567	24	16	5	25	56	15	2
	1974	8,149	2,807	5,342	1,636	820	30	32	10	519	151	12	0
European ldcs	1960-2	181	140	41	12	10	10	53	6	18	0	25	9
	1970-2	477	330	147	38	41	31	84	51	18	4	60	4
	1974	2,164	965	1,199	121	171	67	246	180	69	13	85	1

Table 1.5: Exports from Developing Countries to Selected Areas and World Totals: 1960-2, 1970-2 (Annual Averages) and 1974 (cont.)

(a) $m

Exports from:	Year	All ldcs inc. oil producers	All ldcs exc. oil producers	Oil producing states	Argentina, Brazil, Mexico	Other LA and Caribbean[1]	European ldcs	Middle East and N. Africa[1]	Other African states[1]	ASEAN states[2]	Hong Kong, Taiwan, S. Korea	India, Bangla-desh, Pakistan Sri Lanka	Other Asian ldcs
Exports to:													
Middle East & N. Africa[1]	1960-2	614	415	199	17	35	71	142	43	9	11	80	7
	1970-2	854	660	194	54	44	107	177	58	28	34	155	3
	1974	2,100	1,291	809	193	47	277	283	155	98	91	104	1
Other African states[1]	1960-2	405	296	109	4	2	11	42	126	15	29	54	14
	1970-2	1,196	914	282	25	14	22	71	522	74	87	81	20
	1974	3,180	1,972	1,208	133	72	74	114	905	315	184	163	17
ASEAN states[2]	1960-2	1,988	1,543	445	16	5	21	10	9	1,177	173	53	79
	1970-2	2,415	1,780	635	14	10	2	33	35	1,111	456	84	35
	1974	7,944	4,486	3,458	75	4	34	78	112	3,229	921	293	99
Hong Kong, Taiwan, S. Korea	1960-2	309	245	52	14	4	0	10	14	116	51	26	33
	1970-2	1,213	951	262	49	18	2	58	34	330	363	98	28
	1974	4,185	2,614	1,571	82	60	7	147	88	1,090	981	134	44
India, Bangladesh, Pakistan, Sri Lanka	1960-2	688	408	280	3	6	15	65	70	68	8	104	85
	1970-2	717	451	266	15	5	41	100	90	53	14	60	73
	1974	2,634	904	1,730	104	7	64	74	136	212	43	217	105
Other Asian ldcs	1960-2	202	200	26	5	2	6	5	7	65	54	41	8
	1970-2	543	506	37	20	6	6	7	0	260	146	89	16
	1974	587	524	63	8	1	2	6	0	289	95	121	2
All ldcs inc. oil producers	1960-2	6,390	3,991	2,399	356	356	163	434	326	1,567	374	511	269
	1970-2	12,273	8,308	3,965	1,150	994	318	840	899	1,991	1,347	861	174
	1974	41,871	21,492	20,379	3,522	2,507	854	1,690	2,249	6,501	3,334	1,703	273
All ldcs exc. oil producers	1960-2	5,022	3,408	1,614	318	312	131	346	281	1,417	312	422	230
	1970-2	9,852	7,093	2,759	1,040	941	245	577	804	1,885	1,331	645	163
	1974	35,652	17,167	18,485	2,827	2,354	583	1,121	2,010	5,789	2,484	1,060	232
Other countries	1960-2	706	592	114	144	62	2	103	80	74	58	53	7
	1970-2	1,536	1,121	415	211	136	13	143	284	292	81	70	212
	1974	11,146	4,547	6,041	1,366	537	270	900	522	524	490	180	11
World Total	1960-2	30,774	20,522	10,522	3,222	3,601	1,014	1,803	3,371	4,088	991	2,143	866
	1970-2	64,463	41,291	23,172	6,733	6,634	2,925	3,575	6,200	6,595	6,221	3,252	519
	1974	208,334	97,771	110,563	17,294	15,320	5,908	8,058	12,843	22,337	15,939	5,681	629

Table 1.5: Exports from Developing Countries to Selected Areas and World Totals: 1960-2, 1970-2 (Annual Averages) and 1974 (cont.)

(b) Annual growth rates (%) 1960-2 – 1970-2 and 1970-2 – 1974.

Exports from:	All ldcs inc. oil producers		All ldcs exc. oil producers		Oil producing states		Argentina, Brazil, Mexico		Other LA and Caribbean[1]		European ldcs		Middle East and N. Africa[1]		Other African states[1]		ASEAN states[2]		Hong Kong, Taiwan, S. Korea		India, Bangladesh, Pakistan, Sri Lanka		Other Asian ldcs	
Exports to:	1960/2 to 1970/2	1970/2 to 1974	1960/2 to 1970/2	1970/2 to 1974	1960/2 to 1970/2	1970/2 to 1974	1960/2 to 1970/2	1970/2 to 1974	1960/2 to 1960/2	1970/2 to 1974	1960/2 to 1970/2	1970/2 to 1974	1960/2 to 1970/2	1970/2 to 1974	1960/2 to 1970/2	1970/2 to 1974	1960/2 to 1970/2	1970/2 to 1974	1960/2 to 1970/2	1970/2 to 1974	1960/2 to 1970/2	1970/2 to 1974	1960/2 to 1970/2	1970/2 to 1974
North America	7.4	49.8	8.3	36.4	5.1	18.2	6.4	23.0	4.0	47.5	6.7	32.1	9.1	40.9	4.7	29.5	6.0	52.8	29.6	27.8	2.9	17.4	2.3	0
EEC (9)	6.9	43.2	5.4	28.5	9.0	58.3	6.4	27.5	5.8	18.1	10.9	18.8	6.0	33.1	3.8	27.7	2.7	37.5	18.8	40.3	−1.0	25.0	−4.8	12.4
United Kingdom	2.7	36.9	1.8	21.1	4.0	53.4	1.2	29.2	1.7	19.8	7.8	5.1	2.0	33.6	1.8	15.3	−1.2	17.0	12.4	29.6	−3.4	15.5	−4.0	10.0
EFTA	9.5	41.9	9.5	28.2	9.5	67.7	8.1	26.3	10.0	20.5	13.8	19.8	7.7	33.0	7.5	30.5	1.3	48.3	25.9	39.8	9.6	28.7	4.1	14.5
Australia, New Zealand, S. Africa	0.0	56.8	1.7	54.8	−2.8	61.0	8.6	58.1	1.0	49.8	11.9	44.2	7.8	38.7	−7.6	20.9	−1.1	132.0	18.0	60.1	−2.9	28.3	−12.4	−9.1
Japan	15.3	58.1	13.4	35.2	18.1	81.1	11.5	39.6	16.6	10.8	20.3	53.0	16.6	27.0	24.0	24.0	12.2	62.8	20.8	50.2	12.5	18.3	2.1	−20.4
Total developed market economies	8.0	46.4	7.5	31.4	8.9	64.9	7.2	31.1	6.2	30.2	10.7	19.7	7.3	30.9	5.1	26.5	6.3	52.7	24.3	36.2	2.0	21.4	−12.6	0.3
Centrally planned economies	6.3	29.8	6.3	27.2	5.6	59.5	4.2	54.4	−5.5	44.9	14.8	28.5	7.9	19.5	15.6	18.4	−1.1	49.9	−1 2	71.7	12.6	7.4	−20.3	20.1
Oil producing states	5.9	37.0	7.6	52.7	4.4	16.2	11.2	84.9	1.9	42.4	8.6	54.8	11.6	29.3	7.8	36.0	−3.4	8.87	16.7	43.1	9.3	43.9	−11.9	55.1
Argentina, Brazil, Mexice	7.2	26.1	9.6	46.1	4.0	96.1	12.2	32.2	11.4	55.2	−2.2	45.6	31.5	77.0	9.3	81.1	−11.8	113.0	34.2	39.9	0.6	21.1	−14.0	−63.2
Other Latin America/Caribbean[1]	10.9	69.5	11.3	35.2	10.0	114.9	12.4	55.4	12.9	13.1	23.1	7.7	−1.2	26.0	9.6	26.0	3.9	174.8	16.6	39.2	−7.6	−7.2	n.a.	−63.2
European ldcs	10.2	76.3	9.0	43.0	13.6	101.3	12.2	47.1	15.3	61.0	12.0	29.3	4.7	43.1	23.9	52.3	0	56.5	n.a.	48.1	9.1	12.3	−7.8	−37.0
Middle East and N. Africa[1]	3.4	35.0	4.7	25.1	−0.3	61.0	12.2	52.9	2.3	2.2	4.2	37.3	2.2	16.9	3.1	38.8	12.0	51.8	12.0	38.8	6.8	−12.4	−8.1	−30.7
Other African states[1]	11.4	38.5	11.9	29.2	10.0	62.4	20.1	74.6	21.4	72.6	7.2	49.8	5.4	17.1	15.3	20.1	17.3	62.1	11.6	28.4	21.1	26.2	3.6	−5.3
ASEAN states[2]	2.0	48.7	1.4	36.1	3.6	75.9	−1.3	75.0	7.2	−26.3	−21.0	157.2	12.7	33.2	14.5	47.3	−0.6	42.7	10.2	26.4	4.7	51.6	−7.8	41.4
Hong Kong, Taiwan, S. Korea	14.7	51.1	14.5	40.1	17.7	81.7	13.3	18.7	16.2	49.3	n.a.	51.8	19.2	36.3	9.3	37.3	11.0	48.9	21.7	39.3	14.2	10.9	−1.6	16.2
India, Bangladesh, Pakistan, Sri Lanka	0.4	54.3	1.0	26.1	−0.5	86.7	17.4	90.7	−1.8	11.9	10.6	16.0	4.4	−9.6	2.5	14.8	−2.5	58.7	5.8	45.4	−5.4	53.5	−1.5	12.9
Other Asian ldcs	10.4	2.6	9.4	1.2	3.6	19.4	15.0	−26.3	11.6	−45.0	–	−30.7	3.4	−5.0	n.a.	0	14.9	3.6	10.4	13.4	10.5	10.8	7.2	−50.0
All ldcs inc. oil producers	6.7	50.5	7.6	37.3	5.2	72.6	12.4	45.2	10.8	36.1	6.9	39.0	6.8	26.2	10.7	35.8	2.4	48.4	13.7	35.3	5.4	25.5	−4.3	16.2
All ldcs exc. oil producers	7.0	53.5	7.6	34.3	5.5	88.5	12.6	39.6	11.7	35.7	6.5	33.5	5.3	24.8	11.1	35.7	2.9	45.4	15.6	23.1	4.3	18.0	−3.4	12.5
Other countries	8.1	93.6	6.6	59.5	13.8	144.2	3.9	86.4	8.2	58.1	20.6	174.9	3.3	84.6	13.5	22.5	14.7	21.5	3.4	82.2	2.8	37.0	40.6	−62.7
World total	7.7	47.8	7.5	33.3	8.2	68.4	7.6	37.0	6.3	32.2	11.2	26.4	7.1	31.1	6.3	27.5	4.9	50.2	20.1	36.8	4.3	20.5	−5 0	6.6

1 Excluding oil producers.
2 Including Indonesia.

Source: International Monetary Fund, *Direction of Trade*, 1958-62, 1968-72, and 1970-74.

Table 1.6: Exports to Developing Countries from Selected Areas and World Totals: 1960-2, 1970-2 (Annual Averages) and 1974

(a) $m (fob)

Exports to:	Year	All ldcs inc. oil producers	All ldcs exc. oil producers	Oil producing states	Argentina, Brazil, Mexico	Other LA and Caribbean[1]	European ldcs	Middle East and N. Africa[1]	Other African states[2]	ASEAN states[2]	Hong Kong, Taiwan, S. Korea	India, Bangla-desh, Pakistan, Sri Lanka	Other Asian ldcs
Exports from:													
N. America	1960-2	7,473	6,287	1,186	1,729	1,548	306	542	234	577	452	881	134
	1970-2	15,374	12,650	2,724	3,434	2,835	543	1,132	518	1,279	1,747	1,004	450
	1974	35,287	27,695	7,592	9,174	5,393	192	2,606	980	3,204	4,014	1,682	892
EEC (9)	1960-2	10,828	8,245	2,583	1,105	1,187	738	1,300	1,609	744	278	1,088	196
	1970-2	21,185	16,092	5,088	2,156	2,235	2,463	2,480	3,277	1,354	920	1,019	193
	1974	46,997	32,874	14,123	5,224	7,540	5,689	6,259	5,550	3,254	1,788	1,708	204
United Kingdom	1960-2	3,444	2,701	743	229	374	185	303	533	349	128	590	52
	1970-2	5,287	3,910	1,377	393	596	378	557	724	501	319	435	38
	1974	8,863	6,031	2,832	591	715	611	1,082	993	969	546	456	34
EFTA	1960-2	1,207	1,042	165	227	160	107	148	172	63	45	101	19
	1970-2	2,927	2,447	480	452	310	372	323	519	165	177	105	24
	1974	6,770	5,372	1,398	1,052	564	1,011	720	1,065	403	384	243	37
Australia, New Zealand, S. Africa	1960-2	611	570	41	18	16	27	25	226	107	63	80	20
	1970-2	1,582	1,411	171	32	85	44	98	442	390	250	81	41
	1974	4,442	3,873	569	99	240	143	257	739	1,020	566	327	115
Japan	1960-2	2,194	1,841	353	127	157	28	77	185	529	395	201	268
	1970-2	8,575	7,142	1,433	511	762	119	177	390	2,152	2,591	319	589
	1974	22,772	16,962	5,810	2,133	2,052	345	435	368	5,407	6,023	895	283
Total developed market economies	1960-2	22,275	17,928	4,342	3,237	3,094	1,230	2,136	2,438	2,024	1,234	2,355	638
	1970-2	50,163	40,094	10,069	6,723	6,397	3,629	4,319	5,226	5,347	5,690	2,535	1,300
	1974	116,268	86,776	29,492	17,682	15,789	7,380	10,277	8,702	13,288	12,775	4,855	1,531
Centrally planned economies	1960-2	1,930	1,738	192	106	274	231	283	50	173	201	182	325
	1970-2	3,339	2,770	569	86	35[1]	802	424	202	258	538	408	62
	1974	7,332	5,964	1,368	183	150[1]	1,797	698	511	738	1,141	801	111
Oil producing states	1960-2	2,399	1,614	785	272	208	41	191	109	445	52	280	26
	1970-2	3,965	2,759	1,206	402	538	147	194	282	635	262	266	37
	1974	20,805	18,911	1,894	3,106	5,342	1,199	809	1,208	3,458	1,571	1,730	63
Argentina, Brazil, Mexico	1960-2	356	318	38	123	135	12	17	4	16	14	3	5
	1970-2	1,150	1,040	110	390	436	38	54	25	14	49	15	20
	1974	3,535	2,840	695	901	1,636	121	193	133	75	82	104	8
Other LA/Caribbean[1]	1960-2	256	312	44	80	169	10	35	2	5	4	6	2
	1970-2	994	941	53	236	567	41	44	14	10	18	5	6
	1974	2,570	2,417	153	882	820	171	47	72	4	60	7	1

Table 1.6: Exports to Developing Countries from Selected Areas and World Totals: 1960-2, 1970-2 (Annual Averages) and 1974 (cont.)

(a) $m (fob)

Exports to:	Year	All ldcs inc. oil producers	All ldcs exc. oil producers	Oil producing states	Argentina, Brazil, Mexico	Other LA and Caribbean[1]	European ldcs	Middle East and N. Africa[1]	Other African states[2]	ASEAN states[2]	Hong Kong, Taiwan, S. Korea	India, Bangladesh, Pakistan, Sri Lanka	Other Asian ldcs
Exports from:													
European ldcs	1960-2	163	131	32	15	3	10	71	11	21	0	15	6
	1970-2	318	245	73	12	24	31	107	22	2	2	41	6
	1974	853	582	271	37	30	67	277	74	34	7	64	2
Middle East & N. Africa[1]	1960-2	434	346	88	2	18	53	142	42	10	10	65	5
	1970-2	840	577	263	31	16	84	177	71	33	58	100	7
	1974	1,703	1,134	569	172	32	246	283	114	78	147	74	6
Other African states[1]	1960-2	326	281	45	7	2	6	43	126	9	14	70	7
	1970-2	899	804	95	17	5	51	58	522	35	34	90	0
	1974	2,348	2,109	239	101	10	180	155	905	112	88	136	0
ASEAN states[2]	1960-2	1,567	1,417	150	42	17	18	9	15	1,177	116	68	65
	1970-2	1,991	1,885	106	12	25	18	28	74	1,111	330	53	260
	1974	6,816	6,104	712	116	519	69	98	315	3,229	1,090	212	289
Hong Kong, Taiwan, S. Korea	1960-2	374	312	62	1	12	0	11	29	173	51	8	54
	1970-2	1,347	1,057	290	19	56	4	34	87	456	363	14	146
	1974	3,457	2,607	850	52	151	13	91	184	921	981	43	95
India, Bangladesh, Pakistan Sri Lanka	1960-2	511	422	89	17	33	25	80	54	53	26	104	41
	1970-2	861	645	216	18	15	60	155	81	84	98	60	89
	1974	1,697	1,054	643	32	12	85	104	163	293	134	217	121
Other Asian ldcs	1960-2	269	230	39	9	0	9	7	14	79	33	85	8
	1970-2	174	163	11	2	2	4	3	20	35	28	73	16
	1974	273	232	41	0	0	1	1	17	99	44	105	2
All ldcs inc. oil producers	1960-2	6,378	5,010	1,368	567	596	181	614	405	1,988	309	688	202
	1970-2	12,273	9,852	2,421	1,138	1,675	477	854	1,196	2,415	1,213	717	543
	1974	42,620	36,555	6,065	5,399	8,104	2,152	2,058	3,161	7,641	4,204	2,692	587
All ldcs exc. oil producers	1960-2	3,979	3,396	583	295	388	140	415	296	1,543	257	408	176
	1970-2	8,308	7,093	1,215	736	1,137	330	660	914	1,780	951	451	506
	1974	21,815	17,644	4,171	5,216	2,762	953	1,249	1,953	4,183	2,633	962	524
World total	1960-2	30,583	24,676	5,907	3,910	3,964	1,642	3,033	2,893	4,185	1,744	3,225	1,165
	1970-2	65,775	52,716	13,059	7,947	8,107	4,908	5,597	6,624	8,020	7,441	3,660	1,905
	1974	166,220	131,189	35,031	23,081	24,043	11,329	10,975	12,374	21,667	18,120	8,348	2,229

Table 1.6: Exports to Developing Countries from Selected Areas and World Totals: 1960-2, 1970-2 (Annual Averages) and 1974 (cont.)

(b) Annual growth Rates (%) 1960-2 – 1970-2 and 1970-2 – 1974

Exports to:	All ldcs inc. oil producers		All ldcs exc. oil producers		Oil producing states		Argentina, Brazil, Mexico		Other LA and Caribbean[1]		European ldcs		Middle East and N. Africa[1]		Other African states[1]		ASEAN states[2]		Hong Kong, Taiwan, S. Korea		India, Bangladesh, Pakistan, Sri Lanka		Other Asian ldcs	
Exports from:	1960/2 to 1970/2	1970/2 to 1974	1960/2 to 1970/2	1970/2 to 1974	1960/2 to 1970/2	1970/2 to 1974	1960/2 to 1970/2	1970/2 to 1974	1960/2 to 1970/2	1970/2 to 1974	1960/2 to 1970/2	1970/2 to 1974	1960/2 to 1970/2	1970/2 to 1974	1960/2 to 1970/2	1970/2 to 1974	1960/2 to 1970/2	1970/2 to 1974	1960/2 to 1970/2	1970/2 to 1974	1960/2 to 1970/2	1970/2 to 1974	1960/2 to 1970/2	1970/2 to 1974
N. America	7.5	31.9	7.2	29.8	8.7	40.7	7.1	38.8	6.2	23.9	5.9	–29.3	7.6	32.0	8.3	24.1	8.3	35.8	14.5	32.0	1.3	18.8	12.9	25.6
EEC (9)	7.0	30.4	6.9	26.9	7.0	40.5	6.9	34.3	6.5	50.0	12.8	32.2	6.7	36.2	7.4	19.2	6.2	33.9	12.7	24.8	–0.6	18.8	–0.2	1.9
United Kingdom	4.3	18.8	3.8	15.5	6.4	27.2	5.5	14.6	4.8	6.3	7.4	17.4	6.3	24.8	3.1	11.1	3.7	24.6	9.6	19.6	–3.0	1.6	–3.1	–3.6
EFTA	9.3	32.2	8.9	30.0	11.3	42.8	6.7	32.5	6.8	22.1	13.3	39.6	8.1	30.6	11.7	27.1	10.1	34.7	14.7	29.5	0.4	32.3	2.4	15.5
Australia, New Zealand, S. Africa	10.0	41.1	9.5	40.0	15.3	49.3	5.9	45.7	18.1	41.3	5.0	48.1	14.6	37.9	6.9	18.7	13.8	37.8	14.8	31.3	0.1	59.2	7.4	41.0
Japan	14.6	38.5	14.5	33.4	15.0	59.5	14.9	61.0	17.1	39.1	15.5	42.6	8.7	34.9	7.7	–1.9	15.0	35.9	20.7	32.5	4.7	41.0	8.2	–21.7
Total developed market economies	8.5	32.3	8.4	29.4	8.8	43.1	7.6	38.0	7.5	35.1	11.4	26.7	7.3	33.5	8.0	18.5	10.2	35.5	16.5	30.9	4.1	24.2	7.4	5.6
Centrally planned economies	5.6	30.0	4.8	29.1	11.5	34.0	–2.1	28.6	–18.6	62.4	13.3	30.9	4.1	18.1	15.0	36.3	4.1	42.0	10.3	28.5	8.4	25.2	–15.3	21.4
Oil producing states	5.2	72.6	5.5	88.5	4.4	16.2	4.0	96.1	10.0	114.9	13.6	101.3	–0.3	61.0	10.0	62.4	3.6	75.9	17.7	81.7	–0.5	86.7	3.6	19.4
Argentina, Brazil, Mexico	12.4	45.2	12.6	39.6	11.2	84.9	12.2	32.2	12.4	55.4	12.2	47.1	12.2	52.9	20.1	74.6	–1.3	75.0	13.3	18.7	17.4	90.7	15.0	–26.3
Other Latin American and Caribbean[1]	10.8	36.1	11.7	35.7	1.9	42.4	11.4	55.2	12.9	13.1	15.3	61.0	2.3	2.2	21.4	72.6	7.2	–26.3	16.2	49.3	–1.8	11.9	11.6	–45.0
European ldcs	6.9	39.0	6.4	33.5	8.6	54.8	–2.2	45.6	23.1	7.7	12.0	29.3	4.2	37.3	7.2	49.8	–21.0	157.2	n.a.	51.8	10.6	16.0	–	–30.7
Middle East and North Africa[1]	6.8	26.2	5.2	24.8	11.6	29.3	31.5	77.0	–1.2	26.0	4.7	43.1	2.2	16.9	5.4	17.1	12.7	33.2	19.2	36.3	4.4	–9.6	3.4	–5.0
Other African states[1]	10.7	35.8	11.1	35.7	7.8	36.0	9.3	81.1	9.6	26.0	23.9	52.3	3.1	38.8	15.3	20.1	14.5	47.3	9.3	37.3	2.5	14.8	n.a.	0
ASEAN states[2]	2.4	48.4	2.9	45.4	–3.4	88.7	–11.8	113.0	3.9	174.8	–	56.5	12.0	51.8	17.3	62.1	–0.6	42.7	11.0	48.9	–2.5	58.7	14.9	3.6
Hong Kong, Taiwan, S. Korea	13.7	35.3	13.0	23.1	16.7	43.1	34.3	39.9	16.6	39.2	n.a.	48.1	12.0	38.8	11.6	28.4	10.2	26.4	21.7	39.3	5.8	45.4	10.4	13.4
India, Bangladesh, Pakistan, Sri Lanka	5.4	25.5	4.3	18.0	9.3	43.9	0.6	21.1	–7.6	–7.2	9.1	12.3	6.8	–12.4	4.1	26.2	4.7	51.6	14.2	10.9	–5.4	53.5	10.5	10.8
Other Asian ldcs	–4.3	16.2	–3.4	12.5	–11.9	55.1	–14.0	–63.2	n.a.	–63.2	–7.8	–37.0	–8.1	–30.7	3.6	–5.3	–7.8	41.4	–1.6	16.2	–1.5	12.9	7.2	–50.0
All ldcs inc. oil producers	6.7	50.5	7.0	53.5	5.9	37.0	7.2	26.1	10.9	69.5	10.2	76.3	3.4	35.0	11.4	38.5	2.0	48.7	14.7	51.1	0.4	54.3	10.4	50.5
All ldcs exc. oil producers	7.6	37.3	7.6	34.3	7.6	52.7	9.6	46.1	11.3	35.2	9.0	43.0	4.7	25.1	11.9	29.2	1.4	36.1	14.5	40.1	1.0	26.1	9.4	1.2
World total	8.0	36.2	7.9	35.5	8.3	38.9	7.3	42.7	7.4	43.7	11.6	32.2	6.3	25.2	8.6	23.2	6.7	39.3	15.6	34.5	1.3	31.6	5.0	5.4

1 Excluding trade with Cuba.
2 Including Indonesia.

Source: International Monetary Fund, *Direction of Trade*, 1958-62, 1968-72, and 1970-4.

compared with 3 per cent and 6 per cent respectively in 1960-2. Japan's main ldc trading partners in both periods were the oil producing states and the Asian ldcs, in particular the member states of ASEAN. The pattern of growth of Japan's imports from ldcs, however, indicates that African and European ldcs are increasing their importance as suppliers to Japan – and in 1970-2 African ldcs were running a trade surplus with Japan. Meanwhile, after its exports to Hong Kong, Taiwan, and Korea, Japan's exports to Latin America and the Caribbean had the fastest growth rate. In aggregate, trade between the Socialist countries and ldcs was not particularly dynamic during the decade. But the aggregate conceals wide differences in performance. Thus, trade in both directions between African countries and Socialist countries grew rapidly, as did the trade of European developing countries. Exports from the Socialist countries to Hong Kong, Taiwan, and South Korea also expanded rapidly; but their exports to Socialist countries fell. The importance of bilateral trading agreements between India and the Soviet Union is reflected in the rapid growth of exports from the subcontinent to Socialist countries.

The pattern of trade flows among the developing countries themselves confirms the importance of regional trade, a subject which we discuss in Chapter 8. Most of their trade with developing countries was intra-regional, although it was not the most rapidly growing sector. Outside purely regional trade, exports from Latin American countries to Africa expanded very rapidly, although from an extremely low base. These two groups of ldcs were also the only groups whose exports to other ldcs expanded more rapidly than their trade with the world as a whole. In Chapter 8 we investigate the reasons why this is so. At this stage, we merely note that it is in these areas that the greatest interest in and impetus to regional integration and intra-regional trade have been shown; the figures in these tables are a first indication that these efforts may be having a result.

Note: Country Groupings Used in Tables 1.2, 1.3, 1.5 and 1.6

North America: United States, Canada.

EEC (9): Belgium, Denmark, France, West Germany, Ireland, Italy, Luxembourg, Netherlands, United Kingdom.

EFTA: Austria, Finland, Iceland, Norway, Portugal, Sweden, Switzerland.

Total developed market economies: all above plus Australia, New Zealand, South Africa, Japan.

Oil producing countries: Algeria, Bahrein, Brunei, Ecuador, Gabon, Indonesia, Iran, Iraq, Kuwait, Libya, Nigeria, Oman, Qatar, Saudi Arabia, Trinidad and Tobago, United Arab Emirates, Venezuela.

Other Latin America and Caribbean: Bolivia, Chile, Colombia, Costa Rica, Dominican Republic, El Salvador, Guatemala, Haiti, Honduras, Nicaragua, Panama, Paraguay, Peru, Uruguay, Bahamas, Barbados, Belize, Bermuda, Guadeloupe, French Guiana, Guyana, Jamaica, Martinique, Netherlands Antilles, Panama Canal Zone, Surinam, Virgin Islands, Windward Islands.

European ldcs: Cyprus, Malta, Turkey, Yugoslavia.

Middle East and North Africa: Egypt, Israel, Jordan, Lebanon, Syria, Yemen Arab Republic, People's Democratic Republic of Yemen, Morocco, Sudan, Tunisia.

Other Africa: Angola, Burundi, Cameroon, Cape Verde Islands, Central African Republic, Chad, Comoro Islands, Congo People's Republic, Dahomey, Equatorial Guinea, Ethiopia, French Territory of the Afars and Issas, The Gambia, Ghana, Guinea-Bissau, Guinea, Ivory Coast, Kenya, Liberia, Malagasy Republic, Malawi, Mali, Mauritania, Mauritius, Mozambique, Niger, Reunion, Rhodesia, Rwanda, Sao Tome and Principe, Seychelles, Senegal, Sierra Leone, Somalia, Tanzania, Togo, Uganda, Upper Volta, Zaire, Zambia.

ASEAN members: Indonesia, Malaysia, Philippines, Singapore, Thailand.[19]

Other Asia: Afghanistan, Burma, Kampuchea (Cambodia), Laos, Macao, Maldive Islands, Nepal, Timor, South Vietnam.

Centrally planned economies: Albania, Bulgaria, China, Cuba, Czechoslovakia, E. Germany, Hungary, Mongolia, N. Korea, N. Vietnam, Poland, USSR.

Notes

1. Paul Streeten, 'Trade Strategies for Development: Some Themes for the Seventies', in P. Streeten (ed.), *Trade Strategies for Development* (London, Macmillan, 1973), p.6
2. G. Myrdal, *Economic Theory and Underdeveloped Regions* (London, Duckworth, 1957).
3. Population growth increases the numbers dependent on the resources of the rural sector for their livelihood and, without changes in production techniques, average incomes are likely to drop in consequence.
4. See H. Myint, *The Economics of Developing Countries* (London, Hutchinson University Library, 1967).
5. See, for instance, A.I. MacBean, *Export Instability and Economic Development* (London, Allen & Unwin, 1966).

6. Ibid.; also Commonwealth Secretariat, *Terms of Trade Policy for Primary Commodities,* Commonwealth Economic Papers, No. 4, 1975, pp.15-16.
7. See pp.34-49 (Table 1.4); also Chapters 3, 4, and 5.
8. See Chapter 5 for a discussion of this point in relation to manufactures.
9. See, for instance, R. Prebisch, 'The Role of Commercial Policies in Underdeveloped Countries', *American Economic Review, Papers & Proceedings,* May 1959, and Hans Singer, 'The Distribution of Gains between Investing and Borrowing Countries', *American Economic Review, Papers & Proceedings,* May 1950.
10. A. Emmanuel, *Unequal Exchange* (London, New Left Books, 1972).
11. See, for instance, M. Barratt Brown, *The Economics of Imperialism* (Harmondsworth, Penguin, 1974), p.232.
12. Emmanuel, p.136.
13. See F. Stewart, 'Trade and Technology' in Streeten, op. cit., pp.231-63.
14. See, for instance, O. Sunkel, 'Transnational Capitalism and National Disintegration in Latin America' *Social and Economic Studies,* Vol. 22, No. 1, March 1973, pp.132-76.
15. See Chapter 3 for a discussion of commodity price changes.
16. There is a considerable discrepancy between the figures presented by GATT (used in Tables 1.1 and 1.4) and those presented by the IMF (Tables 1.2, 1.3, 1.5, and 1.6) for world trade totals and the shares of ldcs in any one year, although the broad trends over the years shown by both organisations are similar. Differences in annual statistics result from different recording and estimating systems used in the different organisations.
17. See International Bank for Reconstruction and Development (IBRD), *Annual Report,* 1975; Edith Hodgkinson, 'OPEC Aid: The Programme of the Newly Rich', *ODI Review 2 - 1975.*
18. The shares of manufactures and primary product exports do not quite add up to 100 per cent because of a small residue of unclassified exports in the total.
19. Indonesia is included twice: in oil producing countries and ASEAN. Since ASEAN is the only ldc regional grouping specifically shown in these tables, it is included in order to preserve the unity of the group.

2 THE INSTITUTIONAL BACKGROUND

Over the past thirty years developing countries have moved from being largely passive spectators in a world whose rules were made entirely by the big powers to being active participants – although, many people would say, still in a world whose rules are made by the big powers. Developing countries' problems – in which trade problems play a major role – have over the years become the main focus of attention in United Nations agencies and in GATT, and new concern with commodity trade in the seventies has created new agencies and conferences in which relations between developed and developing countries are being argued out. At the same time, the rules of the world trade 'game' are being perpetually modified and re-written. Major elements in this process of modification are, firstly, the apparent movement in trade patterns (or at least trade treaty links) from 'global' patterns back to regional ties; and, secondly (and probably more significantly) the ever-growing role of governments both in determining the rules of the game and in becoming prime movers and participants in actual trading.

This chapter will examine some of these patterns and try to assess what they mean for developing countries. First, we look at the role played by the main established global institutions – GATT and UNCTAD – in setting out the ground-rules for ldcs' trade and the part ldcs have played in the institutions. Second, we look at the role of national governments in international trade, alone in conjunction with other governments.

GLOBAL INSTITUTIONS: GATT AND UNCTAD

GATT and UNCTAD are the two major global institutions in which developed and developing countries' governments meet to discuss trade issues.[1] Although their secretariats are based only a short walk from one another in Geneva (UNCTAD also has offices in the UN Headquarters in New York) their styles of operation are markedly different. This reflects their respective origins as well as the ways in which they have developed. Nevertheless, the two organisations' methods, successes, and failures have affected each other's development, and governments have been able to use both at once – or, on occasions, one against the other – to pursue their aims.

GATT

The General Agreement on Tariffs and Trade is a treaty which sets out rules of conduct in the field of international trade. Members (Contracting Parties) agree to apply these rules to their trade policy, and the agreement permits sanctions against countries which openly flout the rules. The rules which GATT exists to supervise and enforce cover mainly levels and structure of import duties, export subsidies, and non-tariff barriers (quotas, rules of origin, health regulations, etc.).

Membership

At present, there are eighty-three full members. Three countries have been accepted in principle for membership, but admission has not been ratified by all the members. Twenty-four ex-colonial territories are also subject to GATT rules in an interim way, pending full membership. Thus, although GATT's membership is almost universal, it does not compare in scope with that of UNCTAD. The most notable absentees are the USSR and China, although Czechoslovakia, Hungary, Poland, and Romania are full members.

Basic Conditions

The GATT was first signed in 1947 by twenty-three countries (Australia, Belgium, Brazil, Burma, Canada, Ceylon, Chile, China (Taiwan), Cuba, Czechoslovakia, France, India, Lebanon, Luxembourg, the Netherlands, New Zealand, Norway, Pakistan, S. Rhodesia, S. Africa, Syria, United Kingdom, United States). The signatories expressed their desire to contribute to

> . . .raising standards of living, ensuring full employment and a large and steadily growing volume of real income and effective demand, developing the full use of the resources of the world and expanding the production and exchange of goods. . .[through] reciprocal and mutually advantageous arrangements directed to the substantial reduction of tariffs and other barriers to trade and to the elimination of discriminatory treatment in international commerce.[2]

Table 2.1: GATT Membership as at September 1976

Contracting Parties to the GATT (83)

Argentina	Greece	Peru
Australia	Guyana	Poland
Austria	Haiti	Portugal
Bangladesh	Hungary	Rhodesia
Barbados	Iceland	Romania
Belgium	India	Rwanda
Benin	Indonesia	Senegal
Brazil	Ireland	Sierra Leone
Burma	Israel	Singapore
Burundi	Italy	South Africa
Cameroon	Ivory Coast	Spain
Canada	Jamaica	Sri Lanka
Central African Republic	Japan	Sweden
Chad	Kenya	Switzerland
Chile	Korea	Tanzania
China	Kuwait	Togo
Congo	Luxembourg	Trinidad and Tobago
Cuba	Madagascar	Turkey
Cyprus	Malawi	Uganda
Czechoslovakia	Malaysia	United Kingdom
Dahomey	Malta	United States of America
Denmark	Mauritania	Upper Volta
Dominican Republic	Mauritius	Uruguay
Egypt	Netherlands	Yugoslavia
Finland	New Zealand	Zaire
France	Nicaragua	
Gabon	Niger	
Gambia	Nigeria	
Germany, Fed. Rep. of	Norway	
Ghana	Pakistan	

Acceded provisionally (3)

Colombia	Philippines	Tunisia

Countries which maintain a de facto *application of the GATT (24)*

Algeria	Grenada	Qatar
Angola	Guinea-Bissau	São Tome and Principe
Bahamas	Kampuchea (Cambodia)	Surinam
Bahrain	Lesotho	Swaziland
Botswana	Maldives	Tonga
Cape Verde	Mali	United Arab Emirates
Equatorial Guinea	Mozambique	Yemen, People's Dem. Rep.
Fiji	Papua New Guinea	Zambia

Thus, reciprocal negotiations, conducted on a bilateral or multilateral basis among members, and the extension of all negotiated 'concessions' to the entire group under the most-favoured-nation (mfn) clause, formed the two foundations of the GATT. These principles are still fundamental to the agreement, although a number of exceptions were allowed from the start[3] and many new exceptions (often applying to developing countries) have been allowed as time has gone on.

The Mfn Clause

In GATT, this clause states that 'any advantage, favour, privilege or immunity granted by any contracting party to any product originating for or destined for any other country shall be accorded immediately and unconditionally to the like product originating in or destined for the territories of all other contracting parties'.[4] Thus, no special import duties should be levied on any particular countries' products. Thus import duties should not be levied in a discriminatory manner on any particular country's products. In addition, there should not in general be any provision for special preferences, on the other hand, to be given to any specially favoured supplier countries.

Exceptions to the Mfn Clause

Several exceptions to this rule were allowed from the start. First, existing tariff preferences between Britain and the Commonwealth area, France, Benelux and their colonies, and the United States, its dependencies and the Philippines, were allowed to continue.[6] But it was agreed that the percentage-point gap between mfn rates and those applied to preferred partners could not be enlarged, although mfn tariffs – and hence preferential margins – could be reduced.

Second, provision for the creation of customs unions and free trade areas was built into the GATT.[7] Under Article XXIV, customs unions and free trade areas are intended to eliminate duties 'and other restrictive regulations of commerce' on 'substantially all'[8] trade between the member states, at least in products originating in the countries concerned. Any plan to create a new customs union or free trade area should be submitted to GATT for the approval of the contracting parties, and should contain 'a plan and schedule for the formation of such a customs union or such a free trade area within a reasonable length of time'.[9]

The provisions of the Article have proved extremely vague and flexible. They have been used to justify not only genuine regional trade arrangements – such as the European Community and EFTA –

which have shown clear, well-defined timetabled progress towards internal free trade, but also less defined plans for economic co-operation among more or less equal partners, such as the Latin American Free Trade Area (LAFTA). Until the signing of the Lomé Convention in 1975, the EEC also used the provisions to rationalise its preferences for Yaoundé associates in return for free trade area treatment ('revenue preferences') given by many Francophone African countries to imports from the European Community.[10]

Reciprocity

Developed countries negotiating in GATT are expected to do so on a basis of reciprocity, to gain mutual concessions. This attitude reflects national, mercantilist views of the effects of reductions in trade barriers. Where close attention is paid to the trade balance as an element in the wider balance of international payments, reductions in protective barriers tend to be seen as losses, in increasing imports (negative elements in the balance), rather than as gains in raising the efficiency of use of resources by making more competitive supplies of a product available. Thus, negotiations set off each country or customs area against all the others. They become a long process of requests, offers, and compromises. Because each country sees a concession on tariffs or other barriers as a potential balance of payments loss, each concession given has to be matched by one received, thus enabling negotiations to be presented to the public at home as a 'success' for each participant.

Developing Countries in GATT: Non-reciprocity

Until 1965, no special provisions existed in GATT to cover the trade problems of developing countries. Ldcs had been pressing for some years for recognition of their special problems, following the publication by GATT in 1958 of *Trends in International Trade.* This report had highlighted many trade barriers which weighed particularly heavily on ldcs' exports, such as higher than average tariffs, heavy effective protection of processing, and import quotas. Between 1958 and 1963 a committee of the Contracting Parties (Committee III) made some steps with a view to alleviating some of these problems. But the developed countries undertook no precise commitments. For them, the accent was still heavily on *quid pro quo* as a principle of negotiations; and ldcs were unable to exert any bargaining power.

However, one main aim of the ldcs in GATT in this period was to gain acceptance for the principle of non-reciprocity. In their view, this would mean that, however negotiations among developed countries were conducted, developing countries' need to protect their economies, in particular their infant industries, from imported competition would be recognised. The non-reciprocity clause, as eventually written into GATT, was cautiously worded.

Part IV of the GATT, covering trade and development, was introduced in 1965, while the 'Kennedy' round of trade negotiations was in progress. Its main statement is that developing Contracting Parties 'should not be expected, in the course of trade negotiations, to make contributions which are inconsistent with their individual development, financial and trade needs, taking into consideration past development'.[11] This was the interpretation put on the provision that 'the developed contracting parties do not expect reciprocity for commitments made by them in trade negotiations to reduce or remove tariffs and other barriers to the trade of less developed contracting parties'.[12] The principle of non-reciprocity, as thus set out, was written into the framework for the Kennedy round (in which only a few developing countries were required to make concessions) and was carried forward into the Tokyo Declaration, of September 1973, which formally inaugurated the round of GATT negotiations which effectively began in 1975.

Developing Countries in GATT Negotiations

Since the establishment of GATT as a global negotiating forum on tariffs and other trade measures, six 'rounds' of negotiations have been held. Under the mfn clause, any cuts in tariffs or non-tariff barriers made by any participant are extended to all parties to GATT. Thus any developing country which joins the Agreement gains, as a legal entitlement, comparable treatment to that given to all existing members;[13] and since the introduction of Part IV, ldcs which join GATT have to make few, if any, concessions in return. Nevertheless, it is only really since the 'Kennedy' round of the sixties (the main thrust of which took place under the Johnson and Nixon administrations in the USA) that ldcs have taken part in GATT negotiations.

It is obvious from the outcome of the Kennedy round that the non-reciprocity clause has its disadvantages as well as its advantages in negotiations. The Kennedy round began with a ringing declaration that the developed countries would make 'every effort' to reduce barriers to imports from ldcs without expecting reciprocity. They were also, they declared, ready to consider making tariff reductions deeper than the general rule, proposed to be 50 per cent, on products of which ldcs were the main suppliers.

Developing countries took part in the negotiations by tabling 'affirmative offers' of trade concessions which they were prepared to make. These were held back until developed countries' own offers on products of interest to ldcs were known. But, on the other hand the developed countries took the stand that their own offers would only be extended to countries which were prepared to 'make contributions' to the negotiations; thus, a measure of reciprocity was maintained. (In the event some twenty developing countries took an active part in the Kennedy round negotiations.)[14] Moreover, although the method of negotiation used broadly satisfied the non-reciprocity principle as interpreted by GATT – in that ldcs were not required to give concessions equivalent to those exchanged among developed countries – it also allowed concessions made by developed to developing countries to be made in a spirit of 'take it or leave it' and deprived ldcs of a vital lever – the ability to strike bargains.

Kennedy round tariff reductions by developed countries (which averaged around 35 per cent) affected mainly chemicals, pulp and paper, machinery, transport equipment, raw materials other than fuels, non-ferrous metals, and 'miscellaneous manufactures'. Most of the concessions were negotiated among developed countries and on products mainly of interest to them: either on those traded mainly among them or on those regarded as essential raw materials for industry. To the extent that developing countries were competitive suppliers, they could take advantage of the negotiated concessions through the mfn rule. However, agricultural products in general were excluded from the negotiations because of a conflict of interest between the United States and the EEC. The USA was concerned to gain as much as possible for its farm exports and set off concessions by its trading partners on agriculture against its own concessions on industrial products, while the EEC was in the process of establishing a common agricultural policy, aiming (among other things) at Community self-sufficiency. Tropical products, too, were not generously treated by the main participants. In addition, few non-tariff barriers to ldcs' exports were abolished or even reduced: indeed, these have become more important as tariffs have been reduced. And, as an UNCTAD study[15] pointed out, even after the Kennedy round tariffs levied by developed countries on goods imported from ldcs were still generally higher than those on trade among developed countries, and levels of effective protection[16] remained high.

The GSP

For many developing countries, the main advantage of the introduction of Part IV of the GATT has been that the Generalized System of Preferences (GSP) schemes which have now been introduced by all developed countries were given legal validity within GATT and could not, therefore, be easily abandoned.[17] It is clear that, as far as the body of legal provisions which goes to make up the GATT is concerned, the GSP has become an accepted part of the whole. And one big difference betweeen the situation at the start of the Kennedy round and the present state of affairs in GATT negotiations is that ldcs' negotiating positions start from a point at which a commitment exists to maintain and improve the GSP as an integral part of the present round of negotiations.

Nevertheless, the attitude of developed countries to the GSP within GATT negotiations remains ambivalent. Many developed countries maintain that the GSP is a set of independent, unilateral concessions – 'free gifts' given, not negotiated, by the developed countries – and that, as such, they are not negotiable. Any improvements, while perhaps admissible as contributions to the negotiations, would therefore also be made purely unilaterally. For developed countries which take this point of view, the negotiations proper would presumably be limited to discussions of mfn tariff reductions, cuts in non-tariff barriers, etc.[18]

It is hard to see how this attitude can be maintained consistently with the declaration which opened the current round of GATT negotiations. Even disregarding this, it is a fact that most developed countries have made annual improvements to their GSP schemes and that, although these are unilateral concessions in the sense that developing countries make no concessions in return, they have generally been made after intensive and often continuous consultations with ldcs; even if not within the context of formal international negotiations.

Developing Countries and the 'Tokyo Round'

The inadequacies both of the Kennedy round and the imperfections of GSP schemes have alerted many ldcs to the need for a much more active role in the current Tokyo round of GATT negotiations. In broad terms, developing countries' trade problems have been more clearly stressed than in any previous GATT negotiations:[19] and the negotiations as a whole are also to be wider in scope than any previous series.

The general intention is substantial reductions of virtually every type of trade barrier: tariffs, non-tariff barriers, 'countervailing' duties levied on subsidised exports, 'safeguard' measures taken by governments to prevent imports from threatening established industries, and the wide range of protective measures affecting agricultural products.[20] Industrial and agricultural products are covered, including tropical products and raw materials, 'whether in primary form or at any stage of processing'.[21]

The Tokyo Declaration stressed that developing countries were to be given 'special and more favourable' treatment 'in areas of negotiation where this is feasible and appropriate'.[22] Reciprocity (in the sense already defined) was not expected from developing countries.[23] Tropical products were to be treated as a special and priority sector:[24] and overall, the negotiations were to provide, 'in the largest possible measure, a substantial improvement in the conditions of access for the products of interest to the developing countries and, wherever appropriate, measures designed to attain stable, equitable and remunerative prices for primary products'.[25] This last object is a completely new departure for GATT trade negotiations.

The Tokyo round hung fire until late in 1975. Formally, the delay was due to the United States' lack of negotiating authority: the Trade Act giving this authority to the Administration was passed only in the autumn of 1974. Underlying this lag, however, was a considerable number of real problems: not least, the fact that between 1972, when the round of negotiations was proposed, and 1975 the state of most Western economies had changed from boom to recession. During this period the mood of most developed countries, with growing unemployment, had changed, and most were more concerned with trying to safeguard their own industries than with liberalising trade. Protectionism, far from being on the way out, looked like being on the increase; and in the short run, the only thing which trade negotiations could do was to prevent countries taking too restrictive unilateral action.

Some eighty developing countries are taking part in the Tokyo round (see Table 2.2). For ldcs as a group, a negotiating strategy which would satisfy their common interests and minimise differences among them is difficult to work out. The two basic principles on which ldcs' participation in the negotiations is founded are the maintenance of non-reciprocity and the preservation of preferential advantages which have been gained under the GSP. A third, even more general, is to gain

Table 2.2: Countries participating in Tokyo Round Trade Negotiations as at September 1976

*Algeria[1]	Luxembourg
Argentina[1]	Madagascar[1]
Australia	Malawi
Austria	Malaysia[1]
Bangladesh[1]	*Mali
Belgium	Mauritius[1]
Benin[2]	*Mexico[1]
*Botswana[1]	Netherlands
Brazil[1]	New Zealand
*Bulgaria	Nicaragua[1]
Burma[1]	Nigeria[1]
Burundi[1]	Norway
Cameroon[1]	Pakistan[1]
Canada	*Panama[1]
Chile[1]	*Papua New Guinea
**Colombia	*Paraguay
Congo[1]	Peru
*Costa Rica[1]	**Philippines[1]
Cuba[1]	Poland
Czechoslovakia	Portugal
Denmark	Romania[1]
Dominican Republic[1]	Senegal[1]
*Ecuador[1]	Singapore[1]
Egypt[1]	*Somalia[1]
*El Salvador[1]	South Africa
*Ethopia[1]	Spain[1]
Finland	Sri Lanka[1]
France	*Sudan[1]
Gabon[1]	*Swaziland[1]
Germany, Fed. Rep. of	Sweden
Ghana[1]	Switzerland
Greece	Tanzania[1]
*Guatemala[1]	*Thailand[1]
Haiti[1]	Togo[1]
*Honduras[1]	Tonga[1]
Hungary	Trinidad and Tobago[1]
Iceland	**Tunisia[1]
India[1]	Turkey[1]
Indonesia[1]	Uganda[1]
*Iran[1]	United Kingdom of Great Britain and Northern Ireland
*Iraq[1]	
Ireland	United States of America
Israel[1]	Uruguay[1]
Italy	*Venezuela[1]
Ivory Coast[1]	*Viet-Nam[1]
Jamaica[1]	Yugoslavia[1]
Japan	Zaire[1]
Kenya	*Zambia[1]
Korea[1]	European Communities 9

*Not Contracting Parties to GATT) 28
**Acceded provisionally to GATT)
[1] Countries participating in the Tokyo Round as developing countries

as far as possible the best possible terms of access to developed country markets. Taken in the aggregate, these demands may be self-contradictory.

In the field of tariffs, the only way round the possible contradiction is for ldcs to take a rather pragmatic line. Each product has to be considered individually. Ldcs can fight for the principle of non-reciprocity and the improvement of the GSP, where that seems of benefit to them. On some products where they are already competitive suppliers and which are thus already restricted or excluded from rich countries' GSP schemes or may be in future, they may do better to aim for negotiated reductions in mfn tariff rates. Even these do not necessarily require reciprocal concessions to be made by ldcs.

In the areas of non-tariff barriers to trade, 'safeguards' and countervailing duties, ldcs' negotiating strategies may be easier to define. By and large, it is in their interests to try to negotiate the reduction, generally, of NTBs and to accept some international surveillance of the conditions under which they can be applied. They can (and do) also argue that their export subsidies are necessary to the development of infant industries and should not, therefore, be subject to countervailing duties. And they are probably even more interested than developed countries in adequate international control of 'safeguard' measures taken by developed countries to protect their industries.

Agricultural products are one of the key areas of the negotiation. Here a solution depends largely on the working out of a reasonable bargain between the United States and the EEC. Ldcs' aims, however, are to get as liberal access as possible: to get as many products as possible accepted by the main trading powers as tropical products distinct from the main areas of competition between them: and to improve as much as possible the terms on which their major 'competing' products such as meat, vegetable oils, and fruit and vegetables gain entry to the developed countries. This last is an uphill struggle.

Generally speaking, in a protectionist world, ldcs may find it in their interests to have a greater area of international trading practices subject to international surveillance and control. But these controls must be effective. The problem is how to make them so. The experience of international surveillance which has emerged from the Multifibre Textile Agreement negotiated in GATT in 1973[26] is not encouraging – although it might be claimed that without it importing countries would be even more restrictive and arbitrary in their approach to textile imports. And any measures negotiated in GATT (or anywhere) will necessarily have to be a compromise between exporters' and importers' interests.

The work being pursued in GATT at the 'nuts and bolts' level has its parallel in other organisations. Perhaps the most influential of these, at least at the political level – although, as we shall see, it has also acted as a negotiating body particularly in the field of commodities – is the United Nations Conference on Trade and Development. It is to UNCTAD that we now turn.

UNCTAD

Since its foundation in 1964, UNCTAD has operated side by side (although not always in harmony) with GATT, and even provides advice to ldcs in GATT negotiations. Its area of operations often overlaps (e.g. in the GSP, which was an UNCTAD 'baby'). But its field has been much wider than that of GATT, and its style of operation quite different. GATT has deliberately restricted its operations to the questions involved in negotiations on tariffs and non-tariff barriers to trade: UNCTAD's work has covered the whole field of ldcs' trade and financing problems. GATT negotiations are conducted behind closed doors: UNCTAD conferences, and some routine committee meetings, are conducted in public. The GATT secretariat plays a generally self-effacing role, guiding the meetings of Contracting Parties and negotiating groups from behind: the UNCTAD secretariat has, from the start, taken definite views about the subjects discussed in UNCTAD and has not been hesitant in expressing them in published documents.

Origins of UNCTAD

UNCTAD grew from a resolution passed by the majority of UN General Assembly members in 1961, at a time when developing countries were becoming hostile to what they saw as GATT's domination by the West. The first UNCTAD conference was held in Geneva in 1964, convened under the auspices of the Economic and Social Committee of the UN (ECOSOC). At that time it was simply a one-off conference. Western countries, which had opposed the convening of the conference in the first place, were also against the creation of a standing body which would cut across and perhaps usurp the functions of GATT. But ldcs, with the support of the Socialist bloc, pressed for its establishment as a permanent UN institution. It was, in fact, made into a permanent organ of the UN General Assembly in December 1964.

Since 1964, three more conferences have been held at four-yearly intervals in 1968, 1972, and 1976 (New Delhi, Santiago de Chile and Nairobi). UNCTADS II and III continued the practice of UNCTAD I of being large, lavish, very wide-ranging conferences: they were widely criticised for achieving less than they set out to do (but see below). The fourth conference, by contrast, concentrated particularly on commodity problems, and was a less large and diffuse affair.

Membership and Structure

UNCTAD membership is open to any country which belongs to the United Nations, to any UN specialised agency (e.g. FAO, ILO) or to the International Atomic Energy Agency. Currently some 160 countries are members. Formally, UNCTAD is a subsidiary conference of the UN General Assembly; in practice, it is semi-autonomous with a great degree of working independence. In theory, ECOSOC is supposed to comment on, but not supervise, the activities of UNCTAD. In practice, it is a 'post box' for communication between UNCTAD and the General Assembly.

The main executive arm of UNCTAD is the Trade and Development Board, with sixty-eight members (originally fifty-five). Under it are six committees (originally four), on Commodities, Manufactures, Invisibles and Financing, Shipping, Preferences, and Transfer of Technology, reflecting UNCTAD's six main areas of activity.

Co-ordination: Lists and Groups

UNCTAD member countries are officially classified into four 'lists' from which the Trade and Development Board is drawn. African and Asian ldcs, plus Yugoslavia, are in list A: 'Western' countries – developed countries including Australia, Canada, and Japan, as well as European ldcs like Cyprus and Malta – comprise list B: Latin American and Caribbean countries make up list C: and Socialist states list D.

But the pattern which has emerged in practice has been rather different. One of the most remarkable elements to come out of UNCTAD, and spread its influence over most international agencies and conferences, has been the public solidarity of the developing countries. This began at the end of UNCTAD I, with the Joint Declaration of the Seventy-Seven Developing Countries.[27]

The Group of 77

The group now numbers over one hundred developing countries. It is an informal co-ordinating body with 'a heterogeneous composition. . . vast political ideological and cultural differences. . .varying levels of economic development. . .large numbers, and. . .absence of leadership by a big power'.[28] (While it is true that no one country dominates the Group, a few of the larger or politically more outspoken ldcs – Brazil, India, and more recently Algeria – have tended to play leading roles.)

Originally, the Group existed simply to co-ordinate ldc attitudes in UNCTAD: a co-ordination based on the belief that only united pressure on the developed countries could bring about desirable changes in their policies. However, Group of 77 co-ordination has spread to most other UN bodies, from the General Assembly down. The Group has regional sub-groups which try to assemble common attitudes among their members, which are in turn fused into overall '77' declarations and resolutions. On occasion, other regional bodies, particularly the UN Economic Commission for Africa (ECA), the Organisation for African Unity (OAU), and the Economic Commission for Latin America (ECLA) contribute to this co-ordination.

One important practical effect of the '77's' existence has been to strengthen the element of confrontation in UNCTAD's public debates and in other international bodies. Developing countries as a united group are seen to put pressure on developed countries ('Western' countries in particular) to demand concessions from them, and on occasion to embarrass them. The solidarity shown by developing countries has, in turn, increased the importance of co-ordination among developed 'Western' countries through the Organisation for Economic Co-operation and Development (OECD) and among Eastern European countries (Romania being something of a maverick) through the Council for Mutual Economic Assistance (CMEA). China has, so far, stayed clear of all groups while generally supporting ldc resolutions.

OECD includes in its membership, now twenty-five, all the developed 'Western' economies. Australia and New Zealand, as relatively highly developed countries with Asian-Pacific, rather than European-Atlantic perspectives, and mainly agricultural economies, and Portugal, Spain, Turkey, and Yugoslavia (a member of the '77') as semi-developed countries, are exceptions to this general rule. Within OECD, the main policy lines to be followed by the B group in UNCTAD and other international bodies are worked out, as far as possible.[29] In a confrontation situation like an UNCTAD meeting, such co-ordination may either help or hinder ldcs' efforts. If Western countries accept a particular principle, OECD is a good forum in which to work out the details (as happened, for example, with the GSP).[30]

UNCTAD Programmes and Methods

UNCTAD operates in two main ways. On the one side, there are the four-yearly conferences; on the other, the continuing work of committees and groups throughout the periods between them. The conferences, which are public affairs, serve as places where issues of concern to developing countries are brought into the open, and where attempts are made to gain commitments to particular programmes of action at the international level. In principle, they are also occasions where negotiation may take place, although (as we shall argue below), the atmosphere of the conferences militates heavily against this. The ongoing work of the committees and groups puts flesh on the bones of political declarations made at the conferences, and initiates new programmes of study and negotiation on aspects of international development.

Perhaps the two best-known aspects of international development policy with which UNCTAD has been directly associated are the concept of aid 'targets' – an idea which predates UNCTAD but which the organisation has made one of the cornerstones of its 'lobbying' for developing countries – and the agreement on the GSP. If these were all the organisation had to show for its existence, it could quite well be rated a failure; and many critics – even friendly ones – felt that after the third UNCTAD in Santiago the organisation had indeed achieved little. But if the ongoing work of UNCTAD, and its influence on other international discussions, are considered, the net results of its existence can be seen to be considerably more than these two 'substantive' results suggest.

The Role of the Conferences

As noted above, the three UNCTAD conferences have achieved much less than the organisation's supporters hoped for. One disillusioned commentator put it this way:

> Poor countries present non-negotiable demands: rich countries do not negotiate: meetings disperse after worthy – but debating-society – resolutions about Suez or Vietnam. Journalists enjoy themselves. . .Quadrennial confrontations of unrepresentative élites, from ungenerous rich and unco-ordinated poor countries,

produce unworkable compromises among unclear positions.[31]

This is entertaining and largely true. But it is easy to criticise large ineffectual frustrating conferences. Part of the reason for disaffection with UNCTAD stems from the way in which the conferences operate – in the glare of publicity, with grandiose political declarations for home consumption at every turn; part must be due to the fact that the conferences themselves focus on demands, not on negotiations: and few real negotiations can proceed in such an atmosphere. But to criticise UNCTAD conferences on these grounds is to miss the point. The conferences have served, perhaps more than any other forum, to keep development issues before the eyes of governments and public opinion, particularly in the West. Moreover, UNCTAD's record shows that so far the conferences themselves are places where discussions are started, rather than finished; subjects which remain alive are kept going, and negotiated, in specialised committees or other international bodies. And it would be hard to say that the efforts of the ldcs in UNCTAD to get better trade, investment, and aid terms from the rich countries had been less successful than the lower key GATT negotiations.

The agenda agreed for the fourth UNCTAD conference in Nairobi was more concise and better defined than those of the first three conferences. The key area in which the UNCTAD secretariat and the Group of 77 hoped for action and decisions was that of commodity trade and, in particular, the creation of an 'integrated programme for commodities' which would help to improve the terms on which primary commodities are traded, to the advantage of developing countries.[32] But alongside this proposal for a jointly financed set of commodity agreements went the elaboration of a comprehensive strategy to expand and diversify ldcs' exports of manufactures and semi-manufactured goods, which was in turn linked to ldcs' demands for progress on a preferential basis in the GATT multilateral trade negotiations. Other specific items on the agenda included the determination of a code of conduct for the transfer of technology from developed to developing countries (an important theme of UNCTAD committees since 1972 and an area closely related to ldcs' industrialisation and trade efforts) and decisions on measures to alleviate ldcs' debt problems, an area in which UNCTAD work was closely related to that of the World Bank.

There is no doubt that the commodities issue dominated the Nairobi conference. The ldcs, basing their point of view on a joint declaration of the Group of 77 which had been worked out earlier in the year in Manila,[33] held strongly to the line that the integrated programme was necessary and desirable. Faced with this solidarity, the developed countries of the 'B group' were seriously divided, with the United States and West Germany making the strongest opposition to the proposals and Holland and the Scandinavian countries giving them their support. No agreement could be reached until the very end of the conference (put off for two days in order to continue negotiations) when the meeting at last agreed to continue studies of possible commodity agreements and the principles and problems involved in common financing, and agreed to meet again in plenary session in the spring of 1977.

This decision, however weak it may seem, was a breakthrough for the ldcs and the UNCTAD secretariat. For the ldcs it showed that the commodity agreement idea could still be kept alive; and for the secretariat it meant that at least it could look forward to real negotiations in the near future – increasing the stature of UNCTAD as a negotiating body, and reserving an important area of world trade policy as an UNCTAD preserve.

The Ongoing Work of UNCTAD

Trade in Manufactures: Generalised Preferences[34]

The introduction of the GSP, covering imports of manufactures and semi-finished products, and some processed agricultural goods, from ldcs into developed countries, would probably not have occurred without persistent pressure from ldcs in UNCTAD and the strong advocacy of the principle by the UNCTAD secretariat. The exact 'first statement' of the GSP principle is not clear; but certainly one of the first proposals of the type was made by the British Government in 1962, in the suggestion for the extension of Commonwealth preferences to other developing countries in return for preferential treatment of Commonwealth ldcs' exports by other developed countries – a suggestion which it was hoped, among other things, would help to compensate Commonwealth ldcs for the losses they might sustain as a result of British membership of the EEC. It was further discussed in GATT in 1963 in the form of a proposal to reduce mfn tariffs for manufactures and semi-manufactures of interest to ldcs by 50 per cent in three years, as an advance concession in the Kennedy round: a move which most developed countries were very reluctant to consider. And in preparing for the first UNCTAD conference, Raúl Prebisch, UNCTAD's first secretary-general, urged that preferential tariff treatment was an essential element in increasing ldcs' exports of processed and manufactured goods. The concept of the GSP was thus tossed about for nearly ten years among governments and international organisations before the first scheme was introduced in 1971 by the EEC.[35]

Because most GSP schemes are so restrictive, many critics have claimed that very few ldcs can benefit. Those which have benefited in the first few years of the GSP's operation tend not unnaturally to be the more competitive – which could probably export successfully without preferences. UNCTAD, with finance from the UN Development Programme, has put a considerable effort into advising developing countries, through seminars, on how to take advantage of GSP terms offered. At the same time, UNCTAD secretariat reviews of GSP schemes have contributed to putting pressure on developed countries to improve the terms offered to ldcs.[36]

Commodities[37]

UNCTAD, unlike GATT, has from the start concerned itself with issues of trade in commodities, and in particular with improving the terms on which commodities are exported by ldcs, through international commodity agreements.

Two UNCTAD efforts must in particular be noted. First, UNCTAD has provided the forum and the facilities for the negotiations of successive International Tin Agreements, the most recent of which was concluded in May 1975.[38] Second, the International Cocoa Agreements of 1973 and 1976 were also negotiated under UNCTAD's aegis. But since 1974 the UNCTAD secretariat has been engaged on a much more ambitious exercise in the commodities field than the supervision of individual agreements. This is an attempt to construct an 'integrated programme' for commodities which will combine fair terms of trade for exporting ldcs with secure access to supplies for importing countries.

Basically, the programme[39] involves proposals for an internationally financed network of stockpiles of basic food and raw material commodities. The proposals cover coffee, cocoa, tea, sugar, cotton, rubber, jute, sisal, copper, tin, wheat, rice, bananas, beef and veal, wool, bauxite, and iron ore, with ten commodities as the core. It is hoped that international agreement can be reached on terms for the establishment of international stocks of these commodities, on the finance to run such stockpiles, and on at least the beginnings of a linked programme of aid and trade concessions to encourage diversification out of commodities in chronic surplus and the development of processing industries in ldcs.

Shipping

For most ldcs, the costs of shipping their goods to the main markets may be as important obstacles to the development of trade as overt tariff or non-tariff barriers. Shipping has been one of the fields in which UNCTAD's work has been most energetic and aggressive. The secretariat has pursued inquiries into the operation of the liner conferences, private cartel organisations dominated by Western and Japanese shipping lines, which have historically dominated the shipping trade. A code of conduct for conferences was drawn up for UNCTAD III. Following initial opposition from major shipping countries, an international convention covering such a code was negotiated in 1974 and has already been ratified by some participating governments. UNCTAD has also examined the effects of rising international freight charges on developing countries' export and import costs. This work is still continuing.

For developing countries, the value of such work can show itself in two main ways. First, it can, all being well, bring ldcs into fuller participation in an aspect of trading which affects them directly but over which they and their entrepreneurs have in the past had little or no control. Secondly, it creates wider knowledge and information among ldcs' governments of shipping practices, and also a framework for more informed international negotiation.

Foreign Investment and Multinational Corporations[40]

UNCTAD's work on foreign investment has changed considerably since the first conference, reflecting changing attitudes to the presence and effects of foreign companies. A resolution of UNCTAD I called on capital exporting developed countries to 'avoid measures preventing or limiting the flow of capital from such countries to developing countries and take all appropriate steps to encourage the flow',[41] on developing countries to 'take all appropriate steps to provide favourable conditions for direct foreign investment'[42] and on investors, 'based upon respect for the sovereignty of the host country [to] co-operate with local initiative and capital. . .and [to] work within the framework and objectives of the development plans'.

UNCTAD II was much more detailed and specific. Many developing countries had begun to query foreign investment's benefits and costs. Within the UN family the General Assembly and ECOSOC had begun studies of the promotion of foreign investment and for the transfer of technology to ldcs through foreign investment. The New Delhi conference listed fourteeen points which studies of foreign investment should take into account covering, broadly, ldcs' criteria for accepting foreign investment; forms of foreign participation in ldc industry; use of patents and licences, both by ldcs and by capital exporting firms; taxation of foreign investment; and training. It requested UNCTAD to study the economic effects of foreign investment and recommend policies on 'transfer of technical services and know-how'.[43]

Resolutions on investment at UNCTAD III in Santiago again reflected growing economic nationalism in ldcs and a growing suspicion of the role of foreign companies. A general resolution affirmed 'the sovereign right of developing countries to take the necessary measures to ensure that foreign capital operates in accordance with the national development needs of the countries concerned, including measures to limit the repatriation of profits',[44] expressed concern at foreign investors' 'excessive utilisation of local financial resources' [45] and the effect of marketing contracts on competition in ldcs, and urged developing countries to take appropriate fiscal and other measures to stop 'the tendency for an outflow of capital'.[46] A second, more specific, resolution called for further study of restrictive practices in foreign investment

> . . .including such practices as may stem from: cartel activities; business restrictions practised by enterprises and multinational corporations; export prohibitions; agreements on market distribution and allocation; the tying of the supply of inputs including raw materials and components; restrictions specified in contracts for the transfer pricing between the parent company and its affiliates; monopoly practices[47]

while a third sought to encourage international subcontracting as far as possible.

Since the third conference, much work has been undertaken by the UNCTAD secretariat, and in expert groups, on the sale or 'transfer' of technology from developed to developing countries. Particular studies have been heavily critical of restrictive practices in the sale of patents by companies, and of conditions attached to licensing agreements which restrict exports of the products manufactured under the agreements. A Group of Experts drew up and submitted to UNCTAD IV a Code of Conduct for the transfer of technology, but there was no specific agreement between developed and developing countries on the exact conditions of such a code.

The value of this type of work to developing countries lies both in its possible legal status – although it is not an area where capital exporting and capital importing countries will easily agree – and, perhaps more, in the fund of knowledge and case studies being built up. Ldcs, individually or in groups, need to understand and come to terms with the benefits and risks of foreign investment, and to lay down reasonable laws governing foreign company operations. Such studies can help them to do so.

Other Areas of Interest

The subjects mentioned above have formed the main part of UNCTAD's work, but the organisation has other areas of interest covering most of the external relations of ldcs. It maintains a watching brief on the terms and conditions of aid and other finance for ldcs, and is one of the few organisations to assess the terms of Eastern European aid. It provides technical assistance, with finances from UNDP in various fields: e.g. advice on how to make the best use of GSP schemes. It interests itself in problems of economic co-operation and integration among ldcs (see Chapter 8). And through the International Trade Centre, the only organisation which formally links GATT and UNCTAD, the two international bodies are involved in advising developing countries on export promotion and marketing.

The International Trade Centre (ITC)

ITC was founded by GATT in 1964 and since 1968 has been run as a joint organisation of GATT and UNCTAD, being financed from their budget and by contributions from individual developed countries. In practice it is more or less autonomous. The two organisations contribute equally to the running of the ITC.

ITC undertakes marketing studies for particular countries or particular groups of products; recruits, usually with finance from UNDP, experts to help developing countries solve practical problems in trade and marketing, such as costing and pricing, or product and market development, and organises training courses in export promotions techniques for officials and businessmen from ldcs. It can set up national or regional export promotion projects on request from recipients. Most of its work is now undertaken on behalf of ldcs, in an area which is vital to their trading development.

UNCTAD, GATT and Other International Bodies

As we have seen, the work of UNCTAD has been and remains, a great deal wider in scope than that of GATT. Although on some trade questions – e.g. the GSP – the two organisations have overlapped, on commodities, shipping, insurance, and foreign investment UNCTAD has ventured into fields where GATT has never gone. GATT, at least until the present 'round' of negotiations, has kept its eyes firmly fixed on the detailed issues of negotiations on liberalising trade patterns in the world as a whole. And it does not include in its membership the most significant Socialist countries.

GATT's operating limitations have reflected what has been, in the past, a fundamental difference in attitude, even in ideology, between the two organisations. GATT's aims are essentially related to improving the operation of world markets. The organisation has, until now, based itself firmly on the desirability of free trade as a mechanism for improving world economic welfare. UNCTAD, by contrast, was intended to provide a new approach. Through its more politically-orientated activities and in the evolution of the 'Group of 77' in particular, the UNCTAD system has created a form of international pressure group which it is impossible to ignore, and which spills over into other international conferences (such as the UN General Assembly itself, and the various special Assemblies which have been held).[48] Broadly, this international pressure group is concerned with planning the structure of international economic relations; and, in particular, with creating a permanent shift of advantage in favour of poorer countries.

GATT, like United Nations agencies, operates on a system of equality of membership, each country having one vote (although few, if any, GATT decisions are voted on). The growing numerical strength of developing countries in GATT increases their importance within the organisation; indeed, participation is the only way in which ldcs can hope to change GATT's legal conditions in ways which will favour them.

But what are such changes likely to be? Many developing countries adhere rigidly to the principles of preference and non-reciprocity, arguing that trade concessions constitute virtually a moral obligation for developed countries and that ldcs cannot be expected to 'give' anything in return. Others, often the more successful trading countries,[49] appear to agree with the view that infant industry protection need not extend to the whole economy or last forever, and some have reduced their levels of domestic protection when it appeared possible that certain industries might be able to stand up to outside competition.

Within international institutions, many ldcs are pressing for reform of GATT by the more complete acceptance of the conditions of Part IV (which are not accepted by all the developed countries) into the General Agreement as a whole. This pressure was supported, in November 1975, by the tabling of a resolution sponsored by the Group of 77 in the United Nations General Assembly, calling for a new 'General Agreement on Trade'.

In contrast to this, a recent study sponsored by the Atlantic Council of the United States[50] called for the introduction in GATT of a system of weighted voting such as exists, for example, in the International Monetary Fund, in which votes are allocated according to the level of subscriptions. The report also suggested that GATT should be supplemented with 'specific codes, of varying membership, to deal with particular kinds of non-tariff trade barriers, such as product standards, etc., which could be administered within GATT by those countries of GATT adhering to them rather than by the GATT organisation as a whole', and, further, that there should be 'an overall code by which the major trading nations, acting on a weighted voting basis, could take more far-reaching action in the field of trade liberalisation than other GATT countries, such as the less developed countries, are able to do, provided that trade liberalising actions are applied to the trade of other GATT countries on a non-discriminatory basis'.[51] These proposals seem on the one hand to suggest the introduction of a series of exclusive 'clubs' within GATT, outsiders to which would be accorded less liberal treatment than their members, and on the other to retain the *status quo* in which it is accepted that ldcs do not need to make trading concessions as large as those by developed countries.

Whatever new pattern of agencies or of inter-agency relations emerges from the haze of resolutions, it is clear that the world in which they exist cannot be governed either by a simple application of the most-favoured-nation principle or by a simple extension of preferences on a non-reciprocal basis to developing countries. Developing countries themselves are unequal in their trading strength. Some may be able to accept international codes of conduct, others need to be treated with extreme generosity. New rules are needed, at the national and international level: to regulate (but at the same time be fair to) the trading practices of large international companies;[52] to ensure that governments do not simply lapse into protectionism and the narrow interpretation of 'national interests' at the first sign of a competitive import from abroad, but at the same time to prevent indiscriminate 'dumping' of goods; to ensure that the growth of trading blocs, such as the EEC/EFTA/Lomé Convention/Mediterranean area, does not mean the emergence of a whole series of neo-colonial exclusive partnerships. Finally, new rules are needed, and effective surveillance and enforcement required, to create freer conditions in the vastly over-protected sector of agriculture.

As ldcs have gradually found in GATT, the only way to shape rules to fit their needs is to take an active part in formulating them. This may mean accepting responsibilities as well as negotiating concessions. Otherwise, international trade rules will continue to be the prerogative of 'rich men's clubs' of big trading powers: or, alternatively, developed countries may lapse into growing protectionism except towards their own equal partners. Neither of these solutions would benefit developing countries.

ROLE OF NATIONAL GOVERNMENTS

The existence of both GATT and UNCTAD bears testimony to the fact that the pattern of international trade is by no means the outcome of the unfettered interplay of market forces. Rather the latter are subject to the intervention of powerful agents which variously influence the composition, direction, volume, and value of international trade. One such agent is the multinational corporation. In certain spheres, the dominance of large international firms in technology, production, and marketing allows them to exert considerable control over world trade flows and to limit competition. Meanwhile, the fact that a large and probably growing proportion of international trade takes place *within* multinational firms allows the firms to adjust the prices of traded goods so as to maximise profits or minimise risks, thereby distorting the value of trade between countries (and also counteracting certain national policies). These and other aspects of foreign firms' involvement in the external trade of developing countries are discussed in Chapter 6. Here we concentrate on probably the most important agent of all: the national government.

National governments have always exerted some control and influence over the economic and social activities of private individuals and institutions through legislation, taxation and their control of the national currency. And in the area of international trade there is a long history of government intervention to protect markets for producers and traders and for revenue raising purposes which accords ill with textbook notions of free trade. After a brief interlude of *laissez-faire* policies in the nineteenth century, the extent of government involvement in, and direction of, economic and social affairs has increased considerably during the twentieth century. In the so-called centrally planned economies of the Eastern bloc countries, this change is most obvious, but it is also a characteristic of the Western developed countries with so-called 'market economies', and of developing countries. And with this change, there has been an increase in the ways in which governments directly or indirectly influence and control the volume and pattern of international trade in their pursuit of various, and not always consistent, domestic and foreign policy objectives. In discussing some of the more important ways in which governments affect the international exchange of goods and services, we will attempt to distinguish between those government policies and actions which are primarily intended to restrict, promote, or regulate trade and those which do so but are not primarily intended to do so. The main point of emphasis is not that governments on balance restrict or encourage external trade – which would be extremely difficult to assess – but rather that governments play a major part in determining the conditions and extent of such trade.

Import Restricting Policies

A variety of government policies operate so as to restrict imports. Some have this effect on virtually all imports but generally such policies are selective. That is to say, they do not apply equally to all imported products and, often, are applied so as to restrict the same import from different countries to varying extents. Where government policies actively discriminate in the latter way, this generally reflects the existence of one or more exclusive inter-governmental agreements on trade and related matters – with the major exception of the discrimination in tariff treatment arising from the existence of the GSP, under which individual governments have *unilaterally* extended preference to developing countries. Intergovernmental agreements are discussed separately below.[53] The restrictive effect of a given policy instrument may in any case vary according to the exporting country. For instance, the various government regulations concerning the quality of certain imported products tend to inhibit exports from ldcs more than from developed countries.

There are two main reasons why governments adopt policies deliberately to restrict imports: to protect certain domestic industries and to ensure balance of payments equilibrium. The protection of domestic industries in developed countries is often undertaken in response to pressure from employers – sometimes in state-owned industries – or workers, or both, whose livelihoods are threatened by external competition. Protectionist measures can form part of governments' regional or industrial policies which may ultimately entail the run-down or modernisation of the affected industry. In some cases – and agriculture is a prime example – protection of an industry which is not internationally competitive is deemed necessary for national security reasons. Among developing countries, protectionist policies have formed an important element in industrial development programmes designed to encourage import-substituting industries.[54] Import restricting customs levies, or tariffs, and certain excise taxes which can only restrict external supplies (for instance developed countries' excise taxes levied on solely tropical products, such as coffee and bananas) also serve a third government purpose, namely revenue raising. For developing countries, customs levies are often a, if not the, major source of revenue, and are of particular importance as such because of the administrative difficulties of levying other sorts of taxes domestically. The main types of policy instrument adopted by governments which have the effect of restricting imports or of strengthening the competitive position of import competing producers are noted below.

Tariffs

A tax levied on an import, by value or by quantity, which raises its price and hence reduces domestic demand for that item. Developing countries, on the whole, tend to impose higher tariff duties than developed countries for protection, balance of payments, and revenue raising reasons. Developed countries' tariffs, however, are not insignificant and, leaving aside the impact of preferential tariffs, tend to have a greater trade restricting effect on developing countries' exports for two reasons. First, many of the industries which developed countries seek to protect with tariffs are labour-intensive ones in which developing countries now have a comparative advantage, e.g. textiles. Hence developing countries' exports would most benefit from the removal of these tariffs and are worst affected by their existence. Secondly, developed countries' tariffs tend to increase according to the degree of fabrication, e.g. cotton yarn tends to face lower tariffs than cotton fabrics which tend to face lower tariffs than cotton clothing. This has the effect of inhibiting ldcs' export diversification out of raw materials exports into manufactured and processed goods.

Import Surcharges, Variable Levies, etc.

Certain other policy instruments have equivalent effect to that of tariffs, increasing the price of imports relative to domestic goods, and vary only in that they are not levied as customs duties. Some, like import surcharges and multiple exchange rates,[55] are chiefly used in response to balance of payments problems although they tend to be applied selectively with consequent protective effects. Others are purely protective devices, as for instance variable levies. The most important use of variable levies is in the context of the EEC agricultural policy where they bring the price of certain agricultural imports in line with EEC prices, so virtually eliminating the possibility of price competition by exporters. A further instrument, with similar restrictive effect to a tariff, but used primarily for revenue purposes, is the excise tax applied in the way noted above.

Quantitative Import Restrictions

Governments adopt a variety of measures designed to impose absolute or discretionary limits to the value or volume of certain imports. Import quotas, 'voluntary' export restrictions and import licensing are the most frequently found measures.[56] Quotas are established for a given period usually on a global or country-by-country basis. 'Voluntary' export restrictions are effectively quotas, being agreements to restrict exports on the part of an exporting country secured by the importing country. Quotas are administered by a system of import licensing, whereby permission to import is given only if the quota is unfilled. Import licensing itself is, sometimes, used in the absence of a pre-established quota as a means of import surveillance, and control on a discretionary basis. Both quotas and import licensing are used by Western developed countries mainly as for protecting particular industries. In developing countries they are more often used as a means of dealing with payments problems as well.

Quantitative restrictions are also effected by governments or individual public sector organisations in their roles as producers, consumers, and investors by the adoption of procurement policies designed to favour domestic suppliers.[57] In Western developed countries, such public sector procurement policies affect a wide range of imports. In addition, publicly owned trading organisations with monopolistic control over domestic and external trade in a particular product have often discriminated in favour of domestic suppliers and imposed quantitative restrictions on imports. In the Eastern bloc, external trade is subject to pre-established quantitative limits as agreed under bilateral barter arrangements made under state auspices. The barter system and the accompanying quantitative limits are not themselves intended to restrict trade. Nonetheless they do in fact both restrict the volume and affect the direction of international trade.[58]

The quantitative restrictions applied by developed countries on manufactures and food products tend to have a disproportionately adverse effect on ldcs, in that products of particular export interest to ldcs rather than other countries are most affected, e.g. textiles and clothing. Further, those ldcs seeking to establish themselves as exporters of a restricted product have an additional problem in that it is difficult for new entrants to gain a share of a restricted market where to do so means displacing external suppliers with established links with importing institutions.

Marketing and Product Regulations

Mainly for the protection of the purchaser, governments – particularly of Western countries – have introduced a wide range of regulations relating to the quality and marketing of given products. Thus, for instance, imported and domestic electrical products have to meet certain safety standards, and methods of beef production must meet the health regulations of the consuming country. Although such regulations are generally not applied with the intention of restricting market access of foreign suppliers, some are – for instance the requirements to label imported products with the country of origin in the context of 'buy domestic' campaigns – and others often have that effect, since details of the various regulations imposed by different countries are not always readily available to exporters, and the lack of standardisation between countries also makes the exporters' task difficult. These regulations are often a greater impediment to developing country exporters than to developed country exporters for two reasons. First, production conditions in many ldcs are such that would-be exporters tend to have difficulties in conforming with the requirements of developed countries, which are relatively sophisticated in comparison with those, if any, imposed by their own governments. Second, ldc exporters' access to information about the regulations is often hampered by the relative lack of established information channels in ldcs as compared with developed countries.

Taxes, Subsidies, and Cheap Credit

The competitive position of import competing domestic industries can be enhanced by governments' fiscal, investment, and loan policies. In the context of agricultural, regional, and industrial policies and programmes, individual public and private producers and investors variously benefit from such measures as capital grants or cheap investment loans, tax relief on capital and income, employment subsidies, and injections of state finance in the form of equity capital. While policies of this sort directed towards the agricultural sector in developed countries have a strong protectionist bias, in regional and industrial programmes they are often only incidentally protectionist in so far as they give a boost to import competing industries. Nonetheless, in developed countries, both regional and industrial policies do tend to have a significant protectionist effect since they are often intended to bolster those industries, frequently located in economically backward regions, which are least competitive in international terms. The British Government's support of the textile industry, and of the car industry in 1975, provides illustrations of this point. The forms of job preservation and job creation, particularly evident in developed countries' regional programmes, tend moreover to boost the more labour-intensive industries in which developing countries now have a comparative advantage.

Export Promoting Policies and Activities

We have noted some of the main areas of government activity which can restrict market access for imports and enhance the competitiveness of domestic producers. Such policies and actions also affect the ability of domestic producers to compete in external markets. Government tax concessions and incentives to import competing producers can enhance their competitive position overseas. At the same time, such government support tends to alter the pattern of exports (as well as imports) in so far as it delays the movement of resources out of declining industries into new industries which are more competitive internationally, or diverts resources out of existing uses into import competing industries. This is especially true of specifically protectionist devices, such as tariffs and import controls, which sometimes act also as disincentives to existing export industries. Governments do, however, adopt measures to encourage exports as part of general economic growth and balance of payments policies. Some of the policy measures are 'compensatory', designed to offset the export restricting effects of other policies. Others are designed to give special advantages to domestic exporters so as to improve their competitive position *vis-à-vis* foreign producers. A number of the more important government policy instruments and export-promoting institutions are noted below.

Export Subsidies

GATT rules are somewhat ambiguous on the question of export subsidies, in particular on those employed by developing countries. Whether or not they are sanctioned by GATT, both developed and developing countries effectively subsidise at least some exports. EEC surplus agricultural products, for instance, are sold abroad at subsidised prices under the Common Agricultural Policy. Fiscal policies in both developed and developing countries are adapted so as to provide incentives to exporters: exporters variously receive tax remissions on import duties, on sale taxes, on value-added taxes, and sometimes on direct taxation as well. With the help of government subsidies, credit is sometimes extended to exporters on softer terms than are normally available to business. Some governments offer special encouragement in the form of grants, tax concessions, and subsidised services, to foreign and/or domestic investors intending to export most of their production. Meanwhile state-financed research and development helps to lower the costs of private sector industry, whether competing in the domestic market or abroad: the technological spin-offs from defence expenditure provide an example.

Export Credit

Whether subsidised or not, an exporter's access to officially guaranteed export credit puts him at an advantage as compared with exporters without such access. In this sphere, developing country exporters tend to be disadvantaged because of the relative lack of such facilities open to them.

Aid

One important form of subsidy to developed country exporters results from the extension of inter-governmental development aid. A significant proportion of such aid is conditional on the purchase of goods from the donor country. Exporters in the latter country are thus provided with a 'tied' market and are able to secure at least some export orders which they would not have won in an open market.

Export Promotion

Most governments involve themselves in the business of export promotion for both private and public sector producers. In Eastern bloc countries, where international trade is run by government agencies, government involvement in export promotion follows as a matter of course. But in market economy countries, particularly developed countries, the state also provides a variety of export promotion services, via overseas trade missions established within or alongside diplomatic missions, the sponsorship of trade fairs, and the establishment of information services for exporters both within government ministries and as separate state-financed institutions. The business of export promotion is also pursued *inter alia* through agreements on trade and trade-related matters – and it is to these that we now turn.

INTER-GOVERNMENTAL AGREEMENTS ON TRADE

All countries depend on international trade to some degree. Yet the limits of national sovereignty restrict the ability of individual governments to control and influence their country's trade relations with the rest of the world. In the interests of the nation, a government may, for instance, attempt to promote exports but it cannot unilaterally ensure that its exporters will gain access to foreign markets or that they will not be subject to adverse discriminatory treatment; a government may restrict imports but it cannot prevent retaliatory restrictions on its country's exports, nor can it unilaterally ensure that external supplies are maintained. Individual governments therefore have an interest in extending their control and influence on international trade beyond their national borders to secure both adequate markets for their exporters and external supplies. This interest is reflected not only in the existence of the GATT but in a plethora of inter-governmental agreements of a more, or less, exclusive nature. Contrary to the principles of GATT, most of these agreements implicitly recognise that, in an imperfect world, individual countries' interests will not necessarily be best served by unrestricted international trade. Without attempting to provide an exhaustive list of all the different types of agreement in existence, we identify two main types of agreement. First are those agreements between two or more countries covering a wide range of traded products. These may be termed 'extensive' trade agreements. Second are those made between two or more countries which cover trade in a given product or group of products. Both sorts of agreements generally entail a degree of reciprocity. The main exceptions are to be found in respect of intergovernmental agreements between developed and developing countries, when the latter's explicit reciprocal obligations are often minimal.

'Extensive' Inter-governmental Trade Agreements, Regional Co-operation and Free Trade Areas

Since the Second World War there has been a proliferation of agreements designed to promote trade – and economic and political – co-operation among various groups of countries, usually on a regional basis. Among Western developed countries, the two most important trading blocs to emerge from these sorts of agreement are the European Free Trade Association (EFTA) and the European Economic Community (EEC). The members of EFTA and EEC respectively also extend preferential terms of trade to each other, and the EEC has further entered into a variety of preferential trade agreements with other European and Mediterranean countries. Among the centrally planned economies the members of COMECON (the Council for Mutual Economic Aid, alternatively abbreviated to CMEA) constitute a major trading bloc. Meanwhile a number of smaller trading blocs are emerging in the Third World as a result of various regional agreements on trade and economic co-operation among developing countries, for instance, the Central American Common Market.[59]

As a minimum, these agreements involve reciprocal trade liberalisation affecting a range of products traded between the parties to the agreement: that is, the removal or reduction of tariffs and other trade restrictions in respect of imports from each other. The EFTA agreement is of this kind. Often agreements involve more than this. They may, as in the Central American Common Market arrangement, provide for the establishment of a customs union, with a common external tariff on imports from outside the free trade area, or, like the EEC and COMECON arrangements, they may involve a considerable degree of economic integration. The Treaty of Rome, with which the EEC was established, not only provides for the eventual elimination of trade barriers to intra-Community trade and for a common external tariff but also for the free movement of capital and labour between member countries, for the harmonisation of members' fiscal and monetary policies, and for common policies on agriculture, transport, and industry. If this degree of integration is eventually achieved, third countries would be confronted by a super-nation-state, in which the 'pooling' of national sovereignties permits producers in one member country to compete in the EEC on terms equivalent to those of producers in other member countries and more favourable than those of any third country producers.

There is no doubt that these exclusive trade agreements, whatever the degree of economic integration, affect the pattern of international trade or that they provide more favourable terms of access to the exporters of member, or partner, countries than to third country suppliers. Whether they leave third countries worse off depends on two factors: first, the extent to which exclusive trade liberalisation leads to trade diversion, that is, the switching of import purchases from third countries to partners; and second, the extent to which trade liberalisation, by increasing the size of the 'home' market and the competition between member countries, permits economies of scale and acts as a stimulus to productivity, and hence to economic growth and import demand from which third country suppliers benefit.

The actual effects of such agreements on the external trade of third countries are hard to assess, in the ignorance of what would have happened without them, and will vary according to the economic structures of partner countries. In the case of the EEC, however, the common market arrangement has undoubtedly led to substantial trade diversion in agricultural products. And generally the trade experience of the original six EEC members between 1960 and 1972 suggests that third countries have been disadvantaged: intra-EEC trade accounted for 36 per cent of the total external trade of members in 1960 and 53 per cent in 1972, while EEC imports from the rest of the world in the period grew more slowly than those of other industrialised Western countries (including the USA, which had a lower rate of economic growth). The looser

EFTA arrangement appears to have had considerably less impact on international trade. COMECON arrangements have probably resulted in the most significant trade diversion of all trading bloc agreements. In this case, the deliberate policy to step up intra-bloc trade was encouraged in the post-war period by US-led Western embargoes on trade with the Eastern bloc, but it followed also from the shared characteristics of the economic systems of Eastern bloc countries and their divergence from the West, which would have impeded trade even in the absence of the cold war. Since the sixties, however, COMECON countries have successfully pursued a policy of increasing their trade with third countries with the result that intra-COMECON trade has dropped from 62 per cent of total COMECON imports in 1965 to 49 per cent in 1974.[60] This shift in policy can be related to the easing of political relations with West, the Sino-Soviet dispute, and the emergence of potential client states in the Third World, and to the increased recognition of the economic advantages of trading outside the bloc.

North-south Agreements

These are agreements made between developed and developing countries.[61] Whether on a bilateral or 'plurilateral' basis, these have two main characteristics. First, they tend to be made along 'regional' lines – although not exclusively so. Thus, for instance, in a series of agreements the EEC has developed its trade and other economic relations primarily with African and Mediterranean developing countries, the USA primarily with South American countries, the USSR primarily with Asian developing countries. Secondly, they tend either to involve the offer of more concessions – not only in relation to trade – by the developed countries than by developing countries, and/or to be set in the context of a relationship involving investment and aid flows from the developed to the developing country. Thus, for instance, in the most comprehensive and probably the most important of all such agreements – the Lomé Convention made between the EEC and the ACP (forty-six developing countries in Africa, the Caribbean, and the Pacific) – the developing country signatories receive duty-free access for most of their exports to the EEC as well as various other trade and aid concessions. EEC members' exports to the ACP, on the other hand, are only guaranteed most-favoured-nation treatment.

In some respects, these agreements may be seen as providing a framework for continuing a colonial-type trade relation between developed and developing countries on a more rational geographical basis. In return for the encouragement given to developing countries' exports in their markets or for financial flows, developed countries look to the agreements as a means of preserving and enlarging their market opportunities in a particular area of the Third World and of ensuring raw material supplies. But while the agreements may help the achievement of these objectives, they by no means guarantee it. Developing country parties, meanwhile, gain from the special concessions offered them by developed countries – and only lose in so far as the maintenance or intensification of their economic links with particular developed countries – or developed countries *per se* – is undesirable.[62] There can be little doubt that these 'North-South' agreements do foster trade and other economic relations along 'regional' lines and effectively discourage the development of extra-'regional' trade, thus affecting the pattern of international trade.

Barter Deals

Until the oil crisis bilateral barter trade deals – that is, agreements between two countries to balance trade flows – were almost exclusively associated with COMECON countries, trading with each other and the rest of the world.[63] Since the oil crisis, there have been a number of bilateral barter-type arrangements between oil exporting and oil importing, so-called market economy, countries, for instance between India and Iran. These have been sought by certain oil importing countries in order to secure oil supplies and/or to reduce the balance of payments impact of increased oil prices by ensuring export sales to oil exporting countries. For the oil exporting countries, the arrangements can lead to cheaper imports, as well as providing access to foreign expertise – often included as part of the trade deal.

Inter-governmental Agreements on Individual Products

The most significant of these agreements are those regulating markets for particular products. A variety of other agreements exist, however, which do not have this aim. Some international product agreements, for instance, involve consultations among producers and consumers but have no machinery for market intervention.[64] Some, like 'voluntary' export restrictions on certain products which are the outcome of informal bilateral agreements, are primarily akin to unilateral protectionist measures. Others, like the EEC-Bangladesh trade agreement on jute products, are primarily intended to improve market access on a preferential basis.

Those agreements concerned with market regulation are of three broad types – which, since they are discussed fully elsewhere, will only be summarised here. It should be noted that where the agreements are of an exclusive nature, and where they involve restrictions on supply and demand beyond what is required to stabilise prices, they inevitably affect the pattern of world trade in the commodities concerned. The first and most important are those chiefly designed to promote price stability of primary export products by regulating supply and demand. Those agreements are mainly multilateral, involving virtually all exporting and importing countries. Some, like the sugar agreement in the Lomé Convention, are exclusive, involving only some exporting and importing countries and are also concerned with problems of securing supplies and market access.[65] The second type of agreement is concerned primarily with market access. In this category comes the Multi-fibre Textile Arrangement, which again involves both exporters and importers, and is intended to regulate on a multilateral basis the growth of textile and clothing exports and the restrictions on market access for these products.[66] Both the above types of agreement involve exporters and importers and, whether biased in favour of one or other group, represent some degree of compromise between their conflicting interests. The third type of agreement involves only exporting countries and is designed to promote and safeguard their particular interests by market intervention. In this category come the OPEC agreement among oil exporting countries and the CIPEC agreement among copper exporting countries.[67]

Notes

1. Another global institution – the International Monetary Fund – also provides a forum for the discussion of trade issues in relation to balance of payments problems. See Chapter 7.
2. General Agreement on Tariffs and Trade, *Preamble.*
3. See below.
4. Article I, para.1.
5. Article III.
6. Article I.
7. Article XXIV.
8. Article XXIV, 8 (a) (i) and (b).
9. Article XXIV, 5 (c)
10. The Lomé Convention, which does not provide for reciprocal trade concessions, is justified in GATT terms by the EEC as a case of the application of Part IV on trade and development. A working party

was established by GATT in the autumn of 1975 to examine whether, in fact, such unilateral preferences were justifiable under the General Agreement.
Note also that the Yaoundé Convention was not uncritically accepted by other members of GATT; notably non-associated ldcs like India, and developed countries like the United States which were opposed to the favourable treatment given to France and other EEC members in the African associates.
11. GATT, Annex I, Ad Article XXXVI.
12. GATT, Article XXXVI, para.8.
13. In practice virtually all developing countries receive mfn treatment in all major markets. The Socialist countries are the only group to which mfn treatment is not generally applied: and the GATT members among them do benefit from mfn terms. So this provision is not really of critical value.
14. The main ldcs concerned were Brazil, Chile, India, Hong Kong (represented by the United Kingdom), Dominican Republic, Peru, Turkey, Israel, Yugoslavia, Malawi, South Korea, Jamaica, and Trinidad and Tobago.
15. See UNCTAD TD/56, *The Kennedy Round – Estimated effects on tariff barriers,* 1972.
16. See Glossary.
17. The first GSP scheme was introduced by the EEC in July 1971. Most other developed countries introduced similar schemes in 1972, with the exception of Canada and the USA, whose schemes were introduced in 1974 and 1976 respectively. See also pp.169-75.
18. See below, pp.60-3 where the present round of negotiations is discussed.
19. The Declaration of Tokyo is published in GATT, *Basic Instruments and Subsidiary Documents* – BISD – 20th supplement, pp.19-22.
20. Tokyo Declaration, para.3 (e) and 4.
21. Ibid., para.4.
22. Ibid., para.5.
23. Ibid., para.5.
24. Ibid., para.3 (f).
25. Ibid., para.2.
26. See Chapter 5.
27. UNCTAD I, *Proceedings,* vol.1, pp.67-8.
28. Branislav Gosović, *UNCTAD, Conflict and Compromise* (Leyden, Sijthoff, 1972).
29. See Gosović, p.294; P. Tulloch, *The Politics of Preferences* (London, Croom Helm for ODI, 1975), p.46.
30. Tulloch, pp.47-8.
31. Michael Lipton, 'UNCTAD SCHMUNCTAD', *The Round Table,* July 1972.
32. See Chapter 3.
33. TD/195: *Manila Declaration and Programme of Action,* 12 February 1976.
34. See also Chapter 5.
35. The history of the GSP is set out in Tulloch, chapters 5 and 6.
36. For a recent view of ldcs' concerns about the GSP, see UNCTAD document TD/B/C.5/SR, 59-70 of 24 April 1975.
37. See Chapter 3.
38. See UNCTAD documents, TD/TIN/2, TD/TIN/4 and TD/TIN/8 of June 1975. See also Chapter 3.
39. See Chapter 3.
40. See Chapter 6.
41. UNCTAD I, Annex A.V.12 para.A.1.
42. Ibid., para.B.3.

43. UNCTAD II Resolution 33 (II), New Delhi, 28 March 1968.
44. UNCTAD III Resolution 56 (III) 19 May 1972, para.1.
45. Ibid., para.2.
46. Ibid., para.4.
47. UNCTAD II, Resolution 73 (III).
48. Most recently in April 1974, when the proposals for a 'New International Economic Order' (See Chapters 3 and 9) were approved by a majority of the Assembly: and in September 1975 in New York.
49. E.g. Brazil, India or Mexico
50. 'Beyond Diplomacy', First Interim Report of the Special Committee of the Atlantic Council on Intergovernmental Organisation and Reorganisation, 1975. The Atlantic Council is an unofficial body uniting many of the US economic and political establishment.
51. Ibid., p.46.
52. See Chapter 6.
53. See p.82
54. See pp.23-4 and pp.193-6.
55. See Chapter 7.
56. See Chapter 5.
57. These policies can constitute a non-quantitative restriction on trade if preference for domestic supplies is based on a price margin.
58. See Chapter 5.
59. See Chapter 8.
60. GATT, *International Trade 1974/75*, p.189. Figures relate to USSR and Eastern European CMEA countries only and data for Mongolia and Cuba are included with the rest of the world.
61. They are to be distinguished from GSP arrangements in that they involve inter-governmental agreements while individual GSP schemes are the result of unilateral government action.
62. See Chapters 1 and 8.
63. See Chapter 5 for a discusssion of barter arrangements between COMECON countries and ldcs.
64. See Chapter 3.
65. See Chapters 3 and 4.
66. See Chapter 5.
67. See Chapter 3.

3 COMMODITY TRADE AND ECONOMIC DEVELOPMENT

Lack of diversity, and lack of ability to change, are two of the main symptoms of underdevelopment. Many poor countries lack the financial and technical capacity, and the market for goods and services, to support a wide range of industries, and particularly of secondary industries capable of exporting. Historically, the first stage of 'economic development' for many ldcs was the creation of plantations to export tropical crops to imperial powers, or the exploitation of mineral resources also for export. These plantations or mines tended to form foreign-controlled 'enclaves' with little beneficial impact on the development of agriculture or local industries. The cash economy of many ldcs became based almost exclusively on the export of a few commodities, in their raw or virtually unprocessed form, through channels controlled by companies based in the West and heavily influenced by the activities and attitudes of Western governments.

In the past ten to fifteen years, much progress has been made in bringing some developing countries at least out of overdependence on exports of a few commodities. Table 3.1 illustrates this by comparing ldcs' exports in 1960 and 1973/4.[1] During this period, exports of manufactures and fuels from ldcs grew much faster than exports of primary products. In 1973 – even before the action taken by the OPEC countries to raise the price of petroleum – fuels accounted for 40 per cent of ldcs' exports to the world as a whole, as against 28 per cent in 1960. The share of manufactures in their exports other than fuels had risen from 20 to 43 per cent. And the share of primary products as a group had fallen from 80 per cent of the non-fuel total to 57 per cent.

Despite the rapid increase in ldcs' exports of manufactures, taken in aggregate, there are still relatively few developing countries for whom exports of manufactures account for more than 20 per cent of total exports. And it is still true that many countries are heavily dependent on the export of a few basic commodities for the major proportion of their foreign exchange earnings. The development of exports of manufactures, and the conditions under which this has taken place, are discussed in Chapter 5.

Table 3.1. Primary Commodities in ldcs' Exports, 1960, 1973, and 1974

Exports to		Developed market economies			Centrally planned economies			Developing countries			Total exports		
Product groups		1960	1973	1974	1960	1973	1974	1960	1973	1974	1960	1973	1974
Food	$m	5,885	16,790	21,290	349	2,160	3,260	1,460	4,170	6,390	8,070	23,330	31,270
% of non-fuel total		41.4	36.4	35.0	28.7	46.9	48.9	38.9	28.5	31.2	41.0	34.9	34.7
Agricultural raw materials	$m		6,050	6.630		1,220	1,510		2,230	2,790		9,660	11,080
% of non-fuel total		5,595	13.1	10.9	775	26.5	22.6	1,100	15.3	13.6	7,640	14.4	12.3
Ores and minerals	$m	39.4	4,000	5,820	63.6	350	600	29.3	430	590	38.8	4,880	7,150
% of non-fuel total			8.7	9.6		7.6	9.0		2.9	2.9		7.3	7.9
Primary products (exc.fuels)	$m	11,480	26,840	33,740	1,124	3,730	5,370	2,560	6,830	9,770	15,710	37,870	49,500
% of non-fuel total		80.9	58.1	55.5	92.3	80.9	80.5	68.3	46.7	47.7	79.8	56.6	55.0
Other products	$m	2,720	19,340	27,020	94	880	1,300	1,190	7,780	10,720	3,990	29,020	40,510
% of non-fuel total		19.2	41.9	44.5	7.7	19.1	19.5	31.7	53.3	52.3	20.3	43.4	45.0
Total exports (exc. fuels)	$m	14,200	46,180	60,760	1,218	4,610	6,670	3,750	14,610	20,490	19,700	66,890	90,010
% of total exports		74.6	56.9	37.1	99.8	90.4	87.2	62.4	62.6	44.1	72.0	59.8	40.4
Fuels	$m	4,840	34,920	103,140	2	490	980	2,260	8,740	25,960	7,650	44,990	132,640
% of total exports		25.4	43.1	62.9	0.2	9.6	12.8	37.6	37.4	55.9	28.0	40.2	59.6
Primary products (inc. fuels)	$m	16,320	61,760	136,880	1,216	4,220	6,350	4,820	15,750	35,690	23,360	82,860	182,140
% of total exports		85.7	76.1	83.5	99.7	82.7	83.0	80.2	67.5	76.8	85.4	74.1	81.8
Total Exports	$m	19,040	81,100	163,900	1,220	5,100	7,650	6,010	23,350	46,450	27,350	111,800	222,650

Sources: GATT, *International Trade 1975/76: UN Monthly Bulletin of Statistics*, 1964.

Developing countries which are too heavily dependent on a few commodity exports can try to improve the situation in any of three main ways. They can try to diversify into new exports, either based on or quite different from traditional lines of production. They can try to realise in cash terms importers' dependence on regular and reliable sources of supply, either by negotiating long-term supply contracts with importing firms or countries, by joining in international commodity agreements in which both producing and consuming countries take part, or – if their bargaining position and their unity is strong enough – by banding together into export cartels to regulate production and maintain prices. Or they can try to reduce their overall need for export earnings by redirecting their own development programmes into more autarkic channels. In each case, an increase in ldcs' own control over the goods they export and the channels through which they are traded is likely to be a major feature of the strategy.

WHAT DO WE MEAN BY COMMODITIES?

Broadly speaking, we can include in primary commodities any products which are farmed, mined, or hunted, or are based on such products, but which do not contain any substantial manufacturing input. Thus, rubber can be counted as a primary product, but not rubber tyres or shoes; copper ore and ingots of copper, but not copper wire; live and dead animals, meat and hides, but not leather shoes or jackets. Some of the distinctions made between commodities and manufactures are obvious; others merely arbitrary.[2]

Again, we can broadly divide primary commodities exported by ldcs into five main groups: fuels (given a group to themselves because of their importance in world trade); raw materials for industry, in two categories, minerals and agricultural materials; tropical foodstuffs; and 'competing' agricultural goods – those grown in both developed and developing countries.

DEVELOPING COUNTRIES: SITUATION IN MAIN COMMODITY GROUPS

Table 3.2 shows the shares of ldcs in production and world trade for the major commodities in each of the five main commodity groups except fuels. Ldcs have a high share of production and exports of tropical crops, excluding cotton; their share of output and trade in

Table 3.2. Production and Exports of Selected Commodities, 1971-3

Commodity	Production: Volume ('000 tonnes) 1971-3	Production: Ldc share (%) 1971-3	Exports: Volume ('000 tonnes) 1971-3	Exports: Ldc share (%) 1971-3	Exports: Value ($m) 1971-3	Exports: Ldc share (%) 1971-3
(a) *Tropical beverages and foods*						
Cocoa beans	1,483	100.0	1,202	99.2	805	99.0
Coffee	4,542	98.6	3,489	97.2	3,407	96.0
Bananas	34,209	95.5	6,603	92.1	596	87.9
Tea	1,486	69.5	629[1]	90.6	580[1]	90.3
Pepper/pimento	n.a.	n.a.	192	85.9	160	86.9
Cocoa butter	n.a.	n.a.	154	51.9	231	29.4
(b) *Agricultural raw materials*						
Copra	4,000	100.0	1,161	99.6	190	99.5
Manila hemp	66	100.0	56	98.2	17	94.1
Rubber (natural)	3,184	99.9	3,062	98.5	1,243	97.8
Sisal	654	98.5	501	97.4	97	96.9
Jute and kenaf	3,631[2]	80.4	956	96.0	232	96.1
Cotton	12,767	45.4	4,229	59.4	3,292	62.2
(c) *Minerals (excluding fuels)*						
Copper (ores)	7,003	39.4	808	59.6	4,495[4]	54.1
(unwrought metal)	7,312	30.0	3,397	50.1		
Bauxite	68,782	52.3	26,702	75.0	278[4]	72.7
Alumina	23,383	20.9	8,204	42.6	n.a.	n.a.
Iron ore	430,800	19.2	186,433	47.1	2,649[4]	37.7
Tin[3]	225	65.5	n.a.	n.a.	638[4]	85.4
(d) *Competing agricultural goods*						
Rice	306,604	55.5	9,334	38.6	1,506	32.9
Sugar	75,936	47.6	16,847	79.3	2,630	81.2
Tobacco	4,742	38.6	1,141	50.8	1,579	35.0
Beef	40,073	26.1	2,260	33.0	2,988	29.2
Maize	306,974	22.1	39,261	20.5	2,926	18.0
Wheat	359,583	20.6	62,048	4.2	5,103	3.9

1 Excluding tea re-exports from developed countries.
2 Production of 'jute and jute-like fibres' (FAO).
3 Mine production: ore and metal exports.
4 1970-2.

minerals varies considerably; and in competing agricultural goods, as might be expected, their share in world output is, except for rice, less than half, although they account for the majority of world exports of sugar and tobacco.

Although many developed countries have substantial reserves of *fuels*, including coal, gas and oil, the role of oil as a fuel for industry and personal consumption in rich countries grew so rapidly in the 1960s that developed countries became increasingly dependent on imports of oil from developing countries. It was this very dependence, and the ability of the oil producing countries to agree on and put into effect a joint price and production strategy through OPEC[3] and OAPEC,[4] which enabled the exporters acting together to raise the world market price of oil so dramatically in 1974. Although the effect of this on developing countries which did not have oil (the majority, including many of the poorest countries) has been, on balance, highly unfavourable, the example of OPEC in taking joint action to increase the group's returns from exports is one which many commodity producing countries wish to follow.[5]

In other minerals, the shares of ldcs in trade and in output vary a great deal. Ldcs are majority suppliers in world trade of tin (85 per cent of the value of world exports in 1971-3), bauxite (73 per cent), and copper (54 per cent), and have a substantial minority share in world trade in iron ore (38 per cent). Ldcs' share in world output of these minerals is, however, much smaller.

Demand both for fuels and for other minerals is governed very largely by the state of the developed economies. Generally, during the 1960s, a period of fairly steady economic growth in developed countries, demand was relatively strong; and the period from 1971 to 1973 saw a peaking of demand for all types of raw materials. Substitution is difficult for most minerals, in contrast to many agricultural raw materials, although metals can to some extent be substituted for one another (e.g. aluminium alloys for copper in some industrial, military, and building applications) and plastics can also be used sometimes for metals (e.g. in pipes). During the sixties, many ldc exporters of minerals, including non-ferrous metals, increased their exports fairly rapidly; Mauritania (iron ore), Angola (copper), Liberia (iron ore), Zambia (copper), Peru (copper, iron ore, and other metals), and Caribbean bauxite exporters (Jamaica, Guyana, Surinam, Dominican Republic) among them. But the dependence of developed countries on these sources of imports, and the economic and political unity among the exporting countries, were not sufficient to enable any joint cartel-type action to be undertaken by any group of these ldcs.

Phosphate rock is the only non-fuel mineral on which monopoly power has been exerted. The supply of phosphates from ldcs is dominated by Morocco, and phosphates are an essential raw material in the manufacture of one range of artificial fertilisers. The other main range, nitrogenous fertilisers, are highly dependent on oil as a basic raw material. The oil price rise of 1973-4 allowed Morocco to seize the advantage and raise its own export prices more than five-fold.

In *agricultural raw materials,* among which we include rubber, cotton, and other industrial fibres such as jute, hemp, and sisal, the situation is rather different. Ldcs account for almost all world exports of natural rubber. But natural rubber itself accounts for less than half of the world rubber market; the rest is supplied by synthetic rubber produced very largely in developed countries. The two are not perfect substitutes – in particular uses, such as radial tyres, natural rubber has an advantage over synthetic – but are closely substitutable. Similarly, the main fibre crops are in close competition with other natural or artificial substitutes. Cotton grown in developing countries competes with cotton grown in the United States and the USSR, as well as with artificial and synthetic synthetic fibres. Jute, largely used for sacks and for carpet backing, competes with paper and plastics in the first use and with foam, generally synthetic, rubber in the second. Similarly, sisal competes with polypropylene for the market for twine and string.

Generally, except in periods of short supply or when speculation bids prices up, countries producing agricultural raw materials have been in a relatively weak position. The price which they can command for their products is governed directly by the cost of production of the nearest substitutes. Although the oil price rise has benefited producers of agricultural raw materials to some degree by increasing the production costs of substitutes, these benefits do not seem to be very large; and the possibility that many oil producing countries may soon also become major producers of petrochemicals, plastics, and synthetic fibres may depress prospects for jute and sisal in particular.

The one group of products in which ldcs are both the major producers and the major exporters are the *tropical crops*, including cocoa, coffee, tea, some fruits, and spices. Western demand for the main tropical beverages has grown less rapidly than income since the

1950s, and with numerous producing countries competing for the sluggish demand, prices and export revenues have tended to stagnate.

We devote a separate chapter (Chapter 4) to the problems faced by developing countries in trading in *agricultural products which compete with those produced in the developed countries* – a large group including grains, vegetable oils, sugar, meat, and tobacco. These products face two different types of trading problem. Vegetable oils, meat, sugar, and tobacco compete directly with production in developed countries which provide the main demand. The condition of the world market for any of these products is thus dictated very largely by the policies followed by developed countries in the field of agriculture. In grains, although some developing countries are exporters, the majority – and most of the poorest countries – depend heavily on imports for their food supply. If these are in short supply, they are the first to suffer.

And, as will be seen in Chapter 4, the effects of developed countries' policies towards grains, meat and vegetable oilseeds are all to some degree interconnected.

DEVELOPING COUNTRIES' DEPENDENCE ON COMMODITY EXPORTS

Table 3.3 shows how far many ldcs still depend on the export of a relatively few products, particularly of agricultural products, for the bulk of their export earnings. Over fifty countries gain half or over of their trading receipts from agricultural commodities, and in over thirty of these the bulk of revenue comes from three or fewer products. Moreover, there are few cases in which any one developing country has a large enough share of the world market to be able to influence – to raise or to stabilise – world prices through its own activities.

Most ldcs which depend on a few commodities are, therefore, highly vulnerable to changes in world market prices, and to variations in their own crop yields. If in a particular season most countries exporting a particular commodity have good crops, and can export a large quantity, the world price will tend to fall: a country which for one reason or another has had a bad crop-year will find its export earnings from the commodity falling much more than the average. If world prices are stable, individual ldcs may find that their own export earnings vary considerably from year to year with the quantity they can export. In most cases, individual ldcs' attempts to raise prices received for exports by cutting back production, or to

Table 3.3: Developing Countries Arranged by Share of Commodity Groups in Total Exports (1959-60 and 1969-70, or nearest available.

	Agricultural goods			*Three main agricultural products*			*Fuels, ores, minerals*			*Manufactures*		
	Country	Share of total exports 1959-60	1969-70	Country	Share of total exports 1959-60	1969-70	Country	Share of total exports 1959-60	1969-70	Country	Share of total exports 1959-60	1969-70
1	Gambia	99.9	99.2	Gambia	96.3	98.9	Zambia	96.7[12]	99.1	Hong Kong	79.2	88.1
2	Sudan	99.9	98.9[1]	Guadeloupe	96.3	96.0	Bolivia	91.5	92.8[2]	S. Korea	13.1	79.5
3	Cambodia	96.7	98.7[2]	Mauritius	98.7	94.8	Surinam	80.9	90.4	Lebanon	40.5	59.0
4	Mauritius	99.8	98.5	Reunion	85.6	91.2	Chile	86.1	88.2	Pakistan	25.7	57.2
5	Ethiopia	93.3	98.2	Somalia	81.9	87.8	Mauritania	3.6	85.8	India	43.6	50.0
6	Sri Lanka	98.3	98.0[2]	Ethiopia	76.3	86.5	Zaire	55.0	84.1	Israel	31.8	38.4
7	Malawi	98.3[3]	96.3	Sri Lanka	89.3	85.2	Sierra Leone	74.9	79.0	Jordan	3.6	35.4
8	Chad	94.0[4]	96.1	Ecuador	90.9	83.7	Trinidad	83.6	77.9	Singapore	19.6	30.6
9	Guadeloupe	96.3	96.9	Uganda	81.5	81.6	Liberia	45.0	73.9	El Salvador	5.0	30.0
10	Upper Volta	91.8[5]	96.0	S. Vietnam	91.7	81.4	Nigeria	6.5	70.7	Mexico	12.2	28.9
11	Niger	99.5	94.6	Cuba	84.9	80.8	Jamaica	47.7	63.0	Barbados	1.7	27.4
12	Somalia	92.7[6]	94.1	Niger	91.8	80.4	Gabon	24.1	58.6	Egypt	12.8	27.2
13	Martinique	97.5[7]	93.9	Ghana	81.4	80.0	Peru	45.0	53.9	Guatemala	2.7	26.7
14	Ecuador	98.5	92.7[2]	Chad	81.4	79.8	Guyana	27.4	51.0			
15	Ivory Coast	97.2	92.4	Uruguay	70.9	78.4	Indonesia	38.0	49.9			
16	Reunion	85.6	91.5	Ivory Coast	90.5	78.3	Tunisia	24.5	44.9			
17	Uruguay	95.2	91.4[1]	Malawi	75.4	77.4	Laos	56.6	43.5			
18	Burma	94.6	91.3[2]	Sudan	75.2	77.3	C.A.R.	12.2	43.2			
19	Paraguay	92.1	91.2[8]	Martinique	84.9	75.8	Angola	20.5	41.9			
20	Mali	96.3[9]	91.1	Dom. Republic	70.9	72.5	Rwanda	80.5	37.7			
21	Dahomey	95.2	90.3	Burma	77.2	71.4	Cyprus	51.0	36.1			
22	Uganda	90.7[6]	90.1[1]	Colombia	78.3	76.4	Israel	30.1	34.7			
23	Mozambique	89.6	88.7[2]	Panama	91.9	67.4	Morocco	37.7	32.8			
24	Dom. Republic	92.0	87.5[2]	Cambodia	84.6	64.9	Togo	n.a.	29.4			
25	Cuba	91.8	87.0	Cameroon	61.9	63.0	Malaysia	20.4	28.8			
26	Argentina	55.1	85.4	Costa Rica	84.9	61.8	Singapore	11.5	25.8			
27	S. Vietnam	96.0	84.7	Egypt	77.7	60.5						
28	Madagascar	91.0	83.8[1]	Honduras	77.9	60.0						
29	Honduras	93.6	82.8	El Salvador	86.6	60.0						
30	Nicaragua	95.9	82.1	Mali	73.7	58.8						
31	Cameroon	76.9[4]	81.5[1]	Philippines	69.1	58.5						
32.	Ghana	83.3	80.8	Rwanda	14.3	57.1						
33	Costa Rica	95.8	80.0	Togo	77.3	54.6						
34	Colombia	79.6	78.6	Congo	76.8	52.5						
35	Brazil	89.2	78.2	Syria	61.3	52.3						
36	Afghanistan	87.9	77.9[2]	Senegal	85.7	51.7						
37	Tanzania	86.8[6]	76.9	Paraguay	55.7	51.9						
38	Panama	99.6	75.3	Guatemala	85.1	51.4						
39	Syria	81.6	75.3	Upper Volta	82.1	51.4						
40	Kenya	86.6[9]	74.8	Kenya	53.5	49.6						
41	Guatemala	96.1	73.3	Malaysia	60.9	49.4						
42	Thailand	91.1	72.6	Barbados	95.0	48.7						
43	Philippines	85.4	70.7	Afghanistan	61.0	47.7						
44	El Salvador	94.8	68.4	Brazil	67.6	46.0						
45	Egypt	83.1	68.3	C.A.R.	72.1	42.8						
46	Congo	84.2[4]	68.2	Guyana	61.0	42.0						
47	Senegal	91.4	64.6	Tanzania	55.0	39.3						
48	Malaysia	75.6	61.6	Angola	51.7	37.9						
49	Rwanda	18.8[10]	61.2	Dahomey	85.0	36.8						
50	Togo	96.2	60.1	Indonesia	52.3	35.0						
51	Barbados	98.3	59.9	Gabon	60.7	33.2						
52	Morocco	54.5[7]	57.6	Mozambique	56.0	32.3						
53	Cyprus	48.0	56.7[2]	Pakistan	57.2	30.4						
54	Angola	75.4	54.3	Liberia	50.3	18.8						
55	C.A.R.	85.4[7]	53.5	Nigeria	54.1	18.1						
56	Mexico	63.7	51.2	Mauritania	69.3	3.8						
57	Indonesia	61.2	48.3[2]									
58	Guyana	70.7	45.4									
59	Peru	52.2	44.1[2]									
60	Jordan	59.6	44.1[1]									
61	Pakistan[11]	73.8[6]	40.9									
62	Singapore	62.7	40.5									
63	Lebanon	59.1	37.2									
64	Tunisia	64.7	36.0									
65	Gabon	61.7	33.6									
66	Nigeria	91.1	27.8									
67	Liberia	51.7	22.9									
68	Mauritania	69.9	9.3									

[1] 1970-1 [2] 1968-9 [3] 1964 [4] 1960 [5] 1960-1 [6] 1961-2 [7] 1960 [8] 1968 [9] 1961 [10] 1963 [11] Including Bangladesh [12] 1964-5

Source: Adapted from GATT, *International Trade, 1973-74*, Table F.

stabilise export earnings by creating stockpiles from which supplies can be released or into which they can be put, are likely to fail.

'WORLD PRICES'

In principle, the world market price of a commodity is the price at which the commodity is bought or sold internationally, among several buyers and several sellers all of whom are operating independently of each other. In this situation buyers and sellers are said to be operating 'at arm's length'. Some commodities are traded in this way, among them coffee, cotton, and – in part – grain crops such as wheat and rice. But in many cases, a large proportion of international trade is not conducted freely at arm's length. For example: most bananas sold in Britain and other Western countries are marketed by two companies, which buy the crop from plantations (which may themselves not be independent) in a number of developing countries. The companies are virtually monopoly purchasers who can set 'world' prices at a level to suit their own interests. Again, quite a high proportion of the sugar which enters international trade is bought and sold under special agreements between governments, of which the most important now are the Soviet Union's agreement with Cuba and the European Communities' contracts, under the Lomé Convention, with a large number of sugar producing countries. This means that the 'world price' for sugar, far from being determined in a free market, is governed by the surpluses or shortages which occur outside the special arrangements. Since the latter account for nearly half of sugar traded, 'world' prices tend to be considerably more volatile than in a situation of complete free trade.[6] Many metals are, also, not (or have not been in the past) freely traded. Bauxite is a case in point. Much of the world's bauxite output is owned by, or at least contracted to, the major aluminium producing companies. In this situation, trading is not at arm's length between independent buyers and sellers, and it is difficult to talk in terms of a free market price.

PRICE AND EXPORT REVENUE INSTABILITY

Most world prices for commodities vary from year to year and over shorter periods, with changes in supply and demand. Over the past twenty years, however, commodity prices have, in general, been relatively stable. There have been only two periods when prices swung violently upwards: the Korean War boom, when growing demand for materials due to world economic reconstruction was supported by a sudden growth of military consumption, and the period from 1971 to 1973 when industrial expansion in the West coincided with currency instabilities, and speculation in commodities as a hedge against devaluations boosted the inflationary effects of strong demand. But even in the intervening 'normal' period – say from 1953-4 to 1970 – the prices of different commodities showed very different degrees of variation. The World Bank and the IMF estimated that the average world price variations in commodities of interest to ldcs, around a predicted trend, ranged from 19 per cent for zinc down to 2.4 per cent for phosphates.

REASONS FOR PRICE INSTABILITY

The price instability of primary commodities can be attributed variously to fluctuations in the quantity supplied and in the quantity demanded. Commodities exported by ldcs may broadly be divided into those for which world demand remains fairly stable, while supply fluctuates; those for which both demand and supply fluctuate; and those for which demand tends to vary more than supply.

The first group includes most edible agricultural commodities, such as coffee, bananas, tea, cocoa, and foodgrains. Demand for these products is fairly stable and slow-growing. Supply, however, is greatly affected by variations in the weather and other conditions of husbandry and small changes in export supply have in the past tended to result in relatively large changes in world prices. Producers' responses to short-term price movements, i.e. a reduction or an increase in planting, can, moreover, perpetuate and also accentuate price instability: high prices due to a shortfall in output in one year can lead to increased planting and hence output in the next year, which in turn lowers prices, leading to reduced planting and lower output in the year after and a consequent increase in prices – and so on. In the case of perennial crops, such as cocoa, where there is a lag of several years between planting and the realisation of output, short-term price instability may similarly generate cyclical fluctuations in export supply and prices.

The second group includes most agricultural raw materials, for instance rubber, sisal and jute. The factors underlying supply side variations are essentially the same as those for the first group. Demand, however, is less stable, since it tends to vary directly with the rate of economic growth in importing countries. The influence of shifts in both supply and demand on the price of many commodities in this group, however, tends to be affected by the existence of synthetic substitutes, e.g. for natural rubber and fibres. In general, the availability of synthetic substitutes, especially close substitutes, tends to lessen the de-stabilising effects of fluctuations in supply and demand on the export price – and usually the export earnings – of the natural products affected.

In the last group come most metals and minerals. In the short term, supply is unlikely to vary significantly, except as a result of industrial action, war, or other catastrophe. Demand, however, tends to fluctuate in line with the level of economic activity in the importing country. Since increases in production capacity tend to require large-scale investment with several years' gestation, upward fluctations in demand are unlikely to produce a rapid supply response unless there was previously idle capacity. In consequence demand fluctuations are likely to induce short-term price instability, with prices for these commodities being generally more volatile than the quantities exported, and a tendency to cyclical variations in prices.

It should be noted that where price instability stems mainly from demand fluctuations, the direction of the effect on the export earnings of each individual producer is likely to be similar – unless trade flows in the commodity concerned are very much governed by bilateral supply contracts, in which case the varying growth rates of different markets would bring about different results for each supplying country.[7] Where, however, price instability stems from supply fluctuations it is more probable that individual producers' export earnings will be variously affected according to their individual supply position, particularly where climatic variations, rather than lagged producers' responses, are the cause of changes in the world market supply.

DECLINING TERMS OF TRADE

One of the problems which is said to affect ldc commodity producing countries is a long-term, continuing decline in the prices which they receive for their exports. While there is little evidence for this, taking all primary commodities together, prices of primary products exported by developing countries did fall substantially against those of manufactures in the twenty years 1950-70 (see Table 3.4). Figures produced for the UN General Assembly Special Session on Raw Materials in 1974 show that although the dollar prices of most

Table 3.4. Prices Changes Affecting Main Ldc Export Commodities

	Price changes, where prices are expressed in $ (%)			Price changes measured relative to unit value of exports of manufactures (%)		
	1950-60	1960-70	1970-3	1950-60	1960-70	1970-3
Food, beverages, tobacco						
Coffee	−23.9	45.7	30.1	−37.9	22.1	−7.2
Cocoa	0.9	18.7	102.4	−17.6	−0.6	44.4
Tea	0.0	−20.0	−6.0	−18.4	−33.0	−32.9
Sugar	−26.6	19.0	98.6	−40.1	−0.4	41.6
Rice	−10.1	12.4	170.0	−26.6	−5.9	92.6
Fruit	(2.2)[1]	−14.7	39.5	(−5.1)	−28.6	−0.5
Maize	−20.7	19.6	91.8	−35.3	0.1	36.8
Beef	126.1	42.3	131.1	84.6	19.2	64.9
Fish	23.0	65.9	92.1	0.4	39.0	37.0
Tobacco	27.4	16.1	24.1	4.0	−2.7	−11.5
Agricultural raw materials						
Palm kernels	7.2	2.9	34.6[2]	−12.5	−13.8	16.6
Copra	−11.0	3.5	102.6	−27.4	−13.3	44.5
Rubber	0.7	−49.3	92.2	−17.8	−57.6	37.1
Sisal	(22.8)[3]	−41.4	343.9	(14.0)	−50.9	216.7
Jute	32.2	−7.0	−1.9	7.9	−22.1	−30.0
Palm oil	−16.5	14.9	44.8	−31.9	−3.8	3.3
Coconut oil	−18.1	16.1	92.7	−33.1	−2.8	37.5
Groundnut oil	−1.8	24.5	(24.1)[4]	−19.8	4.3	(7.5)
Groundnuts	15.8	20.9	(69.2)[4]	−5.5	1.3	(46.6)
Palm kernel oil	6.6	8.0	(66.4)[4]	−1.0	−9.6	(44.2)
Cotton	−37.7	2.0	130.1	−49.1	−14.6	64.2
Timber	34.6	11.4	109.4	9.9	−6.7	49.4
Oilseed cake	10.1	28.7	161.6	−10.1	7.8	86.6
Minerals						
Bauxite	7.4	90.4	(13.7)[5]	−12.4	59.5	(−25.2)
Tin	6.1	67.8	−48.6	−13.4	40.6	6.0
Tin ore	7.4	67.8	54.8	−12.3	40.6	10.4
Manganese ore	−9.9	−34.7	66.2	−16.4	−45.3	18.6
Copper	36.4	106.7	37.8	11.3	73.1	−1.7
Crude fertiliser	17.6	15.0	13.0	−4.0	−3.7	−19.4
Iron ore	74.6	−5.8	22.7	42.5	−21.1	−12.5
Copper ore	39.7	113.7	42.7	14.1	79.0	1.8

1 1954-73.
2 1950-73 (third quarter).
3 1954-73.
4 1950-73 (third quarter).
5 1950-72.
Source: UN General Assembly Document A/9544, April 1974.

agricultural products (both food and raw materials) rose in the sixties after falling from the Korean War peaks of the early fifties, the barter terms of trade for the majority of these commodities against prices of manufactures continued to deteriorate. This was not the case for most minerals of importance to developing countries, whose prices rose both in dollar terms and relative to manufactures during the sixties. Overall, the UN price index for all primary commodities stood at approximately the same level in 1970 as in 1950, as against a rise of about two-fifths in the prices of manufactures.[8] For policy makers in developing countries at the end of the sixties, then, the problem was how to maintain export revenues in the face of rising import costs.

THE SITUATION SINCE 1971

Since 1971 the course of world commodity markets has been unusually unstable and disorganised (see Table 3.5). Some developing countries have done well out of exceptionally high prices and buoyant export revenues. Others have been selling their products at high prices, but at lower volumes, so that total revenue has not risen markedly. Developing countries exporting commodities not in strong demand, or without major commodities to export, have generally done extremely badly.

Boom conditions during 1972 and 1973 in the West increased demand for all types of raw materials: not only metals such as copper, bauxite, and tin, but also agricultural materials, such as timber, oilseeds, and cotton. At the same time, crop failure over large areas of the world boosted grain prices to crisis levels. The USSR virtually cornered the American grains market in 1972 after a drastic fall in domestic output: monsoon failures in Asia caused a severe rice and wheat shortage and increased still further demand for imports from the West. The failure of the Peruvian anchovy fishing haul contributed to the crisis, increasing demand for alternative protein-rich sources of animal feed, such as soya and other oilseeds: while in turn drought in Africa cut supplies of tropical oilseeds. Shortages and high costs of foodgrains, feedgrains, and other agricultural raw materials highlighted the potential conflict between the demand of livestock producers for feed and that of human consumers for food. By 1974 producers of beef, pigs, and poultry in Western countries were cutting their losses, by large-scale and often premature slaughtering of unprofitable animals, which have contributed

Table 3.5: Price Changes in Selected Commodities, 1970-5 (Prices expressed in US $ and as index, 1970 = 100)

Commodities	1970	1971	1972	1973	1974	1975	1974-quarterly average				1975-quarterly average			
			(annual averages)				1	2	3	4	1	2	3	4
Tropical foods and beverages														
Coffee (per 100 lb)	55.8	44.7	52.5	69.2	73.3	82.6	71.0	75.4	65.1	63.3	73.4	74.3	86.9	95.7
(Brazilian, New York)[1]	(100)	(84)	(94)	(124)	(129)	(148)	(132)	(140)	(121)	(117)	(131)	(133)	(156)	(172)
Cocoa (per 100 lb)[2]	33.3	25.7	30.5	59.9	94.4	68.0	73.1	113.6	101.9	89.9	78.5	60.7	69.4	64.0
(Ghanaian, London)	(100)	(77)	(92)	(180)	(283)	(204)	(220)	(341)	(306)	(270)	(236)	(183)	(208)	(192)
Tea (per 100 lb)[3]	49.6	47.8	47.6	48.1	63.4	62.4	58.1	66.4	61.1	67.1	69.8	63.0	59.7	58.0
(London, average auction)	(100)	(96)	(96)	(97)	(128)	(125)	(117)	(134)	(123)	(135)	(141)	(127)	(120)	(116)
Agricultural raw materials														
Copra (per 100 lb)[4]	10.2	8.6	6.4	16.0	30.0	11.6	36.0	33.2	28.4	23.0	14.9	11.4	10.8	9.4
(Philippine, European ports)	(100)	(84)	(63)	(155)	(299)	(114)	(356)	(329)	(281)	(228)	(146)	(111)	(106)	(92)
Sisal (per 100 lb)[5]	7.3	8.4	11.5	24.4	47.9	28.1	n.a.	48.1	48.5	48.5	42.7	31.2	20.6	18.1
(East African, London)	(100)	(115)	(158)	(334)	(656)	(385)		(659)	(664)	(664)	(585)	(427)	(282)	(248)
Jute (per 100 lb)[6]	12.4	12.9	13.5	13.1	16.0	16.6	14.1	15.8	17.6	21.5	21.4	18.9	15.3	14.4
(Bangladesh, Chittagong-Chalna)	(100)	(104)	(109)	(106)	(129)	(134)	(102)	(114)	(127)	(155)	(172)	(152)	(123)	(116)
Rubber (per 100 lb)	21.1	18.0	18.1	35.2	39.8	29.9	48.2	39.1	31.0	26.7	29.3	29.0	31.0	30.3
(All origins, London)	(100)	(85)	(85)	(167)	(188)	(142)	(243)	(198)	(157)	(135)	(139)	(137)	(147)	(144)
Groundnuts (per 100 lb)[8]	10.3	11.4	11.5	17.8	33.5	19.6	n.a.				25.2	19.5	18.0	16.6
(Nigerian, London)	(100)	(111)	(112)	(173)	(325)	(190)					(245)	(189)	(175)	(161)
Groundnut oil (per 100 lb)[9]	17.2	20.0	19.3	24.8	48.8	38.9	n.a.				47.2	34.3	39.2	34.9
(West Africa, UK)	(100)	(116)	(112)	(144)	(283)	(226)					(274)	(199)	(228)	(203)
Palm oil (per 100 lb)[10]	11.8	11.8	9.9	17.1	30.4	19.5	n.a.				23.7	18.0	19.2	17.4
(Malaysia, UK)	(100)	(100)	(84)	(145)	(258)	(165)					(201)	(153)	(163)	(147)
Minerals														
Tin (per 100 lb)[11]	166.7	158.7	170.7	218.4	371.3	310.2	337.6	416.0	400.3	333.8	341.8	316.9	303.4	283.9
(All origins, London)	(100)	(95)	(102)	(131)	(223)	(186)	(203)	(250)	(240)	(200)	(205)	(190)	(182)	(170)
Copper (per 100 lb)[12]	64.2	49.1	48.5	80.8	93.1	55.9	106.5	126.1	78.2	62.0	57.7	57.0	56.1	53.0
(UK, London)	(100)	(77)	(76)	(126)	(145)	(87)	(165)	(196)	(122)	(97)	(90)	(89)	(87)	(83)
Phosphate rock (per metric ton)[13]	11.0	11.3	11.5	13.8	54.5	68.0	n.a.				68.0	68.0	68.0	68.0
(Morocco, Casablanca)	(100)	(103)	(105)	(125)	(495)	(618)					(618)	(618)	(618)	(618)

N.B. Quarterly statistics for 1974 for groundnuts, groundnut oil, palm oil and phosphate rock are not quoted in source.

1 Brazilian, Santos No. 4, annual and quarterly averages of daily quotations.
2 Ghanian, good fermented grade, averages of daily quotations, London spot markets.
3 All teas, London average price at auctions.
4 End of month prices, averaged.
5 End of month prices, averaged.
6 Bangladesh, raw, fob, Chittagong/Chalna. Average of daily quotations.
7 Malaysia, R.S.S. (ribbed smoked sheets) No. 1 in bales, fob, Singapore.
8 Nigerian, shelled, cif European ports.
9 West Africa, cif United Kingdom.
10 Malaysia, 5 per cent bulk, nearest forward shipment, cif European ports.
11 All origins, minimum 90.7%, London Metal Exchange, average of daily cash prices.
12 Wire bars, London Metal Exchange, average of daily cash prices.
13 Morocco, fas Casablanca, average of daily quotations.

Source: International Monetary Fund, *International Financial Statistics*.

1975 to high meat prices world-wide. Meanwhile, the poor in many developing countries starved.

Semi-processed materials for industry and agriculture – woodpulp, non-ferrous metals, iron, manufactured fertiliser – were also in short supply. The GATT secretariat suggested that investment in productive capacity in materials processing industries, particularly in the United States, had turned down in 1969-71 (reinforced in many cases by pollution control measures), leading to shortages just at the time when an upsurge in demand required extra output.

Throughout this period there was also a good deal of speculation on international commodity markets, both simply in the expectation of profit and as a hedge against currency depreciation,[9] particularly following the floating of the major Western currencies in 1972. Since the main commodity trading currencies, the dollar and the pound sterling, were consistently weak, speculation in commodities was particularly encouraged.

The 'genuine' rise in raw materials prices, together with speculative activity, helped to create an inflationary atmosphere which itself encouraged further speculation, in a general flight from money. The inflationary spiral was given a final twist by the action of oil producing countries, members of OPEC, between October and December 1973, in raising the posted price[10] of crude oil from $3 to $11.65 per barrel.

THE IMPORTANCE OF OPEC

The enormous increase in the price of oil had three contrasting and conflicting effects on ldcs. First, it put the balance of payments and the financial reserves of a good many at risk, at least in the short term. At a stroke it quadrupled the cost of fuels, demand for which in many developing countries could not easily be reduced, and diverted large amounts of foreign exchange from other equally essential imports. The costs of many oil-based products on which many ldcs had come to rely, such as fertilisers and agricultural chemicals, were also suddenly and drastically increased, and industry's profitability was also threatened. Second, the OPEC action radically changed, again at least in the short term, the balance of international wealth and financial power. Although some oil producing countries, such as Nigeria, Indonesia, or Venezuela, have had the potential absorptive capacity to use their new wealth for effective investment in industrial or agricultural development, and others such as Iran, wealthy but still relatively underdeveloped, are also likely to develop extremely rapidly, the smaller oil exporting countries, such as the Gulf sheikhdoms, have largely to invest their funds outside their own economies, either in the West or in other developing countries.

Third, it became even more urgent for non-oil producing ldcs to find ways of improving their own terms of trade. And the example of OPEC in gaining control and bargaining power against international companies and consumer governments led many commodity exporting countries to wonder whether similar cartels, aimed at raising export prices, might not be feasible for other products. We argue below that OPEC has been very much a special case. But the oil crisis showed other developing countries that, in certain circumstances, 'the shrewd and determined use of new policy levers can be made to work'[11] while, at the same time, it brought home to the developed resource consuming countries their dependence on regular and reasonably priced sources of supply.

LDCS' AIMS FOR THE NEW INTERNATIONAL ECONOMIC ORDER

The new urgency and new demands of the developing countries have found expression in calls for the establishment of a New International Economic Order (NIEO). Developing countries' stated aims in the field of commodities include the following:

(i) to improve *access* to markets in developed countries, and expand markets for natural products in relation to synthetics,[12]

(ii) to *regulate and stabilise* world markets for raw materials and primary commodities, and set up 'remunerative and equitable' principles of pricing for commodities;[13]

(iii) to *improve the terms of trade* for commodities exported by ldcs, in order

> . . .to establish a just and equitable relationship between prices of raw materials, primary commodities, semi-manufactured and manufactured goods exported by developing countries and [those] imported by them, and to establish a link between the prices of exports of developing countries and the prices of their imports from developed countries.[14]

These aims may overlap, and are not necessarily consistent one with another. Different countries may pursue differing aims at different times following a view of the best trade strategy for exports of a particular commodity. But these three points, which we shall now discuss in some detail, summarise the basis on which most ldcs' commodity trade policies are currently founded.

Access

The terms on which Western countries will import particular commodities vary greatly. Broadly, commodities regarded as essential raw materials for industry get free access. Those which are basic consumer goods but which do not compete with domestic production enter freely but may bear consumption taxes. Those which compete with domestic output, including the processed forms of 'non-competing' products, face varying levels of tariff and non-tariff barriers.

Raw Materials

Minerals and metals in their unprocessed form (e.g. copper, tin, bauxite, iron ore, zinc, lead, manganese, phosphates) face few, if any, direct barriers to trade in developed countries. The introduction of Generalised Preference (GSP) schemes by developed countries has meant that most fabricated metal and mineral products can now also enter duty-free. In general the growth of ldcs' exports of these products has been rapid.

Similarly, many *agricultural raw materials* (e.g. raw jute, hard fibres, raw hides, raw cotton, natural rubber – and some important raw materials for the farm and livestock industries themselves (e.g. oilseeds, and oilseed cakes and meals) may be admitted tariff- and quota-free. This is not, however, as universally true as is the case for metals and minerals, particularly where a product competes with domestic farm output, and processed goods made from these raw materials are also generally less liberally treated.[15]

Tropical Foods

Tropical food products which do not compete with production in developed countries (tea, coffee, cocoa, and bananas) are, in general, reasonably liberally treated by importing countries. Tea, coffee, and cocoa beans face few direct tariff or non-tariff barriers, although internal revenue taxes, which may contribute to lower consumption of these products, are common in many European countries and Japan. However, once again, duties escalate as processing progresses. Tariffs in the United States are generally low – non-existent on tea or coffee in any form, and ranging up to only 5 per cent on cocoa products. EEC duties on packaged tea have been suspended under the GSP, but a 15 per cent tariff is imposed on instant coffee, while rates on cocoa products range from 4 per cent on cocoa beans to 16 per cent on unsweetened cocoa powder and a mixed tariff of 6 per cent *ad valorem* under the GSP and a variable levy on the sugar content of sweetened chocolate. Japan levies 25 per cent on cocoa butter, 15 per cent on unsweetened cocoa powder, and a massive 35 per cent on chocolate confectionery.[16]

This tariff escalation, combined with the structure of ownership and marketing in trade in these commodities[17] has ensured that few ldcs have yet made significant progress in building up processing industries for tropical foods. In coffee, Brazil is the only developing country which has built up a large export trade in instant coffee – and that only after a major dispute with the United States resulting in a restrictive 'voluntary' export agreement in force up to 1973. And the Netherlands remains the world's largest exporter of cocoa butter.[18]

A number of developed countries maintain import controls on bananas, which are often designed to assure preference for particular suppliers. For example, within the EEC, which maintains in principle a 20 per cent import duty on all imports other than those from Lomé Convention members and external dependencies, the individual member states' markets are covered by various 'derogations' and exceptions to the general rule. West Germany, which imports most of its bananas from Latin America, has a special tariff quota which allows sufficient to enter duty-free to meet its requirements. France imports most of its bananas from its Overseas Departments (Guadeloupe and Martinique) which account for two-thirds of the market, and from independent Franc Zone countries such as the Ivory Coast, Cameroon and Madagascar. Small quantities are imported from the Canary Islands under a bilateral agreement with Spain. Italy, which historically took most of Somalia's output,[19] operates a 'global' quota system on imports of bananas from countries outside the Lomé Convention. And the United Kingdom's guaranteed quotas on bananas imported from the Windward Islands have been continued under Lomé Convention arrangements.

Switzerland and Japan also levy substantial import duties on bananas; in Switzerland a duty of S.Fr. 0.20 per kilo is equivalent to over 20 per cent *ad valorem*, and the Japanese tariff (which is applied in a discriminatory way to favour packing in Japan) is 60 per cent.

PRICE STABILISATION AND THE MAINTENANCE OF THE TERMS OF TRADE

We have already noted that world prices for primary commodities fluctuate from year to year, or even over shorter periods; and that the prices which ldcs received for their exports have, in general, fallen *vis-à-vis* prices of manufactures on world markets. Developing countries' desire to regulate the markets for primary products, therefore, has two aims which are not necessarily consistent. The first is to iron out short- or medium-term fluctuations in the world prices of particular commodities or in the revenue which ldcs derive from these exports. The second is, if possible, to reverse the long-term deterioration in ldcs' terms of trade.

These aims have often, in the past, been confused. One reason why 'traditional' commodity agreements involving producing and consuming countries have often seemed unsatisfactory to exporting countries – and why so few have been successfully operated – is that, while they are perhaps quite good instruments for smoothing out short-term fluctuations in world prices, they have also been expected to deal with the long-term problem, which they cannot solve. New kinds of arrangement, either made by producers unilaterally or in concert with consumers, are one of the main international themes of the mid-seventies.

THE ROLE OF INTERNATIONAL COMMODITY AGREEMENTS

International commodity agreements, in which both producing and consuming countries participate, have generally aimed at price stabilisation: at ironing out short- or medium-term fluctuations in world prices for particular commodities. Since the Second World War, agreements covering five major commodities have been concluded, for tin, coffee, sugar, wheat, and cocoa. All have utilised one or more of a common mix of measures with the intention of stabilising prices: export or import quotas, buffer stocks, and 'floor' and 'ceiling' prices below which exports are cut or bought in by the buffer stock and above which export quotas are raised or the buffer stock sells. Appendix I sets out in summary form the conditions contained in the different agreements.

Since 1970, the operation of international commodity agreements has been particularly difficult, for various reasons. One main difficulty concerns the 'floating' of most currency exchange rates since 1972. When national currencies maintain a constant relationship to each other, or their values change relatively seldom, world prices can safely be denominated in virtually any currency taken as a point of reference. But when the values of national currencies against one another are perpetually changing, a 'real' world price may be difficult to define, and movements of exchange rates will change the world market values of the payments importing countries make and exporting countries receive for their goods, frequently and unpredictably.

The International Tin Agreement[20] is the only one of the international commodity agreements set up in the post-war period to have survived the international currency upheavals of the 1972-5 period. To date, there have been four five-year agreements on tin, and a fifth, to run from July 1976 to June 1981, was negotiated during 1975, under the auspices of UNCTAD. It is based on an international buffer stock, price floor and ceiling levels which govern the operation of the buffer stock, and the possibility of export controls if world prices fall too low. Thus it should tend both to stabilise and to raise prices.

The buffer stock set up under the Agreements has throughout been set at 20,000 tonnes of tin metal, or its cash equivalent. This is raised by compulsory contributions from the producing countries and voluntary contributions from consuming countries which are members of the Agreement. The United States (the world's largest consumer, and holder of stocks which far outweigh the 'international' stockpile held by the International Tin Council), although a member of the Agreement, does not contribute to the buffer stock. Since the start of the first Agreement in 1956, the buffer stock has once, in 1958, risen as high as 23,700 tonnes. During the second Agreement (1961-6) there were no buffer stocks for most of the time, and its highest level was around 3,300 tonnes. Since that time, the highest level the buffer stock has reached was 12,400 tonnes in 1972; and by the end of the fourth Agreement in 1975, the buffer stock was again virtually exhausted as prices more than doubled between mid-1973 and mid-1974.

The structure of ITA price margins and the way in which the buffer stock operates is intended to dampen any general upward or downward movement in prices. Upper and lower price bands are fixed by the council in relation to one another at any one time. The buffer stock manager must buy if the world price falls below the floor. In the bottom third of the price range he may buy, if he feels that prices should be supported. In the middle third he may not buy or sell unless expressly authorised by the council to do so. In the upper third he may sell to prevent prices rising too fast, and above the ceiling level he must sell. But in practice the efficacy of buffer stock operations as a stabiliser will depend very highly on how flexibly the price floor and ceiling are operated and on the size of the initial stock.

During the four Agreements, changes in floor and ceiling prices were not made often. In general, they were only adjusted after market prices had been rising consistently for some time. Over the twenty years of the Agreements, floor and ceiling prices have been changed substantively only nine times, and only once downwards. Since the beginning of the second Agreement in 1961, tin prices have consistently tended upwards, with only relatively short periods of falling prices. Given the way the buffer stock works, it can be easily seen that unless price ranges were adjusted upwards as prices rose, the stock would always tend to run out – which is what happened both in the Second and Fourth Agreement periods when prices outran the ceiling levels. But it is equally clear that, if price ranges had varied to keep pace with market price changes, the operations of the buffer stock would always tend to follow, and support, any general price movements. In a generally increasing price trend, in order that stocks should not run out, the manager would have to take advantage of any temporary fall into the bottom third of the range to replenish stocks, thus supporting prices at the bottom. In order to keep the buffer stock in business, the price levels would have to be continually raised, with a kind of ratchet effect. Similarly, if prices were tending generally downwards, the buffer stock would tend to run out of funds to buy stocks; thus, in the top part of the price range tin would have to be sold, contributing to the downward pressure on prices.

Despite the presence of both producer and consumer countries in the Agreement, the onus of its operations has always fallen on the producers. Their contributions to the buffer stock, or fund, are compulsory while those of consuming countries have always been merely voluntary – and France and the Netherlands are the only consuming countries which have ever contributed to the buffer stock fund, to the tune of £671,000 and £1,215,000 respectively in the Fourth Agreement which began in 1971. Since tin has, throughout the four Agreeements, been more consistently in short supply than in surplus, consuming countries presumably do not want to contribute to faster rises in price by adding to stocks.

Mention must also be made here of the role of the United States' General Services Administration in administering US stocks of tin. We have seen that the United States has never been a member of the ITA, and that US Government stocks have always been much larger than ITA buffer stocks, with the possibility that they could be used to drive down world prices. In fact, the United States has released major amounts of tin from its stocks in two periods during the Agreements: in 1963-6 and from mid-1973 onwards until the end of the fourth Agreement. In neither of these periods, however, have US sales been able to prevent the market price of tin from rising rapidly, in the first period to a peak of £1,715 per long ton in October 1964 and in the second to the equivalent of around £2,100 per ton in mid-1974.

The ITA has, despite its problems with buffer stocks, apparently worked satisfactorily. However, a good deal of the credit for this must go to the fact that tin is a metal for which demand is strong and supply historically short – a situation in which producers are likely to be satisfied while consumers must grin and bear it. The Agreement may have helped to smooth out some short-term fluctuations in price, but has had rather little effect on long-term trends, which have been consistently upwards.

The International Coffee Agreement began in 1959 with an agreement among exporting countries. In 1963 the first Agreement including both importing and exporting countries was established; and a second, which lasted until its breakdown in 1972, was concluded in 1968.

Both Coffee Agreements were based on a system of export quotas, with no buffer stocks: exporting countries were left to manage their own stockholdings. A 'global' export quota was set annually, related to the volume of exports in the previous year and the actual level of world prices. Within this, individual exporting countries were allocated export quotas in proportion to their productive capacity (the area of coffee planted and bearing). Indicator floor and ceiling prices were fixed quarterly, in relation to world market price levels: if actual market prices rose above the 'ceiling' and remained there for fifteen days in succession, export quotas were raised, and if they fell below the floor for the same length of time, exports were restricted.

The indicator price system was again mainly geared to smoothing out short-term price fluctuations. There is no evidence that the system was intended to prevent longer-term price changes: and none that it did so. After a rise of 35 per cent in coffee prices in 1963, when export quotas were first set up, the world price declined by 19 per cent between mid-1964 and mid-1969. In 1970, with a short crop in Brazil because of frosts, world prices rose again by 55 per cent in fifteen months, to fall almost as fast once more in 1971.

The devaluation of the US dollar in December 1971 caused a crisis in the coffee market. Brazil, the main producer and for whom the United States was the main market, demanded an upward adjustment of the indicator price, which was denominated in dollars, to offset the fall in export revenue through devaluation. When this was rejected, most exporting countries resolved to withhold a proportion of supplies from the market – a move which brought prices back up by about a quarter in 1972. Since then, following the breakdown of the International Coffee Agreement, a new producer organisation, Café Mondial, largely supported by Brazilian finance, has been buying up low-priced stocks of coffee with the intention of reselling at a more favourable time.

The market situation faced by coffee producers is quite different from that of tin. First, coffee, unlike tin, is not in strong demand, and production has historically tended towards surpluses. Second, within the market there is one very large producer – Brazil – and a large number of smaller ones. Brazil's importance as the main producer *and stockholder,* in the absence of an international buffer stock, cannot be overemphasised. Although Brazil has the capacity to flood the world market, it is clearly not in its interests to do so. On the contrary, it is for Brazil as the main 'price-maker' to hold back supplies from the market in a surplus year in order to maintain prices. Other producing countries, by contrast, stand to gain if they can increase their output, as long as Brazil maintains a 'responsible' attitude to stockholding. The fact that annual export quotas were determined according to productive capacity supported this type of behaviour. In practice, during the period of the ICA, African countries in particular increased their coffee output considerably.

The International Coffee Agreement illustrates well that there need not be any strong community of interest, at least in the short term, among producers of a commodity. It was in Brazil's interest to keep the Agreement – or at least a stable system of export quotas – in being. Other producers could, in the short term, increase their exports without greatly depressing prices, as long as they did not go too far. But the interests of all producing countries were opposite to those of coffee buyers, particularly the companies producing instant coffee, who were interested in buying at the 'best' (i.e. lowest) price.

Not all world exports of coffee were included in the Agreement. Exports to the Soviet Union and Eastern Europe, as well as to developing countries (including the Middle East) counted as 'new' markets and were excluded from the export quota provisions. This provided a certain safety valve for surpluses and a measure of extra export revenue for some producers. But the risk that non-quota markets would be used as illegal *entrepôts* to get round the export quotas for the main markets (this smuggling was known in the trade as 'tourist coffee') meant that strict certificates of origin had to be introduced for imports to the main Western consuming countries.

Following the pattern of the coffee and tin agreements, an *International Cocoa Agreement* was signed in 1973. Its provisions included both floor and ceiling price levels, with export quotas, and a buffer stock. World prices for cocoa have fluctuated considerably over the years, and the commodity would seem to be a good candidate for a commodity stabilisation agreement. Unfortunately, the first two-year Agreement suffered from remarkably bad timing. World cocoa prices had risen three-fold between 1972 and 1974, owing to shortages and speculation: and although they had fallen back considerably by mid-1975, they were still historically very high. It was not a good time to try to establish a buffer stock, which in fact never began operations, nor to try to gain agreement between producers and consumers (again, the United States refused to join the agreement). In the short term, therefore, the attempt to establish an Agreement for cocoa was a failure. A second, scarcely more auspicious, agreement was drawn up to start operations in October 1976. Again, the US has refused to join. And some of the leading producers, including Ivory Coast, have joined only reluctantly, with the reservation that intervention prices must be raised if they are to remain inside the Agreement.

The two other international commodity agreements with 'global' status, on sugar and wheat, face very different market situations, which are discussed in Chapter 4.

ASSESSMENT OF COMMODITY AGREEMENTS

Four conditions at least must probably be fulfilled for global commodity agreements to succeed.[21] The first is that all producers and consumers of a commodity, but particularly the largest of them, should be members. Second, the market shares supplied by large and small producers should remain relatively stable during the life of an agreement. It is obvious that a dominant producer which remains outside an agreement at least creates a risk of disruptive market behaviour, for example by undercutting floor prices in order to gain a competitive edge: while inside an agreement the dominant producer will have a vested interest in maintaining or improving agreed trading terms. But the opposite risk is that small producers, who individually may have little or no effect on world prices dictated by the balance between bigger producers and consumers, will try to increase their share of world markets inside an agreement, either by straightforward negotiations on the basis of a growing volume of production, by producing a different strain of product which satisfies different tastes, or again by undercutting the agreement price. This was in fact one of the most serious problems faced in the International Coffee Agreements under pressure of increasing supplies of African *robusta* coffee.[22]

Third, all export and import transactions should be included in an Agreement. Again, the exclusion of most exports to East European countries from the International Coffee Agreement's quota provisions meant that strict documentary safeguards, in the shape of certificates of origin, had to be introduced to prevent trade with these states being used to circumvent the Agreement; and even the small percentage of world sugar supplies actually traded on 'free' world markets weighed heavily against the success of the International Sugar Agreement.

Lastly, as far as possible, synthetic substitutes should be included in commodity agreements, to regulate the extent of substitution for natural products. This may well be an insuperable obstacle to international agreement on trade in easily substitutable commodities, such as rubber or sisal, where the interests of natural and synthetics producers are likely to differ widely or even to be directly opposite. None of the arrangements in force in the sixties related to a commodity for which synthetic substitutes were significant. If synthetics are absent from an agreement, the upper limit on prices achievable will continue to be the point at which consumers turn to substitutes.

But in addition to the conditions listed above, the international commodity agreements of the sixties show how important the global political and economic environment may be. The International Tin Agreement is the only one to have survived the currency upheavals of the 1971-4 period intact; and this was probably due more to the supply and demand conditions for tin itself than the particular provisions of the Agreement.

PERMANENT IMPROVEMENT IN LDCS' TERMS OF TRADE?

As we have seen, conventional commodity agreements do not seem to have been a good vehicle for influencing commodity prices in the long term. Ldcs exporting primary commodities are still very much concerned to find some way of bringing about a permanent shift of international trade prices in their favour. The commodity price inflation of 1973-4 did not achieve this, although it favoured some developing countries, including agricultural raw materials producers, in the short term. It was followed in its turn by inflation in developed countries which worked its way into the costs of the manufactures which ldcs import just as, in late 1974 and early 1975, many commodity prices were once again falling; and when many ldcs were also being very seriously affected by high prices for basic foodgrains. The cost of fuels and fertilisers – the two principal raw materials which ldcs import – also hit many ldcs hard, and is a continuing burden, while, with low world grain stocks, wheat and rice prices will most likely remain high.

Thus it is unlikely that the terms of trade for ldcs' exports against their principal imports have been substantially improved by the developments of the last few years. Obviously exporters of petroleum and phosphates have gained significantly, while some agricultural raw materials – such as rubber, jute, and hard fibres – may also have benefited from the effect of the oil price rise on synthetic substitutes.[23] However, these latter price increases are hardly likely to offset the rises in prices of both oil and manufactures.

There are only two main ways in which ldcs can possibly change this situation. One is, where possible, to try to follow the path shown by OPEC in taking joint action to raise the price of a particular commodity. The other is to continue to negotiate with developed countries in the expectation that the disruptions of the early seventies will have changed their view of price maintenance in real terms as an objective for commodity agreements which aim to offset good terms for commodity exports against regular and reliable access to supplies.

In purely economic terms, the action taken by the OPEC countries in late 1973 consisted of bidding up the price of a needed, and scarce, raw material whose price had been falling in real terms for a considerable number of years, to the point at which demand began to fall, or was curbed by governmental administrative action, and at which substitutes (coal, nuclear power, other sources of energy such as solar or marine power) began to be more seriously considered. It is clear that this could not have been done without a substantial shift of bargaining power from consuming to producing countries, first by the producers exerting national authority over 'their' natural resources and over the mainly Western-owned companies involved in oil exploration and extraction, and secondly by acting together as a cartel.

So far, no other group of commodity producing countries has been in a position to emulate OPEC in bidding up the price of its major product. Whether any other could do so is doubtful at the least. But there is no doubt that many groups of ldcs would like to follow OPEC's example both in gaining control of their own resources and in shifting the terms of trade in their favour. Interest in this has grown rapidly. A number of groups of producing countries with these aims have been established – principally for copper (CIPEC), bauxite (IBA), coffee (Café Mondial), and bananas (UBEC), while the Cocoa Producers' Alliance, dating from 1962, is being strengthened.

What are the conditions for the success of 'producer power' in this field likely to be? Several can be listed, of which the most significant may be the following:

(1) The location in member countries of a dominant share of world output and/or exports of a commodity. Ldcs' shares in specific commodity exports were noted in Table 3.2. But exports also vary widely as a percentage of total world output. If ldcs account for a high proportion of production as well as trade, their potential bargaining power will obviously be strengthened. For example, bauxite producing ldcs are in a stronger position with 88 per cent of world exports, particularly since Australia is also a member of the International Bauxite Association, than ldc exporters of iron ore or copper with 42 per cent of world trade.

(2) Control of the means of production. This may, although it need

not, mean outright nationalisation of foreign capital assets. Alternatives to total nationalisation may be majority local ownership, public or private, taxation policy, or regulations limiting the rate of extraction in the case of minerals, as Norway has introduced for North Sea oil. Historically, however, many attempts to regulate the conditions under which commodities, particularly exhaustible resources, are produced seem to have involved a move towards total nationalisation, with a greater or lesser degree of friction between host governments and foreign companies. Zambia's gradually phased nationalisation of foreign copper interests may be contrasted with the events in Chile under Allende, or with some Latin American attempts to take control of banana plantations, [24] Guyana's outright nationalisation of the bauxite industry with Jamaica's partial local ownership,[25] and Papua New Guinea's renegotiation of foreign investor contracts.

(3) Control of (or at least lack of monopolistic foreign domination of) the channels through which commodities are marketed. The degree of 'freedom' in commodity markets varies considerably. Few conform to a model of perfect competition. In some commodities trade may be carried on between two or more parts of a highly integrated company, as are the major bauxite and copper concerns, the main trading companies, or the international oil companies.[26] Within a vertically integrated industry controlled by a few large firms 'international' transactions take place at prices determined within the relevant firms, and these may be quite different from hypothetical 'free' market prices. Where a government is attempting to tax or limit company profits, an integrated trading company may at one and the same time avoid tax and extract 'surplus' profits from its export operations by undervaluing production exported from one country to its own branch in another.

(4) A common policy among all major exporting countries. Probably the only way to bid up world prices for a commodity is to withhold supplies from the market. Both OPEC and CIPEC were, at the time of writing, doing this – OPEC with the aim of keeping money prices for oil high in order to maintain 'real' returns; CIPEC faced by a rapid decline in copper prices between 1974 and 1975, caused by industrial recession in developed countries and large-scale sales of Japanese surplus stocks.

While a producer association may be able to withold supplies, individual countries which wish to increase their share of a market or maintain export income in a period of falling prices may break ranks and go for growth. Zambian copper output in 1966-72 faced

> . . .the strong likelihood of a copper surplus by the early 1970s [which actually materialised] resulting in a weakening of the copper price. . .for the government it is an additional reason why they should want to see capacity increased. When Zambian producers have, by themselves, only a small and diminishing influence on world price, it is important from the government view-point that as price falls production should increase so that losses in foreign exchange earnings are at least minimised.[28]

Of course if the forecast had been wrong and the price had risen the country would have both gained foreign exchange and strengthened its share of the market!

> (5) Reasonable diversity in the direction of exports. Close connections between particular ldcs and importing developed countries may break up the unity of a producer group. Preferential stabilisation arrangements may tie groups of ldcs into trading links which have more advantages than the 'free' market. These may destabilise world markets for exporting countries which remain outside and hinder attempts to conclude global commodity agreements.

Until recently, the only preferential marketing and price supporting arrangements of this type were those on sugar; for example, the Commonwealth Sugar Agreement which provided a guaranteed price for stipulated quotas of cane sugar imported into Britain from Commonwealth countries and the United States' import quotas under the American Sugar Act[29]

Since the enlargement of the European Communities in 1973, new 'regional' preferential arrangements for some commodities have been drawn up under the Lomé Convention signed in February 1975. The Convention includes an export revenue stabilisation scheme, known as STABEX, which applies to the export earnings of the forty-six Lomé Convention countries in Africa, the Caribbean, and the Pacific, from thirteen commodity groups (bananas, coffee, cocoa, cotton, coconut oil, copra, groundnuts, hides, palm products, sisal, tea, timber, and iron ore). The aim of STABEX is to compensate these countries for shortfalls in their export earnings in any one year below the average value in the preceding four years. Presumably, the size of compensatory payments will depend on the size of the shortfalls: and if both prices and revenue from commodity exports fell rapidly from the reference levels, a considerable payout would be necessary. The funds provided initially by the Community under STABEX (the equivalent of $400 million over five years, or less than 4 per cent of the value of eligible exports from the Lomé Convention countries to the Community in 1973) may be inadequate to the task.[30]

AN INTEGRATED PROGRAMME FOR COMMODITIES

Past commodity agreements or bilateral arrangements have, in the main, aimed to stabilise prices or earnings in money terms. In a period of continuous and rapid inflation in prices of manufactures, many commodity-dependent ldcs seek more than this: they hope to conclude agreements which will raise the prices of their exported commodities in parallel with those of their imported manufactures, or to 'index' export prices to those of imports.[31]

At the same time, some of the developed importing countries seem more sympathetic to the idea of long-term agreements aimed at stabilising or maintaining commodity prices as a *quid pro quo* for an assurance of access to supplies of raw materials. An ambitious 'integrated' programme for the future regulation of world commodity trade, or at least part of it, has been under discussion in UNCTAD and other international institutions since 1974 and formed the main item on the agenda for the fourth UNCTAD conference held in Nairobi in 1976.

Ten 'core' commodities are suggested for the programme (with the possibility of including others) – coffee, copper, rubber, tea, tin, sugar, cotton, cocoa, jute (and jute manufactures), and sisal. The programme proposes the establishment of international agreements based on buffer stocks, internationally financed from a common fund, and with floor and ceiling price levels. The indexation of prices to compensate for deteriorations in commodity producers' terms of trade is also proposed as an essential element.

Even within the group of commodities treated by UNCTAD as the 'core', examples of practically every commodity situation can be found. Coffee, cocoa, and tin are all products for which international commodity agreements are, or have been, in force. But their amenability to buffer stockbuilding is very different. Tin, as a metal, can be stored over long periods while both coffee and cocoa deteriorate over time; thus stocks of coffee and cocoa would have to be differently managed than those of tin. Tea is hardly amenable to stockpiling.

Again, the extent to which ldcs are dominant – or even majority – producers of the commodities in question varies enormously. While obviously they are the main growers of coffee, cocoa, and tea, cotton faces strong competition both from American and East European producers and from synthetic fibres, increasingly produced in developing countries, particularly those with oil, while other fibres and rubber, as we have seen, also contend with the threat of synthetics. Moreover, probable price developments in the various commodities differ considerably, as do projections of supply and demand.

There are thus considerable practical difficulties with the grand design. But there is also a more fundamental economic drawback to the creation of international stockpiles, even if this is feasible technically. This is that their existence may, in the long run, tend to depress, rather than raise, prices.

In the long run, the only way to bid up the price of any product is to create a scarcity. Scarcity results from either excess demand for the product or shortage of supply. And the only way artificially to create a shortage of supply is to restrict production – as OPEC countries have (successfully) done and CIPEC countries are (perhaps less sucessfully) attempting to do. Without supply restriction, international stockpiles aimed at raising the money prices of commodities and maintaining the 'real' prices could grow continually larger. Not only would this be enormously expensive for the financing bodies and their subscribers; it would, in fact, depress prices as world markets reacted to the existence of growing stocks and to the possibility, even if remote in theory, of their release. Without production restrictions the strategy could, therefore, become self-defeating.

In any commodity programme, therefore, regulation of international trade would have to be combined with strict production controls, also administered on an international basis. The possibility of production in one country, or group of countries, being encouraged at the expense of output in others – as happened in tea with East African and Malawian production displacing to some extent Sri Lankan and Indian exports – would also have to be minimised. Stresses and strains on the various agreements from the producer side, as well as between producing and consuming countries, would be bound to occur.

If production were successfully limited, however, new employment would have to be found for the people and equipment put out of their previous work. New sources of employment are among the most difficult elements of an ldc's development strategy to promote successfully. But two possible directions – at least in the area of agriculture – can be indicated. The first is a much greater move to processing of raw materials for export in developing countries themselves – a move which, in turn, as we have seen, would require a new attitude on the part of both governments and processing firms in developed countries. The second is a move away from production for export to domestic food output in the commodity producing ldcs. This would in many cases require an equally radical change in attitude and in policies in many developing countries which have, until now, actively encouraged industry as a means of 'development' at the expense of rural development.

The implications of a global programme for commodity trade thus go far beyond the conditions under which the commodities themselves are produced and traded. They involve potentially enormous changes in policy in both developed and developing countries. And they may lead to a net decrease in the volume, if not the value, of world commodity trade. If as a result, the pattern of world trading relationships became more appropriate to the needs of the majority of the world's population for basic foods this could not be regarded as a bad thing.

Notes

1. See also Table 1.4
2. Neither of the international classification systems (the Standard International Trade Classification (SITC) and the Brussels Tariff Nomenclature (BTN) used in presenting international trade statistics provides an adequate basis for distinguishing between commodities and manufactures.
3. Organisation of Petroleum Exporting Countries. Current membership: Abu Dhabi, Algeria, Ecuador, Indonesia, Iran, Iraq, Kuwait, Libya, Nigeria, Qatar, Saudi Arabia, Gabon (associate).
4. Organisation of Arab Petroleum Exporting Countries. Current membership: Algeria, Bahrain, Egypt, Iraq, Kuwait, Libya, Qatar, Saudi Arabia, Syria, United Arab Emirates.
5. See below, pp. 104-5.
6. See Chapter 4.
7. If the market were so organised, a 'world price' for the commodity concerned could have a limited meaning. See p.98 above.
8. See S. Harris and T. Josling, 'Can World Commodity Prices be Explained?', *National Westminster Bank Quarterly Review*, August 1974.

9. See e.g. Barry Wilson, 'Speculators force up sugar prices', *Action for Development,* VCOAD, London, November 1974.
10. The posted price is set by producing countries, in negotiation with oil extracting companies, as an accounting base on which royalties and taxes paid to the producing countries are calculated. Such royalties and taxes are generally set as percentages of the posted price, and thus rise as it rises. An example of the relationship between 'posted price' and production costs (before and after tax) is given in a US Tariff Commission document, 'World Oil Developments and U.S. Oil Import Policies' (US Tariff Commission Publication 632, October 1973). The figures for Saudi Arabian crude oil for July 1972 (before the 'oil crisis) were as follows:

	$ per barrel
1. Posted price	2.479
2. Royalty (12.5% of (1))	1.310
3. Real extraction cost	0.130
4. Posted price less (2) and (3)	2.039
5. Tax (55% of (4))	1.121
6. Total cost of extraction to company (2+3+5)	1.561

11. G.K. Helleiner, 'Standing up to the world: the new mood in the less developed countries', *Development Dialogue,* No. 2, Uppsala, 1974.
12. UN General Assembly, Sixth Special Session, Document A/9556 (Part II), 'Declaration on the Establishment of a New Economic Order, Programme of Action', Part I: paras. 3(a)(ii) and 1(f).
13. Ibid., para.3 (a) (iii) and (viii).
14. Ibid., para.1 (d).
15. See Chapter 4.
16. See Glossary: *Effective Protection.*
17. See below, pp.116-17.
18. See Appendix II, Table A2.3, Chapter 3.
19. However, the closure of the Suez Canal since 1967 has presented Somalia with great difficulties in exporting bananas to Italy. In recent years, Somalia has been able to develop new markets in the Arab states.
20. See UNCTAD documents TD/TIN.5/4, 'The International Tin Agreements in Operation, 1956-1975', 2 April 1975, and TD/TIN.5/10, 'Text of the Fifth International Tin Agreement'.
21. See e.g. M.A.G. van Meerhaeghe, *International Economic Institutions,* 2nd edn. (London, Longmans, 1971).
22. See J.W.F. Rowe, *The World's Coffee* (HMSO, 1963).
23. But see Appendix III and *FAO Commodity Review and Outlook, 1973-74.*
24. See M. Faber and J.G. Potter, *Towards Economic Independence in Zambia* (Cambridge University Press, 1971); also e.g. M. Niedergang, *The Twenty Latin Americas* (Harmondsworth, Penguin, 1971); and Chapter 6.
25. See I. Litvak and C. Maule, 'Nationalisation in the Caribbean Bauxite Industry', *International Affairs* (London, January 1975).
26. Ibid., and E. Penrose, *The Large International Firm in Developing Countries* (London, Allen and Unwin, 1968).
27. See R.J. Barnet and R.E. Muller, *Global Reach* (New York, Simon and Schuster, 1974), pp.158-9. See also Chapter 6.
28. Faber and Potter, op. cit., p.63.
29. See Chapter 4.
30. See P. Tulloch and E. Hodgkinson, 'Europe and the Developing Countries', *Grindlays Bank Review,* July 1975.
31. See UNCTAD TD/B/C/1/188, 'International arrangements for individual commodities within an integrated programme', July 1975. Also Chapter 7.

4 COMPETING AGRICULTURAL GOODS: FOOD, FODDER AND FARM POLICIES

One large group of commodities traded by ldcs faces problems which can be clearly distinguished from those discussed in the last chapter. These are the products in which exports from ldcs compete directly with domestic production in Western and Socialist developed countries, or in which ldcs compete directly with the farm and food industries of the developed world for supplies. These goods account for around 30 per cent of the primary commodities, other than fuels, exported by ldcs.[1]

The first set of products includes such items as oilseeds and vegetable oils, meat, and sugar. The other category comprises the principal foodgrains, mainly wheat, maize, and rice. The problems the two sets of products face, though different, have common features in that they are all tied into the structure of agricultural production as managed by the developed countries, including those of Eastern Europe.

The situation of world supply of foodgrains, and their distribution throughout the world, has been given particular focus by the marked shortage of supplies of recent years. On one hand it has become apparent that many developing countries do not appear to have the capacity to feed their growing populations – although many would argue that this is a crisis of organisation rather than of physical growing capacity, and that it is rooted rather in the inability of very poor landless people to grow or buy food, in which case the measures which should be taken to right the situation are quite different to those which would be necessary if ldc production had really run up against a physical constraint. But the domestic farm and food policies of the governments of developed countries are also significant in determining the level of world demand for and supply of foodgrains, since they are consumed both by people and, to an increasing extent, by animals in these countries.

The other products face problems stemming from direct competition between developed and developing countries. Such competition, in many cases exacerbated by high levels of protection in developed countries, inhibits or destabilises markets for exports from ldcs.

The two problems, though separate, are linked. Grain shortages increase competition between food for people in poor countries and fodder for animals in rich ones. High grain prices in turn worsen the trade balances of grain importing countries, increase farm costs in meat producing developed countries, and drive up the prices of products such as vegetable oils which compete with grains in the fodder market. The agricultural policies of developed countries, particularly in regard to meat and dairy products, are the main determinants of world market prices for many grains, oilseeds, and oils, while their policies on the production of less essential foodstuffs such as sugar and fruits can affect the ability of ldcs to earn the foreign exchange necessary to import needed products, including foodstuffs.

In this chapter, we shall deal first with world trade in grains, and the situation during and since the world food crisis of 1972; and second, with trade in other 'competing' agricultural goods. The aim is to illustrate both the differences and the similarities among ldcs' positions in respect of both groups of products.

GRAINS

Wheat, maize, and rice are the world's principal foodgrains. Table 4.1 shows the world production and trade situation for wheat, Table 4.2 for maize, and Table 4.3 for rice. Exports accounted for rather small proportions of world output in the period 1971-3 in all three cases: over a sixth for wheat, around one-eighth for maize, but only 3 per cent in the case of rice. The main wheat exporting countries were the United States, Canada, Australia, and Argentina, with over three-quarters of world exports among them. The main maize exporters were the United States, Argentina and South Africa, again with over three-quarters of world exports. And in rice, China, Thailand, and the United States accounted for almost two-thirds of world exports.

In the period 1971-3, developing countries as a group were net exporters of maize, but substantial net importers of rice and, particularly, of wheat, where ldcs' imports were more than eight times the volume of their exports, with Brazil, India, Egypt, and Pakistan among the main importing countries. Ldcs' imports of rice during the same period were, at 6.6 million tonnes, more than double their exports; and despite the high proportion of world rice production in Asian developing countries (over 90 per cent of production in ldcs, or 50 per cent of world output), Thailand, Burma,

Pakistan, and Nepal were the only Asian ldcs which were net exporters of rice.[2]

Historically, foodgrain supplies entering world trade have fluctuated considerably more than total production. In most countries grains are generally grown primarily for home consumption and only secondarily for export. Canada, and the United States, are probably the only

Table 4.1. Wheat: Production and Trade, 1971-3 (Annual Averages)

Country	Production '000 tonnes	Exports '000 tonnes	Exports $m	Imports '000 tonnes	Imports $m
USSR	98.204	5,238	426	8,533	559
USA	44,218	24,974	2,138	5,458	449
EEC	40.902	6,850	742	10,662	1,139
China	34,102	–	–	5,162	454
India	25,055	224	24	1,954	202
Canada	15,346	12,997	989	–	–
Turkey	11,983	198	14	251	18
Australia	9,056	7,693	445	–	–
Argentina	6,693	1,817	131	–	–
Brazil	1,644	–	–	2,169	188
E. Germany	17,132	–	–	1,802	139
Egypt	1,729	–	–	1,602	123
Pakistan	6,936	4	–	783	55
Japan	309	–	–	5,286	456
Total listed	313,609	59,995	4,909	43,662	3,782
World total	359,583	62,048	5,103	59,394	5,115
Ldcs	74,012	2,589	199	21,739	1,908
Ldcs' share (%)	20.6	4.2	3.9	36.7	37.3

Source: FAO, *Production Yearbook 1974,* and *Trade Yearbooks 1974.*

Table 4.2. Maize: Production and Trade, 1971-3 (Annual Averages)

Country	Production '000 tonnes	Exports '000 tonnes	Exports $m	Imports '000 tonnes	Imports $m
USA	142,734	22,822	1,608	38	5
China	29,643	–	–	1,815	153
EEC	14,807	5,046	526	16,703	1,541
Brazil	14,540	498	29	3	–
USSR	10,622	258	20	3,460	195
Mexico	9,413	242	13	450	1
Argentina	8,497	5,011	341	–	–
Romania	8,522	404	31	100	6
Yugoslavia	7,876	127	19	363	24
India	6,036	–	–	155	7
S. Africa	7,477	2,041	131	1	47
Egypt	2,424	–	–	64	4
Japan	–	–	–	6,276	495
Lebanon	1	3	–	120	9
Singapore	–	70	5	189	14
Chile	278	–	–	291	20
Malaysia	5	1	–	196	15
Total listed	262,875	36,573	2,723	30,224	2,536
World total	306,974	39,260	2,926	38,971	3,193
Ldcs	67,905	8,036	527	3,616	301
Ldcs' share (%)	22.1	20.5	18.0	9.3	9.4

Source As Table 4.1.

Table 4.3. Rice: Production and Trade, 1971-3 (Annual Averages)

Country	Production '000 tonnes	Exports '000 tonnes	Exports $m	Imports '000 tonnes	Imports $m
China	108,249	2,640	383	2	0
India	63,384	14	3	263	41
Indonesia	19,005	–	–	962	238
Bangladesh	16,107	–	–	464	60
Japan	15,119	545	86	13	2
Thailand	13,354	1,526	182	–	–
Vietnam	10,424	23	4	1,477	197
Burma	8,031	485	40	–	–
Brazil	7,288	62	5	5	1
S. Korea	5,635	1	–	388	37
USA	3,992	1,714	395	30	4
Pakistan	3,509	390	64	20	1
Egypt	2,438	423	58	–	–
Nepal	2,413	217	57	–	–
Other Asian ldcs	9,708	292	49	2,217	409
Total listed	293,833	8,332	1,326	6,565	1,104
World total	306,754	9,334	1,506	9,344	1,626
Ldcs	170,032	3,606	496	6,605	1,176
Ldcs' share (%)	55.4	38.6	32.9	70.7	72.3

Source: As Table 4.1.

exceptions to this rule; and even in these main exporting countries the volume produced and available for export depends very much on the encouragement given by governments through the farm price and income support system. In most countries, then, exports come from surplus, marginal supplies, and any shortfall in supply can mean a dramatic change from a world trade surplus to deficit.

The World Food Crisis of 1972-4

In 1972, just such a change took place. From the mid-sixties, world grain supplies had been generally in surplus. North American wheat output was expanding, Japan was aiming for self-sufficiency in rice, and EEC farm policies were also encouraging the expansion of many areas of output. Even in the Indian sub-continent the food supply situation appeared to be improving with the introduction of new varieties of wheat and rice. A series of projections published by the FAO in 1971, looking ahead to 1980, suggested that world output of cereals, as well as that of oilseeds, could seriously outrun demand and cause major problems both to farmers and to governments.[3]

These optimistic projections were completely exploded in 1972. Between 1971 and 1972, world rice production fell by 14 million tonnes, or more than the total volume of world trade. Wheat output fell by 6 million tonnes, or 10 per cent of world exports. Maize output also declined by 1 million tonnes. By 1973, world stocks of rice, wheat and coarse grains had fallen by 65 per cent, 59 per cent and 34 per cent from their 1970-1 levels. A second decline in world grains production occurred in 1974.

The crisis was in large measure a result of natural disasters, mainly in countries which were grain importers. Crops had failed in 1972 over a large area of the world. The principal and most dramatised failure among developed countries was in the Soviet Union, whose wheat output fell by 13 per cent between 1971 and 1972. The USSR contributed to the gravity of the crisis by buying, in almost total secrecy, 19 million tonnes of grains in the United States and virtually 'cornering' the US export market. Among developing countries, large areas of Africa and Asia were seriously affected in their turn by droughts and monsoon failures, which caused severe shortages of all three principal foodgrains.

At the same time, the world surplus situation of the period up to 1971, and the large stocks of grain which had been built up, had led exporting countries, particularly the United States, to reduce the area planted with grains and compensate farmers for growing less grain. Thus the capacity to respond to the crisis did not, in the short term, exist.

The Effect of the Food Crisis on Developing Countries

The effects of the world food crisis have been very unevenly spread in the world and among developing countries. Broadly, three main groups of ldcs have been identified in this context:

(a) countries with a basic 'structural' food problem;
(b) countries which are fairly near self-sufficiency in food or which spend only a low percentage of export earnings on food imports;
(c) food exporting countries.[4]

The first category would include India, Bangladesh and most of the 'least developed' countries of Africa. All are heavy net importers of foodgrains. Most (with the notable exception of India) have a small range of exports, mainly of commodities, to set off against purchases of foodgrains. In the short term, these countries have few options open to them. Their immediate need, following the crisis, was to be able to import food supplies from abroad. The costs of these imports had to be met either from export earnings, or from running down already low foreign exchange reserves, or from international aid and foreign borrowing. In the short run, the last has been the only feasible alternative.

The second group of countries, where only a small shift in land use is required to offset an internal food deficit, includes the Philippines, Pakistan and Brazil. These countries can exercise a choice at the margin between using their land for domestic food production or for export crops. For example, cotton production competes for land with wheat or other grains. The relative movements in world prices of various commodities can help farmers and governments to decide whether it is more sensible, for example, to grow cotton and import wheat, or to grow more wheat and ignore possible export earnings from cotton. But the choice may not be easy, even where two alternative crops are both annuals; as, for instance, when the prices of both wheat and cotton on world markets are high. It will be even more difficult to respond to price changes when one or both of the crops is a long-term investment like oil palm or coffee.

The third group, which includes such countries as Argentina and Thailand is in the enviable position of normally having an export surplus over 'domestic' consumption. Severe malnutrition may still exist in grain exporting countries, however, as a result either of important, but not necessarily fundamental, problems such as poor transport and distribution facilities, or more seriously from gross maldistribution of rural income (for example as a result of inequitable patterns of land tenure) or high unemployment in towns. In this situation, the capacity of a country to export foodgrains may not be a sign of its prosperity, but rather of social inequality and distorted patterns of development.

Grain Stocks and World Trade

Any global strategy to rebuild the world balance of foodgrains must take account of two factors. The first is, as mentioned above, that world stocks fall drastically after 1972 and must be built up again. The policy which would best square with international comparative advantage would be for countries with the greatest capacity as efficient grain producers to increase their output as far as possible, while others imported grains and exported other goods. With this, however, there is a clear need to create adequate buffer stocks against future shortfalls in supply; and there is a good case for the international financing of such stocks – if only since it is clearly in the interests of importing countries, even more than exporters, that they should exist. The World Food Conference of 1974 stressed the urgency of international action to increase world 'food security'.

A recent proposal by the United States[5] suggested the establishment of reserves of 30 million tons of wheat and rice (25 million tons of wheat and 5 million tons of rice) over and above 'normal working stocks' of 100 million tons.[6] These stocks would be 'equitably shared' among participants, in proportion to their exports of foodgrains, gross domestic product, and variance in production around a calculated trend. The United States proposal, however, made no suggestions for the international financing of such buffer stocks: rather, members of the reserves agreement, which would be administered through the International Wheat Council, would bear the costs of managing their own reserves.

A further contribution could be made to rebuilding grain stocks by reducing the amount of grains used in animal feeds and, in consequence, the proportion of developed countries' farming devoted to the highly intensive rearing of animals for meat. At present, nearly half the world's grain supplies are fed to livestock, including poultry. If this proportion could be reduced, a buffer against famine would be more readily available.[7] In addition, a reduction in intensive meat production in developed countries would allow more easy access for beef, in particular, from developing and developed countries which have a comparative advantage in extensive range-based beef production.[8]

It is doubtful, however, that even grain importing countries, particularly developing countries, would be wise to concentrate exclusively on the 'trade-related' type of policy outlined above, for two main reasons. First, their dependence on the policies followed by principal exporting countries would be substantially increased; particularly if, as in the American proposal, exporting countries were made solely responsible for financing stocks. Second, it would greatly enhance the importance of grain importing countries in turn being able to export other goods to pay for imports of grain. There is no guarantee that they would be able to do so. On the one hand, as we have seen in Chapter 3, the demand for many of the commodities which ldcs export is neither flexible nor fast-growing, while many also face intense competition from synthetic substitutes. Where exports of other competing agricultural goods are concerned, moreover, developed countries are as a rule intensely protectionist. Unless some substantial reduction in trade barriers could be negotiated in GATT or elsewhere at the same time, which at present seems remote, a rapid increase in ldc exports of these products seems most unlikely.

Developing countries may therefore find it more desirable or advisable to concentrate on increasing their own 'food security', either individually by encouraging production for the internal market or collectively by trading with other developing countries.[9] Such a policy may be desirable in the long term even though it appears more costly in the short run than the 'trade-related' alternative.

A third reason why this type of policy may not altogether appeal to ldcs relates to the growing realisation that one of the main reasons for the existence of persistent malnutrition and starvation is simply that many people are too poor to buy food even if it is available on the market. The problem has to be attacked from the other end; by creating the capacity either to grow, or to buy, the means of subsistence. Demand, rather than supply, is often what is lacking.[10]

This problem cannot be attacked solely through the creation of larger world food reserves based on production in existing exporting countries. In so far as the objective is to enable peasants to *grow* more of their own food, the developing countries themselves are the only places where such changes can take place. The need is for a drastic improvement in the state of the small-scale, subsistence sector. This may require wide-ranging, even revolutionary, changes in the economic and social fabric of particular countries. It would in any case not be a trade creating policy. In so far as the objective is to enable people to *buy* the necessary food, other sources of income – crops or industries – must be found. This strategy would imply an expansion of the cash economy and could be related to trade. In these circumstances, a better global balance between supply and demand would still be desirable.

OTHER PRODUCTS

We have seen that developed countries dominate the world markets for the three principal grains: both as buyers (Europe and Japan) and as sellers (United States and Canada). Developing countries which rely on imported foodgrains are thus almost totally dependent on the balance of supply and demand among the main developed trading countries.

But developed countries also dominate the markets for the other principal competing agricultural goods – meat, oilseeds and vegetable oils, and sugar – exported by ldcs. Plantations or livestock industries originally established to serve European or American markets are now challenged by competition from the farming industries of Europe and America themselves. Most developed countries have followed policies which have protected and encouraged overproduction of these goods, often at high cost both in money and in consumption of other resources. This in turn may harm the prospects for ldc exports of these goods. No doubt in some countries a measure of diversification away from the plantation economy would be desirable. But the structure of international trade in farm products seems to have gone so far away from any principles reflected in the theory of comparative advantage that such diversification may be forced on ldcs as an undesirable alternative.

Meat and Meat Products

Developing countries account for almost one-fifth of world exports of meat (fresh, frozen, chilled, or canned – see Table 4.4). Beef in its various forms is the meat most commonly exported by developing countries, and their share of world exports of beef and beef products is some 30 per cent.

The main beef exporting ldcs are in Latin America: Argentina, Brazil

Table 4.4. Meat: Production and Trade, 1971-3 (Annual Averages)

	Production	Exports		Imports	
	'000 tonnes	'000 tonnes	$m	'000 tonnes	$m
Argentina	2,495	440	503	–	–
Brazil	2,849	163	173	2	3
Uruguay	392	110	100	–	–
Costa Rica	68	21	27	1	0
Nicaragua	77	27	37	0	0
Honduras	52	20	19	0	0
Guatemala	79	16	20	0	0
Botswana	45	18	13	–	–
Other Africa	3,783	120	96	80	60
Other Latin America	3,045	104	112	155	131
S & E Asian ldcs	2,923	13	17	103	81
EEC (9)	13,572	1,661	1,807	2,780	2,788
Australia	2,269	699	713	–	–
New Zealand	1,023	671	520	1	1
USA	16,489	264	264	647	870
Canada	1,579	120	138	113	138
Japan	1,168	6	3	393	442
Total listed	51,908	4,473	4,562	4,275	4,514
World total	87,508	5,232	5,602	5,163	6,019
Ldcs	16,319	1,004	1,081	396	343
Ldcs' share (%)	18.7	19.2	19.3	7.7	5.7

Source: As Table 4.1.

Uruguay, Mexico, Costa Rica, Honduras, and Guatemala are the principal suppliers. Beef accounts for 36 per cent of exports from Uruguay, 18 per cent from Honduras, 15 per cent from Nicaragua and 13 per cent from Argentina. Some African countries – Botswana, Kenya, and the Sudan are examples – also have significant meat exporting capacity.

Developing countries' capacity to export meat is limited by three factors: their capacity to supply meat for the export trade, the degree of competition between ldcs and other suppliers to the world market, and the agricultural and veterinary policies of importing countries.

Supply Constraints

Ldcs' capacity to supply meat for export depends partly on the extent of investment in animal farming and meat processing (including investment in health and sanitary facilities to fulfil developed countries' regulations) and the volume of output which this can sustain, and partly on the balance of demand between home and export markets. Currently, African countries with relatively large grazing lands and a low level of demand for meat in the domestic commercial market show the greatest potential for expansion of meat production for export. The 'traditional' meat exporting – and beef consuming – countries of Latin America have found the balance between exporting meat and supplying domestic consumption increasingly hard to maintain. *Per capita* consumption of beef and veal in Uruguay, for example, fell steadily throughout the sixties and in 1971 was less than half its 1962 level: that in Argentina fell by one-third between 1969 and 1972. Both countries had, during the later sixties and early 1970s, preferred export supply over domestic consumption.

Competition with Other Exporters

Ldcs face two main sources of export competition in world markets for meat. The first is from other efficient producers – principally Australia and New Zealand, both substantial producers of beef and mutton, which in 1971-3 accounted for more than a quarter of world beef exports and around 83 per cent of mutton and lamb exports. The second is from surpluses created by farm policies of other developed countries which have, through high protection, built up their meat industries to a high level of production at high cost.

In a completely free trade situation, exports of meat from other efficient producing countries would be unlikely to threaten meat producing ldcs. Both groups have a comparative advantage in beef production and should find easy markets. In the highly protected state of the world meat trade, however, the efficient producers are set off against each other competing for a small slice of trade.

Developed Countries' Policies

Developing countries face several handicaps in establishing meat exports to Western developed countries. One comes from health regulations imposed to prevent the spread of serious animal diseases such as foot-and-mouth and rinderpest. In general, these regulations are not used as overt barriers to trade. But the differences which exist between acceptable health standards in various countries (for example, whether meat from animals protected against foot-and-mouth disease by vaccination will be accepted for import) can be a barrier to trade. The establishment of commonly accepted standards among groups of importing countries helps developing countries to overcome such problems. It should be noted that common EEC health regulations should be in force among the Nine by 1977, and that GATT negotiations also include discussions of standards.

These problems affect all developing countries, but particularly those in Africa. African exporters, in general only now beginning to break into European markets for fresh or frozen beef, have to overcome disease problems which are both more widespread than in Latin America and of types exotic to Europe.[11] Some countries – Botswana and Kenya are so far the main examples – are now raising beef cattle of a quality acceptable to European markets and establishing disease-free zones where export meat farming can be undertaken. The costs of such programmes have been very high.

Even when disease problems can be overcome, however, exporting is likely to be risky, owing both to the levels of import barriers imposed by some developed countries and – equally important – the rapid changes which have taken place both in world markets and in importing countries' policies. Since 1970, the world market has been particularly unstable. A rapid rise in world beef prices between 1970 and 1972 led to a relaxation of import restrictions in the United States, Britain, and EEC countries, and exports from Latin American and African countries grew rapidly. Argentina's exports of beef increased by 67 per cent in volume and 106 per cent in value between 1971 and 1972. Most Latin American governments were forced to take steps, in the form of new export taxes and quotas, to restrict exports.

At the same time every encouragement has been given to beef and other meat production in Europe and the United States in order to combat high world prices. In Britain, official subsidies and higher deficiency payments encouraged the raising of intensively fed cattle, taking advantage of low world prices for grains and oilseeds. A large proportion of UK meat production and of live cattle reared was, moreover, exported to the original six EEC members, where prices were even higher – closing the differential between British and EEC-consumer prices for meat. At the same time Community meat production was itself being encouraged through higher target and intervention prices; and the combination of high-cost beef and increasing production of intensively farmed pigs and poultry in Europe meant that in all European countries the relative importance of beef and veal in meat consumption was declining. Intensive feeding, moreover, vastly increased the importance of oilseed-based compound feedstuffs in Western farming in this period, affecting in turn the market for vegetable oils and oilseeds.[12]

The crisis in world grain and oilseed markets which began in 1972 and reached its peak in 1974 upset all the projections of the growth of intensive meat production. Farm costs – first of feed, then of fuels – rocketed and, in Britain as well as some other European countries, many farmers were forced to cut back their output through premature slaughtering of animals, often at bankruptcy prices. A short-term glut of meat arose in Europe, just at a time when investment in beef and mutton production in major exporting countries – particularly Australia and New Zealand – was also yielding results. The European Community reaction to this situation was to impose a strict ban on imports of beef, and to export meat at subsidised prices, while Community farmers agitated for still higher support prices to overcome escalating costs.

These events cast grave doubt on the policy of all-out expansion which was pursued by Western meat farming enterprises, and encouraged by governments, between 1970 and 1972. In the short term, the growth of intensive meat farming, now also being questioned as a danger to health in Western countries, may have been stemmed. But the United States is probably the only major Western economy in which a really substantial reduction in the amount of grain and oilseeds used as fodder for intensively raised animals has taken place during 1975: a reduction which one estimate puts at 20 per cent of the 1974 level.[13] Elsewhere, there must remain considerable pressure from consumers to maintain patterns of factory farming for pigs, poultry, and even cattle in order to maintain the patterns of consumption to which people have become accustomed. Farmers who over-expanded output in the 1970-3 period and have since found themselves in difficulties exert even stronger pressure on governments, particularly in Europe.

It would be a pity if the present chaotic state of world meat markets failed to lead to any international reconsideration of the patterns of trade. In the present situation there is at least some scope for a reassessment of patterns of comparative advantage in meat production and export, and of the role which countries with adequate and ample grazing land, in particular, ought to play. The two parts of the world where meat exports could, at reasonable cost, be increased substantially are Australia and New Zealand, and certain African countries, always assuming animal disease problems can be overcome. In this case, it may be in the interest both of these developing countries and of the West for Western aid agencies (including the European Development Fund) to invest in the development of pasture-based meat farming. In the short and medium term, the potential output of beef, and even of 'exotic' varieties like buffalo beef, now being tried experimentally in Brazil and

India, could in most African countries at least outrun the demands of their growing population and provide an exportable surplus. And the diversion of resources in Western countries from intensively raised animal farming, with its high demands for imported feeds, would also take some of the pressure off the markets for grains and oilseeds.

The main international fora for the discussion of international trade in meat are the ongoing GATT negotiations and the FAO Intergovernmental Study Group on Meat. At the time of writing (early 1976) it appears that little progress towards liberalisation of trade in meat has been made in the GATT negotiations. The problems which underlie the lack of progress were highlighted in an FAO report, published in October 1975, which reported that, mainly because of the EEC import ban, world trade in beef and veal in particular had fallen substantially in 1974.[14] At the same time, higher consumer prices, coupled with the general effects of inflation and economic recession in developed countries, including the Community, weakened demand for meat. Although high prices encouraged increases in output throughout the world, they simultaneously discouraged consumption.

EEC import policy on meat during 1975 continued to be very restrictive. Although the outright ban enforced during 1974 was eased, imports were at first allowed only if a corresponding volume of meat was re-exported on to the world market. Later this regulation was eased further to allow for imports of twice the volume of exports. A special quota was additionally opened for Botswana under the provisions of the Lomé Convention.

The strict connection maintained between imports (which are subject to EEC variable levies) and exports (which benefit from export subsidies) helps to ensure that Community meat prices, in general, remain above world levels. While this is, no doubt, very useful for EEC farmers, it operates in a time of surplus to depress world markets. Developing country meat exporters, therefore, remain at a disadvantage.

Oilseed Products

Vegetable oils, fats, and proteins are extracted from a wide variety of sources. Among the most important are soya beans, groundnuts, cottonseed, palm kernels, coconuts, rapeseed and sunflower seed. Castor, sesame, linseed, and tung are also significant.

Table 4.5 shows the value of exports of major oilseeds and their products and the direction of trade. The main producers of rapeseed are Canada and the EEC, and intra-EEC trade is very important. Output in the Community more than trebled in the period 1963-73. Sunflower

Table 4.5. Direction of Trade in Major Oilseeds and Oilseed Products

Product	Total exports (1971-3, $m)	Ldc share (%)	Main exporting countries	Main importing countries
Groundnuts, oil, and cake	595	75	Senegal, Nigeria, India, Sudan, Brazil, Argentina, USA, China	W. Europe (France, UK, W. Germany), Poland, USSR
Copra, coconut oil, and cake	438	90	Philippines, Papua/New Guinea, Indonesia, Malaysia, Sri Lanka	W. Europe (W. Germany, Netherlands, UK), USA
Palm nuts, palm kernel oil, palm kernel cake, palm oil	483	82	Nigeria, Sierra Leone, Ivory Coast, Cameroon, Malaysia, Indonesia, Singapore, Netherlands	W. Europe (Netherlands, W. Germany, UK), USA Japan
Cottonseed, oil, and cake	575	74	Sudan (oil, cake and seed), Nigeria, Mali, Ivory Coast, Dahomey, Ethiopia, Thailand (seed), Brazil, India, Turkey (cake), USA, USSR, Nicaragua, Argentina (oil)	Japan (seed), W. Europe (W. Germany, Denmark, Sweden, UK) (oil and cake), E. Europe (Poland, Czechoslovakia) (cake), Egypt, Yugoslavia, Venezuela (oil)
Soya beans, oil and cake	3,601	13	USA, Brazil, W. Germany, Netherlands	W. Europe (W. Germany, France, Netherlands, Italy, Denmark, Belgium, Spain), Japan, E. Europe, Cuba, Venezuela
Rapeseed, oil, and cake	424	2	Canada, France, W. Germany, Denmark	Japan, Italy, France, W. Germany, Algeria, Morocco
Sunflower seed, oil, and cake	336	16	USA, Bulgaria, Yugoslavia, Australia (seed), Argentina, W. Germany (cake), USSR, Romania, Argentina (oil)	W. And E. Europe (W. Germany, France Netherlands, Switzerland, Poland, E. Germany, Czechoslovakia), Algeria, Cuba

Source: FAO, *Trade Yearbook 1974.*

seed, while grown in a number of developing countries, is best known as an East European export.

The import market for oilseed products is dominated by Western Europe and Japan. The United States produces a high proportion of its oilseed requirements and, as we have seen, is a major exporter. The Soviet Union is an important market for groundnuts, and Eastern Europe generally for cottonseed and sunflower cake. But Western European countries account for almost three-quarters of world imports of groundnuts and groundnut products, two-thirds of world imports of palm and soya bean products, and over half of imports of coconut products.

Uses of Oilseed Products

A few oilseeds (e.g. groundnuts and soya) are in part marketed for human consumption. But the two main uses of oilseeds are for the extraction of vegetable oils and the manufacture of oilcake and meal. In quantity terms, oilcake accounts for the largest share of products processed from all oilseeds except coconuts (copra), but in value terms vegetable oil is more often the more important.

Vegetable oils have six main uses: as culinary oils for cooking and salads, in the manufacture of cooking fats, in margarine, in soap and detergents, in paints and varnishes, and as lubricants. The following table shows broadly the extent to which different vegetable oils substitute or contrast with each other in use.

Table 4.6. Uses of Vegetable Oils

Margarine and other foods	*Cooking fats*	*Directly in cooking*
Palm	Palm	Whole group,
Coconut	Groundnut	plus olive oil
Groundnut	Cottonseed	
Soya bean		
Cottonseed		
Sunflower		
Rapeseed		
Sesame seed		
Soap and detergents	*Paints and varnishes*	*Lubricants*
Coconut	Linseed	Castor
Palm kernel	Tung	Rapeseed
	Castor	
	Soya bean	

The main use of oilcake, by contrast, is in the manufacture of compound feeding stuffs for farm animals. The demand for oilcake therefore depends directly on that for meat and other animal products such as dairy products.[15] The rapid growth in meat consumption, particularly of intensively reared pigs and poultry, which has taken place in all developed countries, including those of Eastern Europe, in recent years has meant that consumption of oilcake has grown very rapidly. The total quantity of oilcakes imported by developed Western and Socialist countries grew by 39 per cent between 1969 and 1974, with consumption in the USSR and Eastern Europe growing more than three-fold. Since oilcake substitutes closely for grain in animal feeds, the grain shortage of 1973-4 also drove up the price of oilseed products, and the corresponding increase in exports in volume terms was of the order of 300 per cent (450 per cent in the USSR and Eastern Europe).[16]

In the past decade, the market for all 'edible' oils has also grown steadily. Production of tropical oilseeds, except soya bean output in Brazil, has not, however, kept pace with the development of demand to the same degree as edible oil output in developed countries. Soya bean production in the United States grew by 118 per cent between the early sixties and the peak year of 1973, and the USA increased its dominance of world oilseed markets; and during the same period EEC output of rapeseed more than trebled. Against this, groundnut output grew by only 10 per cent, and exports of groundnuts, taken up to 1972, fell 44 per cent as Nigerian production suffered a serious decline after 1969. Similarly, palm kernel production was only 20 per cent higher. Palm oil exports, however, have forged ahead as ldcs' capacity has grown and new uses developed. Table 4.7 illustrates the growth of production and trade in major oilseeds.

Although the main export trade in oilseed products is from developing to developed countries, a high proportion of most oilseeds is consumed in the country of origin. In many producing countries, cottonseed is fed directly to animals or used as fertiliser or fuel (e.g. in India less than half of cottonseed supplies are crushed for oil). Most sunflower seed, by contrast, is crushed for use in Eastern European countries either directly as edible oil or in margarine and cooking fats, which in turn are domestically consumed. Again, all Indian production of groundnuts and groundnut oil (34 and 53 per cent of world totals respectively) is domestically consumed, as is virtually all of China's output (15 per cent of production of

Table 4.7. Annual Growth Rates of Production and Exports of Selected Oilseeds and Oils 1961-5 (Annual Average) – 1972, 1973

	Production 1973 ('000 tonnes)	Growth rate since 1961-5 (%)	Exports 1972 ('000 tonnes)	Growth rate since 1961-5 (%)
Groundnuts	17,195	+1.1	696	–4.1
Groundnut oil	n.a.	n.a.	409	+ 2.0
Palm kernels	1,282	+2.0	382	–3.7
Palm oil	2,510	+6.5	1,230	+11.1
Soya beans	61,917	+7.6	12,870	+11.1
of which: USA	41,964	+9.0	11,804	+10.4
Soya oil	n.a.	n.a.	942	+5.1
Rapeseed	7,065	+5.9	n.a.	n.a.
of which: EEC (9)	1,131	+13.8	n.a.	n.a.

Source: FAO, *Monthly Bulletin of Agricultural Economics and Statistics.*

groundnuts). Little of the world production of sesame seed is crushed for oil: most is used as a popular sweet in the countries of output. Only the Sudan, Ethiopia, and Nigeria are substantial exporters.

By contrast, relatively high proportions of coconut and palm nut output are crushed for oil. Palm oil extraction has to be located in the growing areas as it is the outer pulp of the palm nut which is used; thus Malaysia, Zaire, and Indonesia are both the biggest producers and the biggest exporters of palm oil, most of which is destined for sale to Britain, West Germany, the Netherlands, and the United States. The same developed countries are the main importers of palm kernels and extractors of palm kernel oil (which technically can be undertaken either at source or destination). Although palm oil and palm kernel oil differ markedly in technical composition, there is some overlap in their end-uses – the former going mainly into the manufacture of edible fats while the latter is in addition used for soaps and detergents.

Developed Countries' Import Policies

The policies which developed countries follow towards imports of oilseeds and oilseed products reflect, as one might expect, their own needs for animal feedstuffs and raw materials for food processing industries. Thus, most developed countries import oilseeds duty-free and without any other restriction. Vegetable oils, which may compete with domestic production, are less liberally treated. Oilcake, as an essential raw material for agriculture, also enters most developed countries free of import restrictions. At the same time, most developed countries subsidise oilseed and vegetable oil production in one way or another.

EEC. Production of oilseeds and vegetable oils in the EEC is subsidised through the mechanisms of the Common Agricultural Policy. Thus olive oil, rapeseed, and sunflower seed production is encouraged by internal support prices.[17] Subsidies based on the area cultivated are also paid on cottonseed and soya beans. Oilseed crushing industries, which would in a situation of free trade buy from the cheapest source, receive subsidies equivalent to the difference between the internal target price and the world market price, when this is lower, to ensure that supplies from within the Community are purchased as readily as those from other sources. The combination of price supports and subsidies to crushers has enabled oilseed production in the Community to expand substantially.

Table 4.8. Imports of Oilseeds and Oils into Enlarged EEC, 1973, and Annual Growth Rate, 1961-5 (Average) – 1973

	Imports 1973 '000 tonnes	Growth rate since 1961-5 (%)
Groundnuts	525	–3.6
Groundnut oil	384	+5.8
Palm kernels	226	–4.8
Palm oil	700	+6.2
Soya beans	7,004	+10.2
Soya oil	182	+12.2
Rapeseed	(700)[1]	+15.0
Sunflower seed	(280)[1]	+14.0

1 Including internal trade.

Sources: Commonwealth Secretariat, *Vegetable Oils and Oilseeds* and *Tropical Products Quarterly*.

Imported oilseeds generally enter duty-free, although variable compensatory levies may be imposed on any subsidised exports from third countries, such as sunflower seed exports from Eastern Europe. Vegetable oils, by contrast, bear import duties of up to 20 per cent *ad valorem*. Lomé Convention member states benefit from duty-free access – a concession which is of considerable value both to these countries and to EEC consumers since such major vegetable oil exporters as Nigeria, Senegal, Zaire, and Dahomey are on the list. Oilcake imported for animal feed also enters the Community duty-free, and this has been of crucial importance in promoting the use of oilcake (including particularly soya) in the meat industry as against feeds based on grains, which bear full variable levies.

United States. Soya is the most important oilseed produced in the United States. In recent years it has also become the most important in world trade, owing to the wide range of culinary and industrial uses to which it can be adapted. No other oilseed has so many potential uses. United States farm support policies have, over the years, provided a firm base for the expansion of soya production. Being an annual crop, the supply of soya is highly responsive to price incentives; it has expanded under the impetus of three main factors – the actual market price, the level of support given by the government, and the prices of competing commodities, particularly grains.

The two main external sources of demand for United States' soya exports have been growing consumption in the EEC and Japan, and food aid. The EEC countries have become the largest importers of soya since the late sixties.

The importance of American soya supplies to the delicate balance of grain and oilseeds in world trade has been evident since the grain crisis of 1972, since when they have twice fallen short of world demand. In 1972 export quotas were imposed to safeguard domestic supplies. This measure caused an enormous outcry from the EEC and Japan in particular, as well as from importing ldcs, and the experiment was not repeated. However, in the autumn of 1974, when it became evident that there would be another poor grain and soya crop largely as a result of frosts, a system of prior approval for any export sales of grains, soya beans, and soya meal was introduced. Although this was abandoned in March 1975, all export sales have since then still had to be reported to the government.

As an important producer and exporter of oilseeds and oilseed products (Table 4.9) the United States is not a large importer. Its main impact on the developing countries' exports of oilseed products lies in the competition which soya products provide for other oilseeds. Soya is more versatile in its uses than most other oilseeds and thus is in heavy demand both as oil and most importantly as high-protein oilcake for animal feed (not to mention a growing use as a meat substitute in human food). In the present situation of high world demand for oilseed products little harm is done by rapidly growing US exports of soya. But if, as the ITC study[18] suggests, growing grain and dairy surpluses in Europe in particular reduce the overall demand for oilseeds, the dominance of soya could have adverse consequences for some ldc exporters.

Table 4.9. US Trade Flows in Oilseeds and Oils, 1973 and Annual Growth Rate 1961-5 (Annual Average) – 1973

	Exports 1973 '000 tonnes	Annual growth rate since 1961-5 (%)	Imports 1973 '000 tonnes	Annual growth rate since 1961-5 (%)
Groundnuts	183	+19	–	–
Groundnut oil	46	+11.8	–	–
Soya beans	13,013	+10.4	–	–
Soya oil[1]	432	–1.3	–	–
Cottonseed	12	+3.4	–	–
Cottonseed oil[1]	244	+1.1	–	–
Linseed	10	–6.7	–	–
Linseed oil	95	+13.2	–	–
Copra	–	–	195	–2.8
Coconut oil	–	–	320	+8.4
Palm kernel oil	–	–	45	+1.85
Palm oil	–	–	173	+30.8
Castor oil	–	–	45	–0.8

1 Including PL 480 aid sales.
Source: As for Table 4.7.

Of the main tropical oils and oilseeds, palm nuts and kernels are imported into the United States duty-free, while other oilseeds bear import duties usually levied on a 'specific' basis of so many cents per lb. These provide higher protection when world prices are low than when they are high and thus are likely to have a greater protective effect than *ad valorem* rates year by year. Vegetable oils, again with the exception of coconut oil from the Philippines and Pacific Trust Territories, bear duties which are generally higher than those on oilseeds.

Japan. Japan is a major importer of vegetable oilseeds and oils, particularly soya and rapeseed, domestic production of both of which has declined markedly since 1960. The farm policies pursued by Japan have encouraged the development of other crops, such as pulses, potatoes, and grass, in former soya bean growing regions.[19] Currently Japan produces only some 4 per cent of its own requirements of soya, and is heavily dependent on imports from the United States.

Table 4.10. Japanese Imports of Oilseeds and Vegetable Oils, 1973, and Annual Growth Rate 1961-5 (Average) to 1973

	Imports 1973 ('000 tonnes)	Annual growth rate since 1961-5 (%)
Groundnuts	75	+ 20.4
Soya beans	3,577	+ 9.3
Cottonseed	157	–0.5
Cottonseed oil	19	+ 12.3
Rapeseed	677	+ 26.9
Rapeseed oil	17	n.a.
Sunflower seed	5	–4.7
Copra	132	+ 3.9
Palm kernels	12	–4.3
Palm oil	99	+ 20.25
Linseed	110	+ 1.5
Castor seed	45	+ 2.4

Source: As for Table 4.7.

Although Japan is, in general, still a highly protected economy compared to the USA or EEC, with a closely planned agricultural import programme under central direction, most oilseeds enter duty-free (including soya beans, rapeseed, and cottonseed). Oils, however, continue to bear substantial import duties.

Sugar

Cane and beet sugar compete directly with one another. Although the technical processes involved in refining the two are significantly different, the end product is chemically identical. Most cane sugar entering world trade is produced and exported raw by developing countries for refining in developed countries, while beet sugar is a temperate crop grown and refined mainly in developed countries. Cane sugar accounts for 58 to 60 per cent of world sugar output, and this proportion has remained relatively stable over the past fifteen years. Overall, however, only 30 per cent of world sugar production enters international trade, and of this more than three-quarters in volume is cane sugar exported by ldcs.

A large number of ldcs export sugar. As Table 4.11(a) shows, the five largest exporters are Cuba, Brazil, the Philippines, the Dominican Republic, and Mauritius. Sugar accounts for more than half of export earnings from Mauritius, Reunion, Cuba, and Guadeloupe.

Over the past twenty years world production of sugar has doubled, and world consumption *per capita* has increased from about 14 kg in the early fifties to about 20 kg at present.[20] In recent years, however, the balance between production and consumption has deteriorated in developing countries and improved in developed; developing countries' taste for sugar has grown while consumption in developed countries has perhaps reached saturation point, aided by medical evidence, often disputed, about its effect on health.[21] At the same time unit costs of production have fallen in developed countries, and some at least of the advantage which ldcs previously possessed in the production of raw sugar has been lost.[22]

'World' market prices for sugar have fluctuated considerably over the past twenty years, as Table 4.12 shows. This has been in part in response to real fluctuations in production and export availability, but it has been exacerbated by the fact that the 'world' market has historically been, and remains, strongly affected by the surplus disposal patterns of exporting countries. About half of the sugar entering international trade has been exchanged under bilateral trading arrangements or long-term contracts, the most significant of which have been the United States Sugar Act and the Commonwealth Sugar Agreement (CSA), both of which are described below, and the bilateral agreement under which, since 1960, most of Cuba's sugar has been sold directly to the Soviet Union. Since 1974, the US Sugar Act has been inactive and the Commonwealth Sugar Agreement has been superseded by new EEC arrangements concluded under the Lomé Convention and a parallel agreement with India. But they have been of crucial importance for the development of the sugar trade.

Table 4.11 (a). Production and Trade in Raw Sugar (Beet and Cane), 1971-3 Annual Average

Country	Production '000 tonnes	Exports '000 tonnes	Exports $m	Imports '000 tonnes	Imports $m
Cane producers					
Cuba	5,346	3,809	597	–	–
Brazil	6,456	2,198	370	–	–
Philippines	2,058	1,369	235	–	–
Dominican Republic	1,175	1,041	159	–	–
Mauritius	682	617	89	–	–
Mexico	2,631	577	103	–	–
Peru	916	423	74	–	–
Guyana	330	289	44	–	–
Jamaica	371	283	40	–	–
Thailand	686	226	31	–	–
Mozambique	353	211	26	–	–
Colombia	802	193	30	–	–
Trinidad	216	185	37	–	–
Reunion	206	180	42	–	–
India	3,916	153	22	–	–
Guadeloupe	118	112	23	–	–
Ecuador	271	101	16	–	–
Guatemala	235	101	16	0	0
Nicaragua	160	93	15	0	0
Costa Rica	131	88	16	0	0
Other Ldcs	9,067	1,711	224	2,049	324
Beet producers					
W. Europe	12,088	146	34	3,104	512
EEC	(9,888)	(146)	(34)	(2,562)	(335)
USSR and E. Europe	12,749	21	3	2,065	384
USA (beet and cane)	5,528	–	–	4,722	827
Total listed	66,285	13,989	2,246	11,940	2,047
World total	75,936	17,204	2,668	16,101	2,645
Ldcs	35,920	13,822	2,209	2,049	324
Ldcs' share of world total (%)	47.3	80.3	82.8	12.7	12.2

Table 4.11 (b), Trade in Refined Sugar, 1971-3, Annual Average

	Exports '000 tonnes	Exports $m	Imports '000 tonnes	Imports $m
W. Europe	2,217	500	1,618	365
USSR and E. Europe	1,082	166	948	164
USA	1	0	47	8
Ldcs	1,053	177	2,537	517
Ldcs' share of world total (%)	22.7	19.8	45.6	45.9

Source: FAO, *Production Yearbook and Trade Yearbook*.

Table 4.12. Trends in World Sugar Prices and CSA Prices, 1956-74 (£)

	Average world price (cif UK)	Average Commonwealth Sugar Agreement (cif UK)
1956	35.75	40.75*
1957	46.98	42.17*
1958	31.38	43.84*
1959	27.31	45.14*
1960	28.48	44.44
1961	25.68	48.20
1962	25.59	48.80
1963	71.70	50.60
1964	51.13	51.10
1965	21.51	51.15
1966	17.87	51.25
1967	19.36	51.50
1968	21.83	52.10
1969	33.83	52.10
1970	40.06	53.25
1971	46.18	53.25
1972	72.63	62.82
1973	99.46	66.90
1974	305.13	120.93

* 1956-1960 (based on pre-war freight and insurance rates).

Source: *World Economic Interdependence and Trade in Commodities*, Cmnd. 6061 (HMSO, May 1975).

United States. The United States Sugar Act was passed in 1948 and expired at the end of 1974. It created a system of national supply quotas within a global total determined annually by the US Secretary of Agriculture. Around 60 per cent of supplies were drawn from 'domestic' production (from mainland beet and cane growing areas, Hawaii, Puerto Rico, and the US Virgin Islands) and the remaining 40 per cent from the Philippines (which after the breach of United States relations with Cuba in 1960 accounted for about 25 per cent of 'foreign' supplies), the Dominican Republic, Brazil, Peru, Australia, and Commonwealth Caribbean suppliers. From 1962 to 1965, the system was protected by variable levies intended to protect United States production when world prices were lower than domestic. From 1965 onwards, domestic producers were protected by fixed rates of specific import duty together with annual regulation of the quota system.

After the end of 1974 the system was abandoned in the face of a serious domestic shortage. Global quotas were not pre-allocated among exporting 'foreign' countries; instead, competition up to the quota level was encouraged on a first-come-first-served basis: a system which would work well enough when there was a world shortage, but which might give rise to a scramble among exporting countries in the event of surpluses re-emerging, to get inside global quota limits.

Commonwealth. The Commonwealth Sugar Agreement was in effect from 1950 to 1974. Under it, the United Kingdom contracted to buy pre-determined quantities of sugar (1.7 million tons by 1974) at negotiated prices from Commonwealth exporting countries (Australia, the West Indies, East Africa, Fiji, Mauritius, Swaziland, India, and until 1965 Rhodesia). A single negotiated price was applicable to all Commonwealth exporting countries; it was negotiated annually until 1965 and irregularly thereafter on the basis of a 'cost plus' formula designed to reflect changes in wages and other costs since a base year (1958) and to be 'reasonably remunerat-ave to efficient producers'. Imports from CSA countries historically accounted for some two-thirds of British sugar consumption; and in fact all CSA exporters, except the East African countries, typically sold more to the UK than their CSA negotiated price quotas. Excess supplies were purchased at a figure equivalent to the world price plus a refund of UK import duty. British domestic production was limited by a strict ceiling on the acreage which could be planted with sugar beet. New Zealand and Canada also took part in the CSA as importing countries.

In most years from the Second World War onwards the CSA price was above 'world' levels as measured by the London import price (see Table 4.12). The Korean War price boom of 1950-2, and cyclical shortages in 1957 and 1963, were the only occasions before 1970 when the London free market price rose above the CSA level. But although, with unstable prices on the 'world' market, CSA price and quantity guarantees gave a welcome degree of stability to Commonwealth suppliers until 1970, the rapid increase in 'free' market prices for sugar between 1970 and 1974 (actually stemming from disinvestment by producers in the cyclically low price period of 1966-7) made the CSA price level seem increasingly unrealistic. From 1971 onwards it came under great pressure as 'world' prices skyrocketed with shortages and speculation combining. The growing gap between CSA and world prices, plus a realisation that sugar supplies could be used as a bargaining counter in negotiations with the enlarged EEC, led to the withholding of export supplies from the British market during 1974 by major Caribbean Commonwealth exporters: a gambit which – in the short term at least – succeeded.

EEC Association. The arrangements for sugar contained in the Lomé Convention, concluded between the enlarged European Community and forty-six African, Caribbean, and Pacific (ACP) countries in 1974, are intended to continue the satisfactory access terms for Commonwealth producing countries which had been a feature of the CSA. They have been called 'a model for the kind of treatment the ACP countries were looking for on other commodities'.[23]

These arrangements, which are in principle indefinite in duration, unlike the Lomé Convention itself which is a five-year agreement (although they are to be reviewed at the end of seven years, in 1981), commit the sugar exporting countries to supplying an annually negotiated volume of sugar. For sugar supplied to the Community the exporting countries receive a price which is linked directly to EEC support prices, and hence at least partially 'indexed' to inflationary trends;[24] any Community member state which wishes to pay more than this guaranteed price in order to assure sugar supplies is free to do so – as the United Kingdom did in 1974, offering ACP countries a supplement bringing the price received by them up to £260 per ton, as against a Community support price of around £140.

The total amount of sugar which the Community undertook to buy from the ACP countries and India in 1975, the first full year of the Lomé Convention sugar provisions, was some 1.3m tonnes. Almost 500,000 tonnes were allocated to Mauritius, the largest single supplier; just over 400,000 to the West Indies and Guyana (Guyana and Jamaica being the largest suppliers among this group), 160,000 to Fiji, and the rest divided among the other supplying countries (Swaziland, India, Belize, Kenya, Uganda, Tanzania, Malawi, Congo, Malagasy and Surinam).[25]

Unlike the provisions of the Commonwealth Sugar Agreement, which ensured that any shortfall in shipments from any one exporting country would be made up by others, the Lomé provisions state categorically that any country falling short of its export quota in one year shall be allocated a correspondingly smaller quota in the next. The EEC Commission has the authority to decide whether unused quotas shall or shall not be allocated to other Lomé suppliers. There is thus no automatic assurance that the Community will take a stable volume of sugar from Lomé producers.

This particular provision is important in the light of the situation of the enlarged EEC in the world market. Before Community enlargement, the United Kingdom had deliberately restricted the amount of sugar it produced, through strict controls on the area which could be planted to sugar beet, while the EEC of six was a substantial net exporter of sugar. It is estimated that the enlarged Community also has the ability to be a net exporter from its own production.[26]

Thus, although purchases from ACP countries by the EEC are assured as long as export quotas are fulfilled, there can be no guarantee that sugar bought by the EEC will actually be sold in the Community's domestic market. If the exporting ACP states agree, and 'in exceptional circumstances',[27] such sugar may be sent directly to a 'third' country. It is equally possible that in a situation in which the Community domestic sugar crop were in surplus or balance, an equivalent amount of sugar to that imported from the Lomé countries could simply be re-exported on to the world market – just as was done during 1975 with meat.

The effect of such action would be to drive down 'world' prices. If these were at the time high, owing to shortages or speculative pressures, exports of this type might help to stabilise world prices in money terms at least. But if (as may be more likely) such exports were made at a time of general world surplus, when prices were low, the effect would be to destabilise 'world' prices still further. Since many of the ACP countries themselves export a substantial proportion of their sugar on to the 'world' market,[28] this would harm them as well as other countries.

For sugar, then, developing countries still face a world in which their ability to trade at remunerative and stable prices is determined by the actions of the main developed countries. If the United States and the Community between them do not in future have sugar surpluses, the market for ldcs' cane sugar will be assured. If, however, the effect of these countries' domestic farm policies is to create self-sufficiency or oversupply in home-produced sugar, ldcs will have to put up with instability at least or depressed markets at worst for their output.

CONCLUSIONS

In this chapter, we have dealt with ldcs' trading problems in four areas of agricultural production which are of major importance to them. One of these areas – grains – is a field in which ldcs have major importing as well as exporting interests: in the others, developing countries are mainly exporters. Two, grains and sugar, are products which in recent years have been in short supply on world markets; with much more serious consequences in the case of grains than in that of sugar. Prices of oilseed products and of meat have been directly affected by the world grains shortage: the former directly in so far as oilseed products and grains are close substitutes, the latter indirectly as costs of grain-based and oilseed-based animal foods have increased.

A factor common to all groups of farm products is that the ability of ldcs to trade in them is directly influenced by actions undertaken by the main developed countries, particularly the United States and the European Community. US policies largely determine the terms on which ldcs can purchase grains. In turn, US and EEC policies on meat production, in terms both of volume and of techniques of production, determine how much meat other exporting countries can export to them and, in a situation of tight world supplies, the world prices for the basic feeding stuffs for meat producing animals, which may also, in some cases, be basic foods for people. And the conditions of the world sugar market can also, to a large degree, be determined by developed countries' policies with respect to sugar beet production, which can be varied more easily than that of sugar cane.

All developed countries are highly protective towards their farmers, partly for reasons of national food security, partly for employment purposes, and partly because of the sheer strength of farm lobbies on the political scene. The means used to protect farm output – tariffs, quotas, price supports, and variable levies – are highly efficient regulations of the volume of imports permitted to enter, and are strictly tuned to the needs of each country as seen by its government at any given moment. In this situation, developing countries are in a very weak bargaining position.

There is, however, some realisation that over-protection is self-defeating. Protecting, for example, EEC meat producers' interests through high support prices has begun to show diminishing returns in the volume of meat consumed. Budgetary costs of farm support have become very high at the same time as prices have become prohibitive. It is at least possible that the common interests of consumers and Exchequers may, in time, contribute to more rational policies allowing for a more even balance between domestic production and imports, and at least a partial return to some semblance of comparative advantage. Such a move should, on balance, be in the interests of developing countries.

Notes

1. See *Ceres,* FAO Review, Vol.5, No.2, March/April 1972, p.64.
2. Note that Vietnam and Cambodia, in peace time, should also have the capacity to export substantial volumes of rice.
3. FAO, Agricultural Projections 1970-1980 (Rome, 1971)..
4. See United Nations World Food Conference, 1974, Volume II, *Proposals for International Action.*
5. Statement to the International Wheat Council, 29 September 1975.
6. Compared with actual world stocks of 50m tons of wheat and 12m tons of rice in 1971.
7. See John A. Schnittker, 'Grain Reserves – Now', *Foreign Policy,* December, 1975.
8. See below, p.132ff.
9. See Chapter 8.
10. This point is brought out in Ministry of Overseas Development, *Report of the ODA Advisory Committee on Protein* (London, ODA, 1974).
11. See Ursula Wasserman, 'Import Regulations for Meat into Europe', *Journal of World Trade Law,* Vol.8, No.2, March-April 1974.
12. See below, pp.138-45.
13. Schnittker.
14. See 'World meat trade outlook gloom', *Financial Times,* 2 October 1974.
15. See International Trade Centre, *The Major Import Markets for Oilcake,* (Geneva, 1972).
16. See FAO, *Trade Yearbook 1974.*
17. Rapeseed production is likely to continue to grow rapidly. One trade forecast has predicted rapeseed output in the UK as growing to 200,000 tons per annum, compared with 31,000 tons in 1973 (3,000 tones annual average in 1961-5). See 'Europe boosting rape crop area', *Financial Times,* 25 November 1975.
18. *The Major Import Markets for Oilcake* (Geneva, International Trade Centre, UNCTAD/GATT, 1972), p.153.
19. See Kenzo Hemmi, 'Structural Adjustment of Japanese Agriculture', in Kiyoshi Kojima (ed.), *Structural Adjustments in Asian-Pacific Trade* (Tokyo, 1973); also OECD, *Agricultural Policy in Japan* (Paris, 1974).
20. See S. Harris and G. Hagelberg, 'Effects of the Lomé Convention on the World's Cane Sugar Producers', *ODI Review 2–1975.*
21. See e.g. John Yudkin, *Pure, White and Deadly* (London, Davis-Poynter, 1972).
22. Harris and Hagelberg, p.42, text and footnotes.
23. Ibid., p.40.
24. Ibid., pp.40-1, footnote, which suggests that the real value of Community farm support prices may have been falling.
25. Ibid., p.43, Table 1.
26. Ibid., p.47.
27. Declaration by the Community in the Procès-Verbal to the Lomé Convention.
28. Harris and Hagelberg, p.48, estimate that the proportion of sugar exported to the free market by major Lomé Convention countries ranges from 3.5 per cent (West Indies and Guyana) to 42 per cent (Fiji).

5 LDCS AND THE EXPORT OF MANUFACTURED GOODS

Historically, the less-developed countries have been exporters of primary products and importers of manufactures. While this pattern broadly persists today, the importance of manufactured goods in ldcs' exports is increasing. Indeed, while for the majority of ldcs manufactured exports account for less than 10 per cent of their export proceeds, for a few such exports now form the main source of their foreign exchange earnings. Whether the majority of ldcs can follow the lead of the few is a moot question. The world market for manufactures is expanding faster than that for primary commodities, and therefore diversification into manufactures would appear to offer better prospects for increasing foreign exchange earnings and stimulating development than continued dependence on primary product exports. But these prospects depend on the extent to which ldcs' manufactured goods are allowed access to export markets, and on the ability and willingness of ldcs to overcome domestic impediments to the growth of export industries. This chapter sets out first to examine the main trends in ldcs' manufactured exports and then to consider the main demand and supply problems and possibilities facing ldc manufactures exporters.

STRUCTURE AND GROWTH OF LDCS' EXPORTS OF MANUFACTURES

Manufactures – and semi-manufactures – are distinguished from raw materials or primary products are processed to some extent, they receive. Since virtually all products are processed to some extent, the dividing line is blurred and in practice several ways of classifying manufactures are used. For instance, UNCTAD often uses a broad classification which includes some barely processed metal, mineral and petroleum products as well as agricultural processed goods and other manufactures. GATT, on the other hand, uses a more restricted classification which excludes agricultural processed goods and petroleum products but still includes some barely processed metals and minerals along with other manufactures. The choice of definition does not affect the broad picture of ldcs' exports of manufactures – as can be seen in Table 5.1 – but it does inevitably affect more detailed analysis. Therefore, since available statistics do not permit one definition to be

Table 5.1. Ldc Exports of Manufactures to Developed Countries, by Different Definitions, 1962 and 1971

	1962 $m	% total ldc exports[1]	1971 $m	% total ldc exports[1]	Average annual growth %
1. GATT (SITC 5-8)	2.71	13.4	9.50	20.6	15.0
2. GATT (SITC 5-8), excluding unworked non-ferrous metals (SITC 68)	1.64[2]	8.1	7.14	15.5	18.0
3. UNCTAD (including agricultural processed goods, unworked non-ferrous metals and petroleum products)	5.29	26.1	12.62	27.3	10.0
4. UNCTAD (as above, but excluding unworked non-ferrous metals and petroleum products)	2.42	11.9	7.52	16.3	13.5

1 Total exports according to GATT, which is slightly different from UNCTAD totals.
2 Approximate figure only.
Sources: GATT *International Trade 1965 and 1973/4,* and UNCTAD, *Trade in Manufactures of Developing Countries: 1972 Review,* TD/B/C.2/124, June 1973.

used throughout, the data presented below should be read with care.

A major distinguishing feature of ldcs' export trade in manufactures is its rapid growth relative to the rest of their exports. By the first GATT definition,[1] such exports have increased by over 15 per cent a year between 1961-3 and 1970-2, as compared with the 9 per cent annual growth of all ldcs' exports. As a result, ldcs' exports of manufactures constituted 24 per cent of their total exports at the end of the period as compared with 15 per cent at the beginning. And since their growth rate was slightly faster than that of world exports of manufactures there was an increase in ldcs' share of the latter. This share, however, remains extremely small at 6.6 per cent of the total (see Table 5.2).

Ldcs' exports of manufactures have tended to be concentrated among a few product groups, generally resource-based or labour-intensive or both, such as textiles, leather goods, and semi-processed

Table 5.2. Summary of Ldc Exports of Manufactures 1961-3 and 1970-2 (Annual Averages)

	1961-3				1970-2				
Ldc exports of manufactures[1]	Value $ billion (fob)	% of total	% of world exports of manufactures	% of total ldc exports to region	Value $ billion (fob)	% of total	% of world exports of manufactures	% of total ldc exports to region	Annual average growth[5] 1961-3 to 1970-2
to industrial areas[2]	2.74	63.4	6.0	13.3	10.30	67.3	6.6	21.8	16.0
to ldcs[2]	1.34	31.0	6.9	20.9	4.12	26.9	9.3	32.4	13.5
to eastern trading areas	0.09	2.1	0.1	5.7	0.61	4.0	2.4	18.6	23.5
to world[3]	4.32	100.0	5.5	14.7	15.30	100.0	6.6	23.8	15.0
of which:[4]									
non-ferrous metals / iron & steel	1.44	33.3	12.6						10.5
non-ferrous metals				n.a.	2.95	19.3	25.9	n.a.	
iron & steel				n.a.	0.59	3.8	3.2	n.a.	
chemicals	n.a.	n.a.	n.a.	n.a.	1.16	7.6	4.6	n.a.	n.a.
engineering products	0.26	6.0	0.9	n.a.	2.25	14.7	2.6	n.a.	n.a.
road motor vehicles	—	—	—	n.a.	0.08	0.5	0.2	n.a.	n.a.
textiles & clothing	1.21	28.0	15.0	n.a.	4.26	27.8	19.1	n.a.	15.0
other manufactures	1.42	32.9	5.3	n.a.	4.02	26.3	9.5	n.a.	n.a.

1 Defined as SITC sections 5 to 8 inclusive.
2 Turkey and Yugoslavia included in industrial areas.
3 Includes data for South Africa, New Zealand, and Australia not elsewhere specified.
4 Except for textiles and clothing and non-ferrous metals and iron and steel, product groups are not comparable between the two periods.
5 Calculated to the nearest ½ percentage point.

Sources: 1961-3, GATT, *International Trade 1965,* Table 8, p.36; 1970-2, GATT, *International Trade 1973-74,* Appendix, Table C.

metals. While this tendency remains – exports of textiles and clothing and of base metals accounted for 61.3 per cent of the total in 1961-3 and 50.9 per cent in 1970-2[2] – there has been a marked diversification of manufactures both within and between product groups, the nature of which will be more fully discussed below. The three most notable shifts in composition have been the relative decline of textiles, the increase in clothing exports, and the rise in light non-resource-based manufactured goods exports.

Main Exporters and General Direction of Trade

Exports of manufactures are not a significant source of export earnings for most ldcs. As can be seen from the analysis of eighty-five ldcs, set out in Table 5.3, slightly over half received less than 5 per cent of their export proceeds from manufactures and a clear majority received less than 10 per cent. Only thirteen countries, listed with nine others in Table 5.4, received 20 per cent or more of their export earnings from manufactures. In general, ldc manufactures exporters tend to be richer and/or have larger populations than those countries for whom manufactures exports are least significant. Leaving aside Taiwan, the twelve countries separately listed accounted for 67 per cent of ldcs'

Table 5.3. Population and Income Levels of 85 Ldcs, classified by the Share of Manufactures Exports in their Total Exports

Percentage of manufactured exports in total exports, 1967-9	Number of ldcs	Average GNP per head 1971 ($)	Average population in mid-1971 (m)
More than 20% (including India)	13	170	57.0
More than 20% (excluding India)	12	346	15.8
Less than 20% but more than 10%	13	356	20.1
Less than 10% but more than 5%	15	355	13.4
Less than 5%	44	259	9.7
Less than 5% excluding oil exporters	37	210	8.0
Total	85	246	19.2

Source: Based on K. Morton, *A Hand Worth Playing* (ODI, 1974), pp. 21-6, Table 4, excluding Spain and Greece.

Table 5.4. Major Ldc Exporters of Manufactures

Ldcs with 20% or more manufactures exports in total exports	Population mid-1971 (m)	GNP per head 1971 $	Manufactures exports as % of total exports 1967-9	Share of total ldc manufactures exports to the world, 1970, %
Hong Kong	4.0	900	92.1	20.2
South Korea	31.8	290	73.3	6.6
Israel	3.0	2190	69.7	5.6
Yugoslavia	20.7	730	58.3	10.4
Lebanon	2.8	660	51.6	1.2
India	551.1	110	51.6	10.8
Pakistan	62.7	130	51.0	4.1
El Salvador	3.7	320	29.8	0.6
Egypt	34.1	220	25.2	2.1
Singapore	2.1	1200	24.0	4.4
Guatemala	5.4	390	21.2	0.8
Tunisia	5.2	320	20.1	0.4
Taiwan	14.9	430	64.3	n.a.
Other major ldc exporters				
Mexico	52.4	700	19.3	3.3
Costa Rica	1.8	590	17.0	0.4
Argentina	23.6	1230	11.3	2.3
Colombia	22.3	370	10.6	0.6
Philippines	37.9	240	9.5	0.8
Brazil	95.4	460	9.3	3.8
Malaysia	11.2	400	6.4	0.5
Thailand	37.3	210	4.6	0.3
Chile	10.0	760	3.5	0.4

Sources: First three columns, as for Table 5.3, last column UNCTAD, TD/B/C.2/124.

manufactures exports in 1970, and with a further nine countries – all Asian or Latin American – accounted for 80 per cent of total manufactures exports.

In regional terms, Asia accounts for well over half of total ldc exports of manufactures, Latin America roughly 20 per cent and Africa less than 10 per cent, with the remainder accounted for by the Middle East and European developing countries. Exports from Latin America have experienced the most rapid growth over the last decade.

The direction of ldcs' manufactures exports is broadly similar to that of the rest of their exports. Western developed countries form their main market, accounting for 67 per cent of ldcs' manufactures exports in 1970-2. Trade among ldcs accounts for the bulk of the remainder while Eastern bloc countries account for only 4 per cent of ldcs' total manufactures exports. Exports to developed and to Eastern bloc countries have grown more rapidly than those to ldcs. This growth pattern reflects, among other things, the growth of import substituting manufacturing production within ldcs, the dynamic growth of the Western markets, and commercial policy changes in the Eastern bloc.

Manufactures Exports to Developed Countries

Among developed countries, the United States, Britain, and West Germany accounted for over two-thirds of total ldc manufactures exports to the West.[3] The direction of such exports is, however, changing. The two major ex-colonial powers, Britain and France, which in 1962 accounted for 40 per cent of developed country imports of ldc manufactures, accounted for only 20 per cent in 1971. Meanwhile West Germany, Japan, and the United States have increased their share from a total of 41 per cent to 60 per cent over the same period. And in respect of all developed countries, with the exception of Britain and France, there was an increase in the share of ldc imports in total manufactured imports (see Table 5.5).

As with total ldc manufactures exports, the export trade with developed countries is dominated by relatively few ldcs. In 1971, seven ldcs were responsible for 67 per cent and nineteen for almost 90 per cent of such exports. These nineteen ldcs experienced – on average and with the important exception of India – a considerably faster growth in manufactured export earnings than the rest of ldcs: between 1962 and 1971 their earnings grew by an average of 17 per cent a year, while those of the rest grew at only 6 per cent a year.[4]

Underlying the shifts in the direction of ldcs' exports of manufactures and their rapid growth among the major exporting countries are significant changes in export composition. In 1962, ldc exports of manufactures to developed countries were heavily concentrated among fairly simple, often labour-intensive, resource-based manufactures. Textiles, processed foods, drink and tobacco, wood and furniture products, and leather and footwear, made up two-thirds of such exports. By 1971, these product groups accounted for only 42 per cent of the total. Meanwhile, clothing exports together with less traditional exports of miscellaneous light manufactures and engineering and metal

Table 5.5. Imports of Manufactures[1] from Ldcs by Main Developed Countries or Areas[2], 1962-71

Importing country or area	Imports of ldc manufactures ($m)		Individual country's share of developed country imports of ldc manufactures (%)		Share of imports of ldc manufactures in total developed country manufactures imports (%)		Average annual growth of imports of manufactures from ldcs (%)[4]
	1962	1971	1962	1971	1962	1971	1962-71
EEC[3]	1,391.5	3,164.6	57.5	42.1	5.4	4.0	9.5
of which:	(825.5)	(2,036.7)	(34.1)	(27.1)	(4.5)	(3.3)	(10.5)
France	439.1	453.3	18.1	6.0	11.6	3.3	0.5
Germany	222.3	966.4	9.2	12.8	4.0	4.7	17.5
UK	536.6	1,045.1	22.2	13.9	10.0	8.1	7.5
EFTA[3]	103.0	347.7	4.3	4.6	1.3	1.7	14.5
	(664.4)	(1,456.0)	(27.5)	(19.4)	(4.6)	(4.0)	(9.0)
Australia	66.2	170.1	2.7	2.3	3.9	4.3	11.0
New Zealand	16.5	73.0	0.7	1.0	3.1	6.5	18.0
Canada	64.3	220.7	2.7	2.9	1.5	1.7	14.5
United States	730.0	3,168.7	30.1	42.1	9.2	10.0	17.5
Japan	48.8	376.7	2.0	5.0	3.2	7.2	25.0
Total	2,420.3	7,521.6	100.0	100.0	4.9	4.9	13.5

1 According to the UNCTAD classification, including processed agricultural products but excluding petroleum products and unworked non-ferrous metals.
2 Based on data relating to 21 developed market economy countries.
3 EEC and EFTA data relate to current member countries, figures in brackets relate to membership before enlargement of the EEC.
4 To the nearest ½ percentage point.
Source: UNCTAD, TD/B/C.2/124, June 1973, Table 2.5.

products increased their share from 18.5 per cent in 1962 to 43 per cent in 1971: the growth rate of these exports was between 22 per cent and 30 per cent a year. From a smaller base, exports of rubber products, iron and steel, and worked non-ferrous metals grew by some 20 per cent a year increasing their share of the total from 3 per cent in 1962 to 6 per cent in 1971 (see Table 5.6).

This diversification has been most noticeable among the more established manufactures exporters. Of the recorded annual growth of

Table 5.6. Imports of Manufactures from Ldcs by Main Developed Countries[1] by Product Group, 1962 and 1971

Product group	Imports from ldcs ($m)		Share of product group in total imports from ldcs (%)		Share of imports from ldcs in total imports (%)		Average annual growth of imports from ldcs[3] (%)	Share of imports from leading ten ldc exporters[4] (%)
	1962	1971	1962	1971	1962	1971	1962-71	1971
Food products	408.9	850.3	16.9	11.3	16.0	16.4	8.5	71.5
Drink and tobacco	305.1	101.0	12.6	1.3	27.4	4.4	−13.0	71.7
Wood and furniture	251.7	664.6	10.4	8.8	11.2	11.8	11.5	81.1
Rubber products	5.8	27.8	0.2	0.4	0.9	1.3	19.0	90.0
Leather and footwear	96.1	396.8	4.0	5.3	12.2	14.2	17.0	90.5
Textiles	551.7	1,174.2	22.8	15.6	13.1	11.7	8.5	91.2
Clothing	233.0	1,453.2	9.6	19.3	18.3	24.7	22.5	96.5
Chemicals	223.2	510.3	9.2	6.8	4.5	3.3	9.5	60.6
Pulp paper and board	16.2	44.5	0.7	0.6	0.5	0.7	12.0	93.9
Non-metallic mineral products	23.9	72.0	1.0	1.0	2.2	2.4	13.0	96.1
Iron and steel	49.7	277.7	2.0	3.7	1.3	2.6	21.0	97.6
Worked non-ferrous metals	28.4	140.5	1.2	1.9	3.0	5.1	19.5	98.0
Road motor vehicles	9.9	42.7	0.4	0.6	0.3	0.2	17.5	94.6
Other engineering and metal products	92.5	1,010.6	3.8	13.4	0.6	1.9	30.5	91.3
Miscellaneous light manufactures	124.3	755.2	5.1	10.0	5.2	8.6	22.0	92.5
Total A[2]	2,420.4	7,521.6	100.0	100.0	4.9	4.9	13.5	75.3
Petroleum products	1,582.2	2,693.3	30.0	21.3	48.2	39.4	6.0	n.a.
Unworked non-ferrous metals	1,285.1	2,402.4	24.3	19.0	46.5	39.8	7.0	n.a.
Total B[2]	5,287.7	12,617.3	100.0	100.0	9.5	7.6	10.0	58.3

1 Based on data relating to 50 developed, market economy countries.
2 Total A represents manufactures as defined in Table 5.5; total B is the sum of total A plus petroleum products and unworked non-ferrous metals.
3 To the nearest ½ percentage point.
4 Leading ldc exporters defined according to their share, by value, in each product group and in total imports of manufactures from ldcs by developed countries.

Source: As for Table 5.5, p.35 and Annex, p.6.

manufactures from the nineteen leading exporters between 1962 and 1971, 53 per cent was due to increases in exports of clothing, miscellaneous manufactures, and engineering and metal products; for the remainder of ldcs, whose exports grew more slowly, the figure was 31 per cent. Three factors have had an important bearing on the changes in ldcs' export composition. First, the developed countries' sluggish demand for traditional exports, e.g. textiles (not clothing), its growth inhibited by protectionist measures and the slow economic growth of an important market – Britain. Second, during the sixties, more ldcs – notably Brazil, Mexico, Pakistan, and Yugoslavia – have joined the few, predominantly Asian, ldcs – Hong Kong, South Korea, Taiwan, and Singapore – in adopting an export-orientated rather than an import substituting approach to industrial development. These countries, already established as manufactures producers, were in a position to diversify into products with more growth potential than the traditional ldc exports and have sought to do so. Finally, ldcs' export promotion activities – in particular the establishment of export processing zones – have been accompanied and encouraged by the emergence of a new form of export activity – part processing.

Either within a multinational firm or under contract, ldcs have increasingly become involved in the export of a wide range of, usually, labour-intensive processes of manufactures for developed countries – most notably the United States and Japan. Thus, for instance, automobile parts – radio antennae in Taiwan, lamps in Mexico and so on – are manufactured for US, UK, and Japanese firms, while garments, gloves, luggage, and baseballs are sewn together in the West Indies, S.E. Asia, and Mexico for US and Japanese firms.[5] Such exports cannot be easily quantified but an attempt to do so in relation to the United States reveals their growing importance: imports from ldcs under the US value-added tariff schedules (which permit import duties to be levied only upon value-added abroad where inputs originated in the United States) accounted for 4 per cent of total imports of ldc manufactures to the USA in 1966 and 14.3 per cent in 1969 – and these imports do not include all such imports from ldcs.[6]

Manufactures Exports among Ldcs

Exports of manufactures among ldcs have grown relatively slowly on average, reflecting individual ldcs' efforts to industrialise and the protectionist policies adopted by them. Nevertheless ldcs' imports of manufactures from other ldcs have grown faster than those from other sources, and so increased their share of total ldc manufactures imports from 6.9 per cent in 1961-3 to 9.3 per cent in 1970-2. Moreover, the growth of both Latin American and Western Asian manufactures exports to other ldcs exceeded the average for their total manufactures exports (see Table 5.6).

Ldcs' exports of manufactures to other ldcs were as usual dominated by relatively few countries – twenty-three countries accounted for roughly 80 per cent of the total. A more significant feature of this trade however, is its concentration at the regional level: the majority of ldc exports of manufactures to each other takes place between countries of the same region. At the broad regional level this feature is most marked in Latin America (see Table 5.7) but it becomes clearer there and elsewhere when smaller regional groups are considered, reflecting in part efforts towards regional integration among ldcs.[7]

The product composition of manufactures trade among ldcs differs from that for the aggregate of ldc manufactures exports. Chemicals, for instance, fertilisers, medicines and plastics, and machinery occupy a greater share of total trade than average – respectively 13.1 per cent and 21.4 per cent as compared with 9.6 per cent and 15.6 per cent, while miscellaneous manufactures (SITC 6 and 8 minus SITC 68) have a smaller share – 65 per cent as compared with 75 per cent. This difference is to be expected given the overall pattern of import demand for manufactured goods in ldcs: nearly two-thirds of their imports consist of machinery and chemical goods.

Ldcs' Exports to the Eastern Trading Bloc

The Eastern trading bloc comprises both industrial and non-industrial countries, yet the pattern of trade between these countries is considerably different from that between either group and the less developed countries outside the bloc, with which this section is concerned. Whereas manufactures exports from the Asian Communist ldcs – China, North Vietnam, and North Korea – to the Communist countries of Europe account for more than half of total exports, non-Communist ldcs' manufactures exports have been only a small proportion of total exports, to either Communist Asian countries or European countries. With their imports from Communist countries consisting largely of manufactures, the non-Communist ldcs' trade pattern with the Eastern bloc thus conforms closely to that of the centre-periphery model.

The export pattern of non-Communist ldcs, henceforward referred to as ldcs has, however, changed considerably over the sixties. Following

Table 5.7. Trade in Manufactures among Ldcs, 1970, and Average Annual Growth 1962-70

Manufactures exports from	Manufactures exports to						
	Latin America	Africa	Western Asia	South & East Asia	All ldcs	World	Share of exports to ldcs in total exports 1970 (%)
Latin America							
Value $m	685	13	0	14	712	1855	38.4
% value to each region	96.2	1.8	0	2.0	100.0	n.a.	
Annual growth 1962-70	29.1	–	0	4.3	29.3	26.7	
Africa							
Value $m	5	215	30	12	262	903	29.0
% value to each region	1.9	82.1	11.5	4.6	100.0	n.a.	
Annual growth 1962-70	–2.3	12.0	4.0	14.7	9.6	12.3	
Western Asia							
Value $m	11	57	168	59	295	800	36.9
% value to each region	3.7	19.3	56.9	20.0	100.0	n.a.	
Annual growth 1962-70	35.0	21.5	23.5	16.0	20.4	15.4	
South and East Asia							
Value $m	88	257	172	957	1497	4943	30.3
% value to each region	5.9	17.2	11.6	63.9	100.0	n.a.	
Annual growth 1962-70	4.9	8.3	14.4	7.0	7.5	13.6	
Total ldcs							
Value $m	809	595	406	1102	2919	9628	30.3
% value to each region	27.7	20.4	13.9	37.8	100.0	n.a.	
Annual growth 1962-70	16.9	11.7	16.2	7.1	10.9	15.2	

Source: UNCTAD, TD/B/C.2/124

a rapid growth of manufactures exports, such exports in 1970-2 accounted for 18.6 per cent of total ldc exports to the Eastern bloc, compared with 5.7 per cent in 1961-3.

The USSR is, as might be expected, the main importer of ldc manufactures. On the exporting side, six ldcs account for virtually all ldc manufactures exports to Communist countries. Yugoslavia predominates, accounting for half such exports – 83 per cent of which are machinery and miscellaneous manufactures, excluding textiles. In order of importance, India, Egypt, Pakistan, Iran, and Israel account for most of the remaining exports, 49 per cent of which are textiles and 37 per cent miscellaneous manufactures, excluding textiles. The composition of ldcs' exports to Communist countries and their growth rates are set out in Table 5.8. It will be noted that the most rapid growth rates have, with the exception of that for miscellaneous manufactures exported by ldcs other than Yugoslavia, occurred in product groups which still constitute only a small part of the total.

Table 5.8. Ldc Exports of Manufactures[1] to the Eastern Bloc

	Exports by Yugoslavia			Exports by other ldcs		
Product group[2]	Value 1970 $m	% of total	Annual growth 1962-70 (%)	Value 1970 $m	% of total	Annual growth 1962-70 (%)
Chemicals (5)	52	13.0	24.5	48	11.7	13.9
Machinery (7)	159	39.7	14.2	9	2.2	31.6
Textiles (65)	15	3.7	40.3	201	49.1	23.1
Miscellaneous manufactures excluding textiles (6 + 8 minus 65 and 68)	175	43.6	20.6	151	36.9	33.5
Total	401	100.0	18.4	409	100.0	24.5

1 Defined as SITC groups, 5, 6, 7, and 8 excluding SITC 68, unworked non-ferrous metals.
2 Figures in brackets refer to SITC code for the product group.
Source: UNCTAD, TD/B/C.2/124, p.61.

MARKET CONDITIONS FOR LDC MANUFACTURES EXPORTS

Compared with most primary products, the demand for manufactured goods tends to be more responsive to changes in price and to grow more rapidly with increases in income. Ostensibly then, ldcs' export opportunities for manufactured goods are greater than for primary products. However, one of the major factors in ldcs' favour – their ability to produce labour-intensive goods more cheaply than the high-wage developed countries – is in itself a source of pessimism about their export prospects. Because equivalent industries in developed countries tend to be in a weak competitive position, they constitute an actual and potential source of protectionist pressures, and have in the past been successful in limiting ldcs' market access: the textile industry provides a case in point. The growth and diversification of ldcs' manufactured exports has, however, led to suggestions that this pessimism is both exaggerated and outmoded. True, only a few ldcs have so far benefited significantly from the growth in ldc manufactures exports, but it can be argued that this situation owes much to the supply conditions in many ldcs, and in particular their inward-looking protectionist policies. Nonetheless, one may question whether the majority of ldcs can hope to emulate the few leading ldc manufactures exporters or whether the latter's performances can be sustained. Already there is some concern that, in seeking to exploit opportunities for exporting manufactures, individual ldcs will find themselves competing with each other on terms which are such as to limit considerably their gains from exporting. On the one hand, there is evidence that ldcs are competing, via tax concessions and the like, for export-orientated investment by 'footloose' foreign manufacturing firms.[8] On the other hand, the growth in the capacity of certain manufacturing export industries in individual ldcs increases the possibility of price cutting competition between ldcs, which – in turn – could exacerbate protectionist pressures in developed countries. And at present, recession in ldcs' main markets casts doubt on their export prospects in general.

In this section, we focus on the market conditions facing ldc manufactures exports, looking first at some of the trade barriers faced by ldcs and then at the extent to which such barriers are or could be removed or offset by other factors favouring ldc exports. Market conditions in each of the main groups of countries – developed, developing, and Eastern bloc countries – are considered in turn, although conditions in developed countries receive most attention for reasons both of their relative importance and of the lack of data on other markets.

Market Conditions in the Developed Countries

Barriers to trade: tariffs

Barriers to ldcs' manufactures exports are of two kinds: tariff and non-tariff. Such barriers may simply aim to protect domestic producers or other national interests but they may also be designed to encourage and protect trade relations with certain other countries. Thus trade barriers vary according to the product imported and to the country from which it is imported. On both counts, ldc exporters have tended to face more barriers than others exporting to developed countries. At the same time, the effects of the methods of protection employed are such as to weigh more heavily on ldc exporters seeking to establish themselves as manufactures exporters.

In the case of tariff barriers, however, efforts have been, and are being, made to reduce them generally and to lessen their discriminatory impact on ldcs' exports, with the result that they are now considerably less important than non-tariff barriers, and their importance is likely to diminish. Even so, a substantial portion – between a third and two-fifths – of all ldcs' exports, including a significant quantity of manufactured and agricultural processed goods, are still subject to tariffs.[9] Here we consider first the structure of developed country tariff barriers that faced ldcs prior to the introduction of the Generalised System of Preferences (GSP), and then the the extent to which the GSP has altered and is likely to alter this situation. Ldcs' prospects in the ongoing Tokyo round of GATT negotiations on trade liberalisation are considered in a later section.[10]

The mfn tariff structure facing ldc exporters of manufactures has historically possessed two important features. First, such tariffs tend on average to be higher than those facing developed country exports. Second, the structure of tariffs is such that the effective protection is often considerably greater than nominal tariffs suggest. Tariff duties levied on imports raise their price and hence reduce their competitiveness *vis-à-vis* domestically produced goods. The extent of protection afforded to domestic producers is dependent on the structure of tariffs on particular products at different levels of processing. Typically, tariffs are low or absent on goods which have received little processing and higher on goods at later stages of processing (see Table 5.9). This increase in tariffs – which are levied

Table 5.9: Nominal and Effective Tariffs in Developed Countries on Imports of Resource-Based Industrial Products from Developing Countries[1]

Country		Weighted average of tariff duties (%) Stage 1	Stage 2	Stage 3	Stage 4
United States:	Nominal	3.5	3.4	11.6	18.2
	Effective		9.6	21.7	31.6
United Kingdom:	Nominal	2.2	6.3	15.3	18.8
	Effective		18.0	32.1	27.1
EEC	Nominal	3.8	7.0	10.5	13.2
	Effective		17.5	18.2	20.2
Japan:	Nominal	5.3	10.6	14.1	14.1
	Effective		42.8	28.1	26.5
All industrial countries:	Nominal	3.4	5.6	11.3	16.9
	Effective		15.7	20.5	28.6

1 Processed products based on the following twenty-two primary commodities — meat, fish, fruit, vegetables, cocoa, leather, groundnuts, copra, palm kernel, palm oil, rubber, wood, pulpwood, wool, cotton, jute, sisal and henequen, iron, copper, aluminium, lead, and zinc. They thus cover almost all important primary commodities exported by developing countries in processed form, the main exception being petroleum. The different tariff duties for each country or group of countries relate to tariffs applied at successive stages of production.

Source: UNCTAD, ***The Kennedy Round: Estimated Effects on Tariff Barriers***, TD/G/Rev.1, Geneva, 1968.

on the total value of the product – according to the stage of processing is known as tariff escalation. Since it is the degree of processing which results in the differences between tariff rates, it is the value added in processing which is *effectively* protected by the higher tariffs. Where, as is often the case in the type of resource-based manufacturing carried out in ldcs, the value added in processing is low relative to the final value of the product, this kind of tariff structure tends to result in high rates of effective protection and to inhibit the development of such industries for export.

The Kennedy round of GATT negotiations brought a reduction in the tariffs on industrial goods but did not radically affect the relatively disadvantaged position of ldc exporters. The average nominal tariff of developed countries on all industrial goods was cut by 40 per cent to 6.5 per cent and that on industrial goods from ldcs by 31 per cent to 11.8 per cent; the average effective tariffs fell by 42 per cent and 32 per cent to 11.1 per cent and 22.6 per cent respectively.[11] Tariffs facing ldc exports remained relatively high and the wide difference between nominal and effective tariffs was virtually unaltered.[12]

Mfn tariffs do not discriminate between the same products exported from different sources and the reason why ldcs' industrial exports as a whole faced higher mfn tariffs than did developed countries is that the kind of industrial goods exported by ldcs faced, on average, higher tariffs than did those exported by developed countries. The diversification of such exports by ldcs has, no doubt, reduced discrimination. The mfn tariff schedule is, however, only one of several. Trade agreements among developed countries, especially European countries, and between developed countries and certain ldcs have resulted in more favourable tariff schedules and generally more favourable terms of access for the countries concerned. All countries outside such agreements consequently have to compete not only with the protected domestic producers but also with third country suppliers receiving preferential treatment. The recent enlargement of the EEC and related preferential arrangements with non-member European countries (and some ldcs under the Lomé Convention) has increased this form of discrimination, and has actually brought some increases in the tariffs (and non-tariff barriers) facing certain ldcs which previously had benefited from Commonwealth preferences and were not offered similar arrangements with the EEC when Britain joined.[13] An important offsetting development, however, has been the introduction of the GSP, to which we now turn.

Generalised System of Preferences

The proposal for a Generalised System of Preference emerged in the UNCTAD forum.[14] The scheme was intended to counter both the bias of the mfn tariff structure on manufactured and semi-manufactured goods and the exclusive preferential arrangements noted above, and was based on the principle that ldcs, being less economically advanced than the developed countries, required not equal treatment with them but preferential (tariff) treatment, without reciprocation by or discrimination between ldcs. As a device for encouraging the establishment of export-orientated manufacturing industries in ldcs and growth in their manufactures exports, there were two basic flaws in its conception. In the first place, unless mfn tariffs were reduced to zero for ldcs, and other barriers to access removed, the inequality of treatment between ldcs and their main competitors – domestic producers in developed countries, individually and within free trade areas – would remain. Second, since ldcs are demonstrably not equal in their export capacity and ability to compete with developed countries, or each other, non-discriminatory treatment of all ldcs constitutes discrimination against the weakest ldc exporters. Both problems were recognised but only the latter, which is less important, was in the event taken into account.

Preference-Givers and Potential Beneficiaries. After lengthy deliberations, the system was put into practice in 1971 and 1972 with the introduction of fifteen separate schemes operated by Western developed nations and some Eastern European countries, namely the EEC, UK, Eire, Denmark, Norway, Sweden, Finland, Austria, Switzerland, Japan, New Zealand, Australia,[15] Bulgaria, Czechoslovakia, and Hungary.[16] The EEC GSP was merged with that of UK, Eire, and Denmark in 1973. Two major importing countries – the USA and Canada – have been slow to introduce their schemes with the result that roughly half of ldcs' manufactures exports to developed market economies were initially ineligible for GSP treatment, and improvements to existing schemes were threatened because of notions of 'burden-sharing' among importing countries. (Improvements in GSP offers might lead to a diversion of trade from non-preference giving countries to preference giving countries so increasing the latter's burden.) However, the enabling legislation for the Canadian and the US schemes was passed in 1973 and 1974 respectively and the Canadian scheme was introduced in 1974 while the US scheme came into operation in 1976.

Most GSP schemes are open to the vast majority of ldcs. There are, however, some minor differences between each preference giving country's list of eligible countries; for instance Israel, Hong Kong, Cuba and Spain do not appear in some lists. This is hardly surprising given that the definition of an ldc is somewhat arbitrary and that the offer of trade concessions implies political recognition of and some minimal friendship with the potential recipient.[17] In addition, certain exports of a small number of countries have been specifically excluded from some GSPs, e.g. textiles from Hong Kong.

Product Coverage of the GSP. The GSP was originally intended to cover all dutiable semi-manufactured and manufactured goods exported from ldcs. Available data make it difficult to assess the precise extent to which this intention has been realised. UNCTAD estimates based on 1970 trade figures show that only 25 per cent of all dutiable imports from potential beneficiaries to preference giving Western countries (excluding Canada and the US) were covered by the schemes in operation in 1974, and that agricultural goods, which constitute 48 per cent of dutiable imports, account for only 19 per cent of the imports covered (see Table 5.10). Similar estimates for the USA and Canada indicate that 33 per cent of all dutiable imports from potential beneficiaries (or 18 per cent after allowing for estimated exclusions) would be covered by their schemes, and that agricultural imports, which constitute 32 per cent of dutiable imports, account for only 9 per cent of imports covered (this low percentage is, however, raised to 16 per cent if one allows for exclusions to *all* eligible imports since the exclusions affect only industrial goods). These estimates, however, were made before certain improvements to the schemes, for instance, the 1975 revision of the EEC scheme, and are based on data for primary as well as manufactured goods while the schemes were intended to cover the latter only. Nevertheless, it is clear that the various GSP schemes are far from offering preferential treatment to all manufactures. Major exports, such as textiles, petroleum products, and leather goods, as well as minor exports, such as china and glassware, furniture, cycles and motor cycles, and many processed agricultural goods, are subject to exclusions from, or restrictions on, preferential GSP treatment under the various schemes.

The Limitations on Preferential Treatment. The inclusion of a product within a GSP scheme is by no means a guarantee of duty-free preferential access for the potential beneficiary. In the first place, the margin of preference accorded to such products does not always mean that access is duty-free. Secondly, ldcs' ability to compete with domestic producers and third country suppliers on equivalent or, in the latter case, more favourable terms is further limited by the restrictive nature of origin requirements and safeguard clauses.

The margin of GSP preference varies according to the particular scheme and the product concerned. Under most schemes, only proportional cuts in the mfn tariffs have been granted on those few processed agricultural goods included. In general industrial products receive better duty-free treatment – the Austrian scheme, however, permits only a partial cut in mfn tariffs on industrial goods, and

Preference giving country or area		Imports from Beneficiaries: Total $m	Dutiable $m	Eligible for GSP $m	Dutiable imports as % of total imports	Eligible imports as % of dutiable imports	Dutiable imports not covered by GSP as % of total imports
EEC:	Agricultural goods	4,683	3,850	376	82.2	9.8	74.2
	Industrial goods	13,492	1,629	1,071	12.1	65.7	4.1
	Total	18,175	5,479	1,447	30.1	26.4	22.2
Japan:	Agricultural goods	1,059	640	29	60.4	4.5	57.7
	Industrial goods	5,847	3,344	743	57.2	22.2	44.5
	Total	6,906	3,984	772	57.7	19.4	46.5
Others[2]:	Agricultural goods	755	434	82	57.5	18.9	46.6
	Industrial goods	1,187	348	276	29.3	79.3	6.1
	Total	1,941	782	358	40.3	45.8	21.8
Total:	Agricultural goods	6,497	4,924	487	75.8	9.9	68.3
	Industrial goods	20,525	5,321	2,090	25.9	39.3	15.7
	Total	27,022	10,245	2,577	37.9	25.2	28.3
USA[3]:	Agricultural goods	3,421	1,387	122	40.5	8.8	37.0
	Industrial goods	4,425	3,153	1,285(606)	71.3	40.8(19.2)	42.2(57.6)
	Total	7,846	4,539	1,407(728)	57.9	31.0(16.0)	39.9(48.6)
Canada[3]:	Agricultural goods	242	133	22	55.0	16.5	45.9
	Industrial goods	669	143	143(127)	21.4	99.9(88.8)	— (2.4)
	Total	911	276	164(148)	30.3	59.4(53.6)	12.3(14.1)
Grand total:	Agricultural goods	10,159	6,444	630	63.4	9.8	57.2
	Industrial goods	25,620	8,617	3,517(2,823)	33.6	40.8(32.8)	19.9(22.6)
	Total	35,799	15,060	4,148(3,453)	42.1	27.5(22.9)	30.5(32.4)

1 Estimates of imports eligible for GSP treatment relate to imports in 1970 which would have been eligible under GSP schemes, current, or proposed, in 1974. Since there have been improvements in the schemes since then, the potential coverage is underestimated. On the other hand, the estimates do not take account of limitations on the GSP treatment extended to eligible products. On balance, the proportion of imports estimated to be eligible for GSP treatment is likely to be in excess of the proportion of imports actually eligible and certainly in excess of the proportion actually receiving GSP treatment.

2 Includes Finland, Norway, Sweden, Austria, Switzerland and New Zealand. Excludes imports by New Zealand from beneficiaries belonging to the Commonwealth Preference Area.

3 Estimates based on GSP proposals. Figures in brackets relate to estimates of products eligible for GSP after allowance has been made for the likely exclusion of certain products.

Source: UNCTAD, *Review of the Schemes of Generalised Preferences*, TD/B/C.5/9 (Geneva, 1973).

some other schemes make exceptions to the duty-free treatment; for instance, Japan gives only a 50 per cent duty cut on textiles, footwear, leather goods, and toys while permitting most other GSP industrial products duty-free entry.

If the GSP is to encourage the establishment of manufacturing export industries, the preferences granted should be guaranteed for the minimum period required for such industries to become competitive in international markets. Most schemes are, in fact, designed to operate for an acceptable minimum period (usually ten years). However, this preferential access is hedged by safeguard measures: limitations on the value of exports – tariff quotas – eligible for preferences, and escape clauses allowing the suspension of preferences should exports cause, or threaten to cause, some injury to domestic producers or market disruption in the preference giving country. The latter form of safeguard is employed exclusively by all preference giving countries except Japan and the EEC. In principle, one would expect that the uncertainty created by this safeguard would inevitably deter ldcs seeking to build up their export trade via the GSP. In practice, such an effect is hard to determine.[18]

Tariff quotas are employed by the EEC and Japan on all but agricultural processed goods (which are subject to an escape clause).[19] The EEC system consists of three types of quotas: overall quotas for each product which are calculated according to the value of imports in a base year (initially 1968 and changed to 1971 in 1974) plus a supplement of 5 per cent of the value of imports from all other sources in the most recent year; ceiling quotas, for each product, limiting the share of the tariff quota which may be filled by any one beneficiary (to between 15 per cent in the case of a few sensitive products and 50 per cent); and quotas allocating shares of the global quota to each EEC member state. In principle, exports of all industrial products included in the GSP are limited by such quotas, but in practice they are applied only to a list of sensitive products and, if deemed necessary, semi-sensitive products – i.e., those products which are considered to be competitive with domestic manufactures. The Japanese system consists of two kinds of quota for each product group – a global quota, calculated in a similar way to that of the EEC, and ceiling quotas, limited to 50 per cent of the total quota. As with the EEC scheme, tariff quotas exist for all industrial products but are only applied to 'sensitive' items – which are more numerous than those in the EEC GSP. In many cases, the tariff quotas are exceeded by the value of ldc exports to Japan, so that the scheme fails to promote additional exports of 'sensitive' goods.[20] While considerably less restrictive, the EEC scheme tends to operate in a similar way with regard to principal suppliers of 'sensitive' goods, with ceiling quotas – and, to a lesser extent, importing country quotas – limiting preferential treatment of their exports. Since total EEC and Japanese quotas have often been left unfilled, the ceiling quotas may be regarded as a means of restricting preferential treatment of established ldc suppliers rather than of encouraging exports from other ldcs – although the latter effect may none the less occur.[21]

In order to receive preferential treatment under GSP schemes, ldcs' exports must conform to the rules of origin set out by the preference giving country. These rules vary between schemes but broadly are of three kinds. The first specifies that goods are deemed to have originated from the preference receiving country if they have been produced there either wholly or by substantial transformation of imported materials. The specification of 'substantial transformation' varies but is frequently restrictive.[22] The second requires that goods must be consigned directly from preference receiving to preference giving country; although exceptions are made for some land-locked countries' exports which are often consigned in the first instance to a neighbouring country's port. The third requires the beneficiary to furnish details of its procedures for certification of origin. Failure to comply with this rule has resulted in the exclusion of some otherwise eligible exports from the schemes.

Impact of GSP. The various limitations on the eligibility of products for GSP treatment clearly restrict its potential benefits (estimates for which were presented in Table 5.10). Available UNCTAD estimates of the extent to which products covered by the GSP schemes actually receive preferential treatment provide some indication of the shortcomings of the schemes in operation. Thus, for instance, in the first half of 1973 only 47 per cent of eligible products received GSP treatment under Finland's scheme, and only 37 per cent did so under the Norwegian and Swiss schemes.[23] The EEC Commission's own estimates of the utilisation of the GSP for 1974 indicate that around two-thirds of ceilings opened for manufactures were actually taken up. Earlier estimates for the Japanese scheme indicated that the combined effect of the various limitations was to reduce the value of eligible industrial products from $743 million to roughly $100 million or 3 per cent of dutiable industrial imports from ldcs.[24]

Although the product coverage and preferential treatment of the GSP schemes are generally being steadily improved,[25] their most striking feature so far is the low proportion of ldc manufactured, dutiable exports which are eligible for and receive GSP treatment. This feature is reflected in beneficiaries' assessments of the schemes. UNCTAD reports that

> while stressing that the GSP has a significant role to play in increasing exports, many [beneficiary] governments insisted that they could not take full advantage of the tariff concessions because of exclusion from the system of products of major export interest to them. A number of governments also indicated that their exports were confined to agricultural products which were mainly outside the scope of the GSP. And, while some stated that the GSP had made some contribution to their export growth, many governments indicated that the GSP had had little or no impact on investment decisions in the private or public sector, mainly because of the limitations in product coverage and the uncertainty surrounding its operation.[26]

Given these assessments, it is hardly surprising that, although other ldcs are increasingly taking advantage of the schemes, the main beneficiaries[27] still tend to be the more prosperous established suppliers. While processed agricultural goods and some resource-based traditional manufactures important to the poorer ldcs remain excluded or subject to restricted access, the GSP can have but a limited effect in encouraging exports from such sources.

Non-tariff Barriers

Non-tariff barriers (NTBs) consist of a wide range of policy measures, not all of which are related to commercial policy or adopted with the object of restricting trade. The precise effects, and to a lesser extent the incidence, of NTBs are far from clear. Nevertheless, it is widely thought that NTBs are now more important than tariffs in their trade restricting effects. And, as with tariffs, NTBs to trade in manufactured and semi-manufactured products tend to affect ldc exporters more adversely than developed country exporters. This is partly due to past liberalisation among developed countries, and the product composition of ldcs' exports. But it is also due to the fact that certain types of NTB are more difficult for ldc exporters to overcome, frequently because of supply conditions in ldcs.

Main Types of NTB. A useful method of classification is that adopted by UNCTAD[28] which puts NTBs into three groups according to the policy intention of the importing country. The first group comprises those commercial policy measures primarily designed to restrict imports in order to protect specific domestic industries. Among these measures, quantitative restrictions, e.g. 'voluntary' export restraints and quotas, predominate; others include import licensing, state import monopolies, together with a variety of other trade restricting devices, such as government procurement policies favouring domestic suppliers, variable levies as applied under the EEC's Common Agricultural Policy, and subsidies to import competing industries. More than half of the 3,000-odd developed country NTBs on manufactured and semi-manufactured goods that have been identified[29] are of this type.

The second group comprises measures designed to deal with problems not directly related to commercial policy questions but which, sometimes intentionally, have the effect of restricting imports. Most common among NTBs of this sort are regulations relating to safety and industrial standards, customs regulations, and health and sanitary requirements.

The third group comprises measures consistently applied *without* trade distorting intent but which, nonetheless, have that effect. These include general balance of payments policies and domestic policies such as those designed to stimulate regional development.

Within each of these three categories, NTBs may be further subdivided according to the way in which they restrict trade. Broadly, they fall into two groups: first those, like quotas, which impose quantitative limitations on the volume or value of trade in a given product; and second, those, like variable levies or health regulations, which restrict trade by raising the costs or prices of the products affected. Despite the fact that post-war liberalisation of NTBs has mainly focused on quantitative restrictions to trade, these NTBs are probably the most important of all. Meanwhile in the second group NTBs of all three types have been increasing. To a large extent, this reflects the growing involvement of governments in the regulation of economic and social activities.

NTBs and Ldc Manufactures Exports. Work on the restricting effects of different types of NTBs on ldcs' – or developed countries' –

manufactures exports as yet provides only rough guidelines as to their importance. It has concentrated on the first two types of NTBs and on establishing the quantitative importance of the products subject to such restrictions – and the number of restrictions imposed – rather than dealing with the more complex issue of the extent to which the volume and growth of exports are restrained as a result of NTBs. (Table 5.11 sets out the results of one effort of the former type to establish the incidence of NTBs on exports of interest to ldcs.) In general, nevertheless, it is thought that quantitative restrictions are the most important in limiting ldcs' exports, followed by variable import levies, standards regulations relating to the imported product, and domestic procurement policies.

The NTBs discriminate against ldcs partly because of intra-developed country liberalisation. More important, however, are factors relating to the product composition of ldcs' exports and to the differential effect of NTBs on less well-established or would-be exporters as compared with those that are better established. Quantitative restrictions, for instance, tend to operate in favour of established suppliers, while lack of published information about the various product and marketing regulations affecting imports inhibits new entrants. Meanwhile, the range and variability of the NTBs in operation present greater difficulties to ldc, as compared with developed country, exporters since frequently they lack the expertise and flexibility to adjust to, or overcome, such barriers. And as with tariffs, a tendency for the incidence of NTBs to increase with the level of fabrication constitutes an additional barrier for the ldc trying to move away from dependence on primary product exports.[30]

Quantitative Restrictions on Ldcs' Exports. A study of quantitative restrictions[31] applied by developed countries, has found that such restrictions affected 10.4 per cent of their imports of manufactures and semi-manufactures (excluding textiles and clothing) from ldcs but only 2.3 per cent of their imports from all other sources. This finding partly reflected the fact that 62 per cent of all restrictions fell on agricultural processed products which constituted 11.2 per cent of imports from ldcs but only 5.5 per cent of imports from elsewhere. The main agricultural processed goods affected were processed meat, cereal, fruit and vegetable products, edible oils and fats, alcoholic beverages, and tobacco. Among industrial goods (but excluding textiles and clothing) quantitative restrictions fell most frequently on petroleum and chemical products and engineering and metal goods.

Table 5.11. Incidence of Non-tariff Barriers Applied by Industrial Countries on Manufactures of Export Interest to Less Developed Countries, 1969

Product group	Index of NTB incidence[1]	Value of ldc exports to OECD countries $'000
Clothing	11.1	1,074,925
Processed food[2]	4.28	–
Electrical and light transport equipment	3.97	448,423
Textiles	3.03	937,825
Chemicals	1.98	538,422
Industrial materials[2]	1.21	–
Miscellaneous manufactures	0.98	578,276
Footwear and other leather, plastic and rubber products	0.91	175,635
Optical and control instruments	0.40	39,997
Miscellaneous metal manufactures	0.30	77,024
Non-electrical machinery	0.25	136,464
Transport equipment[1]	0.00	108,961
Furniture[1]	0.00	51,840

1 Zero incidence does not necessarily imply that no NTBs are applied: those which do exist may have become negligible via averaging. The method used assumes that NTBs, whether, for instance, a quota or a customs classification difficulty, are equal in their effects; that the more countries and the more NTBs applied to a product, the greater the incidence; and that the larger the size of the market in the country applying the NTBs, the greater their incidence. NTB incidence was measured according to the formula:

$$Wj = [Ni(Yi) + \ldots + Nn(Yn)] / \sum_{i=1}^{n} Yi$$

Where Wj is the weighted incidence of NTBs applied to product j adjusted for the market size of the applying country; Ni is the number of NTBs imposed on j by country i; Yi is the GNP (indicator of market size) of country i; $\sum_{i=1}^{n} Yi$ is the combined GNP of all countries considered;

2 Sufficiently detailed data are not available to indicate value of ldc exports involved in this product group.

Source: C. Pestieau and J. Henry, ***Non-Tariff Barriers as a Problem in International Development*** (Private Planning Association of Canada, 1972), p.84.

Footwear and other leather goods and wood and furniture products are among those goods which are most frequently subject to 'voluntary' export restraints, which are accepted by the exporting country for fear of the imposition of more restrictive measures on their exports.

The Textiles and Clothing Case. Textiles and clothing, which account for over a third of ldcs' manufactures exports to developed countries are the products most affected by quantitative restrictions. Between 1962 and 1973, quantitative restrictions on cotton textiles and clothing were regulated by GATT agreements, starting with the five-year Long Term Arrangement on Cotton Textiles. Under the agreements – which aimed to promote the orderly growth of trade and prevent market disruption – trade in cotton textiles grew more slowly than in other textiles. While the agreements may have prevented a greater degree of protectionism, they were scarcely favourable to ldc exporters.[32] The partial nature of these agreements, however, encouraged ldcs to diversify into different textile exports, notably knitted fabrics and man-made fibres, and into the export of clothing, which were not covered by the GATT agreements. This diversification led to moves among developed countries to increase protection for other sectors of their domestic textile and clothing industries mainly by recourse to quantitative restrictions of a bilateral or unilateral nature, and to press for a new GATT agreement which would extend beyond cotton textiles.

Such an agreement – the Multifibre Textile Arrangement (MFA) – was reached in December 1973, and underwent a major triennial review in December 1976/January 1977, at a time when imports of textiles were a very sensitive point for developed countries. Its signatories include all the main exporting and importing countries and it covers virtually all classes of textiles and clothing, except those certified as 'handicraft' or 'cottage industry' products. It is designed to permit orderly trade expansion in these products, regulating restrictions while providing safeguards against market disruption in importing countries. All existing restrictions have to be brought into line with the provisions of the MFA or eliminated, and countries restricting imports under the MFA are required to adopt 'appropriate economic and social policies (i.e. adjustment assistance measures). . .to encourage businesses which are less competitive internationally to move progressively into more viable lines of production or into other sectors of the economy and provide increased access to their markets for imports from less developed countries'.[33]

The two main provisions for restrictions are contained in Articles 3 and 4 of the MFA. Under Article 3, unilateral action by importers may be taken to restrict disruptive imports (if consultation with the exporters concerned fails to produce an agreement within sixty days) to the previous year's level of imports in the first year of restrictions; thereafter imports must be allowed to rise by a minimum of 6 per cent a year. Article 4 of the agreement provides for bilateral agreements on export restraint which should permit a higher growth rate than the minimum under Article 3. Ldcs, particularly new entrants, should receive more liberal treatment, i.e. higher basic quotas and growth rates, than other countries and where a country's exports have a small share of a particular market, they should not be restricted.

Details of all restrictions on the products concerned in operation before the MFA or introduced subsequently have to be submitted to the Textiles Surveillance Body. This body has a chairman and eight members representing parties to the agreement on a rotating basis. It is intended to supervise the MFA and can make recommendations to participant governments regarding their actions in relation to the MFA, and in the event of disputes. As a last resort, disputes may be referred to the GATT Council. The Surveillance Body is weak in that it has no mandatory powers but its establishment is significant since it is almost the only body of its kind empowered to initiate reviews or make recommendations of its own accord.

While the MFA contains liberal sentiments, it is far from ideal for ldcs. The minimum growth rate specified under its provisions for restrictions is significantly below the actual growth of developed countries' imports of textiles and clothing from ldcs. The definition of 'market disruption' which may prompt restrictions is loose, and there are no time-related, specific provisions for the adjustment assistance measures which the import restricting country is required to adopt under the MFA.[34] Even so, the MFA is almost certainly better than no agreement for ldc exporters.

Other Main NTBs on Ldc Exports. The other main NTBs on products of interest to ldcs are variable levies, product standards and health regulations, and domestic procurement policies, all of which have tended to increase since the Second World War.

Variable levies on manufactures are used – mostly by the EEC – in combination with tariffs to make up the difference between world and domestic (EEC prices of agricultural processed (and unprocessed) goods, thus preventing any price advantage accruing to foreign exporters. The main imports affected are meat and dairy products and cereal and fruit products. In an UNCTAD inventory of NTBs[35] affecting products of interest to ldcs, twenty-seven of the forty processed agricultural products exported by, or of potential export interest to, ldcs were subject to variable levies.

Technical standards regulations for imports are generally designed to protect the consumer but the co-existence of disparate, and variable, regulations in different markets and the methods of ensuring compliance frequently constitute barriers to trade (and in some cases are intended to) by increasing the costs facing the exporter. A wide range of manufactured goods, such as electrical appliances and equipment, of existing or potential interest to ldcs are affected, usually more so than exports from developed countries since ldcs often lack the necessary technical and physical resources (and the information as to standards regulations) to set up national organisations to ensure that external export standards are met. A similar situation – mainly affecting ldcs' exports of processed foods and certain chemicals – prevails in respect of health and sanitary regulations, and more generally in respect of packaging, labelling, and marketing requirements.[36]

Domestic procurement policies have been adopted explicitly (e.g. the US 'Buy American' Act of 1933) or implicitly by most Western governments, with the effect that outside suppliers face considerable discrimination over a wide range of products. In relation to ldcs, these policies constitute obstacles to such exports as clothing, footwear, and office equipment.

Safeguards and Adjustment Assistance

Underlying the plethora of tariff and non-tariff barriers to ldcs' exports and the shortcomings of liberalisation efforts to date is the developed countries' intent to protect domestic producers from low-cost competition. Such studies as have been undertaken on the displacement effects of manufactured imports on domestic industry and employment in developed countries indicate that ldcs' exports have a greater impact than exports from other developed countries.[37] Nonetheless, the displacement effects of imports are generally less, often considerably so, than those arising from changes in productivity and demand within developed countries. Meanwhile, protection reduces welfare in the country applying protectionist measures (as in the exporting country), denying consumers access to cheaper goods and preventing an efficient allocation of domestic resources. Why then does protectionism persist?

There appear to be several reasons. First, while the gains from the removal, or avoidance, of protectionism are widespread but on average small for each beneficiary, the losses are concentrated among relatively few – workers and employers – and on average are considerable for those affected. If the gainers do not adequately compensate the losers it is not surprising that the losers resist import growth: cheap shirts, for instance, are small recompense for a textile worker who loses his job. Second, while those made redundant or suffering reduced profits as a result of productivity or demand changes will be viewed as unreasonable, and regressive, if they seek to stop change to protect their interests, it is somehow more acceptable to attempt to prevent import-generated unemployment by stopping or reducing the flow of imports. Partly this acceptability derives from the fact that the problems created by imports often are, or threaten to be, more acute in the short term. And since these effects tend to be regionally concentrated, often in areas which are anyway relatively backward economically, the social and political pressures to prevent them are often intense – and consequently effective.

Protectionist policies may, in the first instance, be designed to provide a breathing space for the affected industry to adjust to changed market conditions. However, a date for the removal of trade barriers is rarely set and protection tends to slow adjustment by insulating the industry from the very factors which would encourage it. Thus, the spectre of unemployment and bankruptcy should barriers fail to be erected remains an obstacle to their removal.

To block any recourse to protectionist measures would be unacceptable: the extent of potential damage may be exaggerated, but an influx of imports can cause considerable hardship in the short term. Moreover, countries justifiably wish to protect themselves from market disruption caused by 'dumping' – an inflow of goods at prices below those prevailing in the country of origin. At the same time, the benefits of trade will be limited if protectionism continues – as it will perforce, if industrial adjustment is not encouraged.

At present no international agreement exists on measures which will permit short-term protection accompanied by adjustment, and Sweden is virtually alone among Western countries in pursuing such measures effectively.[38] There are two international provisions under GATT which permit countries to impose trade barriers when external competition threatens to disrupt domestic industries – Article 6 (the anti-dumping code) and Article 19 which authorises emergency import restraints when market disruption is not caused by 'dumping'. Article 19 has largely been ignored by GATT signatories mainly because the emergency action it sanctions has to be across the board, rather than discriminatory, and so invites retaliation.[39] From our viewpoint, it is unsatisfactory because, in taking such 'emergency action', governments are not committed to any time-scale for the removal of the import restraints: 'emergency' protection can become permanent. The textile agreement, discussed above, is at least likely to ensure that restrictions imposed will be consistent with its provisions and it does seek to encourage adjustment measures. But it suffers from the shortcoming of the general GATT rules in that it has no time-related provision for the removal of protection or the instititution of adjustment policies.

It has been suggested that new rules for international safeguards should be drawn up to conform with the following three principles.[40] First, emergency protection should have a finite time limit and be progressively cut back over the period. (The time-scale will presumably vary from sector to sector.) Second, it must be accompanied by a visible effort by the importing country government and the industry concerned to adjust, modernise, or diversify into competitive lines of production. Finally, some multilateral body, presumably GATT, should act as referee over both safeguard and adjustment measures. As with the MTA, such rules could be designed to encompass measures taken prior to their establishment.

Clearly, however, there are limits to the effectiveness of any international body seeking either to specify or to regulate national government's policies. The problems of adjustment may be basically similar but the actual policies required to bring it about will vary according to the country – and more specifically the region and industry – involved. It would thus be virtually impossible to construct, let alone apply, an adjustment code which did more than specify basic principles. Meanwhile, it is difficult to see what kind of sanctions could be employed by an international body against a country flouting such an agreement, given that most governments would be unwilling to surrender their right to regulate their own affairs in these areas. Indeed the latter fact makes an effective international agreement on this issue remote.

Nevertheless, a greater commitment than presently exists to adopt measures to encourage adjustment is needed if existing protectionism is to be reduced. It would not necessarily entail programmes specifically related to imports. Most Western governments are involved to some degree in the re-organisation of non-competitive industries, and in encouraging the movement of workers out of run-down sectors through retraining, removal grants, and so on. Within Britain, the phased post-war reduction of the coal-mining industry as part of a broader – and now altered – fuel policy provides a case in point; in the EEC, the executive of the European Coal and Steel Community has performed a similar function in relation to those industries, and similar measures are to be applied to the agricultural sector. It does, however, entail a specific commitment to ensure that such policies can be implemented to cope with industrial changes brought about by trade factors.

The GATT Tokyo Round and Ldcs' Manufactures Exports

The Tokyo round – the successor to the Kennedy round of GATT negotiations – was inaugurated at Tokyo in September 1973, but only began to get under way in mid-1975. In principle, it could have an important effect on ldcs' export prospects although a certain scepticism as to its actual outcome is warranted.[41] So far as their manufactured exports to developed countries are concerned, ldcs as a group have something to lose and something to gain from the negotiations. What they may lose are the margins of preference over third country suppliers accorded to certain of their exports under the GSP. What they may gain is improved market access for those exports – constituting a substantial proportion of the total – which are subject to restrictions and currently do not receive unlimited and duty-free access under the GSP. Particular groups of ldcs may lose additionally to the extent that the preferential treatment they receive under special trade arrangements, e.g. the Lomé Convention, is eroded. How far the gains offset the losses depends on the nature and extent of the trade liberalisation that occurs as a result of the negotiations: some of the possible outcomes are considered below in order of their desirability to ldcs. An important limit on ldcs' potential gains is the probable exclusion of textiles and clothing products from the negotiations, given that the recently enforced Multifibre Textile Arrangement is scheduled to last until 1978.

The most desirable outcome for ldcs would be liberalisation of tariff and non-tariff barriers on all products of export interest to them within the framework of GSP. If this takes the form of guaranteed unlimited and preferential access to developed country markets for ldc exports, the gains would certainly exceed any losses from the virtually inevitable erosions of their preferential tariff margins. Given that NTBs are more important obstacles to ldcs' manufactures exports, a reduction in those on products of export interest to ldcs, even on a non-preferential basis, would be more desirable than liberalisation of tariffs alone, although liberalisation of both tariff and non-tariff barriers would be preferable to either on its own. The worst outcome for ldcs would be if the negotiations concentrated solely on cutting mfn tariffs on those manufactured goods currently included in the GSP, since ldcs would lose their margins of preference and would only gain where the resultant mfn tariff treatment was better than that offered under the GSP, and ldcs' competitive position *vis-à-vis* other producers was not harmed. The desirability of each of the above outcomes – and any other – would be enhanced by progress towards the adoption of liberal safeguards and adjustment assistance measures by the developed countries.

Developing countries' prospects in the GATT negotiations largely depend on developed countries' willingness to liberalise trade particularly in areas of interest to ldcs.[42] The recessionary and somewhat protectionist climate of world trade does not augur well for any trade liberalisation effort despite the potential advantages to all parties. Ldcs' particular prospects are further clouded – as they were in the Kennedy round – by the weakness of their bargaining position. This weakness stems not only from their relatively minor role in the world economy: in this respect their position has improved, given developed countries' increased interest in securing raw material supplies, and in locating certain industrial processes in ldcs. It stems also from the principle of non-reciprocity, which underlies ldcs' negotiating approach. Negotiations are based on the notion that both – or all – parties should gain from a process of give and take, not that one side should give and the other take. The non-reciprocity principle means that ldcs opt out of the negotiating process, which may encourage the existing tendency for developed countries to focus on problems of trade among themselves.

Encouragement to Ldc Manufactures Exports

Co-existing with the obstacles to ldc manufactured exports are certain factors encouraging them, besides the GSP and the various, exclusive, trade agreements between developed and developing countries. There is less contradiction in this state of affairs than might appear since the effect of these positive factors is partly, at least, to encourage ldcs to diversify out of the export fields which most threaten domestic industries in developed countries, and to overcome obstacles to trade which are not actually intended to be restrictive.

Export Promotion Organisations. Developed countries have, with varying degrees of enthusiasm, supported the view that the development of export industries, and specifically manufacturing industries, should be an important part of economic development in ldcs. And a significant part of bilateral financial and technical assistance has been directed, *inter alia,* to this end. Meanwhile, recognising the existence of specific problems in adapting products to the requirements and tastes of foreign countries, and of organising marketing and promotional activities, a number of export promotion agencies have been set up with Western support in both developed and developing countries. Virtually every Western donor, and some twenty multilateral organisations are involved in their operations.[43]

The largest of these agencies is the UNCTAD/GATT International Trade Centre (ITC) in Geneva. It carries out research on market information and export promotion techniques and provides training and trade promotion advisory services for ldcs, and liaises with the UN Export Promotion Programme, which coordinates the various UN bodies concerned with export promotion.[44]

Both these agencies, and certain others financed mainly by individual – or groups of – Western countries,[45] operate on both the supply and the demand side,[46] encouraging the development of ldc institutions and industries geared to exporting as well as providing information and advice on market opportunities. Other agencies, set up by individual developed country governments or by quasi-government or private organisations, are more specifically geared to marketing in the importing country, for instance the Dutch Centre for the Promotion of Imports, and the recently established British Import Opportunities Office for Developing Countries.[47] Their function is to provide information to ldcs on market opportunities, commercial regulations and other import-related issues and to assist contacts with potential buyers. All these agencies are concerned with the promotion of primary, as well as manufactured, exports from ldcs.

Value-Added Tariffs. Perhaps the single most important development in ldcs' exports of manufactures in recent years has been the growth of process exports, noted above. This growth reflects the increase in 'foot-loose' activities by developed country-based firms, that is, the shifting of labour-intensive stages of manufacture from their own high-wage economies to countries where labour costs are relatively low, either by direct overseas investment or by subcontracting to overseas firms. The use of value-added tariffs in the USA and to a lesser extent in Japan, has provided an additional incentive to this development.[48]

A value-added tariff is an import duty levied only on that portion of the value of an imported commodity which is added in the exporting country. At present, these are applied instead of tariffs on the total value of the import when its inputs originated in the importing country. The transfer of processes from high- to low-wage economies is profitable so long as the saving on labour costs outweighs the additional costs of processing overseas, including transportation and government trade levies. The value-added tariffs reduce the import duty costs and hence encourage the transfer of processes to low-wage economies, thereby boosting the latter's exports. Thus in the USA imports of manufactures subject only to value-added tariffs have been increasing relative to total manufactures imports, and imports of the former from ldcs have increased particularly rapidly, accounting for 6.4 per cent of all imports under the value-added tariff schedules in 1966 and 24.4 per cent in 1970.[49] Arguably, it is in the sphere of process exports that ldcs have the greatest export potential. And the wider application of value-added tariffs in developed countries, for instance by the EEC where the adoption of a system of value-added tariffs has been under discussion, could encourage this type of export development.

Conditions in Other Markets

The long-established historical links with Western developed countries and the fact that these countries together constitute the world's largest export market help to explain the predominance of ldcs' manufactures exports to the West and the insignificance of such exports to other countries. But the difficulties of gaining access to markets elsewhere are also important factors. Indeed protectionism in Western countries would be deemed less troublesome by ldcs if access elsewhere were easier.

Trade in Manufactures among Ldcs

The advantages of increased trade among ldcs are frequently stressed: in particular, it is argued that such trade would help to promote faster, and a more desirable pattern of, industrial development.[50] Yet, in practice, efforts to promote industrial development and balance of payments difficulties have led ldcs to adopt protectionist measures which far exceed those prevailing in developed countries. High effective tariffs together with import controls are widely found. And since the level of protection tends to be greatest on consumer goods, rather than intermediate or capital goods, ldcs' exports of manufactures tend to be more adversely affected than those of developed countries. For instance, it was estimated that the average effective protection for all manufactures in Brazil was 118 per cent but for consumption goods only it was 230 per cent; in the case of Pakistan the respective figures were 271 per cent and 883 per cent.[51] Efforts to move from import substituting to export-oriented industrial development have reduced protectionism in some ldcs but, generally, it remains a major impediment to exports.

As discussed below,[52] protectionist measures inhibit the growth of exports from the country imposing them as well as from other countries. Ldcs have, however, made various moves to promote trade amongst themselves – which help to explain the increasing proportion of imports from other ldcs in total ldc manufactures imports.[53] Bilateral trade agreements between ldcs, increasing in the wake of the oil crisis, are one such move. And the provisions in the Lomé Convention for measures to stimulate trade and co-operation among the ldc signatories is another. The Convention is primarily designed to foster links between the EEC and ldcs, and these provisions were included largely in response to pressures from the ldc signatories. Most notable, however, are the moves towards regional co-operation among ldcs. These are examined in Chapter 8, but a number of points are relevant here. First, the accompanying intra-regional trade liberalisation, combined with the development of institutions geared to promoting economic links within the region, are an important stimulus to intra-regional ldc trade. Second, such co-operation can have important implications for the participants' industrial development and export capacity generally. On the one hand, enlarging the potential market in this way can increase the range of industries which can operate efficiently. On the other hand, the larger markets and the increased scope for investment planning on a regional scale reduce the danger of excess industrial capacity being developed in any one ldc. Moreover, by harmonising their policies towards foreign investors, individual ldcs can reduce the extent to which they limit the gains from manufactures exports by competing for foreign manufacturing investment via government subsidies and tax concessions. It has to be added, however, that, while regional co-operation appears to have had some success in promoting intra-regional trade, attempts to harmonise industrial policies have run into difficulties.[54]

Trade with Eastern Bloc Countries

As yet few ldcs are significant exporters of manufactured goods to Eastern bloc countries. Nevertheless during the sixties efforts were made to encourage such exports. As noted earlier, several of the European Communist countries have introduced schemes of general preferences for ldcs. The USSR now offers duty-free entry to all ldc exports, while others have offered preferences, ranging from proportional tariff cuts to duty-free entry on most products, subject – as in the case of Western countries – to safeguards and compliance with certain rules of origin. On the whole, however, the list of potential beneficiaries for the Communist schemes is more circumscribed than those for the Western schemes.[55] At the same time, the Communist countries, in particular the USSR, have entered into many bilateral trade and credit agreements with ldcs, making special provisions for an increase in their imports of manufactured goods from ldcs.

These policy changes largely explain the rapid growth – albeit from a small base – of developing countries' manufactures exports to Eastern bloc countries. It is difficult to assess ldcs' prospects for expanding these exports still further. There are, however, at least two important reasons for supposing that the Eastern bloc will not become a major market for ldcs' manufactures exports. The first is associated with the fact that most of ldcs' trade with the Eastern bloc is via bilateral trade agreements, usually barter agreements. The second is related to the growth of East-West trade links.

The bilateral trade agreements, and particularly the barter agreements, between the Communist countries and ldcs are designed to balance trade flows between both parties to the agreement. and generally to avoid the use of scarce convertible currencies. The requirement that trade flows should be balanced and the bureaucratic procedures involved in establishing and monitoring such trade arrangements restrict the growth of trade. Although the provision of tied credits by the Eastern bloc countries and the development of state trading organisations in ldcs have eased the working of the agreements, they are essentially a cumbersome framework for trade. The aim of conserving convertible currencies tends to restrict the growth of 'barter' trade since both parties wish to exchange those goods which cannot earn convertible currency elsewhere, yet both want to receive in return goods which would otherwise have had to be bought with convertible currency. In the absence of complementarity between the industrial sectors of Eastern bloc countries and ldcs, these aims obviously limit the scope for an exchange of manufactured goods – as opposed to the exchange of manufactures for raw materials from ldcs.

The recent spurt in manufactures imports from ldcs is attributed to a variety of underlying factors, for instance the Sino-Soviet dispute, the economic reforms in the Eastern bloc, and the efforts of the Eastern European countries to reduce their dependence on the USSR. Notwithstanding professions of interest in expanding their manufactures trade with ldcs, the Eastern bloc countries are, however, thought to be chiefly interested in forging trade links with the West: trade with ldcs is seen as a surrogate for the East-West trade they need but cannot always get.[56] Thus the residual nature of ldcs' manufactures trade with the Eastern bloc is likely to become more manifest as East-West detente grows.

SUPPLY CONDITIONS AND CONSTRAINTS

The existence, or the threat, of barriers to ldcs' manufactures exports to developed countries has given rise to a school of thought or despair – known as export pessimism – which stresses demand restrictions as the main constraint on the expansion of such exports. But, while demand factors are undoubtedly important, the export pessimists' view gives a somewhat distorted picture of the factors affecting ldcs' present and potential exports. The variation in individual ldcs' export performance, despite the similarity of conditions in their export markets, and the apparent scope for increasing their currently small share of world export markets indicate that supply as well as demand conditions have an important influence on ldcs' manufactures exports, and that changes on that side can therefore be expected to alter their prospects.

The balance between supply and demand factors is hard to judge and clearly varies among ldcs. Hong Kong, for instance, faces more demand restrictions and fewer supply constraints on its manufactured exports than, say, Upper Volta or any other small, poor country offered preferential access to developed country markets. But since supply factors limit the range and quantity of manufactured goods that the poorer countries may export, any restrictions on their market access within that range of goods has a greater impact than in a more advanced ldc, because of their limited scope for export diversification. Among semi-industrialised countries, government policy has clearly had an impact – beneficial and otherwise – on manufactured exports.[57] It does not follow, however, that if all such countries had adopted the export-orientated policies of, say, Hong Kong, they could have matched Hong Kong's growth performance in the export of manufactures. A more widespread export drive would increase the danger of excess supply and damaging price competition among ldcs. Moreover, it is probable that some of their export products, at least, would have encroached too successfully on developed country markets and so been subject to restrictions. Even so, while demand considerations suggest that the performance of the leading ldc manufactures exporters was in part possible precisely because of the laggards, in both cases, supply-side factors must be regarded as important determinants of their respective performances.

Resource Endowments

A country-by-country analysis of ldcs showed, not surprisingly, that income levels per head, population size, and natural resource endowment were related to the extent to which countries engaged in the production and export of manufactures.[58] Countries with incomes per head below $100 tend to have only a small industrial sector, with manufactured output consisting largely of simple consumption goods (e.g. textiles, beverages) produced almost entirely for the domestic market. Countries with incomes per head above $100 tend to have a larger and more diversified industrial sector but its development and that of manufactures exports is also related to natural resources and population size. Resource-rich countries, such as Malaysia, having less incentive to find alternative sources of foreign-exchange earnings, tend to lag behind the resource-poor countries, such as Taiwan, in their development of manufactures exports. And countries with large populations have tended to develop a capacity for manufactures exports at lower average income levels than countries with small populations.

While far from giving a complete explanation for differences between countries, this analysis points to the importance of economic size and natural resources in determining a country's scope and incentive for the production and export of manufactured goods.

Especially at the early stages of development, but also later on, the problems of exporting manufactures are largely those that the country faces in its attempt to industrialise. The lack of entrepreneurial, managerial and technical skills, the general inexperience of the workforce, and lack of capital and technological know-how inhibit the development of manufacturing activities. The inadequacy of the physical infrastructure – for instance, the transport and energy systems – is also an obstacle. Meanwhile, unless the country can successfully enter external markets, the kind of productive activities it can develop will be restricted by the pattern and level of domestic demand. In virtually every field of manufacturing, individual firms or productive units have to reach a certain minimum level of output before they can operate efficiently. If domestic demand for the product concerned is less than this minimum level – as is likely to be the case with consumer-durable, intermediate, and capital goods – then such products can be produced,in the absence of an export outlet, only at high cost to the economy compared with the alternative of importing such products.

Manufacturing for export can widen ldcs' range of choice and speed their industrial development – and indeed this path was successfully taken by some countries, such as Taiwan, Hong Kong, and Singapore, which had limited prospects for developing primary products for export or industrial products solely for domestic consumption. However, while exporting can help to solve the capacity constraint on manufacturing development, it poses additional problems, which apply to all countries but especially to the least developed countries, since producing for export is both riskier and more taxing than producing for the domestic market. And these problems – as also the export pessimism of many ldcs – help to explain why relatively few countries have sought to base, or succeeded in basing, their industrial development on èxports.

External v. Internal Markets

Any successful producer has to identify opportunities for producing saleable goods, produce them to meet the standards and tastes of the consumer, and enter the market and sell at a price which leaves him a profit. A number of factors make these operations easier for the local entrepreneur in the home than in external markets – particularly in the case of manufactured goods, for which external marketing channels are neither so closely organised nor so well established as in the case of primary commodities.

In the first place, the identification of market opportunities requires access to information not only about foreign tastes and the existing supply situation but also about regulations governing access to potential consumers, such as tariff schedules or product regulations. Such information is likely to be easier to come by and less complex for the producer's home market than that in relation to foreign markets. This is particularly so in ldcs where institutional sources of information on overseas markets are less well established than in developed countries.

Secondly, it is probable – particularly when selling to developed country markets – that product standards will be higher and require more rigorous quality control than is necessary for home production. The difference between what can be sold in a less developed country market and what can be sold abroad may reflect the protection from external competition often accorded to ldc producers,[59] but it also reflects greater consumer sophistication in foreign markets: milled broken-grain rice or matches with a one-in-three (or more) failure rate may be acceptable to the low-income domestic consumer but not to high-income foreigners. If the would-be exporter is already producing for the home market, the organisation and supervision of production will probably have to be altered to meet higher product standards. In this case, ensuring higher quality will involve an increase in the use of scarce skills – and possibly capital as well.[60]

Finally, the would-be exporter has to sell his product in an unfamiliar environment. This brings problems of persuading buyers to purchase his product rather than that of established suppliers, and, of maintaining supply – which may pose difficulties on the production side. His share of the market, moreover, will be at greater risk from other competitors and from adverse changes in market conditions than will an established share in the domestic market, since he is less able to know about or influence such occurrences.

All these factors, in addition to the costs and problems of transportation – which may be considerable for countries which are landlocked or are selling to distant markets, or both – increase the producers' costs, especially in the initial period of selling abroad, relative to those of supplying only the home market. Exporting may be highly profitable but the high costs of entry, for ldc producers in particular, are a significant barrier. This barrier, however, may be reduced for the individual enterprise, in a number of ways, through government action or by resort to foreign expertise and capital.

Government Policy

Negative Effects

In many ldcs, government policy has tended to deter rather than encourage export, and institutional developments which might have helped exporters have been neglected This situation is largely due to the protectionist measures with which most ldcs have attempted to encourage industrial development sometimes, but not always, with a view to eventual self-sufficiency. For a variety of reasons – because initial costs of production are high, or there are market imperfections or external economies – an investment which is profitable in real terms may not be undertaken, and measures may be required to correct for these factors. The need for such measures in ldcs is widely accepted. The problem is, however, that the policy measures employed have frequently been blunt in effect: the incentives to industrial investment and production have not also been incentives to efficiency.

Protectionism through tariffs, administrative controls on imports, and overvalued exchange rates, have been a major element in ldcs' industrialisation and balance of payments policies.[61] It has encouraged manufactured production for the domestic market but discouraged exports of both primary and manufactured goods at some cost to the economy. Reducing external competition by raising the prices of manufactured imports has allowed an uncompetitive cost structure to develop in the manufacturing sectors of ldcs. Domestic competition has tended to lead to surplus capacity, since, with high domestic prices, production at low capacity is profitable. Meanwhile, the structure of protection, and the over-valuation of the exchange rate that accompanies import controls, has reduced capital costs, thus favouring capital-intensive rather than labour-intensive industries and resulting in a neglect of comparative advantage. The overvaluation of the exchange rate renders exporting, as against producing for the domestic market, unprofitable in terms of domestic currency. At the same time, the structure of industry and its high costs reduce the possibility of competitive exports. Other ldc policies, such as tax holidays to investors and minimum wage legislation, have also tended to encourage the development of externally uncompetitive manufacturing enterprises by artificially increasing the cost of labour relative to capital.

Positive Effects

That government policy can encourage manufactured exports is shown by the various success stories among ldcs. For countries which have pursued protectionist policies, however, the switch to export promoting policies may be costly. And just as import substitution policies can result in inefficiency and waste of resources, so there is a danger that export promotion can have similar results. Thus it is important to promote export industries not in such a way that the benefits exceed the cost to the rest of the economy, but to ensure that development elsewhere is not similarly at the expense of export activity while at the same time attempting to offset the specific disincentives to exporting arising from the country's underdevelopment. This suggests a combination of policies to correct for the failure of market prices to match real costs and benefits, and to provide services whose absence inhibits development. It is not possible to discuss here the whole range of activities that governments may seek to influence or the policy options open to them. Two areas, however, are directly relevant to the issue of manufactures exports: the use of commercial policies allied with exchange rate changes to effect industrial development, and the provision of export-orientated services.

Commercial Policy. As we have noted, most ldcs have used protectionist policies to stimulate industrial development resulting in a bias against export-orientated industries. One way of offsetting this bias is to reduce protectionism. But this will generally entail a significant loss of revenue from import duties, and the adoption of alternative measures for balance of payments adjustment. Where the resultant increase in manufactured exports is unlikely to contribute greatly to foreign exchange earnings in the medium term, this approach may be regarded as too costly and disruptive. A less costly and therefore attractive alternative is to offset the adverse effects of protectionism on export-orientated industries by introducing a system of export subsidies.

Such a combination of tariffs and export subsidies has been adopted by many ldcs, for instance India and Pakistan. While better than straight protectionism, it does, however, pose similar problems. As in the case of tariffs, the compensation to the producer is not directly related to the particular difficulties which have to be overcome to make the industry competitive, for instance, a wage bill which is higher than the real resource cost of labour inputs, or the costs of training skilled labour. Nor is the level of export subsidies likely to apply to different industries in such a way as to reflect their need for protection. Moreover, such incentives to export may contravene GATT rules,[62] and result in protectionist pressures in importing countries on the grounds that the selling of exports at prices below domestic prices in the exporting countries constitutes dumping.

As a rule, export incentives – or incentives to industrial investment and production – which are not directed towards the removal of specific problems limiting exports or industrialisation may permit or even encourage a misallocation of resources and uncompetitive production. This being so, there is case[63] for more radical policies, reducing the level of protection and correcting internal price distortions by taxes and subsidies, and for the provision of services to promote industry and manufactured exports. The burden of balance of payments adjustment then falls on the use of financial measures, such as external borrowing, demand, management and exchange rate changes rather than the commercial policy instruments of tariffs, export subsidies and import controls. And reliance on tariffs as a source of revenue has to be reduced. It is thus an argument for a more open, outward-looking economy.

Whether such adjustments are worthwhile will depend partly on the country's export prospects. In the case of at least some agricultural and other primary product exports, there are grounds for supposing that, given sluggish overseas demand, an increase in such exports would tend to lead to a fall in export prices and so worsen the country's terms of trade. In such cases, taxes would have to be employed to curb domestic producers' incentives to export.

Export Processing Zones. A modified version of an open economy to encourage exports has been pursued by a number of the more prominent ldc manufactures exporters, which have set up industrial free trade areas or export processing zones. These are to be distinguished from free trade zones, which are mainly to accommodate warehousing and entrepot trade, in that they are designed to encourage the development of enterprises engaged in the manufacture, processing, and assembly of export products. Such encouragement takes three main forms: the waiving of import duties and controls on producer inputs; the provision of tax incentives to investors, usually to foreign investors specifically;[64] and the supply of infrastructural services usually on a ready-made industrial site.

The establishment of export processing zones or their equivalent began in the mid-sixties, led by Taiwan, Mexico, South Korea, and Singapore. A number of other countries have set up or are in the process of setting up similar zones, for instance, Thailand, Malaysia, and Mauritius. From the evidence of the longer-established zones, they have been successful in promoting manufactures exports and employment, based on foreign capital. The Taiwan Kaohsiung Export Processing Zone, for instance, which was set up in 1965, accounted for $72 million (or 13 per cent) of Taiwan's manufactured exports to advanced countries in 1969, and provided employment to 28,803 workers at an average total capital cost per worker of *c.* $1,500 (including infrastructural investment as well as, mainly US and Japanese, direct investment costs). And while the majority of inputs, apart from labour, have been imported duty-free, local inputs have been increasing.[65]

Despite the latter finding, one of the chief dangers of export processing zones lies in their tendency to an enclave character.[66] While they may meet employment, growth and export objectives better than alternative approaches, the mainly foreign firms operating in them have tended to develop few direct linkages with the rest of the economy. Given also that relatively small amounts of risk-capital are involved in the type of labour-intensive ventures in such zones, the foreign firms involved have little commitment to their operations in the particular economy concerned, which is thus rendered vulnerable. Ldcs have attempted to counter this by regulations on the minimum local value added in the goods produced in the zones.[67] However, precisely because of the foot-loose character of the investments they are seeking to attract, they have more often tended to increase the costs of so doing, by competing with other ldcs in providing incentives to foreign firms, such as tax holidays.[68]

Provision of Services. Besides encouraging or supplying general services, such as banking facilities, savings institutions, and physical infrastructure, governments can provide those services specifically geared to meet the needs of exporters which are frequently lacking in ldcs. Such services include facilities to provide market information, sales promotion assistance, advice and training, and export insurance and financing. Many ldc governments in co-operation with developed country and multilateral agencies,[69] or with other ldcs, or independently, have started to build up their export marketing advice and training facilities. But these services, and the banking and insurance facilities open to exporters, are as yet underdeveloped and place the developing country exporter at a disadvantage compared with his developed country counterpart.

Foreign Investment and Manufactures Exports. The direct and indirect involvement of foreign firms has played an important part in the growth of manufactured output and, more specifically, manufactured exports in ldcs. Initially foreign involvement was tied up with the development of resource-based, and import substituting, manufactures. Since the sixties, however, there has been a rapid growth in foreign participation in labour-intensive export-orientated manufacture in ldcs, geared specifically to ldcs' competitive advantage arising from their relatively low labour costs.[70] This participation has occurred in two main ways: direct investment and international subcontracting. The precise extent of foreign involvement in ldcs' manufactures exports is not known, but is clearly considerable in some countries. For instance, in 1967, it was estimated that foreign firms were responsible for 34 per cent of Brazil's manufactured exports,[71] while the rapid growth of manufactured exports from the smaller Asian countries is largely the result of the growth of direct foreign investment,[72] and of subcontracting arrangements: for instance, approximately 21 per cent of South Korea's exports in 1969 were the result of subcontracting arrangements with foreign firms, compared with 2 per cent in 1962.[73] Indeed, one commentator has observed that the development of multinational activity in ldcs is such that 'it is something like a truism that competitive exports from ldcs in manufactured goods are already to a significant extent accounted for by internationals [i.e. multinationals]'.[74]

To those countries which can, and wish to, attract foreign investment,[75] or to subcontract to foreign firms, foreign participation can be beneficial to their manufactured export trade in several ways. In the first place, direct investment can provide the scarce skills, technology and know-how, and at least some of the capital,[76] required to produce for export markets. Secondly, when the trade is carried out within the multinational firm or by a local subcontractor to a foreign firm – as in the case of export processing – the ldc avoids the marketing problems referred to earlier and, because of the developed country interests involved, is provided with some insurance against protectionist pressures in developed countries. Finally, foreign firms generally may be expected to have more marketing expertise than ldc-owned and controlled export ventures.

A variety of problems have occurred through reliance on foreign participation and may yet occur, and these are discussed in the following chapter.[77] It should be noted here, however, that while most such problems are soluble, for instance the supposed tendency towards capital-intensive production techniques, and also arise in relation to domestic ventures, dependence on externally controlled firms may put ldcs in a vulnerable position which is difficult to avoid unless they do without foreign investment.

Notes

1. See Table 5.1.
2. See Table 5.2.

3. Using the UNCTAD definition of manufactures which includes processed agricultural goods and excludes unworked non-ferrous metals and petroleum products.
4. UNCTAD, *Trade in Manufactures of Developing Countries: 1972 Review*, TD/B/C.2/124, June 1973, p.38
5. See G. Helleiner, 'Manufactured Exports from Less-Developed Countries and Multinational Firms', *Economic Journal*, March, 1973, pp.21-47.
6. Ibid., p.30. The US value-added tariff concession was originally intended to encourage the export of US intermediate goods and raw materials rather than the export of processes previously carried out in the USA.
7. For instance, between 1960 and 1968, exports of manufactures among members of the Central American Common Market increased by 38 per cent a year. See F. Pazoz, 'Regional Integration of Trade Among Less Developed Countries', in P. Streeten (ed.), *Trade Strategies for Development* (London, Macmillan, 1973), pp.145-86.
8. See below, p.196 and Chapter 6.
9. See Table 5.10 for some indication of this, although it should be noted that the eligibility of dutiable imports for GSP treatment does *not* necessarily mean that no duty is levied on them.
10. See below, p.184.
11. UNCTAD, *The Kennedy Round: Estimated Effects on Trade Barriers*, TD/6/Rev.1, Geneva, 1968.
12. It would be wrong, however, to say that ldcs were worse off relative to developed countries than they were before the round. Although the percentage cuts in tariffs affecting ldcs' goods were smaller than those in tariffs affecting all goods, the absolute cuts were greater and the drop in the total post-tariff import price of ldc exports was proportionately slightly greater than that resulting for all exports.
13. Namely the important Commonwealth Asian ldcs; see P. Tulloch, *The Seven Outside* (ODI, 1973).
14. See Chapter 2.
15. Australia introduced its scheme in 1966 and it is not formally part of the GSP although similar in conception and operation to the other schemes.
16. Neither these Eastern bloc schemes nor the similar ones operated by the USSR and Poland are referred to further in this section.
17. In the US scheme, for instance, ldcs falling into certain categories, e.g. ldcs which are members of cartels or are Communist and do not satisfy other conditions, are excluded, while ldcs in other categories, e.g. ldcs which expropriate US property without adequate compensation, may be excluded 'at the President's discretion'.
18. 'According to information available to the UNCTAD Secretariat, the escape clause has been invoked only once. . .' UNCTAD, *Review of the Schemes of Generalised Preferences*, TD/B/C.5/9 (Geneva, 1973), p.7.
19. The EEC imposes tariff quotas on a small number of agricultural goods as well.
20. In this case, the preferences constitute a form of aid, and price cutting competition among ldcs in order to ensure a share of the quota may result in the importers, not the exporters, gaining from the preferences.
21. See UNCTAD, *Review of the Schemes of Generalised Preferences; Second General Report on the Implementation of the GSP*, TD/B/C.5/22, 1974.
22. For instance, to qualify under most schemes, garments must be manufactured from imported fabrics, and plastic goods must be manufactured from basic chemicals and not plastic raw materials.
23. UNCTAD, TD/B/C.5/22, p.25.

24. UNCTAD, TD/B/C.5/9, p.14.
25. The 1973 estimates for the proportion of eligible products receiving GSP treatment given in the preceding paragraph were all higher than those for 1972.
26. These assessments are based on a survey of thirty-eight preference receiving countries, reported in an UNCTAD document, TD/B/C.5/24, noted in UNCTAD, TD/B/C.5/22, p.22.
27. Namely Yugoslavia, Brazil, Mexico, Argentina, Iran, South Korea, and India, plus Israel and Hong Kong in some schemes. All but India and South Korea have incomes per head in excess of $400 p.a.
28. See UNCTAD, *Liberalisation of Tariff and Non-Tariff Barriers,* TD/B/C.2/R.1, 1969.
29. Ibid., p.41. Attempts to identify NTBs have been confined to identifying the first and second types, since those of the third type are both more difficult to uncover and the least susceptible to liberalisation.
30. C. Pestieau and J. Henry, *Non-Tariff Barriers as a Problem in International Development,* Private Planning Association of Canada, 1972, esp. Table 23, pp.84-9. See also Table 5.11 in text.
31. Most notably quotas, discretionary licensing, and state import monopolies. See UNCTAD, *Liberalisation of Tariff and Non-Tariff Barriers,* TD/B/C.2/83, November, 1969.
32. See B. Bardan, 'The Cotton Textile Agreement 1962-1972', *Journal of World Trade Law,* vol.7, no.1, January/February 1973, pp.8-35; and P. Tulloch, 'Developing Countries and Trade in Textiles', *ODI Review,* no.2, 1974, pp.37-49.
33. GATT, *Arrangement Regarding International Trade in Textiles,* TEX.NG/1, Article 1.
34. See below for a discussion of safeguards and adjustment assistance.
35. UNCTAD, *Inventory of Non-Tariff Barriers,* TD/B/C.2/115.
36. UNCTAD, *Liberalisation of Non-Tariff Barriers,* TD/B/C.2/R5, June 1973.
37. Studies by OECD, ILO, UNCTAD, and the Bureau of Labor Statistics in the USA. See S. Mukherjee, *Free Trade is Good* (London, Political and Economic Planning, 1974), Chapter 6.
38. See Mukherjee, *Free Trade,* and also S. Mukherjee, *Making Labour Markets Work* (London, PEP, 1972).
39. Although it is used by some countries, for instance, Australia.
40. See J. Tumlir, *Proposals for Emergency Protection Against Sharp Increases in Imports,* Guest Paper No.1 (London, Trade Policy Research Centre, 1973).
41. See Chapter 2, for further discussion of the Tokyo round.
42. See K. Morton, *A Hand Worth Playing* (ODI, 1974), for a fuller discussion of ldcs' prospects in the negotiations.
43. See *Development Cooperation: 1973 DAC Review* (OECD, 1973), pp.84-9, for a useful summary of bilateral and multilateral activities in the sphere of ldc export promotion.
44. See also Chapter 2.
45. For instance, the British government-financed Tropical Products Institute, and the Export Market Development programme run by the Commonwealth Secretariat in Britain and financed by Commonwealth countries, including ldcs.
46. Although the ITC is precluded from direct investment in export production in ldcs.
47. This is jointly sponsored by the Ministry of Overseas Development and the London Chamber of Commerce and went into operation in 1974.
48. Britain also operates value-added tariffs but their application is limited to

goods which have not undergone substantial transformation, e.g. cloth which is dyed abroad would qualify but cloth made into garments would not.
49. Helleiner, p.30.
50. See Chapter 8.
51. Figures relate to 1966 and 1963/4 for Brazil and Pakistan respectively, and are calculated in relation to official exchange rates. For details of the method of calculation see the source, I.M.D. Little, T. Scitovsky and M. Scott, *Industry and Trade in Some Developing Countries* (London, OECD and OUP, 1970), p.174. See also B. Balassa, *The Structure of Protection in Developing Countries* (Baltimore, Johns Hopkins Press, 1971).
52. See p.193.
53. See above, p.162.
54. See Chapter 8.
55. UNCTAD, TD/B/C.5/9.
56. See M. Kidron, *Pakistan's Trade with Eastern Bloc Countries* (New York, Praeger, 1972), p.13. As well as providing an interesting case study of Pakistan's trading relations with the East, this book gives a useful account of ldcs' trade with the Eastern bloc and their problems and prospects, on which much of this section is based.
57. See Little, Scitovsky and Scott.
58. See H.B. Chenery and H. Hughes, 'Industrialisation and Trade Trends', H. Hughes (ed.), in *Prospects for Partnership* (Baltimore, Johns Hopkins Press, 1973), pp.3-31.
59. See p.188.
60. See pp.29 and 198.
61. See also Chapter 7.
62. These are somewhat confused on the issue of subsidies, see M. Rowe, 'GATT: Export Subsidies and Developing Countries', *Journal of World Trade Law*, September/October 1968. This is an area of negotiation in the Tokyo round.
63. This is cogently argued in Little, Scitovsky and Scott.
64. South Korea's zone, for instance, is reserved for enterprises with 50 per cent or more foreign equity. See Gy Adams, 'New Trends in International Business', *Acta Oeconomica*, vol.7, Nos. 3-4, 1971, p.354.
65. See Asian Development Bank, *Southeast Asia's Economy in the 1970s* (London, Longman, 1971), p.307.
66. Mexico's zone provides evidence for this. See Anna-Shira Ericson, 'An analysis of Mexico's Border Industrialisation Programme', *Monthly Labour Review*, May 1970, pp.33-40.
67. Asian Development Bank, p.307.
68. See Adams, pp.354-6. Cooperation among ldcs could reduce this sort of competition, see Chapters 6 and 8.
69. See section on export promotion, above.
70. Another, as yet less significant, development in this sphere is the establishment of heavy industries in ldcs as a result of environmental laws or pressure against pollution. Japan has carried out some overseas investment of this sort in nearby Asian ldcs.
71. J. Winpenny, *Brazil: Manufactured Exports and Government Policy* (Hove, Latin American Publications Fund, 1972), p.39.
72. Asian Development Bank, and Adams.
73. S. Wantanabe, 'International Sub-contracting, Employment and Skill Promotion', *International Labour Review*, vol.105, May 1972, p.433.
74. Adams, p.364.
75. See Chapter 6.

76. It should be noted that foreign equity investment in a venture often does not meet total investment requirements, and that local equity participation and loans raised locally are frequently used to finance part of the costs.
77. See also Chapter 1 for a summary of the argument that the concentration of ldc-manufactured exports on developed countries is likely to lead to the adoption of inappropriate techniques. A full statement of the argument is in F. Stewart, 'Trade and Technology', in Streeten, pp.231-63. See also Morawetz, 'Employment Implications of Industrialisation in Developing Countries: a Survey', *Economic Journal,* September 1974.

6 DIRECT FOREIGN PRIVATE INVESTMENT AND LDCS' TRADE

International trade is generally conducted by institutions rather than individuals. While in some countries and in some sectors, state-run enterprises are the major agents of international trade, it is generally private firms that play the most important role in both developed and developing countries. And, with the expansion of multinational enterprises, foreign private investors – always important in the traditional export sectors of ldcs – are of growing significance in the conduct of international trade. While global figures are lacking, it has been estimated, for instance, that US-based multinational firms – which predominate among multinationals – account for one-quarter of total world merchandise exports and one-fifth of world exports of manufactures.[1] A large part of the trade conducted by multinationals is, moreover, carried out between affiliates of the same firm: estimates suggest that between one-eighth and one-quarter of world exports are made in this way.[2] Such trade is clearly likely to possess different characteristics from that conducted by independent agents in an open market setting.

This chapter seeks to examine the role of foreign private direct investment activities in ldcs' export trade. Starting with an attempt to estimate the extent to which foreign firms operating in ldcs are engaged in exporting activities, it goes on to consider the kind of advantages and disadvantages to the host country that foreign investment may bring. Finally, it considers how and to what extent ldcs can cope with the problems that may result from the presence of foreign firms in their economies. This latter section will examine alternative forms of foreign involvement, where the host country has complete or partial ownership and/or control of a venture. Although the main interest here is in the role of foreign firms in ldcs' export trade, inevitably many of the issues raised relate to foreign private investment generally – whether engaged in foreign trade or not.

SIGNIFICANCE OF FOREIGN PRIVATE INVESTMENT IN LDC EXPORT TRADE

Data on the extent to which ldcs' export trade is carried out by foreign concerns are scanty, relating only to some ldcs and some foreign concerns. On the whole, moreover, the full extent of the involvement of foreign firms in ldcs' trade is obscured by the lack of information on the importance of multinational organisations acting only on the marketing side. Yet such firms by the nature of their contractual arrangements with ldc producers or by their organisation of the markets for certain commodities may have considerable control over the volume and value of ldcs' exports.

More data, however, are available on direct foreign private investment of all kinds in ldcs. It is partial to the extent that such investment by non-member countries of DAC is excluded despite its importance in some countries.[3] Nevertheless the available data provide a guide to the scale and scope of direct overseas investment in ldcs on which – together with the less ample evidence on concerns specifically involved in export production and marketing – the discussion of foreign investment and ldcs' trade may be based. Unless otherwise stated the terms foreign investment and foreign private investment refer to foreign private *direct* investment. The latter is to be distinguished from other foreign private investment in that it involves (a) the transfer of productive factors besides capital, and (b) some degree of foreign ownership *and* control.

Geographical Distribution of Direct Foreign Private Investment

The value of total direct foreign private investment assets in ldcs in 1967 amounted to $33.1 billion or 32 per cent of such investment stock in the world outside the Communist-controlled countries.[4] A more recent estimate, for 1971, puts the value of foreign direct investment assets in ldcs at $45 billion.[5] Relative to their economic size, such investment is more important in ldcs than in developed countries: while being hosts to a third of global foreign investment, ldcs accounted for only 16 per cent of the global gross domestic product. The stock of foreign investment is measured by putting a value on the total overseas assets – usually known as the book value – owned by foreign investors at a particular point in time. The stock is increased or decreased according to whether foreign investors make new investments or repatriate the capital previously invested, and these changes are recorded by the net investment flow (i.e. new investment minus disinvestments or repatriation) over a given period, usually a year. In 1971, the total net flow of foreign direct investment in ldcs was approximately $4 billion, and this represented just under a quarter of all such investment by Western developed countries (see Table 6.1).

In terms of both the stock and flow of private overseas direct investment to ldcs, the United States predominates, accounting for half the existing assets in 1967 and over half the new investment flow in 1971. Britain, France, and the Netherlands accounted for a further third of the stock of investment in ldcs, while the investment flows from West Germany, Japan, and Canada, whose existing investments

Table 6.1. Stock and Flow of Foreign Direct Investment in Ldcs by Developed Countries[1]

Home country of Investor	Book value of direct investment 1967 $ billion	% of total in ldcs	Value of direct investment in 1971 $m	% of total to ldcs	% of total direct investment by investing country[2]	Annual growth of direct investment in ldcs 1960-1 to 1970-1
United States	16.70	50.4	2,210.0	55.8	32.2	10.7
United Kingdom	6.59	19.9	357.0	9.0	25.7	3.3
France	2.68	8.1	157.5	4.0	11.8	−5.1
Netherlands	1.69	5.1	282.7	7.1	47.5	8.4
Canada	1.46	4.4	76.0	1.9	11.4	13.8
West Germany	1.03	3.1	247.8	6.3	19.4	14.3
Japan	0.70	2.1	235.5	6.0	12.7	11.0
Italy	0.70	2.1	193.7	4.9	21.0	9.8
Belgium	0.63	1.9	26.2	0.7	11.5	0.4
Switzerland	0.56	1.7	65.7	1.7	36.6	2.3
Others[1]	0.43	1.3	105.3	2.7	n.a.	n.a.
Total	33.13	100.0	3,957.5	100.0	23.6	7.9

1 Australia, Austria, Denmark, Norway, Portugal, and Sweden; other developed market economies are excluded but in any case account for only a very small share of total investment in ldcs.

2 Percentages relate to average direct investment flows in 1970 and 1971.

Source: UN, *Multinational Corporations in World Development*, ST/ECA/190, 1973, Tables 27 and 29, p.173 and p.175.

Table 6.2. Book Value of Foreign Direct Investment by Developed Countries in Major Ldc Host Countries, 1971

Country	Book value of foreign direct investment ($m)	% of total	GNP per head 1970 ($)	Population 1970 (million)
Brazil	5,100	11.3	420	92.8
Venezuela	3,700	8.2	980	10.4
Mexico	2,450	5.4	670	50.7
Argentina	2,215	4.9	1,160	23.2
Nigeria	1,700	3.8	120	55.1
India	1,650	3.7	110	538.1
Panama	1,650	3.7	730	1.5
Libya	1,400	3.1	1,770	1.9
Jamaica	1,000	2.2	670	1.9
Trinidad & Tobago	1,000	2.2	860	1.0
Bahamas	950	2.1	2,300	0.2
Iran	930	2.1	380	28.7
Colombia	900	2.0	340	21.6
Indonesia	900	2.0	80	115.6
Saudi Arabia	890	2.0	440	7.4
Malaysia	880	2.0	380	10.9
Philippines	830	1.8	210	36.9
Peru	820	1.8	450	13.6
Chile	820	1.8	720	9.8
Kuwait	650	1.4	3,760	0.8
Netherlands Antilles	600	1.3	1,380	0.2
Hong Kong	590	1.3	970	4.0
Zaire	561	1.2	90	18.8
Pakistan[1]	524	1.2	100	130.2
Total	32,710	72.6	n.a.	1,175.3
Total of 22 ldcs[2] with over $200 million foreign investment but less than $500 million	7,886	17.1	n.a.	204.8
Total of remaining 92 countries	4,637	10.3	n.a.	365.1
Total all ldcs	45,033	100.0	240	1,745.2

1 Including Bangladesh.
2 Including West Indies (n.e.s.)
Source: OECD, *Development Co-operation: DAC Review 1973* (Paris, 1973), Table IV.4. pp.72-6.

accounted for less than 10 per cent of the stock in 1967, showed the fastest growth between 1960-1 to 1970-1.

The importance of foreign investments in ldcs by companies based in different developed countries varied considerably by region. Thus, for instance, British companies accounted for 41.5 per cent and 30 per cent of the stock of foreign investment in Asia and Africa respectively, as compared with 20 per cent of the total; France accounted for 26 per cent of the stock in Africa as compared with 8 per cent of the total; the USA accounted for 64 per cent of the stock in South and Central America but only 21 per cent in Africa as compared with 50 per cent of the total.[6] Such variations – partly reflecting past colonial ties and geographical location – are even more marked at the country level and in some developing countries the foreign affiliates of companies based in a single developed country account for over 80 per cent of the stock of foreign investment.

More than half – 56 per cent – of the stock of all private overseas investment in 1967 was in South and Central America. Africa accounted for a fifth of the total stock, the Middle East just under a tenth, while Asia accounted for some 15 per cent.[7] There was a marked concentration of such investment at the country level. As can be seen from Table 6.2, ten ldcs had a stock of foreign investment of $1 billion or more in 1971 and these countries accounted for nearly half the total stock. A further fourteen countries had a stock of foreign investment of $500 million or more, accounting for nearly a quarter of the total stock to ldcs. Of the remaining ldcs, twenty-two with a stock of $200 million or more accounted for 10 per cent. In terms of their incomes per head, the major host countries to foreign investment tend to be richer than the average ldc.

Size and Ownership Patterns

The major part of foreign investment in all countries is carried out by a relatively small number of large multinational firms. Some 250 to 300 US-based firms control over 70 per cent of US investment, some 165 firms in the UK control over 80 per cent of UK overseas investment, and 82 firms in West Germany control over 70 per cent of its investment overseas. While affiliates of small foreign firms do operate in ldcs, it is reasonable to assume that the bulk of foreign investment there, as in the West, is owned and controlled by the large multinationals; a fact which has particular significance for ldcs' bargaining strength *vis-à-vis* foreign investors, given the size and international mobility of these organisations.

Table 6.3. Pattern of Ownership of Ldc and Developed Country Affiliates of Multinationals Based in Selected Developed Countries

Companies based in	Affiliates in ldcs: Total number	% wholly owned	% majority owned	% minority owned	Affiliates in developed countries: Total number	% wholly owned	% majority owned	% minority owned
United States[1]	2,597	60.7	20.1	11.0	5,330	67.0	17.6	7.0
United Kingdom[2]	2,033	62.7	12.8	24.5	3,129	60.0	15.8	24.3
Japan[3]	(1,336)	23.2	37.1	35.2	(862)	64.4	18.5	14.5

1 Percentages do not add up to 100 since the pattern of ownership is unknown in a few cases. Data based on a survey of 187 US firms, and relate to 1967.

2 Data relate to 1965.

3 Pattern of ownership unknown in some cases: total in brackets refer to known cases while percentages are based on the total number of affiliates. Data relate to 1970.

Source: UN, ST/ECA/190, Table 16, p.152.

The pattern of ownership of direct foreign investment in ldcs is also significant, and tends to vary according to host country policy on local equity participation and the preferences of the foreign investor, both of which, in turn, vary according to the type of investment activity.[8] As can be seen from Table 6.3, the majority of British and American affiliates in ldcs are wholly foreign-owned or majority owned, but minority ownership is significant, accounting for just over a tenth and just under a quarter of American and British affiliates respectively. (In terms of the book value of the affiliates, however, only a tenth of British firms' affiliates were minority-owned.) By contrast, only a minority of Japanese firms' affiliates were wholly-owned, and 35 per cent were minority-owned. This reflects, in part, the reaction of Asian ldcs to the 'invasion of Japanese foreign private investment' and particularly to its presence in raw material industries.[9]

Concern at the implications of foreign subsidiaries operating in their countries is increasing in other ldcs as well and can be observed in the growth of regulations requiring some measure of local equity participation in foreign ventures. The impact of such moves can be seen in the changes in ownership patterns of US affiliates set out in Table 6.4. On average, wholly owned affiliates have declined relative to majority- or minority-owned affiliates. The extent to which local equity participation is feasible or desirable is discussed elsewhere, as also are the factors which may encourage the investing firm to seek local partners or capital.[10] So far as foreign firms engaged in exporting from ldcs are concerned, it is of relevance to note here that ldcs appear to have secured a greater measure of ownership and control in foreign firms operating in the traditional raw materials sectors than in those in manufactures exports – although in the manufacturing sector generally local participation is more widespread.[11]

Sectoral Distribution of Direct Foreign Private Investment

Table 6.5 sets out the pattern of foreign investment in ldcs by sector and region in 1967. Foreign investment in some sectors in ldcs is primarily export-orientated while in others it is primarily geared to the local market. Thus the sectoral distribution of foreign investment provides some guide to foreign firms' participation in ldcs' export industries.

Broadly speaking, foreign firms engaged in extractive industries (oil, metals, and minerals), in the agricultural sector, and in tourism are primarily export-orientated. In 1967, these three sectors accounted for 44 per cent, 6.2 per cent and 1.4 per cent respectively of the total stock of foreign private investment in ldcs. Foreign firms in the public utilities, trade, and transport sectors mainly serve the local market. In

Table 6.4. Changes in Pattern of Ownership of Ldc Affiliates of 187 US Multinationals by Region, 1939, 1957 and 1967

	1939		1957		1967	
	No.	% of affiliates in region	No.	% of affiliates in region	No.	% of affiliates in region
Wholly owned affiliates in:						
Central and South America	215	68.3	702	66.4	1,195	62.1
Africa, South of Sahara	2	50.0	28	57.1	112	67.5
Middle East	8	50.0	30	62.5	50	56.8
Other Asia	44	72.1	91	66.4	216	51.6
All ldcs	269	67.9	851	65.9	1,573	60.6
Majority-owned affiliates in:						
Central and South America	47	14.9	172	16.3	365	19.0
Africa, South of Sahara	—	—	15	30.6	28	16.9
Middle East	3	18.8	8	16.7	20	22.7
Other Asia	6	9.8	22	16.1	108	25.8
All ldcs	5.6	14.1	217	16.8	521	20.1
Minority-owned affiliates in:						
Central and South America	14	4.4	76	7.2	197	10.2
Africa, South of Sahara	—	—	2	4.1	20	12.0
Middle East	2	12.5	4	8.3	12	13.6
Other Asia	1	1.6	7	5.1	58	13.8
All ldcs	17	4.3	89	6.9	287	11.1

Source: UN, ST/ECA/190, Table 18, pp.156-7.

1967, foreign investment in these sectors accounted for roughly 15 per cent of the total stock.

The manufacturing sector accounted for the bulk of the remaining 34 per cent of foreign investment stock in 1967. As noted in Chapter 5, there has been a considerable expansion in export-orientated foreign investment in ldcs' manufacturing sectors. Nonetheless, the major part of such foreign investment, particularly in Latin America, is primarily geared to local markets. But while the proportion of their output sold abroad is usually small, these firms do often make a substantial contribution to ldcs' manufactures exports. And a study of US foreign investments in the manufacturing sector of Latin America

Table 6.5. Stock of Foreign Direct Investment in Ldcs by Sector and Region, 1967[1]

Industrial sector	Book value of total foreign investment in ldcs: $ billion	% of total	% share of book value of direct foreign investment in each region: Africa	Asia[1]	Middle East	Central & South America[2]
Petroleum of which: :	10.96	33.1	39.4	22.1	89.5	24.3
Production	6.30	19.0	29.5	5.0	47.4	14.2
Refining	2.39	7.2	4.5	10.5	17.2	5.6
Transport	1.20	3.6	1.6	1.6	19.8	2.2
Marketing	1.08	3.2	3.8	5.0	5.1	2.3
Manufacturing	9.63	29.1	18.8	31.0	6.1	36.1
Mining & smelting	3.55	10.7	19.4	5.1	0.2	10.9
Trade	2.60	7.8	6.0	10.1	1.0	9.0
Agriculture	2.05	6.2	7.5	18.8	0.1	3.3
Public utilities	1.57	4.7	1.0	2.4	0.3	7.4
Transport	0.68	2.0	3.4	1.4	0.6	2.0
Banking	0.59	1.8	2.1	2.7	0.9	1.6
Tourism	0.45	1.4	0.7	2.5	0.6	1.4
Others	1.06	3.2	1.7	3.9	0.7	4.0
Total	33.13	100.0	100.0	100.0	100.0	100.0
Total book value in each region $ billion	33.13	–	6.59	4.99	3.10	18.75
% of total	100.0	–	19.9	15.1	9.4	55.7

1 Relates to investment by the DAC countries, listed in Table 6.1.
2 Includes ldcs in Oceania.
Source: UN, ST/ECA/190, Table 30, p.177.

has revealed that, while initially their output was almost entirely produced for the local market to substitute for imports, the proportion of their output which is exported has been increasing.[12]

The pattern of investment varies considerably between regions, reflecting differences in resource endowments, market size, and host government policies. For example, in the Middle East, the petroleum sector accounted for 90 per cent of the foreign investment stock, while manufacturing was the most important area in Asia and South and Central America.

Foreign Firms' Share of Output and Exports

In most ldcs, the agricultural and service sectors – where, generally, there is little foreign investment – account for a large share of their gross domestic products (GDPs). Consequently, the contribution of the output of foreign-owned enterprises to ldcs' GDPs tends to be fairly small, at about 6 per cent.[13] Nevertheless, available evidence indicates that in some sectors, and in some ldcs, foreign investment makes a considerable contribution to both output and exports. Thus foreign investors dominate in many of the extractive export industries in ldcs, although here – as in the agricultural export sector – host governments have sought, with some success, and continue to seek ways of reducing foreign ownership and control, and of increasing the returns to the host country. Foreign participation in manufacturing in ldcs varies widely. In Singapore, for instance, foreign investment accounted for an estimated one-third of value-added in the manufacturing sector[14] but in Hong Kong, the figure was probably nearer 15 per cent.[15] US firms alone in Latin America accounted for roughly a tenth of manufacturing output and over 40 per cent of manufactured exports.[16] Their share of manufactured exports varied between countries, for instance 87 per cent of Mexico's manufactured exports in 1966 were made by US firms while their share was 42 per cent in Brazil.[17]

In Asia, where foreign investment in manufacturing accounts for a significant proportion of the stock of foreign investment, its contribution to manufactured exports tends to be less important than in Latin America, despite the foreign-dominated export processing zones there. In 1972, some 10 per cent of Hong Kong's domestic exports were attributed to foreign firms, and some 12-15 per cent of manufactured exports from Taiwan can be so attributed.[18] In India, it was thought that only 3-4 per cent of manufactures exports were generated by foreign firms, but in Singapore the figure was probably 30 per cent. Overall it has been estimated – somewhat impressionistically – that some 10 per cent only of Asia's manufactures exports in 1972 could be attributed to foreign direct investment.[19] At the same time, exports under international subcontracting agreements with major US, Japanese, and European trading groups are thought to account for a much larger proportion of Asian manufactured exports. Using Angus Hone's estimates of the value of trade involved, one may attribute between 50 and 80 per cent of Asia's manufactured exports to developed countries to such agreements.[20] And the general view of the relatively greater importance of buying groups in Asian manufactured exports is supported by a finding in relation to South Korea that manufactured exports under commercial subcontracting increased from $1 million in 1962 to $130.7 million in 1969, accounting for 21 per cent of total exports in that year and roughly one-third of manufacturing exports.[21]

ADVANTAGES AND DISADVANTAGES OF FOREIGN PRIVATE INVESTMENT

The actual and potential impact of foreign private investment on host ldcs is a matter of controversy. One view lays stress on the benefits to be derived from the resultant transfer of resources, often scarce locally. These resources in combination can increase output, employment and incomes in the host country both directly, and indirectly via the spread of skills, technology, and know-how, and via the stimulus to local economic activity and to external capital inflows provided by the presence of foreign enterprise. Another view questions the extent to which foreign investment actually adds to the stock of productive resources in the host country, and the appropriateness of the resources transferred – in particular technology – to production conditions there. The costs of foreign investment are listed: the outflow of resources in the form of profits, royalties, fees, and hidden transfer payments, and the possibility of negative indirect or 'spread' effects. Foreign investment, it is claimed, tends to promote economic and political dependence and to distort the process of development, stifling local entrepreneurship, introducing inappropriate products and production techniques, exacerbating income inequalities and so on. While some of the ills associated with foreign investment may occur when firms are domestically owned and controlled, and – like the benefits – are certainly not inherent to all foreign investment, it is argued that they are more likely to occur when the firm is both foreign and private and is operating not as an independent unit but as part of a large international concern. Meanwhile, host governments are probably less able to ensure that the foreign firm – as opposed to the domestic firm – operates in the interests of the host country, particularly when it is dealing with a large, internationally mobile, company.

It is not possible here to go into all the wide-ranging and complex issues in this controversy.[22] Nonetheless, given the importance of foreign private investment in ldcs' export sectors, some discussion of its particular advantages and disadvantages is warranted. Issues related to host country policies and to its bargaining strength *vis-à-vis* foreign firms – which can substantially affect the costs and benefits of foreign investment – are discussed in subsequent sections.

Export Marketing

It is no accident that foreign-owned firms in developing countries are often most in evidence in the export sector, or that even in Latin America, where foreign manufacturing firms have primarily been established to serve the host country markets, foreign firms' export performance has been markedly better than that of local firms.[23] For a variety of reasons, foreign-owned subsidiaries tend to be better placed than locally owned firms to engage in exporting – and this constitutes a major factor in their favour, so far as host governments bent on export expansion are concerned.

Unlike the local firm, the foreign-owned firm can often draw on direct experience of market conditions in other parts of the world. It tends to have better access to personnel skilled in overseas marketing, to information on overseas markets and export promotion facilities, and can often make use of established distribution channels. And to the extent that the foreign firm's interests are represented in importing countries, it is better able to defend its access to export markets from protectionist pressures.

In certain spheres, moreover, the foreign subsidiary has a built-in export marketing advantage. A growing number of foreign subsidiaries are being established to supply goods to other parts of the same parent firms. They consequently do not have to seek out an overseas market. This is the case with foreign manufacturing subsidiaries geared to carry out certain stages of a production process which is either initiated or completed in other parts of the firm, for instance, car component manufacturers. Certain foreign firms engaged in primary production for export in ldcs, for instance bauxite mining firms, also operate in a similar way, selling their products to other parts of the firm for further processing or marketing. Given the organisation of such industries, the scope for independent ldc producers entering these fields and marketing their output abroad is limited. And in the manufacturing sector, the foreign firm may have an advantage over the local firm producing a similar product in that it can sell under an established brand-name.

But whether or not, and to what extent, a foreign subsidiary engages in exporting often depends on the global sales strategy of the parent firm. Obviously in certain fields – the production of raw materials and export processing – the subsidiary firm is established primarily to serve an overseas market. In the manufacturing sector, on the other hand, some subsidiaries are established by the parent to serve the local market and sales overseas are subject to restrictions, or even bans, imposed by the parent company. In India, for example, it was found that out of a sample of 737 agreements on foreign direct investment effective in 1969, 32 per cent contained clauses restricting export sales and 15 per cent prohibited them altogether.[24] Such restrictions may only be a formality, reflecting the fact that the subsidiary is competitive only in a highly protected host country market, such as has been enjoyed by many foreign *and* domestic manufacturing producers in ldcs. One may then queston whether the host government should have pursued protectionist industrialisation policies, whether it should have imported rather than attempt to stimulate local production of certain products, but one can hardly criticise the foreign firm – or its domestic counterpart – for not exporting at a loss. On the other hand, such restrictions may indeed act as a brake on the industrial expansion and export growth that might have occurred had the firm been in local control.

Production Advantages

On the production side, foreign firms often have an advantage over local firms as a result of their superior – and sometimes exclusive – access to technology, skills, know-how, and capital. In industries, such as those in the extractive sector, requiring substantial amounts of risk capital the large foreign firm with its greater resources and access to the world's capital markets is clearly at an advantage. And in the technologically more advanced manufacturing industries, foreign investment may be the only means of going into local production. The technology concerned may be proprietary, i.e. it is the exclusive property of the firm which developed it, or it may only be worked efficiently with the skills and know-how possessed by foreign firms. The resources at the foreign subsidiary's disposal thus give it advantages in both marketing and production in many spheres.

Given these advantages, ldcs may benefit considerably from permitting foreign firms to participate in their economies. Their activities can diversify output and exports and directly increase employment and incomes (in the form of wages, taxes, and consumer gains) accruing locally. And indirectly, the country can gain further if, for example, the skills and technology transferred become available to local producers or if the firm stimulates local economic activity on the part of suppliers, competitors, distributors and so on.

Limitations on the Benefits

Obviously these benefits do not occur with each and every foreign firm and, besides the outflow of resources in the form of profits and other transfers to the foreign investor,[25] certain costs may be incurred locally. On the whole, the negative effects sometimes associated with foreign investment are less likely to occur with export-orientated foreign investment. Local entrepreneurs, for instance, are unlikely to be displaced by such investment since, as noted above, the export-orientated foreign investor often makes use of resources and skills unavailable or scarce locally, and in certain cases the production or marketing links between the subsidiary and the parent firm are essential to the former's operations. The diversion of scarce local resources, particularly capital, into the employ of the foreign firm from alternative productive uses can reduce its contribution to the host economy – and can lead to negative effects to the extent that such resources yield lower returns to the host economy than they would otherwise have done. To the extent that export-orientated firms use locally unavailable resources, this diversion is unlikely. Moreover, local capital – at least as equity finance – is less likely to be used to finance export-orientated foreign subsidiaries. For parent firms generally seek to retain greater control over their activities than over those of subsidiaries producing for the local market, and local equity interests could hamper such control.[26]

Apart from issues relating to the dependence creating effects of foreign investment, a major criticism of such investment is that it transfers inappropriate technologies to host ldcs: for instance, foreign firms may introduce labour saving production techniques better suited to conditions in industrially advanced countries for which they were developed, than to those in ldcs. Certain export-orientated foreign firms, specifically those engaged in export processing, are not open to this criticism. They are located in ldcs precisely because of the production conditions there and the technology used is geared to take advantage of them, in particular the relative abundance of cheap unskilled labour. Other foreign firms may be more vulnerable to this criticism. Even so, it has to be pointed out that it is the absence of alternative technologies which often leads to the use of inappropriate technologies by both foreign and domestic firms. Moreover, certain factors in ldcs, for instance government minimum wage legislation which artificially raises local wages, may encourage the use, by local as well as foreign firms, of technologies which are inappropriate to local resource availability. And it may be that apparently inappropriate technologies are, in fact, more efficient in their use of scarce resources: as, for instance, when capital-intensive technologies permitting machine-paced production by relatively unskilled labour reduce the need for scarce managerial, organisational and supervisory skills.[27]

Export-orientated firms, particularly export processing firms, are on the other hand more vulnerable to the criticism that they do not have beneficial spread effects: that the diffusion of skills and technology is limited and few linkages are developed with local distributors and suppliers. Export-orientated subsidiaries often have established links with external buyers and suppliers either within or without the multinational enterprise of which they are part. Consequently they are probably less likely than domestic producers and other foreign firms to use local inputs or rely on local distributors.[28] Meeting export orders on time and maintaining the quality of the product, combined with doubts as to the quality and reliability of local supplies, are however significant considerations in the decision to use imported inputs. This is consequently often a reflection on the level of local industrial development more than on the foreignness of the firm.

Restrictions on the diffusion of technology are often imposed by foreign firms to preserve the commercial advantage that the possession of such technology bestows.[29] In the case of export processing firms, however, the technology transfer may be limited because of the relative simplicity of the production processes and in some cases, for instance in sewing together baseballs for export, may be virtually non-existent. The simplicity of such production processes will by the same token inhibit the diffusion of skills, since few new skills are actually needed. And the extent of integration with the parent firm also limits the diffusion of skills. It has been observed that foreign firms do try to employ locals rather than expatriates in their subsidiaries, for political and economic reasons.[30] But since the parent firm often makes the major decisions on production and marketing in export-orientated subsidiaries, the diffusion of higher level managerial and marketing skills is inevitably limited. And, probably in order to ensure greater efficiency and conformity with parent company objectives, there is a tendency for more expatriates to be employed in export-orientated subsidiaries than in those supplying the local market.[31]

Profits and Other Overseas Payments

While certain advantages and disadvantages are associated with different types of foreign investment, most of them do not necessarily accompany such investment. An important and inherent cost of all foreign investment is, however, that otherwise investible resources (and foreign exchange) are transferred out of the host country to the foreign investor, following his initial and potentially beneficial transfer of resources to the host country.

Whether the transfer of profits and other external service payments, such as fees for managerial or technical services provided by the parent firm and royalties on the technology transferred, leave the host country worse off depends on the balance of all the various costs and benefits resulting from the foreign investment. Very often what is of concern is not that the transfer leaves the host country absolutely worse off but that it leaves the host somewhat worse off than it should have been. In other words, there is concern that, in some sense, the foreign investor appropriates an 'unfair' share of the benefit.[32] The most important sense in which this might be true – and sometimes appears to be true – is that tax concessions and subsidies allow the foreign investor to avoid host country taxation on his profits, obtaining a higher rate of return on his investment than the minimum necessary for him to continue producing in the host country.

It is quite clear that, in many ldcs, the tax treatment of foreign firms is different and usually more generous than that accorded to domestic firms. In part this stems from the host countries' independent, and frequently misguided, belief that the various concessions and subsidies are necessary to induce foreign investment. Partly, however, it reflects the superior bargaining – and bribing – power of foreign firms.[33] In either case such concessions represent a loss of tax revenue only if the firm would actually have invested with fewer concessions. As we shall discuss below, the greater the geographical mobility of the foreign firm the greater its monopolistic control over certain inputs, such as technology, and the greater the competition between host countries for particular foreign investments, the more likely it is that tax concessions are the price for obtaining that investment, so far as the *individual* host government is concerned.

Transfer Pricing

In addition to tax concessions, some foreign firms have both opportunities and motives for substantial avoidance of host country taxation. Where various other channels exist for the transfer of funds, as a result of the transactions between the foreign-owned subsidiary in one country and the parent firm or its subsidiaries elsewhere, foreign firms need not declare all their profits for tax. The inputs of capital equipment, technology and other intangibles, such as brand-names, transferred from the parent company may be valued so as to reduce or increase the real rate of profit. And the existence of intra-firm trade in merchandise leaves scope for the transfer of funds via the over-pricing or under-pricing of goods. The scope for such undeclared profit transfers depends on the extent to which the activities of the subsidiary are integrated with other parts of the firm and centrally controlled and on the extent to which goods and services are traded within the firm and not in an open-market situation – at 'arm's length'.[34] Large, vertically integrated manufacturing multinational enterprises such as those making motor vehicles, chemicals, electrical and non-electrical machinery, rubber products and scientific instruments,[35] and those enterprises in the extractive sector where the various stages of production are under oligopolistic control, e.g. in the petroleum and bauxite industries, have the greatest scope for such transfers.[36] Foreign-owned enterprises which are not closely integrated with the parent company and where the scale of the latter's operations is small, and where an open market for such goods traded within the firm exists, have least scope. The pattern of ownership of subsidiaries is also important: local participation limits the extent to which the subsidiary's transactions can be manipulated for the benefit of the company as a whole. Local shareholders may object to the lowering of local profits if funds are siphoned off to the parent company, while the parent company will have less to gain from transactions which increase local profits. The possibility of collusion between the parent company and the local shareholders exists, however, in the former case, and the existence of local shareholders itself may be an incentive to transfer pricing by the parent company.

Two sorts of reason have been distinguished for using transfer prices: to maximise the present value of total profits (i.e. of parent and subsidiary); and to minimise risk and uncertainty about the future value of profits.[37] The first kind of transfer pricing is stimulated by the existence of different rates of taxes, tariffs and subsidies in the countries in which the multinational firm operates, multiple exchange rates which discriminate against profit outflows, quantitative restrictions on profit remittances and service payments, and the expectation of exchange rate changes. The second kind of transfer pricing is induced by the expectation of restrictions on future profit remittances because of balance of payments difficulties; political and social pressures or from a direct threat to profits, e.g. a reduction in the level of protection afforded to the multinational; the introduction of price controls; increases in taxation; or a demand for local participation.

In general, the evidence on the manipulation of profits and the transfer of funds within the company by US-controlled enterprises does not indicate any systematic bias in favour of assigning the greatest profit to the parent company.[38] However, conditions in ldcs are more conducive to the latter practice than to swelling the profits declared in an ldc-based subsidiary – tax and tariff structures, profit controls, balance of payments difficulties, and a political, social and economic environment which tends to be hostile to multinational operations.

The evidence on the actual importance of transfer pricing in relation to ldcs is scanty. Recorded payments for patents, licences, know-how, trade-marks, and management and technical services are a significant balance of payments outflow for certain ldcs, e.g. they were 16 per cent of Mexico's export earnings in 1968, and 8 per cent of Argentina's in 1969.[39] But such payments are not solely within firms, and there is no way of assessing the extent to which the services received were over- or undervalued; although there is a presumption that they were and are overvalued. A study of transfer pricing of merchandise goods in Colombia in 1969, however, revealed a considerable outflow of funds via the over-pricing of imports by fourteen subsidiaries in the pharmaceutical, chemical, rubber, and electrical industries. On conservative estimates, the profits transferred in this way exceeded the value of declared profits in nine of the fourteen firms, and over-pricing ranged from an average of 155 per cent for a wide range of pharmaceuticals to 25 per cent for some chemicals. In the case of pharmaceutical imports alone, the resultant government action brought a saving of $3.3 million annually on an import bill of $15 million.[40] The loss to the ldc host economies and the burden to the balance of payments as a result of such transfer payments could thus be considerable.

HOST GOVERNMENT POLICIES TO REGULATE THE PARTICIPATION OF FOREIGN FIRMS

Foreign private investment can, as noted earlier, be particularly useful in ldcs' export sectors. It can, however, be a costly way of acquiring capital, technology, skills, and know-how. Profits, royalties, and fees paid abroad can be excessive in relation to the gains derived locally from the foreign resources transferred. Frequently, developing countries have had a significant responsibility for the shortcomings associated with reliance on foreign investment. In their eagerness to attract foreign firms, and to stimulate industrial development generally, they have sometimes been indiscriminate in permitting investments, over-generous with their incentives, and lax in curbing practices which conflict with development objectives.

In recent years, developing countries have been looking at foreign involvement in their economies with an increasingly critical eye. And, despite the fundamental limitation imposed by the extent of their dependence on foreign inputs and thus the weakness of their bargaining position *vis-à-vis* foreign firms (discussed below), the majority of ldcs are attempting to increase their gains from foreign investment. Broadly speaking, the policy measures they have adopted fall into two groups. First, there are those designed to regulate the inflow of foreign investment and the framework in which it operates. And second are the more radical measures designed to attack the problems of foreign investment at source by limiting the extent of foreign ownership and control in particular ventures. Most countries employ both sorts of policies – to varying degrees – but generally it is in the countries of Asia and Latin America, which have had the greatest experience of foreign investment and are relatively advanced industrially, that have gone furthest in regulating the activities of foreign investors and restricting the extent of foreign ownership and control in their economies.

Screening Prospective Foreign Investment

If the costs of foreign investment are deemed too high, it is always open to the ldc to exclude such investment. Few ldcs take this view but most are aware of the need for discrimination in permitting the establishment of foreign firms. As a result, foreign investment proposals are subject to some form of appraisal by the majority of host ldc governments. Such appraisal by no means amounts to a cost-benefit analysis and can be extremely perfunctory but, in general, the scrutiny of new investment proposals, and other forms of foreign involvement, is increasing among ldcs, and is an important part of their control over foreign investment. In some countries, special institutions monitor foreign investments, for instance, the Foreign Investment Board in India and the Foreign Investment Commission in Mexico, and a variety of criteria, sometimes amounting to statutory requirements,[41] have to be satisfied before a foreign investment proposal is accepted. The criteria relate broadly to the sector and location of the proposed investment, and its contribution to exports, the development of local industry, the transfer of technology, and the diffusion of skills and creation of employment. The screening process can, of course, be counterproductive, leading to delays and red tape which deter potential investors. In India such deterrent effects were marked prior to the establishment of the Foreign Investment Board, which was designed in part to streamline the screening process.

Sectoral Limitations

Sectoral limitations on foreign investment are intended to serve two distinct, but not mutually exclusive, purposes: first the protection of national sovereignty, which might be endangered by foreign ownership and control in certain key sectors, such as defence and communications, and second, the exclusion of foreign investors from areas where they have little to offer that cannot be provided locally. While these considerations are implicit in any screening of foreign investment proposals, certain countries have made them explicit by drawing up guidelines as to the areas where foreign investment may or may not be accepted or by imposing statutory limitations to this end.

Thus India, for example, has lists – reviewed each year – defining the industries which are of strategic importance or are well established under local control and where, consequently, foreign investment will not be permitted. Further lists distinguish between industries where foreign investment will be permitted and those where foreign investment will be limited to technological collaboration without equity investment.[42] In Indonesia, the Foreign Investment Law prohibits foreign capital from certain fields of defence while no wholly-owned foreign subsidiaries may operate in the sphere of shipping, harbours, public utilities, atomic energy, or the mass media.[43] In Mexico, foreign firms are excluded from, or limited to a minimum 49 per cent equity participation in a number of industries including radio, television, iron and steel, cement, glass, fishing, and fertilisers.[44] And in many countries, foreign involvement in the natural resource sector is subject to restrictions.

Exceptions are made to these general rules on the industrial sectors where foreign firms may participate if the firm proposes to export all or most of its production. In Mexico, for instance, where generally foreign equity participation in a new venture is limited to 49 per cent, wholly foreign-owned investment is permitted in the export processing zone. While, in India, foreign involvement is allowed in areas where domestic entrepreneurs are deemed capable of operating without outside help if a substantial proportion of the output is for export.

These explicit restrictions on the areas open to foreign investors serve a third purpose also: they help to streamline the bureaucratic screening procedures. But like other such simplifications, for instance legal restrictions on the extent of foreign equity participation or expatriate employment,[45] they can lead to inflexibility in the host country's dealings with potential foreign investors, which can lose the country valuable investment, just as can lengthy administrative delays.

Other Aspects of Screening: the Technology Component

The main factors taken into account in screening procedures have been mentioned above. In some countries, such as Indonesia, new investors are required at this stage to make commitments on local participation in their future operations, both financially and in terms of local employment and procurement. Thus at the screening stage, provisions are made to regulate the subsequent activities of foreign investors.

An important element of the screening process in some countries relates to the conditions under which technology is transferred and used. The screening of technology transfers, which is most advanced in the more industrialised ldcs, is carried out not only for ventures with foreign equity participation, but also for various contractual arrangements between foreign firms and locally owned ventures. The aim is to ensure that the technology to be transferred is not otherwise freely available, the associated payments are not excessive, and the restrictions on its use are minimised. Screening with similar intent is also carried out with respect to licensing agreements on trade-marks.[46]

Excessive royalties and restrictive practices are more frequently found in contractual arrangements for technological transfer than when the technology transfer is between the parent firm and the wholly owned subsidiary. This by no means shows that intra-firm technology transfers are less costly or lead to fewer restrictions, rather it indicates that where the parent retains control, the terms of the transfer need not be specified.[47] Understandably, however, where ldcs have attempted to monitor technology transfers they have focused on those made under contract.[48] By requiring such contracts to be registered and making the registration subject to government approval ldcs can have some control over the costs of technology transfers.

Sometimes, as in Colombia, contracts need be registered only if they include royalty payments. Unless it is believed that the contract has offsetting advantages to the Colombian economy, royalty agreements are not approved if they contain export prohibitions (except in some cases), clauses providing for tied purchases, unreasonable price stipulations, restrictions on production of similar goods after the termination of the agreement, excessive royalties, or royalties which increase with sales. The drawback of the Colombian approach is that it encourages the use of alternative methods, such as tied inputs, to obtain royalties, so as to avoid the screening and registration processes.[49] Elsewhere, as in India and Mexico, all contracts between foreign firms and local ventures are subject to screening and registration. The grounds for rejecting contracts are similar to those cited above. As with all screening procedures, however, the extent to which ldcs can ensure a fair deal on the transfer of technology depends not only on the adequacy of their screening but also on their bargaining position (see below). If they seek to impose too many conditions on the transfer of technology, they may end up with no deal at all.

Taxation

On the whole, tax incentives remain an important element in ldc host country efforts to attract foreign investors, and in the new export processing zones there is considerable competition between governments to offer tax holidays and customs duty rebates to attract 'foot-loose' manufacturers. Although such incentives probably do work in the latter case, the general finding is that tax incentives are not significant in determining the location of a foreign firm in one country rather than another.[50] Besides other more important influences on investment location, the effect of tax incentives may be minimised or nullified by taxation on repatriated profits in the home country or reduced by the availability of alternative channels, such as transfer pricing,[51] for repatriating profits untaxed. Meanwhile, all such incentives, whether effective or not, reduce the returns of foreign investment to the host government.

Some ldcs have, however, taken steps to increase their tax revenues from foreign investors. First, some have introduced greater selectivity, linked with the screening processes, into the granting of tax concessions. Thus some are granted only to foreign investments which satisfy certain criteria; for instance, in Malaysia, firms investing in 'priority' geographical areas and industries or producing for export are eligible for a considerably wider range of tax concessions than others.

Second, the countries of the Andean Pact,[52] in particular, have taken the important step of attempting to harmonise their fiscal – and other – policies towards foreign investors, and so remove the self-defeating competition via tax incentives for foreign investment within the region. Finally, a number of ldcs have attempted to limit the scope for tax evasion by foreign firms. The legal requirements for the disclosure of company information have been increased, tax and customs authorities have been strengthened in order to monitor company accounts and intra-firm transactions, and bilateral tax treaties between host and home governments have been signed to reduce tax evasion – as well as remove the disincentive to foreign investors of double taxation. In some countries, for instance India, various intra-firm payments are either prohibited or limited by law, and some attempts are being made to control transfer pricing on intra-firm sales of goods by the introduction of the 'arm's-length' pricing principles, as for instance in Colombia.

Tariff Treatment

High levels of tariff protection to encourage both foreign and domestic investment have been a source of many deficiencies in industrial development, often wrongly attributed to foreign investors.[53] As part of their general development policy, a number of countries have now reduced the extent of such protection. Nonetheless, some, for instance Malaysia, still offer tariff protection as a *specific* incentive to potential foreign investors.

Ownership and Control

Equity Participation and Joint Ventures

The fact of foreign ownership and control is the main source of the problems associated with private foreign economic involvement in ldcs. Logically enough, many ldcs seek to deal with the problems by restricting the extent of foreign ownership of any given venture, hence – it is hoped – gaining some control over the activities of the firm, and thereby reducing conflicts between the firm and the host economy, the outflow of profits, and the vulnerability of external dependence. In the majority of ldcs provision for local equity participation – in a variety of forms – is either a precondition for foreign investment or a major factor in favour of a prospective foreign investor. In some ldcs, established wholly owned foreign subsidiaries are required to allow some local equity participation or to sell out completely to local investors. And in others, local equity participation is regarded as a staging post for complete local ownership.[54]

Local equity participation in foreign firms in ldcs takes different forms. It can amount to no more than shareholding by individual portfolio investors. More usually, however, the division of shares between foreign and local investors is part of some kind of joint venture which in principle involves more than a shared equity interest. It should be noted that local equity participation can and does occur independently of host government preferences. In countries with an established capital market, the public issue of shares is a means used by foreign firms to raise investment finance. So long as the local shareholders are scattered, the firm retains effective control. Joint ventures may be sought by foreign or local firms where their various investment resources are complementary: for instance a brewery was established in Hong Kong financed by a local business providing knowledge of local production and marketing conditions, and by a Canadian firm providing brewing know-how and a brand-name. And host government participation in a foreign venture may be welcomed as a means of raising capital and sharing and reducing risks, or may even be a precondition for the investment. On the whole, however, the growing number of joint ventures in developing countries reflects the desires of the host government rather than those of the foreign investor, who has nonetheless had to bow to necessity.

The local partners in joint ventures range between local businesses, host government corporations, and the host government itself.[55] The availability of indigenous capital and entrepreneurial skills largely determines both the extent of the involvement of the local partner and whether the local partner is a private firm or the government, either directly or through some parastatal organisation. Thus in Africa, it is the government or the development corporation which tends to act as the local partner, whereas in Asia and Latin America private local firms are predominantly so. The extent of equity sharing, required or preferred, varies according to country and to the sector for the proposed investment (see p.222 above). Although there is generally a preference for majority shareholding by the local partners – usually 51 per cent is specified – minority or equal shares are often found. However, it is of interest to note the quite different behaviour of at least one country, South Korea, where foreign investors in the export processing zone have to provide a *minimum* percentage – 50 per cent – of the equity. This does not reflect South Korea's disregard for the issue of ownership control, but rather its concern at the special 'foot-loose' character of this particular form of foreign investment. The minimum equity requirement is to ensure not only an inflow of investment finance, but also some measure of security for the investment.

Shortcomings of Joint Ventures

In encouraging or requiring foreign investment in joint ventures, ldcs are seeking to acquire a degree of ownership and control in foreign ventures. As a business form, however, the joint venture has certain drawbacks, and the experience of ldcs indicates that they tend to give ownership rather than control.

The chief drawbacks of the joint venture are that, where both partners are active, conflicts over management are more likely than in a wholly owned subsidiary, and the need for consultation between partners can reduce decisionmaking flexibility. Even where, as in Europe, joint ventures are established voluntarily, they have a fairly high casualty rate because of such factors.[56] Although most companies investing in ldcs have come to recognise some advantage in setting up joint ventures in terms of the host country's treatment, many remain wary of them. This is particularly true where the parent firm wishes to control such factors as the quality and nature of the product, the use of technology, the allocation of markets, and intra-firm prices.[57] One problem for ldcs is that insistence on local participation in foreign ventures may simply deter prospective investors, except where other factors, such as the size of the market or the presence of certain resources, weigh heavily in their favour or when the foreign investor is able to retain control or ensure returns sufficient to offset the loss of close control.

In practice, foreign firms frequently exercise considerable control over joint ventures in ldcs, even when their equity holdings provide them with only a minority of the voting rights.[58] Day-to-day management is often their responsibility, and the local partner or partners may participate only at general board meetings. And even where the local partner is more active, the need for technical know-how and expertise and continual technological change in production processes may allow the foreign investor to retain *de facto* control. Where neither the joint venture agreement nor the nature of the enterprise gives the foreign investor effective control, formal requirements on, for instance, exports and procurement, dividends and royalties, may be imposed by the foreign partner to limit the joint venture's activities: in general, joint ventures are subject to more explicit restrictions by the parent foreign firm than are wholly owned subsidiaries. Finally, there is no guarantee that a local partner, sharing in the control of the venture, will operate in the interests of the host economy rather than those of the foreign firm. As a result it has been argued that there is no basis for assuming that the joint venture will benefit the host country more than will a wholly owned foreign subsidiary – unless the fact of nominal host country control is regarded as a benefit outweighing other costs.

The joint venture consequently is not a panacea and may simply divert local capital to support essentially foreign enterprises. Nonetheless local participation in a joint venture may be not only a means of obtaining some control over foreign investment but also a training ground for local entrepreneurs, managers and technicians.[59]

Nationalisation and Divestment Plans

Few ldcs have confined their policies for local participation in foreign firms to new investments, although the majority have limited their attempts at partial or complete nationalisation of foreign firms to those operating in key sectors of the economy. A number of important considerations are raised by proposals for the nationalisation of existing firms: the cost to the host economy from compensation and its effects on the subsequent viability of the enterprise; the actual degree of control acquired by local ownership; and the impact on other foreign investors and future foreign investment flows.

On the whole, nationalisation is appropriate when foreign investment in key economic sectors is in a position seriously to harm the interests of the host economy, or when such investment leads to an outflow of funds which is excessive in relation to the contribution of that investment, as for instance when firms continue to extract royalty payments for the use of outworn technology. It has been argued that as economic development proceeds, foreign private investment is less likely to make a positive contribution to the host country. In the early stages of development, such investment usually brings about a transfer of scarce or missing resources to the host country and often performs a teaching function, raising the productivity of local resources. As the latter develop so is it more likely that foreign investment will rather displace local resources and stunt the development of local firms; hence nationalisation is likely to become more desirable.[60]

When the competitiveness of the product depends on continued access to proprietary technological improvements, as in high technology industries, or if marketing channels are controlled by a few foreign firms, complete or partial nationalisation, however desirable on grounds of reducing dependence in key areas of economic activity, is likely either to fail to secure real control or lead to commercial failure. Thus an important reason for the survival of foreign-owned bauxite extracting firms, when many other foreign mineral interests have been nationalised, is the vertical integration of the aluminium industry, combined also with the large investment in infrastructure that is needed to set up independent alumina and aluminium refineries and the wide availability of alumina bearing deposits.[61] And if local entrepreneurial, managerial and technical skills are scarce, local participation acquired through nationalisation of existing industries may, as in the case of joint ventures, fail to lead to actual local control. However this outcome is likely to be less important in respect of raw materials where it is the foreign *ownership* of national resources which is most at issue.

The level and method of compensation is important not only in relation to the host country's costs of gaining some measure of ownership and control in that foreign enterprise but also in the impact on future foreign investment – which, in general, ldcs do not seek to prohibit entirely. A dilemma exists in that compensation which leaves the nationalised foreign investor happy with both the amount and the conditions under which it is given, for instance a lump sum with no restrictions on its repatriation, and which is unlikely to deter new and existing investors, will probably be costly to the host country. Some ldcs have acted as if this dilemma did not exist, creating – for a period at least – considerable uncertainty among other foreign investors. Others, intentionally or otherwise, have been over-generous in their compensation. Many, however, now seek to reassure foreign investors by regulating the conditions under which foreign investment occurs so as to remove or minimise fears of arbitrary nationalisation with inadequate compensation. Having nationalised foreign investments in certain key sectors, certain host governments have – as noted earlier – specified the areas in, and conditions under, which new foreign investment is or is not welcomed, and thus in principle remaining foreign investments no longer face the threat of nationalisation. In Mexico the latest Foreign Investment Law, which reduced the foreign participation permissible in new investment, is specifically not retroactive in effect, providing reassurance to existing investors.

It is, however, clear from experience in ldcs that the acceptable degree of foreign ownership and control in a given enterprise changes over time, notably because of changes in government but also owing to changes in other circumstances in which the enterprise operates. The most dramatic examples of change in host government attitudes are to be found in the mineral sector. Initially ldcs may be prepared to permit foreign investment because of the uncertainties involved and the capital and expertise required in locating, exploiting, and marketing minerals. Once the foreign firm is established and making a profit the perception of the venture changes, and host government concessions made on the basis of an uncertain return often appear far too generous. Given that host government attitudes do change, the foreign investor must inevitably see himself at risk. To meet this situation *and* permit ldc governments to take over foreign firms when their usefulness has ceased, planned divestment of foreign firms has been proposed and incorporated in some countries' policies towards foreign investors. Thus, in the Andean Group of countries, new foreign investments in certain sectors are allowed subject to a provision for subsequent divestment, while in other countries initial agreements permitting foreign investment are for a limited time period only.[62]

Naturally the prospect of divestment might deter some investors if they feel that the time period prior to divestment is too short or that their interests, for instance the security of the technological know-how provided, will not be adequately protected by the proposed arrangements. Difficulties would also occur, as in the case of unplanned divestment or nationalisation, where the foreign firm was closely integrated with the parent. The main problem, however, is that any rigid approach to divestment would almost certainly stunt industrial growth for two reasons apart from its deterrent effect on some investors. First, it would use local capital which might, at times, be better employed in fresh investment. Second, it is likely to slow down the transfer of new technology, given that parent firms overseas will be less willing to transfer certain types of proprietary technology when ownership and control are passing out of their hands. For these reasons, a flexible approach is required, with divestment as an option after some suitable time period rather than a necessity. The establishment of an international divestment corporation to act as an intermediary in the divestment process, as proposed by A.D. Hirschman in relation to Latin America,[63] could lessen some of these problems. Hirschman envisaged that the corporation would act as arbitrator and guarantor of divestment agreements, thus reducing potential conflicts and tensions between host governments and foreign investors, and their deterrent effects. Meanwhile it would also assist in the financing of divestment, raising funds from government and commercial sources, so reducing the possibility that, at any one time, local capital will be diverted from more productive uses.

Foreign Involvement without Direct Investment

Hostility towards direct foreign investment has encouraged a variety of contractual arrangements to develop between ldcs and foreign firms, designed to provide ldcs with elements of the direct investment package without – necessarily – any foreign equity involvement. It should, however, be added that the kind of contractual agreements discussed below are often to be found in joint ventures as well as in locally owned ventures and do often occur without the compulsion of government restrictions on foreign investment. The majority of such agreements relate to the transfer of technology and technical and managerial know-how.[64] On the borderline between such agreements, which clearly result in the direct involvement of foreign private firms in the host economy and the indirect involvement which follows from normal international commerce, are subcontracting agreements where the foreign inputs in the production process are minimal but where foreign firms are important in the marketing of output.

Licensing Agreements

An essential element of a licensing agreement is that it gives the licensee access to proprietary technology: it may or may not involve some foreign ownership. The coverage of licensing agreements varies according to the nature of the product, whether or not brand-names are involved, and the skills possessed by the licensee. In some agreements, the licensor is responsible for the design and construction of the plant, the supply of machinery, the transfer of technical and managerial skills – with or without an obligation to carry out training – quality control, and marketing. And where brand-names are involved licensors frequently seek, at least, to maintain some control over quality and marketing, and restrictive clauses – relating to procurement, exports, and the use by the licensee of the know-how supplied – are often employed as an indirect means of ensuring quality, reducing the threat of competition to the licensor's other activities, and securing higher returns.

As a vehicle for the transfer of technology and know-how, licensing agreements can have two main types of shortcoming. First, the nature of the agreement can limit the licensor's interest in the venture's success; he will be less willing to remedy the licensee's operational problems than if it were a wholly owned subsidiary. This is less likely to occur where the licensor has some equity interest in the venture, where his royalties depend on output, or where brand-names are employed.

Second, although it is difficult to assess the value of the transfer, particularly given the use of proprietary technology, it is likely that the licensee will have to pay a higher price for the technology than would a wholly owned subsidiary. Licensing agreements frequently contain restrictive clauses which can reduce the value of the transfer considerably, as well as providing a source of 'hidden costs' as when certain purchases have to be made from the licensor. Since such restrictive clauses may be considered essential by the licensor to protect his commercial interests, they cannot always be avoided by the licensee or eliminated by host government screening procedures. Nonetheless, the scope for bargaining is indicated by the success of the Indian Government in reducing the incidence of restrictive clauses in licensing agreements and in securing provision for exports and the diffusion of know-how.

Turn-Key Agreements

Under turn-key agreements, foreign firms establish a firm as a going concern and then hand it over to a local entrepreneur. These agreements sometimes include provision for foreign equity participation and the training of local personnel. Proprietary technology is not always involved, and firms exist which will 'standardise, package and sell small, universally needed industries' to ldcs.[65]

Turn-key projects have a number of drawbacks. The most basic is that, while training in the running of the venture may be given to local personnel, the turn-key agreement provides no scope for them to gain experience in the establishment of a commercially viable enterprise. And, even if the agreement provides for the training of local operatives, they tend to receive less external support and assistance than occurs when the foreign firm has greater involvement. (The obverse of this, however, is that the locals have greater control and less, unwelcome, outside interference.) In addition, turn-key agreements sometimes result in the establishment of ventures which are inefficient because of the incompetence of the foreign suppliers, and in the inflation of costs by mark-ups on equipment supplied by the foreign contractor.[66]

Management and Technical Service Contracts

Licensing and turn-key agreements tend to cover several elements of the package otherwise supplied by direct foreign investment. A variety of other contracts exist with more limited scope. One of the most common is the management contract under which the foreign firm supplies management services, with or without training for local personnel, for a fee, which is often at least partly related to the success of the venture. While management contracts can be extremely valuable in overcoming the often severe shortages of local managerial skills, they inevitably involve foreign control of a venture – albeit for a limited period only. The supplying foreign firm, moreover, gains control without risks and with a guaranteed return. Other common forms of contract are engineering and construction agreements which provide one aspect of the turn-key agreement, and technical services agreements, under which the local firm can obtain specific sorts of technical know-how.

International Subcontracting

As noted elsewhere, foreign investment in export processing in ldcs[67] has expanded in recent years. Accompanying, and in some countries far more important than, this development has been the growth of subcontracting arrangements between foreign firms and locally owned ldc enterprises for the manufacture of both final and part-processed goods. This alternative form of global sourcing by multinational companies, usually large retail companies and buying groups, is to some extent equivalent to any normal international commercial transaction. Where it differs is in the strength of the business ties that develop between the selling, subcontracting, firm and the buying, contractor, firm, and the dominant position occupied by the latter.

Under these subcontracting arrangements, the local ldc firm is relieved of the problem of marketing its output. It simply produces to specifications, sometimes under licensed brand-names and patents, supplied by the buying firm. The latter thus performs a valuable intermediary function, given the difficulties and disadvantages ldc firms face in entering export markets and adapting their products to suit external consumers. The drawback of this kind of arrangement lies in the vulnerability of the subcontracting firm to the cessation of orders. Such information as exists suggests that a large proportion of any subcontracting ldc firm's output is produced under contract.[68] Thus, even if the product is not specific to the particular buyer – as when certain components are produced – and the local firm can eventually develop other markets (which may, however, be difficult because of the dominant position of a few large buying groups), the subcontracting firm is likely to suffer considerably if orders are not renewed. Because of the nature of the goods produced under contract, however, other ldc firms can usually compete for contracts. Consequently, the buying firm is often in a position to force down prices, thereby reducing the benefits of export orders to the firm and to the host economy. In this situation, the host country may be worse off with wholly locally owned firms operating under overseas contracts than with 'foot-loose', wholly or partly foreign-owned subsidiaries supplying their output to parent firms, or subsidiaries elsewhere: the 'foot-looseness' of these subsidiaries is at least limited by their investment stake in the host economy.

Bargaining

There is thus no easy way open to a developing country to regulate the activities of foreign firms so as to minimise the costs and maximise the benefits of their participation. Whether foreign involvement is by direct investment or by contractual agreement, the host country's ability to exercise control is constrained not only by the resources at its disposal but also by the fact that if it goes too far in shifting the balance of advantage in its favour, it may simply deter foreign firms from participating. So long as ldcs require the resources supplied by foreign firms, some compromise has to be reached between maximising the host country's returns from foreign involvement and attracting foreign firms. The compromise reached ultimately depends on the bargaining position of the host country *vis-à-vis* the foreign firm. The bargaining position of each party in turn depends not only on the alternatives open to it but also on its awareness of these alternatives and those of the other party. Since the bargaining position of ldcs varies according to the type of foreign involvement proposed, there is a premium on flexibility in the treatment of individual foreign firms, achieved via screening processes or direct government negotiation with foreign firms. Here we consider the factors which strengthen or weaken the host country's 'objective' bargaining position *vis-à-vis* foreign firms, that is, the factors which may lead the foreign firm to prefer involvement with one country rather than another, and those which strengthen or weaken the bargaining position of the foreign firms *vis-à-vis* the host country. The factors affecting the ldc host country's ability to exploit its bargaining position will also be considered.

Factors Affecting Ldcs' Attractiveness to Foreign Firms

Since the bargaining position of an ldc varies considerably according to the type of foreign involvement proposed, this section – which looks at the different factors which lead foreign firms to prefer one country rather than another – will distinguish the types of firms on which they are likely to have most bearing.

Markets. In general, the relatively small size of ldcs' internal markets makes them less attractive investment locations than developed countries. Although market size is a more important consideration for import substituting than export-orientated ventures, it is significant for the latter to the extent that the existence of a home market can provide some kind of insurance against fluctuations in external demand. But such a factor is of minor importance to firms which are largely or exclusively export-orientated, for instance those engaged in export processing or raw-material production. In so far as market size also indicates the economic development of the country concerned, one can, however, expect a general preference among foreign investors for countries with larger internal markets.

The existence of preferential terms of access to external markets and the size of those markets enhances a country's attractiveness to export-orientated firms. Here the generalised preference schemes for manufactured exports from ldcs to developed countries and the various agreements on regional co-operation among ldcs and between ldcs and developed countries involving preferential trade terms are important.[69] Similarly, the geographical proximity of large markets, or producing areas in the case of export processing industries, is an attraction. Conversely, ldcs which are more remote, for instance, the landlocked ldcs and some island-based states, will have less appeal to foreign investors.

Natural Resources. The natural resource endowment of any ldc is an obvious factor in its ability to attract certain types of foreign firms. Furthermore, in the case of non-renewable natural resources, the less widely available they are, the greater the ability of the ldc possessing them to extract favourable terms from foreign firms. And co-operation among ldcs possessing particular resources can further improve their bargaining position *vis-à-vis* foreign firms.

Cheap Labour. The availability of cheap labour in ldcs gives them a comparative advantage in the production of labour-intensive goods and is one of the most important factors leading to the location of export-orientated foreign investments in developing countries rather than developed countries.

Economic and Political Environment. The more developed a country's economic and physical infrastructure – its financial institutions, its transportation, power and communication systems, and so on – the more likely is it to attract foreign firms. At the same time, general economic and political stability is a major factor affecting the investor's assessment of risk. If the risk is high, the level of returns that will be required from an investment will be correspondingly high so as to discount that risk. Other things being equal, fewer foreign investments will take place in a high-risk than in a low-risk environment.[70]

In respect of economic stability, the foreign investor tends to be most concerned over price and balance of payments stability. When a country suffers from inflation and balance of payments problems, the future returns to foreign investment are difficult to assess because of changes in the internal purchasing power of the host country currency and of likely alterations in its external exchange value. Further, since countries with payments problems often resort to some forms of payments restriction to conserve foreign exchange, the foreign investor stands the risk of being unable to repatriate his capital or remit his profits: '. . .among the first candidates for restrictions are payments on foreign capital.'[71]

The importance of political stability to the foreign investor needs little elaboration. It should, however, be added that the interest of foreign private investors in the political stability of actual or potential host countries is related to the host government's stance on foreign investments. Foreign investors, and their home countries, tend to welcome – and indeed have sometimes fostered – destabilising political forces which promise to bring in a pro-foreign investment and usually right-wing government – as experience in Latin America and elsewhere, for instance Indonesia, in 1966, demonstrates.

Policies Towards Foreign Investors. These are a more or less flexible element in ldcs' bargaining position *vis-à-vis* individual foreign firms. In general, foreign firms prefer policies which both offer them liberal treatment and are not subject to arbitrary or frequent changes. On both counts, ldc policies towards foreign investors tend to cause more problems than those of developed countries. Among the policies which foreign investors most dislike are those restricting capital repatriation or profit remittance, imposing bureaucratic controls and making requirements on local equity participation and local procurement.[72] Foreign investors are not always deterred by such policies. Nonetheless a country which does not appeal to foreign investors clearly cannot impose too stringent requirements on foreign firms if it wishes to attract them.[73] Specific incentives tend to be less important in attracting foreign investment than the kind of factors mentioned above; the important exception being internationally mobile investors, who can afford to shop around for the best terms. It is in this latter case that the harmonisation of ldcs' policies towards foreign investors, as in the Andean Group, is an important factor in strengthening an ldc's bargaining position.

Factors Affecting the Bargaining Position of the Foreign Firm

The foreign firm's bargaining position *vis-à-vis* the host ldc depends on how much the latter wants the resources the former can supply, and how much the firm wishes to operate in the particular country. On the whole, the initial bargaining position of a foreign firm is stronger than that after it is established, since it has more to lose and the host country more to gain from expropriation.

Geographical Mobility. Depending on its field of activity, a parent firm can have a broad or narrow choice of location for its overseas investment. At one extreme, foreign firms engaged in the natural resource sector are limited to those countries which possess the relevant natural resources. Foreign firms engaged in export processing activities, on the other hand, have a wide range of initial choice and can use their geographical flexibility as a means of securing concessions from the host country. Somewhere in between are those foreign firms engaged in primarily import substituting activities. These firms may be flexible in their choice of location but may often be forced to invest in a particular country in order to preserve their market there. Once the firm is established, the costs of moving obviously increase. Nonetheless where the foreign investment stake is fairly low and the nature of the operation permits geographical mobility the foreign firm may still retain a strong bargaining position. Where *capital costs* are high, however, the bargaining position of the foreign firm is likely to be more limited even if, in principle, it could operate elsewhere.

Monopolistic Control. Their ownership of proprietary technology and unpatented know-how or their control over marketing channels allows some foreign firms to dominate production in certain fields. The virtual absence of alternatives – or rather their high cost – weakens the bargaining position of ldcs wishing to start domestic production in such fields. And even when foreign firms do not have such monopolistic control, a developing country's alternatives are limited by its lack of domestic capital and entrepreneurial, organisational, and technical skills.

Size. The size of the parent foreign firm can be important to its bargaining position in several respects. First, the larger the firm, the less likely is any one subsidiary or licensing venture to be crucial in its corporate strategy and the more easily can the firm withstand either the failure to reach agreement on a production outlet in a particular country or the expropriation of such an outlet. Second, given its greater resources and the global nature of its activities, a large firm will probably be better able to assess its alternatives and those of its prospective host than a small firm or, indeed, than many developing countries. Meanwhile large firms are more able to put indirect pressure on recalcitrant host countries through their influence on their home governments and international financial institutions. The events following the Allende government's nationalisation of the US copper firms in Chile provide an example of such indirect pressures (which contributed substantially to Allende's eventual downfall in 1973). When Chile nationalised the copper mines in 1971, compensation was refused on the grounds that the, mainly US-owned, companies' excess profits over the years far outweighed the value of their assets. The companies protested and were supported by the US Government. As a result of various pressures brought to bear by the companies and the US Government, credit flows to Chile, including aid from the World Bank, US export credits, and international bank credit, were severely curtailed. This, combined with other factors – including a fall in the price of copper – exacerbated Chile's external payments problems. And in 1972, these problems forced Chile to renegotiate its external debt, half of which was held by the USA. The US Government introduced the issue of compensation into the negotiations and eventually Chile undertook – as part of the debt rescheduling deal – to give 'adequate compensation' to the copper companies.[74]

External and Internal Support

The Chilean example may be extreme but, nonetheless, foreign firms do derive some bargaining strength from the fact that home governments and international financial institutions tend to impose sanctions on developing countries that treat foreign firms too harshly. Meanwhile they receive internal support from an identity, or complementarity, of interest with certain sections of the elite in developing countries – for instance, bankers, traders, and suppliers.[75] And the presence of corrupt, or corruptible, bureaucracies and politicians in many ldcs strengthens – at a price – the ability of foreign firms to prevent the imposition, or reduce the impact, of host government measures which might harm their interests.

The so-called Banana War of 1974 is an example of how foreign firms can draw on internal support to secure their interests. It also, however, provides some corrective to the notion that ldcs – or at least non-oil producing ldcs – are in a state of powerless dependence in their dealings with large multinational companies. The protagonists were, on the one side, seven major banana producing countries in Central and South America, which together formed a Banana Exporters union (known as the UPEB) jointly to impose an export tax on banana exports. On the other side were two large US-based multinationals (United Brands and Standard Fruit) involved in the production and marketing of the bananas in these countries. The companies responded to the tax proposal with a divide-and-rule policy, accompanied by threats of cutting back or stopping banana production completely should the tax be imposed. They were helped in this by the collusion of an influential section of the élite in Ecuador, which was involved in marketing the bananas produced by local peasants to one of the companies. No tax was imposed in that country and the company was able to use the threat of purchasing more bananas from Ecuador to weaken the resolve of other UPEB countries. In several countries, the companies actually did cut back production, and in Honduras one is alleged to have used bribery to secure a reduction in the tax.[76]

In the end, three countries imposed no tax at all. But the companies did not have an outright victory: the other countries bar one imposed a reduced tax and in Panama full tax was imposed (although it was later reduced to be more in line with the other taxes). Panama's success was won with backing – paradoxically – from the US Government which feared that its negotiations on the Panama Canal might be jeopardised and put pressure on the company to settle. The company did so, agreeing not only to pay the tax but also to sell out to Panama by the end of 1977. This was the more important outcome, since the confrontation had demonstrated the difficulty of extracting concessions from the companies while they were in virtually sole control of the production and marketing of an economically important product. In the long run, the recognition of those difficulties is likely to have been the most important result of the confrontation for the banana producing countries. Panama and some of the other banana producing countries, for instance, have plans to set up their own marketing organisation so as to have an alternative outlet for their banana production.[77]

The Bargaining Situation

A country may rely on a set of policies on the participation of foreign firms in its economy without leaving scope for government bargaining with particular firms. More frequently, however, a country's policies towards foreign firms are a framework within which bargaining can take place. The eventual bargain struck in this situation depends not only on the kind of factors noted above, but on the awareness of each party of its respective bargaining strengths and negotiating skills.

At this level the foreign firm is likely to be at an advantage – particularly in the case of the larger firms with world-wide interests dealing with small poor countries with little experience of dealing with foreign investors. It is frequently remarked that developing countries do not possess the resources to find out about, still less to evaluate, the costs and benefits of an investment agreement or a contract with a foreign firm as compared with alternative courses of action, and that even if they are aware of the strength of their bargaining position, their lack of experience in negotiation may prevent them exploiting it fully. The foreign firm, on the other hand, can frequently conceal the real nature of the deal it is offering, and use its often superior negotiating skills to make the most of its position.

It is important, however, to recognise that developing countries are continually adding to their bargaining experience and negotiating ability: it would be wrong to present a picture of ldcs at the mercy of the foreign firms' superior skills and wiles. Moreover, ldcs can increasingly draw on external support in their dealings with foreign firms. This may come from other ldcs as in the case of the banana producing countries. It may also come from developed countries in the form of technical assistance. Individual ldcs have used foreign expertise to assist them in bargaining situations and so counter a lack of information and skills. Meanwhile, ldcs can now draw on an increasing stock of knowledge, relating to sources of technology and to the activities of foreign firms which can limit the benefits and conceal the real costs of their operations to the host country. Various UN bodies have played an important role in it's accumulation and diffusion.[78]

Finally, it must be remembered that bargains struck between foreign firms and ldcs are not immutable. Once an agreement is reached with the foreign firm, ldcs can re-assess the deal and if necessary re-negotiate it. The ldc will then be in a stronger position not only because it will have access to more information on the implications of the deal, but also because the foreign firm can less easily withdraw once it has committed its resources. The extent to which the country can improve the terms of any agreement will, of course, in part depend on the impact of re-negotiations on prospective and existing investors and on their external supporters.

Notes

1. US Tariff Commission, *Implications of Multinational Firms for World Trade and Investment and for US Trade and Labor* (Washington D.C., 1973), pp.8-9.
2. J.H. Dunning, 'The Multinational Enterprise: The Background', in J.H. Dunning (ed.), *The Multinational Enterprise* (London, George Allen & Unwin, 1971), p.32; and UN-ECOSOC, *Report of the Group of Eminent Persons to Study the Role of Multinational Corporations on Development and on International Relations,* E/5000/Add.1 (Part 1), May 1974, p.73, respectively.
3. For instance in Laos, foreign investment is predominantly carried out by investors from neighbouring countries, as is a significant portion of foreign investment in Malaysia. See Asian Development Bank, *South East Asia's Economy in the 1970s* (London, Longman, 1971), Part V.
4. UN, *Multinational Corporations in World Development,* ST/ECA/190, 1973, p.172.
5. OECD, *Development Co-operation: 1973 DAC Review* (Paris, 1973), p.72.
6. See UN, ST/ECA/190, p.175.
7. See Table 6.5.
8. See below pp.213ff.
9. See Charles Sebestyen, *The Outward Urge: Japanese Investment World-Wide* (London, EIU, 1972).
10. See below, pp.225ff.
11. In a sample survey of some eighty foreign private firms in ldcs, mainly operating in the manufacturing sector, it was found that nearly half of the twenty-four export-orientated firms were wholly foreign-owned and in 88 per cent of these firms 50 per cent or more of the equity was foreign-owned, whereas for the sample as a whole the respective figures were 25 per cent and 80 per cent. See Grant L. Reuber, *Private Foreign Investment in Development* (London, Oxford University Press, 1973), p.83.
12. See R. Vernon, *Sovereignty at Bay* (Harmondsworth, Penguin, 1973), p.102ff, and below, p.214 and footnote 23.
13. Estimate for 1970, which, though small, is undoubtedly higher than the equivalent estimate for developed countries. See Reuber, p.4, and above p.204.
14. In 1966, H. Hughes and Yon Poh Seng (eds.), *Foreign Investment and Industrialisation in Singapore* (Australian National University Press, 1969), p.192, quoted in UN, ST/ECA/190, p.20.
15. In 1970 S. Watanabe, 'International Sub-contracting, Employment and Skill Promotion', *International Labour Review,* vol.105, May 1972, p.426.
16. In 1966, R. Vernon, p.107.
17. UN, ST/ECA/190, p.21. A lower figure of 34 per cent for Brazil in 1967 is given by J. Winpenny, *Brazil: Manufactured Exports and Government Policy* (Latin American Publications Fund, 1972), p.39.
18. A. Hone, 'Multinational Corporations and Multinational Buying Groups', paper for Society for International Development European Regional Conference (Oxford, 1973), pp.6-7.

19. Ibid., p.9.
20. Ibid., p.10.
21. Watanabe, p.433.
22. But see, for example, Reuber; articles by P. Streeten and G.H. Meier in J.H. Dunning (ed.), *International Investment* (Harmondsworth, Penguin, 1972); and O. Sunkel, 'Transnational Capitalism and National Disintegration in Latin America', *Social and Economic Studies*, vol.22, no.1, March 1973, and Chapter 1.
23. Between 1957 and 1966, US manufacturing subsidiaries in Latin America expanded their exports by 705 per cent so that in 1966, they accounted for 9.5 per cent of gross manufacturing output but 41.4 per cent of manufacturing exports. Over the same period, local manufacturing firms expanded their exports by 51 per cent. See Jose de la Torre, 'Foreign Investment and Export Dependency', *Economic Development and Cultural Change*, vol.23, no.1, October 1974, p.138.
24. See UN, ST/ECA/190, p.195. In smaller samples relating to Bolivia and Peru 90 per cent and 96 per cent of foreign investment agreements included restrictions or bans on export sales.
25. See below, pp.218-20.
26. Reuber, p.88, found that export-orientated foreign firms financed 70 per cent of their investment from external resources whereas firms producing for the local market used external finance for only 53 per cent of their investment costs.
27. See J. Baranson, *Industrial Technologies for Developing Countries* (New York, Praeger, 1969), and contributions, in particular that by K. Marsden, in Richard Jolly *et al.* (eds.), *Third World Employment* (Harmondsworth, Penguin, 1973), for a useful discussion of the various factors affecting the appropriateness of technology transfer to ldcs.
28. The survey reported in Reuber, found that only 34 per cent of export-orientated firms' cash outlay occurred locally as compared with a figure of around 70 per cent for other firms.
29. It should be observed that the foreign firm is often put in a 'can't win' situation by its critics: if it restricts technology diffusion, it is criticised for limiting the local benefits of the technology transfer; if the technology is spread, however, the firm is said to be spreading inappropriate technology and/or inhibiting local technological research and development.
30. See, for instance, Reuber, pp.201-2, who notes that such a policy keeps down the wages bill, locals being cheaper than expatriates, while at the same time it helps to meet ldc aspirations.
31. Ibid., p.172.
32. See E. Penrose, 'The State and the Multinational Producing Enterprise in Ldcs', in Dunning, *The Multinational Enterprise*, pp.221-39.
33. See below, pp.234-40.
34. This and the remainder of the section draws heavily on S. Lall, 'Transfer Pricing by Multinational Manufacturing Firms', *Oxford Bulletin of Economics and Statistics*, vol.35, no.3, August 1973, pp.173-91.
35. A high proportion of trade by firms in these industries is within the firm. See D. Robertson, 'Foreign Investment, Trade and the Balance of Payments', in Dunning, *International Investment*, p.347.
36. There is a presumption that in the manufacturing sector in ldcs, transfer pricing is a phenomenon mainly to be found among foreign firms producing for the local market, and not those producing for export. The growth of part processing in ldcs suggests that it could also occur in foreign firms producing for export. Evidence that it does occur is to be found in Reuber, p.104 and

passim.
37. Lall, p.175.
38. Vernon, p.139.
39. UN, ST/ECA/190, p.190.
40. Lall, p.186.
41. Embodied in various Foreign Investment Laws. See Asian Development Bank, pp.370-420 for an account of the various laws operating in the countries of South East Asia.
42. This policy was introduced in 1968. For more details see UNCTAD, *Restrictive Business Practices,* TD/B/C.2/104/Rev.1 (New York, 1971), p.29.
43. Asian Development Bank, p.436.
44. Under the 1973 Foreign Investment Law. *The Times,* 'Special Report on Mexico', 19 February, 1975, p.3.
45. In Mexico, for instance, foreign participation at management level can at most be only proportionate to the foreign equity holding. Ibid.
46. Some restrictions, however, derive from national patent and trade-mark laws and cannot be avoided, see UNCTAD, TD/B/C.2/104/Rev.1, pp.32-3.
47. See Vernon, pp.140-4, for a discussion of this point.
48. Although India, for instance, prohibits the payment of royalties by wholly owned subsidiaries.
49. UNCTAD, TD/B/C.2/104 Rev.1, pp.28-9.
50. See, for instance, Reuber, pp.115-9.
51. See above, pp.218-24.
52. Bolivia, Venezuela, Chile, Colombia, Ecuador, and Peru.
53. See Chapter 5.
54. This is particularly so in certain Latin American countries.
55. For a discussion of the different types of joint ventures see J. Tomlinson, *The Joint Venture Process in International Business* (Cambridge, MIT Press, 1970); and for a wide range of case studies as well, see S.G. Friedmann and J.P. Béguin, *Joint International Business Ventures in Developing Countries* (New York, Columbia University Press, 1971).
56. See M.Z. Brooke and H. Lee Remmers, *The MNC in Europe* (London, Longman, 1972), p.67.
57. Vernon, p.140.
58. See Friedmann and Béguin, especially Chapters 1 and 19.
59. C.V. Vaitsos has put forward the proposition that the higher costs that may be associated with joint ventures can, at times, be justified by their contribution to the development of local skills and institutions, e.g. the development of entrepreneurs, capital markets and so on. See Institute of Development Studies, Sussex, *Policies on Foreign Direct Investments and Economic Development in Latin America,* Communication 106, p.19.
60. See A.O. Hirschman, *How to Divest in Latin America and Why,* Essays in International Finance, no.76, November 1969, Princeton.
61. Guyana was able to nationalise its bauxite mines in 1971 because it has resources of calcined bauxite, which is rarer than metal-grade bauxite and does not require expensive processing.
62. Provided that the time period is adequate from the foreign investor's viewpoint, as is usually the case, time period limitations serve also to reassure prospective investors.
63. Hirschman, p.12ff.
64. For a more detailed discussion of these contractual arrangements, see UNCTAD, *The Channels and Mechanisms for the Transfer of Technology from Developed to Developing Countries,* TD/B/AC.11/5, 1971, and UNCTAD, TD/B/C.2/104/Rev.1.

65. See Baranson, p.49.
66. UNCTAD, TD/B/AC.11/5, p.39.
67. See Chapter 5.
68. Information on these subcontracting arrangements is extremely limited but see Hone, and Watanabe.
69. See Chapters 5 and 8.
70. Some multinational firms have elaborate systems for assessing the risk premium for investments in different countries. See C. Tugendhat *The Multinationals* (Harmondsworth, Penguin Books, 1973), Chapter 12 *passim.*
71. Graeme Dorrance, 'Rapid Inflation and International Payments', *Finance and Development,* vol.2, no.2, 1965, p.69.
72. See Sebestyen, p.42.
73. The converse is also true as Vaitsos illustrates: '. . .in the 1960s Bolivia, due to its small market, attracted very few foreign manufacturing investors despite the very generous terms which were offered', while 'Mexico with much more stringent, although sometimes contradictory policies on foreign investment was one of the principal recipients of foreign factor inflows' (p.12).
74. See C. Payer, *The Debt Trap* (Harmondsworth, Penguin Books, 1974), pp.191-8.
75. See Vernon, pp.190-7.
76. See 'Slipping up on a $1.25 million Banana Skin' in *The Sunday Times,* 13 April 1975.
77. See *The Sunday Times Magazine,* 24 August 1975, p.35.
78. See Chapter 2.

7 FINANCE AND INTERNATIONAL TRADE

So far, the focus has been on developing countries' external trade, and specifically their exports. Here we look at those exports in the context of ldcs' other transactions with the rest of the world and in relation to their problems in financing trade and development. Ldcs typically import more than they export, financing their import surplus by grants or capital flows from abroad. Over time, this practice has allowed ldcs to enjoy higher levels of income and probably income growth than would otherwise have been possible. However, for a variety of reasons, ldcs have frequently experienced payments difficulties manifested in a shortage of foreign exchange. Such difficulties can, in principle, be removed or avoided by two sorts of measures which are not necessarily exclusive: first, borrowing, or begging, additional foreign exchange from abroad; second, adjusting external payments and receipts – other than financial inflows – so as to restore balance of payments equilibrium. The latter measures may cause or be accompanied by a desirable redirection of the domestic development effort, resulting in a less import-reliant, less capital-intensive, and more egalitarian mode of development. In general, however, developing countries try to avoid adjustment measures – whatever potentially desirable opportunities they may offer – since they almost certainly entail a cut-back in domestic spending, and often a curb on their current development effort. Ldcs' ability to avoid payments adjustment is, however, limited by the financing facilities open to them.

This chapter is divided into three parts. The first describes the various transactions which make up the balance of payments and relates this description to ldcs, focusing on the particular payments problems of oil importing ldcs, and considering the main factors which make ldcs more vulnerable to payments problems than developed countries. The second part looks at the various balance of payments adjustment measures open to developing countries and considers their drawbacks and advantages. The final part examines the main forms of external finance, proposed or currently available to ldcs, as means of assisting their development and easing or avoiding the process of adjustment.

LDCS' BALANCE OF PAYMENTS

A variety of transactions are made across national boundaries, involving payments and receipts between individuals and institutions in one country and those in other countries. Thus, for instance, goods and services are bought from and sold to other countries; investments, loans, and grants are made to and by governments in different countries, and so on. The payments associated with these various transactions are generally made in the form of an internationally acceptable currency, i.e. foreign exchange, although under barter arrangements, such as are negotiated by Communist bloc countries with their trading partners, payments may be made in kind or in a currency not normally accepted in settlement of international payments.[1]

The payments and receipts arising from an individual country's transactions with the rest of the world are recorded in that country's balance of payments account (except, of course, when such transactions are concealed from the responsible authorities, for instance when smuggling occurs). When payments from all transactions exceed receipts, the account is said to be in deficit, and when receipts exceed payments it is said to be in surplus. The balance of payments account is customarily divided into two main parts, the current and the capital, and relates to a specific period, usually a year, and sometimes a month or three months.

The Current Account

The current account includes all transactions which are completed during the specified period and which will not give rise to further payments or receipts. These transactions are generally classified into three broad groups:

(1) Exports and imports of goods (or merchandise) and 'non-factor service' (or invisibles): the receipts for exports and the payments for imports mirror movements of real resources from and to the country concerned. In the absence of barter arrangements whereby a country matches its exports to another country with its imports from that country, exports to and imports from a particular country do not necessarily have to be balanced and generally are not. 'Non-factor services' – otherwise known as invisibles – include such items as transport, shipping, insurance, tourism, and consultancy services but exclude service or 'factor' payments and receipts on past capital inflows or outflows (see below). As can be seen from Table 7.1, developing

countries as a group have a deficit on their merchandise and invisible trade. This is to be contrasted with the surplus of the developed countries as a group up to the oil crisis in 1974 (see Table 7.2). Ldcs' deficit on goods and services is closely related to their development efforts – as is discussed below. The deficit on invisible trade – which characterises virtually all ldcs' external payments – is also closely related to ldcs' underdevelopment, and hence to their heavy reliance on developed country institutions for services. This is especially marked in respect of freight and insurance, which often constitutes a large debit item in individual ldc's balance of payments. Some ldcs, notably the oil exporting countries, do present a different picture, however, with a surplus on goods and services combined, while certain others – especially during the 1972-3 commodity boom – have managed a surplus on merchandise trade, for instance Zambia and Ghana.

(2) Factor or service payments: these are generally a separate item, or a sub-category of 'goods and services'. They consist of interest, dividends, and profit payments and receipts arising from past external capital investments or loans to and from the country concerned. Sometimes the remittances of migrant workers are also included under this head (otherwise they are usually classified as transfer payments – see below). Although migrant workers' remittances, especially in certain African countries – for instance, Malawi – can make a large positive contribution, net factor services are a negative item in most developing countries' payments accounts. This reflects the fact that, in their pursuit of economic development, ldcs have been – and still are – net importers of foreign capital.[2]

(3) Transfer payments: these are, in effect, gifts in cash or kind made to and from the country concerned. Except that they do not involve further payments and receipts, they are more akin to capital account transactions than those in the current account. They are usually divided into private and government transfers, the latter including bilateral and multilateral development grants, and the former sometimes including migrant workers' remittances. For most developing countries, with the notable exception of the oil exporting countries, the transfer payments item is in surplus (see Table 7.1), mainly as a result of development grants.

Even with these receipts of transfer payments, most ldcs, and non-oil producing ldcs as a group, tend to run current account deficits. The commodity boom of 1972-3 helped to reduce the deficits of many

Table 7.1. Balance of Payments between Oil and Non-Oil Exporting Ldcs and DAC Countries, 1968-70, Annual Average ($ billion)

Balance of payments items	Non-oil exporting ldcs[4]	Major oil exporting ldcs[5]	All lacs
(1) Balance of exports and imports of goods and non-factor services[1]	–8.9	5.2	–3.7
(2) Net investment income[2]	–1.8	–3.8	–5.6
(3) Balance of goods and services (1) + (2)	–10.7	1.5	–9.2
(4) Net transfers	5.6	–0.3	5.3
(5) Current account balance	–5.1	1.2	–3.9
(6) Official long-term capital net flows	4.4	0.1	4.5
(7) Private long-term capital net flows	3.4	0.8	4.2
(8) Long-term capital account balance (6) + (7)	7.7	0.9	8.6
(9) Basic balance (5) + (8)	2.7	2.0	4.7
(10) Short-term capital flows + errors and omissions	–1.2	–1.5	–2.7
(11) Balance on official settlements[3]	+1.5	+0.5	+2.0

1 Non-factor services exclude payments of interest, profits and dividends, i.e. service payments on capital.
2 That is, service payments on capital inflows.
3 If positive, this item signifies an increase in ldcs' reserves as a result of transactions with DAC countries, if negative a decline.
4 These figures obtained by subtracting the second column from the third.
5 Kuwait, Venezuela, Trinidad and Tobago, Libya, Saudi Arabia, Iran, Iraq, Netherlands Antilles, Brunei.

Source: OECD, ***Development Co-operation: 1972 DAC Review*** (Paris 1972), Annex 1, Table 4, p.199.

non-oil producing ldcs – as can be seen from Table 7.2 – but the oil crisis has reversed this situation. Meanwhile, developed countries as a group, until 1974, and oil producing ldcs run surpluses on their current accounts.

The Capital Account

The capital account is a record of changes in a country's assets in, and liabilities to, the rest of the world. An increase in liabilities occurs with

Table 7.2. Balance of Payments between Developed Market Economy Countries and Less Developed Market Economy Countries, 1971-4 ($ billion)

Countries		Trade	Balance on Services & private transfers	Current account[1]	Capital account[2]	Overall balance
Developed countries	1971	7.5	3.9	11.4	–7.6	3.9
	1972	8.3	3.7	12.0	–4.8	7.2
	1973	6.0	5.5	11.5	–9.5	2.1
	1974	–28.5	5.0	–23.5	2.8	–20.8
– industrial	1971	13.1	0.7	13.8	–13.9	–0.1
	1972	11.2	–0.9	10.3	–11.0	–0.7
	1973	11.0	–0.8	10.2	–10.6	–0.3
	1974	–10.0	–1.6	–11.5	–4.5	–16.1
– primary producing	1971	–5.6	3.2	–2.4	6.3	4.0
	1972	–2.9	4.6	1.7	6.2	7.9
	1973	–5.0	6.3	1.3	1.1	2.4
	1974	–18.5	6.6	–12.0	7.3	–4.7
Oil exporting ldcs	1971	10.6	–8.4	2.2	1.1	3.3
	1972	13.0	–10.4	-2.6	1.3	3.9
	1973	21.6	–16.0	5.6	–1.3	4.3
	1974	83.4	–13.4	70.0	–33.6	36.8
Non-oil exporting ldcs	1971	–8.4	–2.9	–11.2	12.7	1.4
	1972	–6.7	–2.4	–9.1	15.5	6.4
	1973	–6.3	–2.6	–8.9	17.3	8.4
	1974	–22.3	–5.5	–27.8	29.0	1.2
– in Africa	1971	–0.4	–1.3	–1.7	1.4	–0.2
	1972	0.1	–1.6	–1.5	1.7	0.2
	1973	0.9	–1.9	–1.1	1.5	0.4
	1974	0.5	–2.4	–1.9	2.1	0.1
– in Asia	1971	–4.1	0.3	–3.8	4.7	1.0
	1972	–3.3	0.8	–2.5	4.8	2.3
	1973	–2.5	0.9	–1.6	4.1	2.5
	1974	–9.6	0.9	–8.7	10.0	1.3
– in Middle East	1971	–1.8	0.6	–1.2	1.8	0.5
	1972	–2.3	1.7	–0.6	1.4	0.7
	1973	–4.1	2.1	–2.0	3.1	1.1
	1974	–5.9	1.5	–4.4	4.6	0.3
– in Western Hemisphere	1971	–2.0	–2.5	–4.5	4.7	0.2
	1972	–1.2	–3.2	–4.4	7.6	3.1
	1973	–0.5	–3.8	–4.3	8.7	4.4
	1974	–7.3	–5.5	–12.8	12.3	–0.5

1 Excludes government transfers.

2 Difference between the overall balance and the current account balance. It includes net errors and omissions, plus reported capital movements, government transfers and, for 1971 and 1972, allocations of SDRs.

Sources: for 1971, IMF, Annual Report 1974; for 1972-4, IMF, Annual Report 1975.

an inflow of external capital via foreign investment or borrowing by government, private firms, and other institutions and individuals; a decrease occurs as external loans are repaid or investment capital is repatriated. An increase in a country's assets occurs when there is an outflow of capital in the form of loans or investment finance, and a decrease when its loans are repaid or investments repatriated. Changes in a country's external assets and liabilities directly affect future factor receipts and payments on the current account. They do not, however, directly bring about real resource movements between countries, i.e. exports and imports, although the latter may be associated with capital movements (for instance, when the foreign investor imports capital equipment to set up his venture), and some capital movements, e.g. commercial export credits, are specifically intended to finance current account transactions.

The capital account is generally divided into two parts:

(1) The long-term capital account, which records foreign private investment flows and long-term public or private sector loans. In most developing countries, this part of the capital account is in surplus – although the relative importance of private and public flows and of equity and loan finance varies between countries. Together with the current account, the long-term capital account makes up what is known as the *basic balance* of payments. In ldcs the surplus on the long-term capital account effectively finances part – or all – of the deficit on current account.

(2) The short-term capital account, which is mainly a record of transactions undertaken by the banking sector to compensate for any surplus or deficit in the basic balance.

Foreign exchange payments and receipts, which cannot be allocated to any of the items in either the capital or the current account are included in a catch-all item called *'errors and omissions'*. This can be positive or negative and quite large: it is thought that a substantial portion of the payments under this head in ldcs' accounts are, in fact, private capital outflows, such as those finding their way to numbered Swiss bank accounts.

As stated above, if the basic balance shows a deficit or a surplus, then – after allowing for 'errors and omissions' – there will be offsetting movements in the short-term capital account. If these movements do not fully compensate for the payments surplus or deficit on all other items, then the country has to add to, or draw on, its foreign exchange reserves to balance the account. Reserves will then increase or decrease accordingly.

In any one period, most countries are likely to have imbalances in both the long-term capital account and the current account which, if they are not offsetting, will lead to accommodating capital flows or changes in the country's foreign exchange reserves. Over time, however, a country which persistently runs an overall deficit on both of these accounts or on the current account alone is likely to run into balance of payments difficulties, that is, have insufficient foreign exchange to meet external payments, as the level of its external liabilities and associated debt service payments rises. Although the pressures for subsequent adjustment so as to restore a payments balance are greater on the deficit or debtor country than on the surplus or creditor country,[3] the latter also needs to restore balance unless it wishes to allow an outflow of real resources and to export capital or accumulate reserves indefinitely.

Most countries have at some time been in balance of payments difficulties, or have had a chronic surplus in their dealings with the rest of the world, and have had to take measures to adjust their payments position. Ldcs, are, however, remarkable in that as a group – with certain notable exceptions such as the oil exporting countries – they have, since the Second World War, generally moved into a situation of chronic current account deficits and surpluses on capital account, and have suffered more frequently than developed countries from foreign exchange shortages and payments difficulties.

IMPORT SURPLUSES AND DEVELOPMENT

Ldcs' development efforts are important in explaining the prevalence of chronic current account deficits – or, more accurately, chronic deficits in respect of goods and services and factor payments. The rate at which a country can develop economically depends on how fast it can increase its productive capacity and hence its national income (and, also, on the distribution of income, which is an important determinant of the actual gain in material welfare achieved by an increase in national income). The rate at which productive capacity can be increased depends on the opportunities for productive investment[4] and the availability of resources to carry out that investment. Unless a country can obtain resources from abroad, in excess of what it can purchase out of its export earnings, what it can spend on investment is limited to the income it can set aside from consumption, i.e. domestic savings. The poverty of peoples in developing countries sets a limit on the income that can be set aside from consumption needs. And, in general, it is held that the opportunities – and, given the poverty in ldcs, the need – for productive investment in ldcs exceeds the savings available domestically. Therefore, if these opportunities are to be realised and if development is not to be held back for want of domestic savings, the country must use external resources to bridge the gap between desired investment and domestic savings.

Where a country uses external resources to overcome a savings deficiency, the inevitable result is an import surplus, i.e. not enough of export earnings to cover import spending. A reduction in investment or an increase in savings would, other things being equal, reduce the import surplus. In some ldcs, particularly the poorer African countries, the lack of savings is probably the prime reason for their need for, and use of, grants and capital inflows to finance their development spending. In some other ldcs, for instance India, however, it is argued that, while eventually the lack of domestic savings may limit exploitation of their investment opportunities without external resource inflows, the lack of foreign exchange is a more important constraint. In their case, although domestic savings could be increased to finance a certain level of investment, their export earnings cannot rise sufficiently to finance the imports which are needed to carry out the investment, since they cannot be produced locally. In other words, these countries need external resources and an import surplus to carry out their investment programme because they cannot transform domestic savings into investment resources.

Thus for lack of savings or foreign exchange, developing countries often need to run an import surplus, financed by grants and long-term capital inflows, to achieve their development potential. And although developing countries' current account deficits are not the result of their development efforts only, the latter are a basic reason for their payments position.

So long as capital inflows, grants, and export earnings are sufficient to finance import requirements and the debt servicing obligations arising from past capital inflows, an import surplus need not cause payments difficulties. But if the balance between these receipts and payments is upset, leading to a deficit, there are likely to be adverse repercussions on the country's development efforts unless it can avoid cutting back imports by borrowing more or by drawing on its reserves. It is because of the close connection between imports and development, as well as the structure of imports, that ldc governments tend to be unwilling to solve or avert payments problems by reducing import demand. The structure of imports contributes to this unwillingness because in most developing countries only a small proportion of imports is inessential either to investment spending or to current production. Besides investment goods, intermediate goods and raw material inputs, including food, make up the bulk of ldcs' imports. Consumption goods, other than food, have a relatively small share of most ldcs' imports as compared with developed countries' imports.

REASONS FOR PAYMENTS PROBLEMS AMONG LDCS

A country has a payments problem when its external payments exceed receipts, or vice versa, and it is unable to meet payments from its reserves, or unwilling to add to its reserves. The former problem – a shortage of foreign exchange – is most common among ldcs, although certain oil producing ldcs now have chronic foreign exchange surpluses. Balance of payments problems may be short-lived, for instance when there is a temporary drop in export earnings, or of a more persistent nature. As will be discussed later, the appropriate solution varies according to the nature of the problem. In this section we look briefly at the main factors, often interrelated, which tend to render ldcs – or more specifically oil importing ldcs – more vulnerable to payments difficulties. Events in recent years – the oil price rise, and the combination of global inflation and economic recession – have greatly increased the vulnerability of many oil importing ldcs and worsened their development prospects. The short-lived boom in the prices of commodities in 1972-3 ameliorated the situation of some ldcs but worsened it for others, the net importers of commodities, such as India and Bangladesh. With the oil price rise, the majority of oil importing ldcs face payments problems of an unprecedented magnitude. (Except in the case of ldcs' indebtedness problem – which is discussed below – fuller discussions of the points raised in this section appear in other parts of the book.)

Inadequacy of Reserves[5]

Foreign exchange reserves provide a cushion against drastic adjustment measures in response to temporary or longer-term payments deficits. Ldcs are more prone to such deficits than developed countries, while at the same time they have greater difficulty in obtaining suitable external finance.[6] As a group, their reserves have in general been at a lower level compared to their external transactions than is the case in developed countries. This fact, in turn, reduces ldcs' ability to cope with adverse movements in their external receipts or payments. Obviously not all ldcs hold inadequate reserves – and certainly not all the time; in 1973, for instance the reserves of most ldcs exceeded, in relative terms, those of developed countries, while the oil exporting ldcs and Latin American and Middle Eastern ldcs have, as groups, maintained relatively high levels of reserves in recent years. Asian and African countries, on the other hand, have had relatively low levels (see Table 7.8).

Rigidity in Current Account Transactions

The greater the ease with which a country can adjust its external transactions to restore payments balance, the less likely is a disequilibriating movement, such as a rise in import prices, or a surge in import demand, to cause payments problems. A comparison of the impact of the rise in import prices and the drop in global export demand in recent years on the current account balances of developed and oil importing developing countries reveals both the greater difficulties and vulnerability of ldcs in the face of disequilibriating movements. While developed countries' aggregate current account (excluding government transfers) deteriorated from a surplus of $11.5 billion in 1973 to a deficit of $23.5 billion in 1974, this deterioration has been halted and their projected deficit for 1975 was down to $11 billion. In the case of the oil importing developing countries, on the other hand, the current account deficit has risen from $8.9 billion in 1973 to $27.8 billion in 1974, and was expected to increase to $35 billion in 1975.[7]

There are three main factors which inhibit ldcs' ability to adjust their current account payments and receipts. The first relates to imports of goods and services. As noted above, ldcs' imports are closely related to their current production needs and development efforts. In the longer term, their pattern of development – and income levels – may be less reliant on imports. But for the present, ldc governments are unwilling to curb import demand in order to avert or solve payments problems. Secondly, a large payments item for most ldcs – factor income payments – is a fixed obligation, resulting from past capital receipts. It can be reduced only by reneging on contractual debt servicing and/or freezing investment income payments or via debt rescheduling on a bilateral basis.[8] In general, any cut-backs in factor payments are likely to have adverse repercussions on future external capital inflows and, in the long term, on economic development.[9] Finally, ldcs' prospects for increasing their export earnings are hampered by the sluggish demand for their major export products (and also by supply side problems).[10]

Fluctuations in Payments and Receipts

Besides factors which increase ldcs' adjustment problems, others make ldcs more prone to payments disequilibria. The payments position of those ldcs – the majority – which have primarily agricultural economies is vulnerable to the variability of the weather and the incidence of crop and animal pests and diseases, which affect agricultural output, and hence import demand and export supply. These and other supply-side factors, combined with developments in external demand for primary commodities, can cause considerable instability in ldcs' export earnings.[11] In general, however, the longer-term deterioration in ldcs' export prices relative to import prices (reversed briefly in 1973) is of more importance than short-term instability in export prices. It is this, together with the steady growth of ldcs' external debt, that causes the more persistent payments problems among ldcs, and it is to the problem of indebtedness that we now turn.

External Resource Inflows and Indebtedness[12]

Ldcs rely on external capital to finance their import surplus. The main types of external capital are:

(1) official development assistance, or aid, including bilateral and multilateral grants and concessional loans;
(2) loans on commercial terms;
(3) foreign private equity investment.

Except for grants, all these inflows add to ldcs' external liabilities and result in debt service obligations, which include repayments of capital (recorded in the recipient's capital account) and payments of interest, profits, and dividends (recorded in the current account). These obligations will be met on a fixed, regular basis in the case of loans, while the level of profits and dividends remittance and capital repatriation arising from foreign private investment varies. The actual value of capital inflows and the true debt servicing costs are often different from that indicated in the balance of payments accounts because of such practices as procurement tying by aid donors and transfer pricing by foreign investors. The level of debt servicing depends on the type and quality of past capital inflows, i.e. the structure of debt outstanding.

As a whole, the record of ldcs' external capital receipts and debt service obligatons shows three main characteristics. First there has been a rapid growth in the level of ldcs' outstanding debt and debt service obligations. Between 1965 and 1971, for instance, ldcs' external public debt, i.e. excluding foreign private loans and investment, more than doubled from $37.5 billion to $79.3 billion.[13] Debt service payments on this debt showed a similar increase, from $3.3 billion to $6.8 billion. (Inflation has, however, eroded the real value of ldcs' outstanding debt.) Second, new inflows of external capital to ldcs have – until very recently – grown relatively slowly. Between 1965 and 1971, external public loans and grants increased by only 57 per cent, from $8.3 billion to $13.06 billion.[14] This, in turn, means that the net transfer of resources to ldcs, i.e. gross capital inflows minus debt service payments, has grown even more slowly – by 25 per cent. And just as inflation has eroded the value of existing debt, so it has eroded the real value of capital inflows, so that the increase in the nominal value of the net transfer of capital has probably not allowed ldcs to increase the volume of imports financed by such capital. This of course ignores the effect of past inflows of external financial resources on ldcs' capacity to finance an increasing level of imports from their own export earnings, but it does indicate that any expansion of ldcs' import capacity, in aggregate, is largely dependent on a greater increase in their export earnings.

Finally, there has in general been a fall in the share of concessional and grant flows to ldcs and an increase in the share of financial flows on commercial terms since the early sixties (see Table 7.3). Although this trend was reversed somewhat in 1974 by an increase in the share of aid to ldcs, the change in composition still implies a hardening of terms on which ldcs receive external finance,[15] and hence an increase in the debt service payments relative to the debt outstanding and so a greater dependence on export earnings to finance import requirements. This effect of the shift in composition is clearly indicated in Table 7.4, which gives the level of debt service payments associated with different types of debt outstanding. Foreign private investment is excluded but it may be assumed that such investment involves an annual outflow of profits and dividends equivalent to at least 10 per cent – probably more – of its book value.[16]

The 'Debt Burden'

The main reason why ldcs have chronic trade deficits financed by

Table 7.3. Composition of Net Flow of Financial Resources[1] from DAC countries to Ldcs, 1961-3 to 1971-3, 1973 and 1974, Annual Averages

($ billion)

	1961-3	1966-8	1971-3	1973	1974[5]
1. Official development assistance	5.47	6.29	8.62	9.41	11.30
% of total	(62.5)	(53.5)	(43.8)	(40.8)	(44.3)
2. Other official flows	0.58	0.56	1.82	2.59	2.11
% of total	(6.6)	(4.8)	(9.2)	(11.2)	(8.3)
3. Private flows[2]	2.71	4.91	9.26	11.07	12.09
% of total	(30.9)	(41.8)	(47.1)	(48.0)	(47.4)
of which:					
4. direct investment	1.64	2.44	4.49	6.65	7.15
% of total	(18.7)	(20.8)	(22.8)	(22.8)	(28.0)
5. export credits	0.60	1.55	1.82	1.15	2.49
% of total	(6.8)	(13.2)	(9.2)	(5.0)	(9.8)
6. Total disbursements	8.75	11.75	19.69	23.07	25.51
7. Grants by private voluntary agencies	n.a.	n.a.	1.10	1.36	1.19
8. Recorded Eurocurrency[3] loans	—	—	4.90	9.35	7.05
9. Grant equivalent of official aid commitments[4]	n.a.	6.88	9.68	11.37	n.a.

1 Gross flows net of capital repayments or repatriation, but *not* interest, profits, or dividends.
2 Besides direct investment and export credits, these also include bilateral and multilateral portfolio investment.
3 Gross commitment figures, based on published data, which understate total commitments, possibly by as much as 50%.
4 The grant equivalent of official aid (which comprises grants and loans) is estimated by deducting the present discounted value of future loan repayments from the face value of the loan. The grant equivalent of an aid loan will always be less than the face value of the loan, but the softer the latter's repayment terms, the nearer its grant equivalent will be to its face value. The grant equivalent of a grant is equal to the grant. See OECD, *Development Assistance 1968 Review,* for details of methodology.
5 Provisional estimates only.

Sources: 1961-8 data, except line 9: OECD, *Development Cooperation, 1972 Review*. 1971-3 data, and 1966-8 data (line 9 only): OECD, *Development Cooperation, 1974 Review;* 1974 data: OECD, Press Release A(75)27.

capital and grant inflows is that this enables them to develop at a faster rate than would otherwise be possible. It can be argued that, so long as they use the resources acquired by such inflows productively, so that the resultant increase in income exceeds the service payments due, they

Table 7.4. Ldcs' Outstanding Debt at End-1972 and Associated Debt Service Payments in 1972

Creditor	Total disbursed debt outstanding		Total debt service payments		Debt service payments as a percentage of debt outstanding[1]
	$ billion	%	$ billion	%	
DAC countries	51.95	69	6.42	71	12.4
of which:					
– government loans	30.63	41	2.15	24	7.0
of which:					
concessional aid	27.99	37	1.80	20	6.4
– suppliers' credits	10.08	13	2.40	27	23.8
– other	11.25	15	1.86	20	16.5
Multilateral agencies	11.02	15	1.05	11	9.5
of which:					
– concessional loans	2.83	4	0.02	0	0.1
– other	8.19	11	1.03	11	12.6
Centrally planned economies	5.55	7	0.52	6	9.4
Ldcs	2.40	3	0.31	3	12.9
Other	4.12	6	0.71	8	17.2
Total	75.05	100	9.01	100	12.0

[1] This column illustrates the difference in debt service obligations arising from different types of debts, which is also indicated by the difference between each type's share of total debt outstanding and the share of debt service payments. It is only an approximation of the level of future annual debt service payments arising from different types of debt outstanding: an accurate measure would have to be based on the specific terms of different loans.

Source: OECD, *DAC Review 1974,* p.152.

are better off than they would otherwise have been. Consequently, the notion that ldcs bear a 'debt burden' has meaning only if it is believed that the countries which supply the financial resources should not seek a return on them but should allow ldcs to retain the whole of the resulting increment from their use of the resources supplied. However, for two sorts of reasons, the debt service payments on ldcs' growing debt can, and do, constitute a problem. First, even if the above assumption is correct, some ldcs may find it hard to finance debt service obligations because of difficulties in increasing their export earnings. Second, the returns on the resources acquired may be insufficient to service the debts incurred. This can occur for a variety of reasons, for instance, the high risks and uncertainties associated with certain investment projects in ldcs, the restrictions on the use of finance by the creditor (e.g. procurement tying), or economic mismanagement by the recipient. Thus debt service obligations may represent a cost of relying on external resources for development that cannot easily be borne.

Other things being equal, a country's ability to cope with its debt service payments – and consequently the extent to which they are a 'burden' – depends on the rate of growth of its export earnings and, in the short term, on the stability of those earnings. Other important factors are the structure and volume of the individual ldc's debt. Countries which, like Ghana in the sixties, accumulated a large volume of debt on hard terms, (i.e. with short maturity periods and high interest rates) are particularly vulnerable to debt servicing problems. But the experience of India indicates that the sheer volume of debt and associated debt service payments can cause difficulties even if that debt is on soft terms.

As Table 7.5 indicates, more than half the total disbursed debt (excluding foreign private investment liabilities) at the end of 1972 was concentrated among the richer ldcs. The debt of the richer countries is moreover on harder terms than that of the poorer countries. This situation is largely explained by richer countries' greater ability to borrow on commercial terms, and the policies of aid donors, who have directed a greater share of concessional aid flows, in particular grants, to poorer countries.[17]

At the country level, the concentration of debt is more marked. Nine countries, listed in Table 7.6, account for half the total debt outstanding and another eleven countries, also listed, for a quarter of the total debt outstanding, and these countries together account also for more than half of total foreign investment liabilities. The picture is changed somewhat when allowance is made for the structure of debt but the geographical concentration remains. Aside from India, Indonesia, and Pakistan, all these countries have relatively high incomes per head. An indication of the importance of their indebtedness is provided in the fourth column of Table 7.6, where debt service is expressed as a percentage of export earnings. The higher the percentage in each case, the more of the countries' total export earnings will have to be devoted to debt servicing and the greater the likelihood of debt problems should foreign exchange receipts drop for any reason. Despite the softness of India and Pakistan's outstanding debt (their discounted debt is only just over 40 per cent of undiscounted debt) debt servicing payments represent a high proportion of their total export earnings. A number of countries not included in Table 7.6 would

Table 7.5. Debt of Developing Countries by Type of Debt and Average Income Level of Debtor Ldc, end-1972.

Ldc debtors	Total disbursed debt outstanding $ billion	% total	Share of debt arising from from govern-ment loans and concessional multilateral lending %	Proportion of total population in ldcs
Oil producers	12.90	17.2	55.0	14.0
Other countries	61.93	82.8	54.2	86.0
of which:				
countries with average GNP per head of:				
$1,000 or more	9.61	12.8	33.4	4.0
$600-999	10.01	13.4	31.3	5.4
$375-599	9.41	12.6	31.8	8.9
$200-374	13.99	18.7	61.6	16.8
Less than $200	16.25	21.7	83.2	42.8
Least developed countries	2.67	3.6	79.9	8.0
Total	74.83	100.0	53.8	100.0

Sources: OECD, *DAC Review 1974,* p.153.

also seem vulnerable to debt problems because of the high ratio of their fixed debt servicing obligations to their export earnings: these include Uruguay, Afghanistan, South Yemen, and Laos.

BALANCE OF PAYMENTS ADJUSTMENT

When a country has a balance of payments surplus or deficit, equilibrium can be restored either by changes on the capital account – or transfers on current account – or by adjusting current account payments and receipts. When payments difficulties are the result of temporary shifts in payments or receipts rather than fundamental disequilibrium, they require different sorts of measures. As we have seen, ldcs' payments problems can be temporary or longer term. Thus, instability of export earnings, bunching of debt service payments, and bad harvests can lead to temporary difficulties while the slow growth

Table 7.6. Main Ldc Debtors Ranked According to Total Debt (Including Undisbursed Debt) Outstanding, 1972

Country	Total medium-and long-term debt outstanding[1] $m		Foreign private investment stock $m	Debt service as % of exports[3]	GNP per head $ (1971)
	Undiscounted	Discounted[2]			
India	11,653	4,728 (2)	1,660	27	110
Brazil	7,747	4,868 (1)	6,150	13	460
Iran	5,928	4,577 (3)	1,000	18	450
Indonesia	5,183	1,970 (12)	1,200	10	80
Mexico	4,842	3,995 (4)	2,650	22	700
Pakistan	4,647	1,993 (11)	485	23	130
Israel	3,864	2,537 (16)	180	16	2,190
South Korea	3,633	2,242 (8)	360	14	290
Argentina	3,576	2,897 (5)	2,300	22	1,230
Chile	3,365	2,300 (7)	765	11	760
Turkey	3,364	1,648 (13)	340	11	340
Yugoslavia	3,041	2,229 (9)	60	5	730
Algeria	2,827	2,120 (10)	250	15	360
Colombia	2,293	1,299 (18)	910	13	370
Spain	2,064	1,641 (14)	2,500	3	1,100
Egypt	2,041	1,486 (15)	100	29	220
Greece	1,744	1,299 (18)	540	9	1,250
Peru	1,677	1,347 (17)	880	19	480
Venezuela	1,629	1,350 (16)	3,700	4	1,060
Taiwan	1,594	1,144 (20)	400	4	430
Total	76,647	47,670	26,430	n.a.	n.a.
Total all ldcs	102,482	63,275	51,553	9	264

1 Including undisbursed debt.
2 Discounted debt is the present value of debt service payments over the next fifteen years, discounted at 10%. This measure understates the debt of countries with service payments on present debt stretching beyond fifteen years, e.g. India. The figure in brackets give the indebtedness rank of countries according to their discounted debt position.
3 Exports of goods and services in 1972.
Sources: OECD, *DAC Review 1974*, pp.284-5.

of exports, the medium-term deterioration in their terms of trade, or the growth of indebtedness relative to capital inflows can cause more persistent difficulties. If reserves are inadequate or suitable external finance is not available, current account transactions have to be adjusted to bring about equilibrium. Here we consider the range of such measures open to ldcs, their appropriateness to the different types of disequilibrium, and, bearing in mind that balance of payments disequilibria occur because governments have chosen to avoid policies which would prevent them, the extent to which they conflict with other policy objectives, especially the development objectives.

Broadly speaking ldcs have a choice of three types of adjustment measures:

(1) exchange rate policy;
(2) commercial policy:
(3) general monetary and fiscal policy.

The first two types of policies encourage – or force – a switch in domestic expenditure from traded goods and services to non-traded goods and services, thus increasing production of the latter, while the third reduces total domestic expenditure – and production. The first two measures will generally reduce expenditure as well, or will have to be accompanied by expenditure reducing measures to be effective. Although each sort of policy is considered separately here, governments rarely put the whole burden of adjustment on any one policy instrument. Ldcs can also take steps to reduce their factor income payments – often a major source of outpayments. These moves tend to take the form of debt rescheduling 'agreements' with creditors – who may have few options in the matter – and are essentially a financing solution to payments problems.[18]

Exchange Rate Policies

Devaluation

The foreign exchange rate of a country is the price of its domestic currency in terms of foreign exchange, usually expressed in one of the major currencies. The official rate (or rates – see below) is that declared by its government, which is expected to maintain that rate by making up any difference between the supply and demand for foreign exchange at that price. 'Floating' exchange rates are distinguished from such 'fixed' rates in that they are allowed to move up and down according to market forces – although some government intervention does often take place. On the whole, ldcs tend to prefer fixed exchange rates both for themselves and internationally (see below).

A foreign exchange shortage means that domestic currency is

overvalued in terms of foreign exchange, and thus there is an excess demand for foreign exchange at the official rate, and the government cannot balance supply and demand by drawing on reserves or borrowing. One obvious way out of this situation is to alter the official exchange rate. Ldcs' currencies are not 'key' currencies, i.e. used for international payments or reserves, and devaluation of an ldc's currency is unlikely to have much impact on international trade. Consequently ldcs, unlike many developed countries, can alter their exchange rates without risking international repercussions. However, unless the currency is left to float, i.e. the government leaves it to market forces to determine the exchange rate which will balance the supply and demand for foreign exchange, the new devalued rate may not restore balance of payments equilibrium. Further, the internal consequences of devaluation have to be considered.

Devaluation increases the internal, domestic-currency, prices of traded goods and services relative to non-traded goods and services, and restores payments equilibrium if these price changes lead to a shift in domestic demand away from imports to domestic output and/or to an increase in exports. Changes in import demand or export supply – or the foreign exchange price for exports – can lead to changes in the terms of trade which will also affect the balance of payments situation.

In the short run, any shift in demand away from imported goods will not increase domestic supply, unless excess capacity exists which can be brought into use. Although unemployment is high in ldcs, an increase in demand for domestic output is unlikely to bring forth additional output in the short term since unemployment is due largely to structural factors rather than lack of demand. Excess capacity may exist in some sectors, particularly in import substituting manufacturing industries, but, on the whole, short-term changes in domestic supply cannot be expected to meet increased demand in ldcs. It follows, then, that in the short term, an increase in demand for domestically produced goods can simply generate inflation and/or a demand for imports, so reducing the likelihood of any improvement in the balance of payments – unless devaluation is accompanied by cuts in domestic demand. But since ldcs' income levels are low and consumption demand cannot easily be reduced, a reduction in spending is likely to affect investment most – and hence development.

In the absence of expenditure reducing measures, devaluation can itself reduce domestic demand where import demand is unresponsive to price changes and/or where spending falls as a result of income redistribution. In the former case, the higher domestic prices for imports act as a tax on expenditure. In the latter case, spending could fall if the shift in real income distribution in favour of producers of exported and import substituting goods and away from consumers – usually wage-earners – brings about an increase in savings which are not invested (assuming that the gainers tend to save more than the losers). But these reductions in spending could simply reduce the level of domestic economic activity and output – as has been observed in Latin America.

In the longer run, devaluation's importance lies in the incentive it provides to move domestic resources into exporting and import substituting production, which should lead to an improvement in the payments situation. Assuming that this incentive is not eroded by the short-term results of devaluation, both its effectiveness and its desirability – in development terms – are in doubt. Price incentives alone are unlikely to overcome the various obstacles to the internal movement of resources and the establishment of new industries. A large proportion of ldcs' imports is made up of intermediate and capital goods which cannot – except at high cost – be produced domestically. Meanwhile an increase in exports is more likely to result from enlarging the supply of traditional exports than from diversifying into new export lines where the lack of skills and know-how is an important obstacle. There is a case for arguing that a reduction in developing countries' dependence on capital imports from the West is desirable, given that such imports embody technologies often inapproprate to ldc production conditions. But the price incentives provided by devaluation are indiscriminate: all import competing production and all export production are encouraged, and all imports discouraged, irrespective of their likely contribution to the country's development efforts. Thus, for instance, imports of high-income-group consumer durables are discouraged as much as capital equipment needed for development or food for low-income groups, while the domestic production of *all* these types of goods is encouraged.

This indiscriminate impact can have adverse consequences for ldcs' terms of trade, and limit the effectiveness of devaluation in restoring payments equilibrium unless accompanied by other measures. In general, the foreign exchange price of ldcs' imports is not likely to be affected by devaluation – or by import restrictions – because individual ldcs account for only a small part of global import demand. The same tends to be true for ldcs' exports, except in the primary products field, where an individual ldc's exports may account for a large proportion of world trade in a particular commodity – for instance Brazil's coffee exports or Ghana's cocoa exports. In the latter case, an increase in export supply can be expected to depress world prices, so turning the terms of trade against the ldc. And total export earnings may also be reduced if external demand were so inelastic that the rise in export volume was more than offset by the fall in the export price. In this case, devaluation would not work unless imports fell more than export earnings. But since import demand in ldcs tends to be inelastic, the payments position would probably be worsened and could only be improved by additional measures to restrict the expansion of exports facing inelastic demand and/or to reduce import demand, which would almost certainly entail a cut in domestic expenditure and output.

Exchange Controls and Multiple Exchange Rates

Rather than relying simply on a straightforward devaluation, with its potentially damaging, indiscriminate, and – in the absence of counter measures – inflationary effects, ldcs can, and frequently do, employ more selective exchange policies to restore equilibrium, namely exchange controls and multiple exchange rates.

Exchange controls restrict the availability of foreign exchange for external transactions and, unlike devaluation, have certain immediate and beneficial effects on the balance of payments position. Further, unlike devaluation, they permit the government to discriminate in its restrictions, between essential and non-essential imports. Some deflationary measures will also be required, if there is no excess domestic capacity, if inflation or reduced exports are not to result from the restrictions on imports.

Exchange controls have two important drawbacks. First, by imposing administrative restraints on imports, the Government is effectively maintaining an 'overvalued' currency and this can have undesirable consequences. An 'overvalued' currency makes those imports which are allowed in cheaper than they would be in the absence of controls, while exporters receive lower returns than they would otherwise, i.e. if the Government devalued the currency. Thus importers are subsidised and exporters taxed. It may well be helpful to encourage development by subsidising essential imports but it can hardly be desirable, in response to payments difficulties, to discourage exports (unless all export demand is inelastic). Meanwhile, since exchange controls are likely to affect non-essential imports, most prices of these on the domestic market will rise – encouraging the production of 'non-essential' import substitutes. Unless exchange controls are only a temporary measure or are accompanied by other measures, such as subsidies to exporters or income redistribution to shift the pattern of internal demand, their long-term impact will be to distort internal resource allocation, without substantially improving the balance of payments position.

Second, exchange controls are only as effective in restricting imports as the administration which implements them. The subsidy given to 'favoured' importers by an overvalued exchange rate stimulates those less fortunate to find ways of overcoming the administrative controls. Black market dealings in foreign exchange and bribery of officials implementing the control system are the almost inevitable result of exchange control measures in ldcs, undermining the effectiveness of import restriction.

Multiple exchange rates are sometimes employed, particularly in Latin America, as alternatives to selective rationing of foreign exchange by exchange controls – although the administrative requirements also leave some scope for black marketeering and corruption. As the term implies, multiple exchange rates, of which the dual exchange rate system is the simplest, entail the setting of different official exchange rates for different classes of external transaction.[19] Thus, a country may devalue its currency selectively. It can, for instance avoid the impact of an across-the-board devaluation on essential imports and exports for which external demand is inelastic, by maintaining the old exchange rate for these transactions and using a separate – devalued – rate for all other transactions. In June 1975, some twenty-nine ldcs maintained dual or multiple exchange rates (see Table 7.7). Like exchange controls, multiple exchange rates operate like a system of taxes and subsidies offsetting some of the effects of a full devaluation. Unlike exchange controls, they do provide some incentives to exporters.

Exchange Rate Policy with Floating Currencies

So far the choice of ldcs' exchange rate (or rates) has been treated as a decision based largely on internal considerations, which is correct so long as the exchange rates of the major currencies of the world are stable. In 1971, however, the relative stability of the international monetary system was interrupted. The rapid growth of the US payments deficit in 1970-1 precipitated an international financial crisis, which in turn led to an agreement – known as the Smithsonian Agreement – among major Western countries on a re-alignment of their currencies' exchange rates. This agreement, which also permitted a greater degree of flexibility in exchange rate values, broke down during

Table 7.7: Exchange Rate Practices Among Ldcs, 30 June 1975[1]

	Multiple/dual exchange rate	Single exchange rate
Exchange rate pegged to a single currency (82 countries)		
(i) US dollar (58 countries)	Afghanistan	*Bahrain
	Argentina	*Bolivia
	*Bahamas	Botswana
	Brazil	*Burundi
	Chile	*Taiwan
	Columbia	Costa Rica
	Dominican Republic	El Salvador
	Ecuador	Guatemala
	Egypt	Haiti
	*Ethiopia	Honduras
	Ghana	Indonesia
	Guinea	*Iraq
	Laos	*Israel
	*Nepal	*Jamaica
	Paraguay	*Jordan
	Peru	*Kenya
	*Somalia	Korea
	Sudan	Lesotho
	Turkey	Liberia
	Uruguay	*Libya
	Venezuela	Mexico
	Vietnam	Nicaragua
	Yemen, Peoples Democratic Republic	*Oman
		*Pakistan
		Panama
		*Rwanda
		Syria
		*Tanzania
		*Thailand
		*Uganda
		United Arab Emirates
		*Western Samoa
		Yemen Arab Republic
		*Zaire
		*Zambia
(ii) £ sterling (9 countries)	Mauritius	Bangladesh
	Sri Lanka	Barbados
		Gambia
		Guyana
		*India
		Sierra Leone
		Trinidad and Tobago
(iii) French franc (13 countries)	–	Cameroon
		Central African Republic
		Chad
		Congo People's Republic
		Dahomey
		Gabon
		Ivory Coast
		Malagasy Republic
		Mali
		Niger
		Senegal
		Togo
		Upper Volta
(iv) Other (2 countries)	Equatorial Guinea (Spanish peseta)	Swaziland (South African Rand)
Exchange rate pegged to SDR (5 countries)		
	*Iran	*Burma
		Malawi
		*Qatar
		*Saudi Arabia
Exchange rate not being maintained within specified margins (12 countries)		
	Khmer Republic	Algeria
	Morocco	Fiji
		Kuwait
		Lebanon
		Malaysia
		Mauritania
		Nigeria
		Philippines
		Singapore
		Tunisia

[1] As determined by the IMF. Of the 99 countries included in this Table, 70 had single exchange rates and 29 maintained dual or multiple exchange rates. An asterisk denotes that the country is availing itself of wider margins, up to ± 2.25%.
Source: IMF, *Annual Report*, 1975.

1972 and 1973, and most of the major currencies have now been allowed to float. The fluctuating values of the major currencies obviously increased the risks and uncertainties of external transactions and of holding foreign currency reserves. And ldcs' decisions as to their exchange rate values have to take account of the new floating régime, whether or not they wish to devalue their own currencies.

Most ldcs have traditionally been members of more or less formal currency areas. Thus, for instance, the colonies and ex-colonies of Britain and France have been part of the sterling and franc area respectively, while the Latin American countries have been part of the dollar area. 'Membership' of a currency area can carry with it certain privileges, such as favoured access to capital markets, and can entail certain restrictions on internal and external policies. But recently, 'membership' has tended to mean little more than that the member holds most of its reserves and conducts most of its external transactions in the particular foreign currency and declares its own exchange rate in terms of that currency. Ldcs' membership of a particular currency area largely reflected their historical and commercial ties and was a matter of convenience, so long as the exchange rates of the major currencies were fixed – or at least infrequently changed – in relation to each other. With the Smithsonian re-alignment of currencies and the subsequent moves towards floating exchange rates, ldcs had to decide whether to retain their links with particular currencies. The alternatives were, and are, to fix their currency value in terms of some other single currency or reserve asset, or a 'basket' of other currencies, or allow their currency to float independently against all others.

Floating increases the risks and uncertainties associated with external transactions. Although these can be limited, at a cost, the financial skills and institutions needed to do so tend to be poorly developed in ldcs.[20] Consequently there is an incentive to 'peg' the home currency to that of one of the major currencies. But while this may ease the problems of traders, financiers and others, if the foreign currency chosen is that of a major trading partner and/or capital supplier, it raises other problems. Movements in the value of that currency will lead to an appreciation or depreciation of the ldcs' currency in terms of other foreign exchange. Such changes, brought about by factors affecting the economy of another country, are likely at least at times, to conflict with the needs and objectives of individual ldcs. At the same time, the maintenance of parity with the currency of a major trading or financial partner will tend to encourage transactions with that partner. This may be undesirable should the ldc be attempting to diversify its external economic relations.

Ldcs can circumvent these two kinds of problem, in the first case by adjusting their exchange rate in terms of the chosen major currency, and, in the second, by linking up with different major currencies in turn or linking up to a group of currencies. These solutions, however, add to risk and uncertainty.

The international floating régime has thus introduced a new set of problems into ldcs' management of their exchange rate and reserve policies. As Table 7.7 indicates, by 1975 the majority of ldcs had opted for 'pegging' their currency in terms of one of the major currencies. Fewer ldcs now retain parity with the £ sterling or the franc, and the majority have opted for parity with the dollar, but without necessarily devaluing with the dollar, but rather 're-pegging' at intervals. Five ldcs have chosen to peg their currencies to the SDR, which itself is valued in terms of a 'basket' of major currencies. Twelve ldcs have allowed their currencies to float.

Commercial Policies

As discussed elsewhere,[21] commercial policies – such as tariffs, quotas, and export subsidies – are primarily designed to encourage import substitution, by providing protection to local producers, and exports, by increasing their profitability through subsidies. Tariffs and quotas, in particular, are widely used in developing countries, and have been employed not only as protective devices but also as a means of restricting imports in the face of foreign exchange shortages. Like multiple exchange rates, commercial policies have the advantage over straight devaluation in that they can be selective. Import quotas moreover, like exchange controls, will immediately improve the balance of payments provided either that all imports are subject to them or that additional measures prevent an increase in those imports not subject to quotas. In the short term, deflationary measures will probably also be required.

Commercial policy measures may improve the balance of payments. In the longer term they, like multiple exchange rates, are likely to distort resource allocation:

> It is exceedingly difficult to arrange a set of tariffs and subsidies, or multiple exchange rates, so as to achieve either uniformity of promotion, or any predetermined desired amount of promotion for each industry. In practice, such a system tends to become highly irrational, with no one knowing (without massive and continuous research) just how much different industries are being favoured.[22]

Frequently, moreover, ldcs rely more heavily on tariffs and quotas than on export subsidies to restore payments equilibrium. This, as noted in Chapter 5,[23] tends to discourage exports and can stimulate high-cost capital-intensive industrial development, which in turn reduces the possibility of competitive exports in the future, with adverse consequences for the country's balance of payments position.

Deflationary Measures

Deflationary measures are an indirect means of restoring payments equilibrium, relying on a reduction in total domestic demand to bring about a lowering in the demand for external resources, and hence foreign exchange. Thus total demand is cut by raising taxes, reducing subsidies or restricting credit creation. Where the balance of payments disequilibrium is the result of an excess of investment or government spending in relation to domestic savings, revenues, and capital inflows, rather than structural problems of expanding export earnings, deflationary measures are more appropriate than primarily expenditure switching measures. Their consequences, however, may be undesirable, particularly in poorer ldcs, since they will tend to curb the country's development momentum.

There is in short, no easy way to restore payments equilibrium. In the absence of excess domestic capacity or exchange controls or quota restrictions, virtually all adjustment requires deflationary measures. Yet because of the latter's impact on development spending and on income levels, ldcs tend to prefer selective controls and to permit internal inflation. Controls, however, are best suited to temporary payments difficulties, since in the longer term they result in inefficient resource allocation and harm the country's export prospects. On the other hand, devaluation and deflation need not necessarily improve the country's long-term payments situation, and by reducing the level of domestic output and investment can harm the country's development prospects and its ability to diversify into new exports.

FINANCING SOLUTIONS

However undesirable balance of payments adjustment measures may seem to the individual developing country, they may nonetheless be necessary in the absence of suitable credit facilities or adequate foreign exchange reserves. Access to some credit facilities, moreover, may be conditional on policies to bring about payments equilibrium. In this final section we look at the different kinds of external finance available to ldcs and at some of the proposals to alleviate their financing problems, which have become particularly acute for oil importing ldcs since 1973.

In principle, both long- and short-term capital inflows can finance a current account deficit (although only short-term finance or reserves can offset a deficit in the basic balance of payments). The availability of different forms of finance and the terms on which it is provided, however, affect its usefulness in solving a payments crisis. Generally, long-term investment finance and development grants can finance an import surplus but they cannot be easily increased or reduced should that surplus rise or fall, or should other items in the balance of payments change. In contrast, short- to medium-term external finance *can* be more readily varied to meet any change in a country's external balance, and as such may be termed 'residual' finance. Accordingly, this discussion of the main types of external finance – proposed or available – is divided into two parts. The first focuses on long-term investment finance, including official aid loans and development grants, foreign private investment, and commercial loans. The second focuses on 'residual' financial facilities: credit facilities (including the SDR Link proposal, which more properly belongs in the first part), debt refinancing, and financial measures designed specifically to ameliorate problems on the export side. Because of the similarity of the role of these types of finance to that of foreign exchange reserves, ldcs' reserve position is also discussed in the second part. It will be noted that the distinction between 'residual' and other external finance is not always clear-cut. In particular, certain aid flows and commercial loans to ldcs, especially in recent years, have been equivalent to 'residual' finance.

Long- and Medium-Term Finance

This includes long-term private investment, international aid, and commercial borrowing. As we shall note, a number of factors limit the usefulness of such finance in solving payments problems and avoiding internal adjustments, although it can provide the means for making such adjustments. Aid resources, for instance, may be used to reduce import needs or foreign investment may be directed to the export sector. In the wake of the oil crisis and the various other events which have substantially increased most non-oil producing ldcs' current account deficits, however, more concessional aid is being used to stave off payments crises, and so help maintain present production and income levels and ease the inevitable adjustment process. In this, aid – or at least some aid – is taking on the character of reserves rather than long-term investment finance.

Official Development Aid. Official development aid consists of grants and concessional loans from governments and multilateral institutions to developing countries to assist economic development. Resources made available for development by private agencies on concessional or grant terms and official finance for non-development purposes, e.g. military aid, are excluded by definition, and are in fact relatively insignificant. Private development grants from DAC countries in 1974 have been estimated as equivalent to some 10 per cent of net official aid flows (i.e. gross aid flows minus capital repayments or amortisation) and some 4.5 per cent of total net resource flows, while other official flows in 1974 were equivalent to 18.7 per cent and 7.9 per cent respectively.[24] Official aid is by far the most important single source of external finance to ldcs. The aid flows originating from DAC countries alone accounted for 30 per cent of the estimated total external resource flow of $37.9 billion to ldcs in 1974; if aid from OPEC, Communist, and other sources were added to DAC flows, official aid would have accounted for at least 40 per cent of the total resource flow in that year. Until recently, DAC countries accounted for roughly 80 per cent of official aid flows to ldcs with Communist countries providing most of the remainder. The OPEC countries have now emerged as significant aid donors. Preliminary data indicate that aid flows from OPEC countries amounted to $2.54 billion in 1974, approximately 22 per cent of DAC aid flows, as compared with $500 million in 1973, or roughly 5 per cent of DAC aid flows. And existing undisbursed commitments by OPEC countries suggest that their share of total aid flows will increase further.

Official aid has generally been viewed as a means of meeting ldcs' longer-term development needs: while ldcs may see aid as a way of supplementing their total resources, donors tend to see it in terms of investment finance to be spent on projects which will increase the productive capacity of the recipient. There are important exceptions, namely aid for disaster relief, for re-organising debt obligations, and to finance recurrent budget deficits and 'maintenance' imports (i.e. imports required to keep production going). These last two forms of aid are intended to overcome deficiencies in domestic resource availability and foreign exchange earnings respectively, which 'bite' even before investment requirements come into the picture, and would reduce income levels if aid were not forthcoming. In that neither constraint can be removed without economic development, aid which alleviates such constraints can be regarded as meeting the country's longer-term development needs even though it will not directly generate increased income. Aid for disaster relief and for debt re-organisation may be similarly viewed, although the economic problems here are generally more acute. To these exceptions is now added emergency aid to offset the effects of the oil crisis, essentially aid to maintain import volumes in the face of mounting import prices and diminished prospects for increasing, and in some cases maintaining, export earnings.

The value of aid to the recipient lies not only in the fact that it increases total resource available but that it is concessional. The financial terms of aid are less likely than commercial finance to strain the recipients' capacity to service debts. Indeed, a large proportion – some 73 per cent in 1974 – of DAC aid net of amortisation is now grants or in grant-like form, involving no debt service or service costs in local currency rather than foreign exchange. Interest rates on aid loans tend to be lower than those on commercial loans while repayment periods are longer, so that a substantial portion of any aid loan constitutes a gift to the recipient. On average, the gift or grant element of DAC aid loans is higher than that of Communist or OPEC loans and, taking grants and loans together, DAC aid tends to be the most concessional.[25] However, aid has three main drawbacks as a source of finance to ldcs, which relate to its total availability, its allocation between ldcs, and the fact that it is rarely an unconditional transfer.

How much aid is available is determined not by ldcs' need for concessional resources, but by the importance that donors attach to aid giving compared with other uses of their resources. The record of DAC country donors in the decade up to 1973 was not encouraging. While their net aid flows increased from \$5.77 billion to \$9.41 billion, these fell as a proportion of their national incomes, from 0.51 per cent in 1963 to 0.30 per cent in 1973, and in real terms, i.e. after allowing for inflation, declined by 7 per cent. In 1974, the downward trends of DAC aid were reversed, but only a small increase was recorded in real terms over 1973. Meanwhile, the emergence of the OPEC countries as major donors contributed to the significant increase in the nominal value of total aid flows. But the 1974 spurt in aid flows has to be set against the dramatic increase in the financing needs of ldcs, brought about by higher costs of oil and other essential imports, such as food, While aid flows from DAC and OPEC countries in 1974 increased by \$3.94 billion, the oil bill which non-oil producing ldcs had to finance rose by around \$10 billion and for their grain imports \$3.2 billion. So the 1974 increase in aid was not enough to offset the income reducing effects of oil and other import price rises on non-oil producing ldcs.

The needs of ldcs for external finance, and in particular concessional finance, vary considerably. The oil producing ldcs, while sharing certain socio-economic characteristics with other ldcs, clearly do not face the same financing problems: indeed many are now providers rather than recipients of external finance. Equally, both before and since the oil crisis, some ldcs have been better able to finance their own development and other import needs either from their export earnings or with non-aid external finance. Those most in need of concessional finance are the poorest ldcs, since for them mobilisation of domestic resources for development – or cuts in income – tend to involve the greatest sacrifice, as would debt servicing payments on commercial terms. Further, since such countries have more limited access to commercial sources of finance, aid is likely to make the greatest developmental impact when channelled to them rather than to countries which can obtain, and better afford, alternative finance. While events of 1972-3 altered the balance of need among non-oil producing ldcs to some extent, income levels remain the most important determinant of ldcs' needs for concessional finance. This is borne out by the UN list of the thirty or so ldcs identified as being most in need of aid because 'most seriously affected' by the oil crisis.[26]

Over the years, however, the relative needs of ldcs have not been closely matched by their aid receipts: donors – in particular bilateral donors – have based their aid allocation policies on a variety of political, economic, and military considerations as well as on the developmental needs of recipients. With the oil crisis and the consequent increase in non-oil producing ldcs' total financing needs, international opinion has increasingly favoured concentrating aid resources on the most needy. Proposals have been made to cut off aid flows to ldcs with incomes above a certain level,[27] and to set aside most aid for the poorest countries. And the establishment of the UN Emergency Fund to channel aid resources to the 'most seriously affected' countries is an attempt to ensure that aid goes where it is most needed. While DAC countries still direct substantial portions of their aid to the richer ldcs, their allocation has undoubtedly improved. Political considerations are, however, clearly a major determinant of OPEC and Communist aid, with pro-Arab Islamic countries and pro-Communist ldcs respectively being the main beneficiaries. In short, ldcs can not yet expect to receive concessional finance in proportion to their needs.

The value of aid is, moreover, often reduced by the conditions attached to it. Not only do the potential recipients' general policies affect their eligibility for aid but also the aid itself is usually given on condition that it be used in specific ways. Where the aid is in grant form, conditions attached to its use merely cut the real, as opposed to the nominal, value of the resource transfer. Where aid loans are concerned, however, such a cut effectively hardens the financial terms on which the aid is supplied since the debt service payments have to be made according to the nominal value of the aid loan. Procurement tying is generally considered to be the most important condition reducing the value of aid. In 1973, over two-fifths of all DAC loan disbursements were wholly or partly tied to the purchase of goods and services from the donor country, and most Communist aid is also tied. The practice has been estimated as cutting the nominal value of aid by 10-20 per cent, and sometimes more.[28] In addition, the donor's interference in the recipient's policies can cause resentment and friction, leading some recipients to seek alternative donors or non-aid finance.

Foreign Private Investment

Foreign private investment is of two sorts: direct and indirect, or portfolio, investment. The latter, which is sometimes broadly defined[29] so as to encompass all private capital flows that are not direct investment, is considered below under the head of 'commercial borrowing'. Direct private investment in ldcs has been discussed in Chapter 6, but a number of points are relevant in this context.

As can be seen from Table 7.2, such investment,[30] net of capital repatriation, constitutes roughly half of net private financial flows to ldcs (excluding private grants and Eurocurrency lending) by DAC countries, which are the main source of foreign private investment in ldcs. As an inflow of capital – together with skills and know-how – foreign private investment supplements ldcs' development resources and can permit them to achieve a rate of economic growth higher than would otherwise be possible. And since a substantial portion of such investment is directed to ldcs' export sectors, it can be an important factor in increasing ldcs' foreign exchange resources. At the same time, foreign investment also leads to a significant, if irregular, outflow of foreign exchange in the form of profits, dividends and other payments, and capital repatriation.[31] This outflow can strain ldcs' balance of payments especially where local loans have been used to finance part of the foreign investment. It can also exacerbate payments difficulties should they occur. A significant portion of private investment in ldcs is financed not by fresh capital inflows but by re-invested earnings. Foreign investors tend to avoid countries with balance of payments problems, whether manifested in foreign exchange shortages or in domestic inflation.[32] Consequently, a country suffering such problems is likely to face not only a reduction in fresh foreign investment but also an increase in the level of remitted earnings and, possibly, repatriated capital.

The majority of ldcs, moreover, are unable to attract significant inflows of foreign direct investment. Such investment is made in response to opportunities for profit, which, after discounting for risk, must be at least comparable to those available elsewhere. As discussed in Chapter 6, economic and political factors in many ldcs, particularly the poorer ldcs, increase the risks and restrict the range of investment opportunities for foreign investors. As a result, the bulk of foreign direct investment in ldcs tends to be concentrated in a relatively small number of countries. Foreign investment thus may be complementary to other external resource flows, but it cannot serve as a substitute. And, as with aid, foreign investment can lead to problems in so far as it reduces, or seems to reduce, the host country's control over its internal affairs.

Commercial Borrowing

Commercial borrowing – or more strictly, borrowing on commercial terms – by ldcs has increased considerably over the last decade. Excluding Eurocurrency loans, ldcs' net borrowings on commercial terms from DAC sources[33] amounted to an average of $1.65 billion a year between 1961 and 1963, or 19 per cent of total net resource flows from DAC countries. By 1971-3, such borrowings amounted to $7.01 billion, or 34 per cent of total net resource flows. In 1974, their relative importance had diminished slightly but at an estimated $7.05 billion commercial borrowing still accounted for a sizeable proportion – 28 per cent – of the total net resource flow from DAC countries to ldcs (see Table 7.2). Short-term commercial loans, with a maturity period of less than one year, are not included in these figures – and data on such loans are poor. In general, international short-term loans to ldcs either by banks or as supplier credits are made to finance trade and tend to be self-liquidating. There is, however, some suspicion that some short-term bank credits are being used to finance capital transactions.[34]

If Eurocurrency lending were added to the above totals for commercial borrowing, the increase in such borrowing would be even more substantial. The full extent of Eurocurrency lending to ldcs – and elsewhere – is obscured by lack of published data, but it has been estimated that from virtually nothing in earlier years *gross* Euroloans to ldcs rose from \$1.5 billion in 1971 to at least \$9 billion in 1973. In 1974, *net* Eurocurrency lending to ldcs was estimated at \$5 billion. The recorded loans are, in the parlance of the Eurocurrency market, 'medium-term': that is, they are for periods of three or more years, generally between five and ten years.

The nature of Eurocurrency lending needs some explanation.[35] The term 'Eurocurrency' refers to deposits of currencies in banks other than banks in the countries in which the currencies were issued. A Eurodollar deposit, for instance, is a dollar deposit placed with a bank resident outside the United States. For a variety of reasons, these sorts of 'off-shore' currency deposits in European banks have increased considerably in recent years and have been the basis for a growth of the market – known as the Eurocurrency market – for Eurocurrency loans. The banks accept Eurocurrency deposits and on-lend these to borrowers. As a general rule, the deposits are accepted for shorter periods than they are on-lent, and deposits have to be 'rolled-over' to finance the loan: for instance, if deposits are accepted for six-month periods – which is generally the case – but are on-lent for three-year periods, new deposits have to be raised since the original deposits will be withdrawn before the loan is re-paid. Since the bank – or more generally banks, as Eurocurrency loans are usually made by a syndicate of banks – cannot estimate the cost of deposits in advance, the interest rates on Euroloans are subject to adjustment at every 'roll-over', i.e. at six-monthly intervals in the above example. The interest rate to the borrower, which includes a margin to cover the overhead costs and the banks' credit risk and provide a profit, is therefore variable and cannot be known in advance. The margin attached to Euroloans to ldcs tends to be higher than for developed countries: interest rates charged have been as high as 15 per cent. Generally Eurocurrency loans are more expensive than other commercial loans. Their rise in popularity among ldcs must be explained at least in part by the lack of alternative finance.

The other main forms of commercial borrowing by ldcs are export, or supplier, credits; bond issues on Western capital markets made directly by ldcs and indirectly by development institutions, such as the World Bank; and loans from banks, of which, however, Eurocurrency loans are the most important. (Trade in equity shares constitutes only a small source of international finance.) On the whole, ldc borrowings are either guaranteed by the developing country government – as with direct bond issues of Eurocurrency loans – or by the lending country's government, as with most export credits, or by the financial intermediary, as with those bonds (the majority of ldc bond issues) issued by development institutions. Thus, until the recent spurt in Eurocurrency lending, ldcs were generally unable to raise commercial credit without the guarantee or backing of some other institution or government. And most external loans are made to ldc governments or public corporations rather than to private firms. The borrowing activities of foreign private corporations in ldcs and the use of export credits by private firms are the main exceptions.[36] These features of ldcs' borrowing indicate ldcs' low credit rating with private commercial lending institutions. And this is underlined by the fact that generally only the richer ldcs have been able to raise significant funds by going directly to international bond markets or Eurolending facilities.[37]

The financial terms of ldcs' commercial borrowing vary considerably and all, except those of Eurocurrency loans, are fixed at the time the debt is incurred. Bond issues usually have a maturity period of more than ten years and interest rates in the region of 7 per cent to 8 per cent. In general, ldcs borrowing on bond markets via development institutions get better terms than if they borrow direct. At the same time, they have to submit more information on their proposed use of the finance and are generally subjected to greater scrutiny. The actual terms of export credits are harder to determine because, it is alleged, exporters sometimes over-price goods sold under export credit schemes.[38] Declared interest rates are in the region of 6-7 per cent. Maturity periods vary: until the early sixties – and before the expansion in the use of export credits – the majority were for periods of five years or less; subsequently the proportion of credits with longer maturity periods rose, but even so maturity periods are generally less than ten years.

Despite the hard terms of commercial loans as compared to aid, it has an advantage over aid – and IMF lending – in that they are generally without strings: commercial lenders' main interest is in the recipient's capacity to repay which is usually judged in terms of the general health of the recipient's economy and its balance of payments situation. The commercial criterion of credit-worthiness obviously limits the capacity of ldcs to resort to commercial borrowing. Equally it can permit, and has permitted, ldcs to borrow on terms which are inappropriate to the use of the funds. If a medium-term loan is used to finance long-term investment, the latter is unlikely to generate sufficient income to meet the debt servicing payments and, other things being equal, balance of payments problems will arise.

Three factors have increased the likelihood of this outcome. First, the relative lack of long-term finance on suitable terms has led some ldcs to seek less suitable commercial finance rather than cut back their development spending. The opening up of the Eurocurrency market to ldcs has, moreover, permitted some ldcs to use Euroloans to finance earlier debts, thus avoiding the arduous and generally unpleasant process of obtaining international agreement – with strings attached – on debt refinancing.[39] Second, the lenders' systems of assessing the credit-worthiness of potential borrowers often provide an inadequate guide to their ability to service debt. This is partly because many ldcs are relative newcomers as international borrowers – and hence less information on them is available – and partly because data relating to their economic affairs, and in particular the full extent of their external indebtedness, are inadequate. Finally, competition to expand export sales in the sixties and to find borrowers for their large Eurocurrency deposits in the seventies has encouraged suppliers of export credits and banks respectively to be less careful in their choice of borrower. Thus, while commercial borrowing has permitted some ldcs to avoid the difficult choice between a cut-back in domestic spending and balance of payments problems, it has led, and is likely to lead, certain ldcs into payments difficulties later.

Reserves and Other Financing Facilities and Proposals

Reserves

There are three main reasons a country holds foreign exchange reserves. First, they are held as liquidity so that a country may avoid cash-flow problems in financing payments, given that receipts and payments at any point in time are rarely balanced. Thus the country has a cushion against temporary payments difficulties, and can avoid adjustment measures which might not be justified by its medium- to long-term balance of payments prospects. Second, they are held to avoid the need for drastic adjustment measures should adjustment be necessary. Third, and linked with this, reserves are held because they give countries greater independence in policy making than does reliance on external credit, to cope with payments deficits. In addition, reserves may be accumulated above what is needed for insurance purposes simply because a country is unable to spend or invest abroad all its foreign exchange receipts. Certain of the oil producing ldcs are in this position but it is rare among ldcs.

The holding of reserves means that foreign exchange is saved rather than used for investment to raise the country's productive capacity. For obvious developmental reasons, this cost of holding foreign exchange reserves appears to weigh heavily in ldcs' decisions regarding reserves. Despite the difficulties and disadvantages of relying on external credit to finance payments deficits, ldcs, as a group, keep their reserves relatively low. As will emerge below, the wisdom of this policy is open to doubt, given ldcs' aspirations to economic independence and the short- to medium-term credit facilities available.

The question now arises as to how to judge whether reserves are high or low relative to a particular country's reserve needs. In practice, there is little agreement on what constitutes a desirable level of reserves for any one country – or for all countries taken together. There is, however, some agreement as to the kind of factors which will lead to higher or lower reserve requirements. For instance, reserve needs are expected to increase with the growth of a country's GNP and trade, although the liquidity demand for reserves is not expected to increase at the same rate. Further, the less easily the country can reduce its external payments – because, for instance, they are fixed obligations, like debt service payments, or there might be adverse domestic repercussions, as when imports are cut back in many developing countries – the more reserves will be needed for a given level of external transactions. Similarly, if receipts are subject to seasonal, or longer-term, fluctuations, then, other things being equal, reserves will have to be higher. Access to financing facilities is another factor; if a country can draw on credit to tide it over short- to medium-term payments difficulties, it need hold fewer reserves relative to the level of its external transactions. But since a country's ability to resort to external credit facilities depends on its credit-worthiness, which in turn partly depends on the level of its foreign exchange reserves, recourse to external credit is not a straightforward alternative to the maintenance of reserves.

Given the nature of their external transactions it would seem that most ldcs – and ldcs as a group – should hold a *higher* level of reserves relative to these transactions than developed countries. This, however, is not the case. The international reserves of a country consist of its official holdings of gold, reserve currencies, SDRs, and, if that country is a member of the IMF – as are virtually all independent countries outside the Eastern bloc – its reserve position in the Fund. (The latter is that part of a country's credit facilities with the Fund that can be drawn unconditionally[40] and has not yet been drawn.) For comparative purposes, reserves in a given year are expressed as a percentage of annual imports: the higher the percentage, the less likely are payments difficulties arising from inadequate reserves. In view of the various factors besides the volume of trade that affect reserve requirements, this measure of relative reserve adequacy is clearly a crude one. It is nonetheless used here. Since the Second World War, reserves of all countries outside the Eastern bloc have fallen relative to imports. This fact caused considerable concern over the adequacy of world liquidity during the sixties and was at the root of proposals for an internationally created and controlled reserve asset, specifically the SDR. In 1948, global (excluding the Eastern bloc) reserves stood at 83.4 per cent of annual global imports, but by 1963 this figure was 48 per cent. Over the same period, developing country reserves fell from 70.1 per cent of their imports to 39.2 per cent.[41]

As can be seen from Table 7.8, relative global reserve levels have since then fallen further, despite some recovery in the seventies. Until 1973, ldcs' reserves relative to their imports were lower than those of developed countries: a situation which is more marked if the United States and the United Kingdom are excluded from the developed country totals, and the oil exporting countries from the ldc totals. As a result of the commodity boom of 1972-3, this situation was reversed in 1973 and 1974. However, by 1974 the improvement of non-oil exporting ldcs' reserve position relative to their imports had been wiped out as a result of mounting import costs: while these ldcs' reserves in 1974 stood at 2½ times their 1970 level, relative to imports they had diminished (see Table 7.8). The ldcs in the worst position were those in Africa and Asia, whose aggregate reserves in 1974 covered less than three months' imports.

The composition of ldcs' reserves makes them more vulnerable to payments problems. As can be seen from Table 7.9, nearly 90 per cent of both oil and non-oil exporting ldcs' reserves in 1974 were held in the form of foreign exchange, with the remainder in gold (5 per cent), SDRs (2 per cent), and Fund reserves (4 per cent). Developed countries, on the other hand, held only 60 per cent of their reserves in the form of foreign exchange, while gold made up nearly 30 per cent. The higher proportion of reserves held in foreign exchange means that any fluctuations in exchange rates have a potentially greater impact on ldcs' reserve position. Such an impact need not, obviously, be adverse and if it is, it may well be matched by gains through reduced external debt liabilities, and be partly offset by the fact that foreign currency reserves earn interest while gold holdings do not.[42] Nonetheless, the need is increased for careful reserve management to minimise the risk of

Table 7.8. International Reserves 1970, 1972, 1973 and 1974 ($ billion)

	1970		1972		1973		1974	
	Reserves at year end	As % of imports	Reserves at year end	As % of imports	Reserves at year end	As % of imports	Reserves at year end	As % of imports
All countries	92.74	31.3	158.97	41.3	184.10	34.8	222.00	28.5
Developed countries	74.45	30.8	126.82	40.5	139.29	32.3	141.18	22.8
Developed countries excluding								
USA & UK	57.13	32.8	108.05	47.7	118.44	37.1	118.84	25.9
Less developed countries	18.29	32.1	32.12	44.7	44.80	45.8	80.82	50.6
of which:								
Oil exporting	5.09	52.5	10.64	78.9	14.61	76.7	46.87	130.6
Non-oil exporting ldcs	13.20	27.9	21.48	36.8	30.19	38.3	33.95	27.4
– in Latin America	4.54	30.7	8.67	46.7	13.75	56.2	14.68	33.8
– in Middle East	1.58	33.7	2.86	49.8	4.26	51.3	5.06	41.6
– in Asia	4.93	26.8	7.26	32.3	9.33	29.3	11.12	21.4
– in Africa	2.03	27.6	2.18	24.8	2.70	25.4	2.94	18.2

Source: IMF, *International Financial Statistics*, April 1975 and November 1975.

Table 7.9 Composition of Reserves, end-1970 and end-1974[1]

	1970										1974									
	Total		Gold		Foreign exchange		SDRs		Reserve position in IMF		Total		Gold		Foreign exchange		SDRs		Reserve position in IMF	
	$ billion	%	$ billion	%	$ billion	%	$ billion	%	$ billion	%	$ billion	%	$ billion	%	$ billion	%	$ billion	%	$ billion	%
All countries	92.74	(100.0)	37.18	(40.1)	44.74	(48.2)	3.12	(3.4)	7.70	(8.3)	222.00	(100.0)	43.70	(19.7)	156.63	(70.6)	10.85	(4.9)	10.83	(4.9)
Developed countries	74.45	(100.0)	33.89	(45.5)	31.21	(41.9)	2.64	(3.5)	6.71	(9.0)	141.18	(100.0)	39.87	(28.2)	84.60	(59.9)	8.94	(6.3)	7.77	(5.5)
Less developed countries	18.29	(100.0)	3.28	(17.9)	13.53	(74.0)	0.48	(2.6)	0.99	(5.4)	80.82	(100.0)	3.83	(4.7)	72.03	(89.1)	1.90	(2.4)	3.06	(3.8)
of which:																				
oil-exporting ldcs	5.09	(100.0)	1.19	(23.4)	3.61	(70.9)	0.08	(1.6)	0.20	(3.9)	46.87	(100.0)	1.48	(3.2)	42.73	(91.2)	0.42	(0.9)	2.24	(4.8)
non-oil exporting ldcs	13.20	(100.0)	2.09	(15.8)	9.92	(75.2)	0.40	(3.0)	0.79	(6.0)	33.95	(100.0)	2.35	(6.9)	29.30	(86.3)	1.49	(4.4)	0.82	(2.4)
– in Latin America	4.54	(100.0)	0.68	(15.0)	3.22	(70.9)	0.22	(4.8)	0.42	(9.3)	14.68	(100.0)	0.71	(4.8)	12.92	(88.0)	0.65	(4.4)	0.40	(2.7)
– in Middle East	1.58	(100.0)	0.50	(31.6)	1.06	(67.1)	0.01	(0.1)	0.22	(0.1)	5.06	(100.0)	0.63	(12.5)	4.24	(83.8)	0.08	(1.6)	0.11	(2.2)
– in Asia	4.93	(100.0)	0.70	(14.2)	3.93	(79.7)	0.10	(2.0)	0.21	(4.3)	11.12	(100.0)	0.77	(6.9)	9.64	(86.7)	0.53	(4.8)	0.19	(1.7)
– in Africa	2.03	(100.0)	0.11	(5.4)	1.72	(84.7)	0.07	(3.4)	0.15	(7.4)	2.94	(100.0)	0.09	(3.1)	2.49	(84.7)	0.22	(7.5)	0.14	(4.8)

[1] Totals may not add because of rounding.

Source: As for Table 7.8.

exchange rate losses. Yet for ldcs, such management is made more problematic by their administrative weakness, lack of technical skills, and remoteness from financial centres.

IMF Credit Facilities

The International Monetary Fund is an important source of credit to ldcs in payments difficulties. The Fund was set up as a result of the Bretton Woods agreement in 1944, and began functioning in 1947. Most independent countries outside the Communist bloc, together with Yugoslavia and Romania, are now members. It is controlled by representatives – the governors – of the national governments. Unlike member states of the UN, and other international agencies, members of the IMF do not have equal voting rights: these are related to the individual country's quota subscription to the Fund, which broadly reflects the individual country's economic power – the US quota in 1975, for instance, was roughly 23 per cent of the total, while that of all ldcs taken together is 27.7 per cent.[43] The purpose of the Fund is to facilitate the orderly expansion of the world economy. To this end, its members are formally required to avoid exchange restrictions and maintain exchange rates stability, except in conditions of 'fundamental disequilibrium' – as determined by the Fund. Members have access to short- and medium-term credit from the Fund to help them meet these requirements and to assist international payments. Access is determined broadly by the size of the country's quota – subject to certain conditions – but additional credit facilities are also available, again under certain conditions. Recently the Fund has taken on an additional role, that of reserve creation, with the introduction of Special Drawing Rights (SDRs) in 1969, which provide members with allocations of unconditional liquidity roughly in proportion to their quotas.

The IMF has not, in practice, played a major role in determining the balance of payments policies of the richer countries. Their economic power and access to alternative sources of credit have generally allowed the richer countries to go their own way in the event of disagreement with the Fund on appropriate payments policies. Developing countries, by contrast, are more dependent on the Fund. Their access to alternative credit facilities tends to be more restricted and, having chosen to maintain relatively low reserves, their potential need for credit is greater. This, in turn, makes it all the more important to ldcs that the Fund is responsive to their particular credit needs. However, the conservative attitude of the Fund to ldcs' needs, and the ldcs' relative inability to influence Fund policies – and their relative weakness in the face of Fund influence on their own policies – has led to criticisms that the IMF, representing the interests of the developed countries, fails to support – and at times impedes – development.[44]

Such criticisms cannot be discussed in detail here but they are not without substance. It is quite clear that, to obtain IMF credit (and aid from major donors made contingent on acceptance of IMF credit conditions), some ldcs have adopted policies, which have arguably been undesirable in development terms, and certainly not desired by the ldc concerned. And it is also clear that certain IMF credit facilities, for instance the compensatory financing facility, could be improved to meet some of ldcs' particular credit needs more adequately, while at the same time preserving the Fund's role as a banker. There is an easy answer to these criticisms, namely, if ldcs do not like the Fund's policies and cannot influence them to the better, they should increase their own reserve holdings, reduce their dependence on the Fund, and quit grumbling. In the short term, this is the only answer for the ldc which is unwilling to accept the kind of conditions which go with Fund credit. But in the longer terms, there is undoubtedly scope for reform. The IMF has not been totally unresponsive to ldcs needs – as will be seen below. Meanwhile, ldcs themselves have acquired a greater voice, if not greater voting rights, in the Fund with the establishment of the Group of Twenty-Four and the Committee of Twenty. The former is the ldcs' equivalent of the developed countries' Group of Ten and consists of twenty-four representatives who discuss and formulate proposals on international monetary issues outside the IMF structure. The latter was instituted by the IMF to negotiate reform of the international monetary system and ldc members make up half the IMF representatives.

Quotas. A country's quota is expressed in SDRs and is equivalent to its subscription to the Fund. Quotas also govern members' voting rights and their access to Fund finances. Quotas for each country are determined by a variety of factors including its national income, its dependence on foreign trade, its reserves – and its political strength.[45] Quotas are reviewed every five years and have been increased on several occasions: by 50 per cent or more in 1959, by 25 per cent or more in 1966 and by 30 per cent in 1970 – a further selective increase partly to take account of the changed economic strength of OPEC countries was agreed in January 1976. Both oil and non-oil producing ldcs have benefited from these increases but their share of the total quotas remains small – if not in relation to either their economic size or to their participation in world trade,[46] then in relation to their liquidity needs and reserve holdings – given the lack of alternative finance. Members subscribe their quota by a payment of 25 per cent in gold and 75 per cent in their own currency. But the 25 per cent gold requirement has been relaxed in the case of some new members, and the IMF reforms agreed in early 1976 are designed to reduce all gold subscriptions – and the role of gold generally in the international monetary system.[47]

The subscription entitles the members to access to Fund credit, known as 'drawing rights', should it require foreign exchange to finance international payments, but not, in principle, to finance speculative currency outflows. A member draws IMF credit by purchasing foreign exchange from the Fund with its own currency. A member can draw up to a limit with the Fund which is expressed in terms of the Fund's holding of the member's currency in relation to its quota. To obtain credit from the Fund, a member makes a deposit of its own currency with the Fund equivalent to its borrowings of foreign exchange – or, put another way, it is allowed to buy foreign exchange with its own currency. The member repays by buying back its own currency with gold or foreign exchange. Thus when a member borrows, the Fund's holding of the member's currency increases, and when it repays, this holding decreases.

Gold and Credit Tranches. At the outset, the Fund holding of each member's currency amounts to 75 per cent of its individual subscription or quota. Each member is allowed to borrow up to 25 per cent of its quota, thereby increasing the Fund's holdings of its currency to 100 per cent of its quota, in any twelve-month period without conditions on the credit (or drawing). This first, automatic, credit is known as the gold tranche. Any subsequent drawings or credit tranches have to be sanctioned by the Fund and the higher the drawings, the more the Fund has to be satisfied that the borrowing country is taking appropriate steps to remove its payments difficulties. A member can draw up to 125 per cent of the value of its quota or, put another way, the Fund will allow its holdings of the member's currency to increase to a maximum of 200 per cent of its quota (although members are permitted, under special credit facilities, to make drawings in excess of this). Each successive 25 per cent credit tranche drawn after the gold tranche bears increasingly onerous terms and conditions. Interest plus administrative charges, although low compared to commercial interest rates, increase with the period of repayment, which generally cannot exceed five years (but see below), and may do so with the amount borrowed in relation to the member's quota. In 1975, interest charges started at 4 per cent for the first year in which the credit was drawn and rose by ½ per cent for each subsequent year the credit remained outstanding.

Extended Credit Facility. As part of recent monetary reforms, IMF credit repayment terms were relaxed in 1974 for members with structural balance of payments problems. Provided that the Fund approves the country's payments policies, a member can now draw up to 140 per cent of its quota on extended repayment terms of 4-8 years, instead of 3-5 years. This is of obvious benefit to ldcs.

Stand-by Credits. In recent years, most countries intending to use their quota drawing rights in the Fund beyond the gold and first credit tranche, have done so under stand-by arrangements. These are contingency arrangements, negotiated with the Fund under which the member country can make drawings up to an agreed limit without its position being further considered by the Fund at the time of drawing. Such drawings are repayable within three years, and stand-by credit may be provided on a revolving basis. Stand-bys are agreed on the basis of IMF approval of a programme, specified in a Letter of Intent, to restore payments equilibrium. The kind of policies that the IMF requires in such programmes and the conditionality of the credit give rise to most resentment in ldcs.[48] In general terms, the conditions are, first, the pursuit of liberal policies on external transactions, for instance, the removal of import and exchange controls; and second – partly to contain the de-stabilising effect of such policies on the balance of payments – the pursuit of deflationary domestic policies, for instance, a reduction in government spending. These policies are consistent with the Fund's risk minimising and conservative approach but are often unpalatable to ldc governments. Their acquiescence to them reflects the relative inadequacy of alternative sources of finance, including their own reserves, and the possibility that aid will not be forthcoming if they do not make the required changes[49] – which gives the IMF greater 'leverage' than would otherwise be possible.

Compensatory Financing and Buffer-Stock Financing Facilities. During the sixties, the IMF established two credit facilities of particular interest to developing countries, both related to export stabilisation. The first, the compensatory financing facility, was introduced in 1963 and improved in 1966. In its present form, it permits a country experiencing a decline in its export earnings which is largely due to circumstances beyond its control to draw up to 50 per cent of its quota – but not more than 25 per cent in any twelve-month period – to compensate for the shortfall. A shortfall is defined as a decline in export earnings as compared with the medium-term trend in such earnings. Repayments are as for ordinary credit drawings but members 'are advised to repay as export proceeds recover'.

As the only export stabilisation measure which attempts to stabilise total export earnings, the introduction of this facility was welcomed by ldcs. In theory, moreover, since drawings under the facility are *additional* to and separate from ordinary quota drawings, they do not lead automatically to more stringent conditions should the country wish to draw on its ordinary credit facilities.[50] In practice, however, a country is at a disadvantage, if it then seeks to draw on its ordinary credit facilities with the IMF. For the Fund is likely to impose more stringent conditions on such a borrower than it would if dealing with a country which had not made compensatory drawings. Further, the compensatory drawings themselves are subject to the condition that the borrowing country satisfies the Fund that it will co-operate to implement the latter's advice on solving its export difficulties. The actual amount of credit available to ldcs under the facility is not large: at an annual rate of $2.4 billion (25 per cent of ldcs' total quota), it would have met a 2½ per cent drop in ldcs' total merchandise export earnings at 1973 levels and 3.3 per cent at 1972 levels. There are, therefore, grounds for supporting the ldc view that the facility should be expanded and, since it involves no net resource transfer, made without conditions as to the borrower's economic policy.[51]

The second facility, for buffer stock financing, was established in 1969 in response to developing country demands. Under this facility which again is separate from, and additional to, ordinary drawing rights, ldcs may draw up to 50 per cent of their quota to finance purchases for international buffer stocks of commodities. If the borrowing country is also drawing compensatory finance – as it might well be, given that buffer stock purchases are usually made when prices are low – its total drawings under both facilities cannot exceed 75 per cent of its quota.

Oil Facility. The oil facility was introduced in June 1974 for a limited period to 'assist members in payments difficulties resulting from the initial impact of increased costs of imports of petroleum and petroleum products'. It has been financed largely by Fund borrowings from the oil exporting countries. As of mid-1975, the Fund had agreed to borrow

SDR 5.6 billion (approximately $7.0 billion) and this was the total amount available for lending to IMF members. The latter's borrowing rights under the facility were additional to their other borrowing rights. The limit to any member's oil facility drawings was determined by the smaller of (a) the increase in its import bill directly resulting from the oil price rise, minus 10 per cent of its reserves, or (b) 75 per cent of its quota. Since potential demand exceeded the funds available, and the needs of ldcs were particularly pressing, about one-third of the funds was earmarked for countries with incomes per head of less than $200 (including all but six of the 'most seriously affected' ldcs). The financial terms of drawings under the oil facility were hard by IMF standards – repayment within seven years and an interest rate of $6\frac{7}{8}$ per cent in the first year, with an additional $\frac{1}{8}$ per cent each subsequent year.

Use of Fund Credit. Ldcs may rightly complain that their quotas and credit facilities with the Fund are inadequate, and that IMF lending conditions are too strict.[52] Nonetheless, besides Britain and Italy, ldcs have been the main users of the IMF's cheap, if conditional, credit over the last decade or so. Both in total and under individual credit facilities, ldcs' share of members' borrowing has exceeded their share of total quotas in most years. Indeed, ldcs have made greater use of Fund credit than developed countries in most years since 1960.

In recent years, virtually all stand-by arrangements have been with ldcs; and between May 1970 and May 1974, eighteen of the twenty countries drawing credit on stand-bys were developing countries. Similarly, virtually all compensatory finance over this period was extended to ldcs, and all buffer stock finance went to ldcs. The oil facility credit was, up to June 1975, more evenly divided between developed and non-oil developing countries. Nevertheless, more than two-fifths of oil facility drawings outstanding at end-June 1975 had been made by ldcs. And over a quarter of *all* outstanding borrowings under the oil facility are held by the 'most seriously affected ' ldcs.

Yet oil importing ldcs as a group have tended to make fairly restricted use of IMF credit in total. This is shown in Table 7.10: only in 1974 and 1975 was their use of fund credit equivalent to more than 25 per cent (but still less than 50 per cent) of their combined quotas.

SDRs and the Link Proposal

IMF Special Drawing Rights (SDRs) are not a credit facility – as the name implies – but an internationally created reserve asset. Unlike

Table 7.10. Use of IMF Credit 1970-5[1]

Areas	Quotas[2]	% of	Use of Fund Credit $m						Share of total use of Fund credit %					
	$ billion	total	1970	1971	1972	1973	1974	1975	1970	1971	1972	1973	1974	1975
All countries	36.79	100.0	3,232	1,455	1,175	1,239	4,579	6,367	100.0	100.0	100.0	100.0	100.0	100.0
Developed countries	26.59	72.3	2,514	680	91	84	2,083	3,272	77.8	46.7	7.7	6.8	45.5	51.4
Less developed countries	10.20	27.7	718	775	1,084	1,156	2,497	3,095	22.2	53.3	92.3	93.3	54.5	48.6
Oil exporting ldcs	1.94	5.3	152	142	125	23	–	–	4.7	9.8	10.6	1.8	–	–
Non-oil exporting ldcs	8.26	22.4	566	633	959	1,133	2,497	3,095	17.5	43.5	81.6	91.4	54.5	48.6
– in Latin America	2.74	7.4	144	168	379	418	487	663	3.5	11.5	32.3	33.7	10.6	10.4
– in Middle East	0.59	1.6	71	121	56	98	179	286	2.2	8.3	4.8	7.9	3.9	4.5
– in Asia	3.48	9.5	234	252	394	455	1,473	1,589	7.2	17.3	33.5	36.7	32.2	25.0
– in Africa	1.44	3.9	147	92	130	161	357	557	4.5	6.3	11.1	13.0	7.8	8.7

1 End of year data in all cases except 1975, when end of June.
2 Quotas as of end-June 1975.
Source: IMF, *International Financial Statistics*.

other reserve assets, which have to be earned or dug up out of the ground, like gold, SDRs are created by the IMF in a quantity determined by its members according to an assessment of global liquidity needs and are allocated to members in proportion to their quotas and voting rights. Originally valued in terms of gold, SDRs have, since July 1974, been valued in terms of a 'basket' of sixteen of the world's leading currencies. As yet, SDRs are used and held only by Central Banks and the IMF. Since the first allocation, in January 1970, of SDR 3.4 billion, two further ones, of SDR 3.0 billion each, have been made in 1971 and 1972. Of the total, ldcs have received SDR 2.35 billion and developed countries SDR 6.97 billion. (A SDR was equivalent to approximately $1.3 at the end of February 1975.)

The distribution of SDRs between member countries has been criticised on grounds of the inequity of *giving* developed countries 75 per cent of the total and ldcs only 25 per cent. Both before and since SDRs were introduced, many observers, ldcs, and some developed countries have held that the creation of such an international reserve asset provides an opportunity to increase ldcs' development resources.[53] Thus, at least a portion of any SDR allocation should be distributed among ldcs only, while the rest should be allocated among developed and developing country IMF members in accordance with some general formula – perhaps quotas – reflecting their reserve and liquidity needs. Under such a system, to obtain larger holding of SDRs than their original allocation, developed countries would have to earn them.

The main opposition to proposals to link SDR creation with development finance – hence the term 'SDR link' – rests on the view that any distribution based on considerations of equity would conflict with managed liquidity creation. Such a distribution would, it is argued, have inflationary effects – for two reasons. First, more of a given total of SDRs would be spent if larger proportions were channeled to ldcs, since they would, for development reasons, spend them on imports rather than hold them as reserves. Second – and this argument is less convincing – ldcs would tend to press for larger allocations of SDRs than the needs for global liquidity justified, since SDR creation would be a source of development finance over which ldcs had some control. Neither argument is particularly compelling as grounds for rejecting the Link proposals since the same sorts of argument apply to any SDR creation, however allocated. A further argument against the Link is that it will not increase ldcs' external development resources since, once it is in operation, donors will cut back their aid giving. This argument is difficult to prove, or to refute, but the possibility that Link development resources will not add to total external development finance makes the *nature* of the Link more important, since this will affect the quality of the resources transferred.

The actual form of the Link between SDRs and development finance is a source of contention. A variety of proposals have been made by both developed and developing countries. Broadly, they fall into three categories. The first type has Link SDRs allocated directly to ldcs in proportion to their IMF quotas. The second has Link SDRs allocated directly but in accordance to some formula reflecting need. The third type of proposal has link SDRs being first channelled to some multilateral aid giving agency – the World Bank soft-lending agency, the International Development Association, is most favoured – and then distributed among ldcs to finance development projects according to existing multilateral aid giving criteria. Although in less than full agreement on the appropriate distribution of SDRs, ldcs, obviously, favour a direct allocation of Link SDRs, since this will not involve donor constraints on their use. The Group of Twenty-Four, which represents ldcs on international monetary issues, has arrived at a compromise formula on allocation, which would give ldcs SDRs in accordance with their quotas, except for the twenty-five least-developed countries, which would be eligible for special additional allocations. The developed countries, understandably, favour an indirect link, where responsibility for allocation and supervision of SDR use is vested in the World Bank, which they control.

The distribution formula proposed by the Group of Twenty-Four is far from being equitable and could be a source of dissension in that, apart from the twenty-five least-developed, it tends to favour the richer ldcs – in particular the oil producing states, most of whom are not in need of additional capital resources. However, ldcs have been united by aversion to donor influence and fears that they might receive smaller allocations under an indirect link proposal: the richer Latin American states think they would lose in a system based on need; the African states doubt their capacity to generate acceptable aid projects; and some radical states fear IDA discrimination. In addition, the advantage of an indirect link to the larger poor countries, such as India, which probably stand to lose under the Group of Twenty-Four proposals, may be outweighed by problems of an administrative nature. Whether additional to total aid resources or not, the Link SDRs would almost certainly greatly increase the resources of any multilateral aid agency through which they were channelled. The administrative burden so imposed could, in turn, slow down disbursement and thus the speed at which ldcs initially received – and benefited from – SDRs.

While any Link scheme would be preferable to the present system of SDR allocation, provided that it led to additional aid resources, in fact ldcs have, to some extent, made up for their smaller share of SDRs by putting them to greater use than developed countries have done. Whereas developed countries have, on the whole, held on to their original SDR allocations and acquired more, ldcs and particularly the African ldcs have been net users of SDR. At the end of June 1975, developed countries were holding SDR 7.36 billion amounting to 106 per cent of their original allocation while non-oil exporting ldcs were holding SDR 1.07 billion, amounting to 55 per cent of their original allocation (oil exporting ldcs were also net users, but less heavily so; holding 88 per cent of their original allocation in June 1975).

Refinancing Debt

Fixed obligations arising from external debt can cause, or worsen, temporary and longer-term payments problems in ldcs – and have done so (as also have outflows of investment income). While inflation is helping to erode ldcs' external debt burden, the foreign exchange costs of debt servicing may still cause some of them problems. An ldc can deal specifically with its debt servicing difficulties by (1) repudiating its debts, (2) unilaterally re-scheduling them, or (3) going to its creditors to seek new debt terms.[54] The problem with the first two courses of action is that they may have adverse effects on capital inflows in the future. In practice, very few ldcs, of which Ghana is one,[55] have unilaterally repudiated or rescheduled their external debts. The number of ldcs – including India and Indonesia – which have sought relief via aid or debt re-organisation from their creditors is not that much greater. This does not mean that there are few ldcs which have faced payment difficulties capable of being reduced by international debt-relief measures. It reflects the unpopularity of such measures with debtors and creditors alike.

The reasons for this unpopularity on the debtor side are to be found in the history of debt-relief measures in the past. Debt re-organisation has tended to provide only relatively temporary relief at the cost of considerable scrutiny of the debtor's internal policies. Typically, ldcs that have got into debt repayment difficulties have had to go cap-in-hand not once, but several times, to their creditors, who – often led by the World Bank – have tended to insist on the pursuit of domestic policies under, or akin to, 'stand-by' programmes. That debt rescheduling is generally unpleasant for the debtor stems partly from creditors' desire to discourage other debtors from viewing it as an easy escape route.

For creditors, too, debt rescheduling does pose difficult problems. These are two-fold. First, how to ensure that the burden of debt relief is borne equally by all creditors: One country, for instance, will not be prepared to relax its repayment requirements if this simply means that others can be repaid on time. Second, how to ensure that debt relief does not constitute an inequitable transfer of resources to debtor ldcs. To some extent, any resource transfer to the debtor country is frowned upon because it is thought to encourage the 'imprudent' at the cost of the 'prudent'. But in the case of some poorer countries, for instance, India, whose debt problems stem partly from the hard terms of earlier aid receipts, the need for debt relief in the form of concessional finance is accepted. These two problems are a major reason for the lengthy negotiations that accompany international debt-relief measures. However, in cases such as that of India, aid donors could help simply by revising the terms of past aid to bring them in line with the terms of their present commitments to the particular recipient. Such a measure might even obviate the need for future debt negotiations. Because of the burden sharing problem, suggestions along these lines have not borne much fruit: only France has unilaterally attempted to cut its recipient's debt burden in this way.

Financing Measures Related to Export Earnings

Export Revenue Stabilisation

Ldcs' export earnings tend to be more prone to fluctuations than those of developed countries and, when reserves are not adequate, such fluctuations can cause payments difficulties. Aside from building up reserves, there are broadly two ways of coping with such fluctuations. The first is to reduce their extent by controlling the volume and price of individual exports. International commodity agreements (discussed in Chapter 3) are examples of this approach. The second is to establish a financial mechanism to offset the effects of fluctuations when they occur. The first approach generally can be employed only to cope with fluctuations in export earnings on a commodity-by-commodity basis, and problems of market organisation limit the extent of its application. The second approach, however, can provide a means of ironing out fluctuations in *total* export earnings.

As yet only two financial schemes exist for the stabilisation of ldcs' export earnings. The first, the IMF compensatory facility, has been discussed above. The second is the recently introduced EEC STABEX scheme, which was discussed in Chapter 3. As a means of combating fluctuations in individual ldcs' total export earnings, the STABEX scheme is deficient in that it applies to only certain export commodities and only if they are exported by the 46 Lomé Associates to the EEC. It can also be criticised on the grounds that the finance provided is likely to be inadequate, and that, for some of the Lomé Associates, it involves a resource transfer – i.e. it is not a self-financing scheme. While a case can be made for resource transfers to counteract falls in the *total* export earnings of poor countries, it is difficult to do so in relation to only *some* commodities. This being said, the STABEX scheme is an advance for the ldcs concerned and may provide a model for a more broadly based, better-financed scheme.

Supplementary Financing Measures

Both the IMF and STABEX schemes are designed to offset fluctuations in export earnings relative to their recent trend. A somewhat different financial mechanism is contained in the proposal for supplementary financing measures. This was elaborated by the World Bank in response to a recommendation by the first UNCTAD in 1964, but has not been implemented.

The proposal is intended to overcome the effects of instability on ldcs' development plans. Instability is determined in relation not to the actual trend of export earnings but to the forecasts embodied in development plans. The amount of supplementary finance made available during the plan period would depend on how much less total earnings were than those projected ('overages', or export earnings above the projected trend, are also taken into account) and also on how much this shortfall would compromise the country's ability to fulfil its development plans. Eligibility for supplementary finance would depend on a prior agreement, between the country and the agency supplying the finance, on its export projections and its plan policy. Although various proposals have been made as to terms, the general idea is that supplementary finance should be concessional, the extent of concessionality being determined by subsequent export performance. (Obviously, for supplementary financing measures to achieve their objective, they would have to be additional to existing aid flows, otherwise development plans could anyway be compromised, to the extent that they are based on the expectation of aid inflows which are then reduced by a diversion of such aid to provide supplementary finance.)

The scheme is open to a number of criticisms, from both the donor and recipient side. Donors particularly have been unhappy about using export projections to determine the need for resource transfers. It has been said that this could simply amount to a reward for bad forecasting. Since additionality is not assured, ldcs whose export earnings are fairly stable have feared that the scheme would result in a reduction in their aid receipts. Finally, the scheme requires considerable policy scrutiny, and hence administrative resources. It is doubted whether any agency could perform the task adequately, while both recipients and the IMF have been uneasy about the powers that would accrue to the supplementary financing body, which would tend to infringe their powers as sovereign states and the main provider of 'residual' finance, respectively.

The two other main criticisms of the proposal are also relevant to other purely financial measures to offset export fluctuations. They are, first, that the proposal deals only with the *effects*, and not the causes, of export instability; and second, that in using export performance as a criterion for additional resource transfers the slowness of export growth should be considered as well as export instability (research suggests that the former is probably more detrimental to development).

Indexation

Another proposal that could help ldcs to avoid payments problems arising from short- to medium-term falls in their export earnings is that of indexation. This also emanates from UNCTAD. The primary objective of indexation is to forestall further deterioration in ldcs' terms of trade *vis-à-vis* developed countries by indexing ldcs' export prices to the prices of their imports from developed countries. Whether it would also stabilise ldcs' export earnings depends on whether the terms of trade to be defended by indexation are appropriate to maintaining equilibrium between supply and demand for ldcs' exports.

A variety of proposals has been made but the one most favoured is for the indexation of the prices of some eighteen primary commodities to the aggregate price of ldcs' imports from developed countries.[56] This is preferred to indexing total export prices to import prices on a country-by-country basis, since the same commodity might have different prices depending on where it was produced. Indexation can be either 'active' or 'passive'. 'Passive' indexation entails developed countries compensating ldcs when the terms of trade deteriorate, and involves a financial mechanism akin to compensatory finance schemes.

'Active' indexation entails increases in the price of exports in step with import price rises, and is preferred for several reasons: it would be automatic and unconditional and would stabilise real prices which, itself, can have beneficial effects. There are, however, many problems of a technical, operational, and political nature associated with the indexation proposal, and while UNCTAD has concluded that it is feasible, its implementation on any broad scale seems remote.[57]

The crucial problem is deciding the level at which to maintain ldcs' terms of trade. Following the OPEC example, some ldcs appear to see indexation as a means not simply of preventing cyclical swings in their terms of trade and offsetting the effects of inflation but also of securing 'fair and remunerative' prices for their exports. There is thus clearly a problem in that the terms of trade to be maintained may be set at a level which is unrealistic in terms of the market forces of supply and demand, resulting in an excess supply of, and reduced demand for, primary products. As a minimum, supply restrictions would then be required to prevent excessive stock-piling and waste of perishable commodities. But even assuming that producers were able to agree on supply restrictions, the maintenance of artificially high prices for primary commodities could lead to a decline in demand such as to reduce total export earnings.

Even if the terms of trade were set at a realistic level, their maintenance would require some form of market organisation to cope with short-term fluctuations in supply and demand – giving rise to the kind of problems associated with commodity agreements. At the same time, the reference terms of trade would have to be altered periodically to avoid supply-demand imbalance, arising from changes in taste and productivity over time.

As a scheme intended to benefit ldcs, indexation has two drawbacks. First, some ldcs, like India, are net importers of primary products. Thus if indexation has any positive effect on primary product prices, these ldcs will lose. Second, some developed countries are important exporters of certain primary products and so will gain along with the ldc primary producers. Without some system of compensatory transfer payments – which the 'active' indexation scheme is intended to avoid – the scheme will benefit some richer countries at the expense of some poorer countries.

The acceptability of the scheme among developed countries is complicated by the issue of burden sharing. Obviously developed countries would be unwilling to back a scheme which resulted in artificially inflated prices for their primary product imports. However, even if the initial terms of trade were realistic, indexation could entail a transfer of resources from developed to developing countries to the extent that, despite devaluations of currencies, their domestic inflation led to an increase in the foreign exchange cost of their exports to ldcs and indexed primary product import prices were then raised in step. In such circumstances indexation would penalise developed countries according to their imports of primary commodities and not according to their contribution to the increase in ldcs' import prices. There is also some reluctance among developed countries to accept indexation of ldcs' exports without at the same time introducing indexation of external assets and liabilities (which would, given the erosive effect of inflation on ldcs' debts, run counter to ldcs' interests).

Because of the problems of indexation on any widespread basis, a more modest approach has been suggested that ldcs should seek indexation within existing commodity agreements. Success at this level – as at any other – will depend on the relative bargaining strengths of the various groups of producers and consumers.

Notes

1. The term 'foreign exchange' used here includes convertible national currencies, gold and Special Drawing Rights (SDRs), all of which may be used to settle international payments. Many ldcs and Communist countries' currencies are not generally acceptable for international payments.
2. See below, p.255 and pp.271-9.
3. This imbalance in pressures was built into the IMF rules, but stems basically from the fact that a debtor, whether a country or individual, is virtually always in a weaker position to resist pressures from his creditor than creditors dealing with pressures from their debtors.
4. The opportunities for productive investment depend on a variety of factors and are not independent of the resources, e.g. technical assistance, obtained from abroad.
5. See below, pp.279-84.
6. See below, pp.281-5.
7. IMF, *Annual Report,* 1975, p.16.
8. See below, p.293.
9. See below, p.293.
10. See Chapters 3, 4 and 5.
11. See Chapters 3 and 4.
12. See also pp.271-9
13. World Bank/IDA, *Annual Report* 1973, p.87. Data relate to eighty developing countries.
14. Includes most export credits and Eurocurrency loans.
15. Until recently the average terms of official aid had improved. In 1974 the terms of both aid and non-aid flows to ldcs hardened.
16. That is, at least $5.06 billion in 1972, according to DAC statistics. See OECD, *Development Co-operation: DAC Review 1974* (Paris, 1974), p.150.

17. Ibid., pp.175-6.
18. See below, p.270ff.
19. A mix of exchange controls and a multiple exchange rate system can be used, as in Brazil in the fifties. There the Government allocated limited amounts of foreign exchange to different categories of transaction and left it to importers to set the various exchange rates by bidding for the foreign exchange available.
20. 'With respect to the problems of uncertainty and exchange rate policy decisions, the less developed countries doubtless suffer a comparative disadvantage in relation to the larger industrial countries. Because of such factors as institutional deficiencies, shortages of technically skilled personnel, limitations of information and communications facilities, and remoteness from major financial centres, many developing countries seem likely to be under som some handicap. . . ' (IMF, *Annual Report,* 1973), pp.32-3.
21. See Chapter 5.
22. I.M.D. Little, T. Scitovsky and M. Scott, *Industry and Trade in Some Developing Countries* (London, OECD and Oxford University Press, 1970), p.133.
23. See pp.193-5.
24. Unless otherwise stated, data refer to resource flows net of capital repayments (amortisation) but not of interest payments.
25. For instance in 1974, DAC aid was estimated to have an average grant element of 87 per cent, compared with an average grant element of 57 per cent for OPEC aid. Both estimates understate the extent of the gift from donor to recipient since they ignore the effect of inflation in reducing the real costs of servicing aid loans.
26. This list includes Bangladesh, Cameroon, Central African Republic, Chad, Dahomey, Ethiopia, Guinea, Haiti, India, Kenya, Khmer Republic, Laos, Lesotho, Malagasy Republic, Mali, Mauritania, Niger, Pakistan, Sierra Leone, Somalia, Sri Lanka, Sudan, Tanzania, Upper Volta, Arab Republic of Yemen, and the People's Democratic Republic of Yemen, all of which have incomes per head of less than $200. A further six countries – El Salvador, Ghana, Guyana, Honduras, Ivory Coast, and Senegal – are also in the list and have incomes per head of $200-$400.
27. For instance, the DAC Chairman and the British Parliamentary Select Committee on Overseas Development proposed that aid should be re-defined – and so, hopefully, redistributed – so that only flows to countries with incomes per head of less than $1,000 and $500 (respectively) counted as aid.
28. See J. Bhagwati, *Amount and Sharing of Aid* (Washington, Overseas Development Council, 1970), p.17 and Mahbub ul Haq, 'Tied Credits: Quantitative Analysis', in Adler and Kuznets (eds.), *Capital Movements and Economic Development* (London, Macmillan, 1967).
29. See, for instance, G.L. Reuber, *Private Foreign Investment in Development* (London, Oxford University Press, 1973), p.53.
30. Including re-invested earnings as well as fresh capital inflows.
31. See Chapter 6.
32. See Chapter 6.
33. Since little data are available for ldc borrowing from other than DAC sources, the data here are confined to ldc borrowing from DAC sources only.
34. See Azizali F. Mohammed and Fabrizio Saccommani, 'Short-term Banking and Eurocurrency Credits to Developing Countries', *IMF Staff Papers,* vol.20, 1973, p.631.
35. For a more detailed exposition of how the Eurocurrency markets function, see K. Pakenham and J. Gore-Booth, 'The Eurocurrency Markets as a Source

of Finance for the Developing World', *ODI Review No.2, 1974.*

36. According to Reuber, nearly one-tenth of net borrowing (including aid) by ldcs between 1965-8 was via 'private firms and agencies' (p.55). Data on the uses of export credits are less easy to come by, but, for instance, slightly over half of the users of British export credits between 1968 and 1971 were private firms (see ODI, *Review 6,* London, 1973, p.85).
37. Nonetheless, by mid-1974, some fifty-five developing countries had tapped the Eurocurrency market. *(DAC Review 1974,* p.147.) Main borrowers, however, are Mexico, Algeria, Brazil, Iran, Greece, and Spain. (Ibid., p.156.)
38. Reuber, p.63.
39. Pakenham and Gore-Booth, p.22.
40. See below, p.284ff.
41. UNCTAD, *The Adequacy of Reserves of Developing Countries in the Post-war Period,* TD/B/C.3/9, November 1965.
42. Analysis of the impact on ldcs of the exchange rate changes in 1971, for instance, suggests that, in aggregate, such gains and losses were offsetting. See G.K. Helleiner, 'The Less Developed Countries and the International Monetary System' (University of Toronto, Mimeo, 1973).
43. At the beginning of 1976 it was agreed, as part of a package of IMF reforms, to increase the level of all quotas and to adjust the relative quotas of Fund members. The main effect of this adjustment will be to increase the quotas of oil producing ldcs relative to all other members.
44. See, especially, C. Payer, *The Debt Trap* (Harmondsworth, Penguin, 1974), and T. Hayter, *Aid as Imperialism* (Harmondsworth, Penguin, 1971).
45. The original quota allocations were arrived at after a series of deals in which the USA was the principal actor. See F. Hirsch, *Money International* (Harmondsworth, Penguin, 1969), p.368.
46. Prior to the 1976 agreement to revise quotas, ldcs' quotas were 27.7 per cent of the total, while their share in world trade outside the Communist bloc was roughly 20 per cent, and their share in world output outside the Communist bloc was less than 20 per cent.
47. The implementation of this reform is geared to benefit ldcs specifically since a portion of the profits made from the sale of IMF gold holdings at market prices are to be used to set up a trust fund for ldcs. This could increase ldcs' access to IMF resources by $400-$500 million a year.
48. And in developed countries, when forced to resort to IMF stand-by credits – as witness the British Labour Government's, and Party's, disgruntlement at having to persent its Letter of Intent in 1967.
49. For instance, US aid to Indonesia in 1963 was contingent on its co-operation with the IMF in such a stabilisation programme.
50. A country can, in addition, request an ordinary drawing to be re-classified as a compensatory drawing (within six months of making the drawing), thereby restoring its ordinary drawing rights.
51. The IMF, in fact, agreed in December 1975, to liberalise the compensatory financing facility with the result that ldcs' potential annual drawings under the facility will be increased by around $1 billion.
52. It should be noted, however that ldcs' annual borrowing facilities in the IMF stand to rise by roughly $3 billion as a result of reforms agreed in December 1975 and January 1976.
53. For a history of the Link proposal, see Y.S. Park, 'The Link Between Special Drawing Rights and Development Finance', *Essays in International Finance,* No.100 (Princeton University, 1973).
54. In the case of investment income outflows, the ldc may stop them either by imposing exchange controls (see above) or by nationalising foreign

investments (see Chapter 6).

55. Although in Ghana's case, Colonel Acheampong's repudiation of some debts and rescheduling of others in 1972 was followed by the offer of the most generous debt settlement package it had ever received from its creditors. See Andrzej Krassowski, *Development and the Debt Trap* (London, Croom Helm for ODI, 1974), p.147.
56. See UNCTAD, *The Indexation of Prices*, TD/B/503, Supp.1, July 1974, also Commonwealth Secretariat, *Terms of Trade Policy for Primary Commodities*, Commonwealth Economic Papers No.4 (London, 1975), pp.16-25, and Chapter 3, for a further discussion of the issues involved.
57. UNCTAD, TD/B/503, p.58.

8 ECONOMIC CO-OPERATION AND TRADE AMONG DEVELOPING COUNTRIES

In Chapter 1, we suggested that there could be many reasons – including the desire to increase self-reliance – why developing countries should want to increase their trade with each other. So far, the growth of this trade has been patchy at best; while trade among some ldcs has grown substantially, others have had less success. In this chapter, we first look at the statistics of trade among ldcs, then examine some of the reasons why ldcs wish to increase co-operation through trade and in other ways, and lastly review some of the new developments in this area.

STATISTICAL BACKGROUND

As we have seen from Tables 1.5 and 1.6, the value and share of developing countries' exports going to other ldcs vary considerably. Overall, in the early seventies, inter-ldc trade accounted for 19 per cent of exports from all developing countries including oil producers, as against 21 per cent in the early sixties. For non-oil producing countries, the corresponding figures for 1970-2 and 1960-2 were 20.1 per cent and 19.7 per cent respectively.

The two sets of figures reflect the much more rapid growth of sales from oil exporting ldcs to the developed Western world over the period than to other countries – 8.9 per cent a year for the former, as against 5.5 per cent for the latter – even in the ten years preceding the 'oil crisis'. For non-oil exporting ldcs, exports to other ldcs grew very slightly faster than those to the world as a whole. Latin American, Caribbean, and African countries' exports to other ldcs grew substantially faster than their exports to other countries, although in some cases (e.g. Latin American trade with Africa) from a very low base.

Trade among countries in the same broad geographical area typically accounts for the largest share of inter-ldc trade – Latin America to Latin America, European ldcs to the Mediterranean area, African countries to other African countries, Asian ldcs to others in the same region. But oil producing states have also taken an increasing share of trade from some developing countries, notably Middle East and Northern African countries (regional trade), the Far Eastern export-based economies, and the Indian sub-continent. Since 1973, balance of payments constraints linked to higher oil costs have greatly increased the importance of exporting to oil producers.

These statistics, though broad and sketchy, give a favourable impression at first glance of trade among developing countries. Tables 5.2 and 8.1 confirm this impression at least where exports of manufactures are concerned. In 1973, 32 per cent of ldcs' intra-trade was in goods broadly categorised as 'manufactures' as against 21 per cent in 1960-2. Here again, trade among ldcs has at least kept pace with, and in certain cases surpassed, trade with the world as a whole. For non-oil producers as a group, over 45 per cent of exports to ldcs were in these categories.

REASONS FOR SLOW GROWTH OF INTER-LDC TRADE

It is easy to point to historical and more recent reasons why trade among ldcs should have developed rather sluggishly. Political and economic ties between colonies and their metropolitan powers, and economic domination even where overt colonial links did not exist – as in the case of Latin America *vis-à-vis* the United States – are one very strong historical reason. Trade 'followed the flag' in the sense that most imports came from and most exports went to the governing power. Transport and communications grew up with the aim of taking plantation and mine products from the interior to ports for export, and capital and consumer goods in the other direction. Shipping lines thus also mainly ran between the colonies and the metropolis – Peninsular and Oriental East of Suez, Union Castle to Africa, from Britain. Investment in farming and extractive industries for export, combined with tied aid, maintained these links. And the existence of different currency areas, with little possibility of or interest in convertibility among the currencies of different developing countries, inhibited the financing of trade in other directions.

Since independence, too, many ldcs' development programmes have tended to inhibit, rather than to encourage, trade with others. This is particularly true where industries have been created to substitute local production for exports. Most ldcs' domestic markets are by definition small. Many do not have the market required to establish competitive industries alone. If several ldcs in the same region start up production in large-scale industries – particularly those like steel, chemicals, or tyre manufacturing, which absorb large capital investment and need high-volume output to remain viable – these industries may only be

Table 8.1. Composition of Trade among Developing Countries, 1973

	%			
	All ldcs	OPEC	Ldcs less OPEC	World
All ldcs				
Total	100.0	100.0	100.0	100.0
Food, beverages and tobacco[1]	17.1	29.2	15.4	19.0
Crude materials, oils and fats[2]	14.2	6.5	15.2	15.7
Fuels[3]	35.3	4.7	39.5	39.6
Chemicals[4]	4.3	4.5	4.2	1.6
Machinery and transport equipment[5]	7.6	12.9	6.8	4.3
Other manufactures[6]	20.1	40.9	17.2	19.0
All ldcs less OPEC				
Total	100.0	100.0	100.0	100.0
Food, beverages and tobacco[1]	24.7	31.0	23.4	29.2
Crude materials, oils and fats[2]	16.9	6.2	19.1	21.9
Fuels[3]	10.6	3.5	12.6	7.9
Chemicals[4]	5.9	4.1	6.2	2.4
Machinery and transport equipment[5]	10.6	10.9	10.5	6.7
Other manufactures[6]	29.1	42.9	26.4	30.3

[1] SITC Sections 0 + 1.
[2] SITC Sections 2 + 4.
[3] SITC Section 3.
[4] SITC Section 5.
[5] SITC Section 7.
[6] SITC Sections 6 + 8.
Source: United Nations, *Yearbook of International Trade Statistics, 1974.*

able to survive behind high protective barriers against imports from outside.

MOVES TOWARDS CO-OPERATION

Despite barriers such as those suggested above – which are only some of the obstacles to inter-ldc trade – some successes have been achieved, and in recent years the movement towards greater economic co-operation among ldcs has grown stronger. (See Table 8.2 for details of economic groupings.) A United Nations study issued in 1973 noted

Table 8.2 Selected Economic Groupings of Ldcs

Organisation	Member States	Date of establishment	Main provisions of agreement
Latin America and Caribbean			
1. Latin American Free Trade Area (LAFTA)	Bolivia, Chile, Colombia, Ecuador, Peru, Argentina, Mexico, Paraguay, Uruguay, Venezuela, Brazil	1960	Free Trade Area leading to establishment of Latin American Common Market by 1985. Distinguishes relatively developed countries (Argentina, Brazil, Mexico), less developed countries (Colombia, Chile, Peru, Venezuela) and under-developed countries (Bolivia, Ecuador, Paraguay, Uruguay). Less developed and under-developed members can obtain preferential treatment from others and have a longer timetable for reduction of tariffs among LAFTA members. No common external tariff. Joint industrial planning through 'complementarity' agreements whereby production is shared among countries.
2. Andean Common Market and Community (ACM)	Bolivia, Chile till 1976, Colombia, Ecuador, Peru, Venezuela	1969 (Cartagena Agreement): Venezuela joined in 1973	Common external tariff by 1980: internal free trade by 1981. Bolivia and Ecuador (less developed members) have longer time-table for removal of customs duties. Common policy on foreign investment stipulates 51 per cent local control within 15 years (20 years for Bolivia, Ecuador) of initial investment. Andean Development Corporation (1967) serves as common development bank. Agreements on merchant shipping and on treatment of migrant workers.

Table 8.2. (Contd.)

Organisation	Member States	Date of establishment	Main provisions of agreement
Latin America and Caribbean *(contd.)*			
3. Central American Common Market (CACM)	Costa Rica, El Salvador Guatemala, Honduras,* Nicaragua. (*Honduras, while still officially a member, has re-imposed tariffs on other members)	1960	Common external tariff and internal free trade (largely achieved). Intra-regional trade increased tenfold 1963-73. Aims at common customs administration, fiscal policy, industrial policy, etc.
4. Caribbean Community (CARICOM)	Antigua, Barbados, Belize, Dominica, Grenada, Guyana, Jamaica, Montserrat, St. Kitts – Nevis – Anguilla, St Lucia, St Vincent, Trinidad and Tobago.	1973 (Treaty of Chaguaramas) – succeeding CARIFTA (1968)	Common external tariff and protective policy against imports from outside. Common scheme for incentives for industry envisaged. Joint planning in agriculture, aiming at greater self-sufficiency and intra-regional trade, covers most items produced in the region for regional consumption. Slower timetables for integration of less-developed members (all those except Guyana, Jamaica, Trinidad and Tobago, and Barbados). Caribbean Development Bank (1970) lends to public and private development projects.

Table 8.2. *(contd.)*

Organisation	Member States	Date of establishment	Main provisions of agreement
Africa			
5. East African Community (EAC)	Kenya, Tanzania, Uganda	1967	Intra-Community free trade, modified by 'transfer taxes' (internal import duties) imposed by deficit countries (Uganda and Tanzania against Kenya). Common external tariff inherited and adopted from colonial administration. Common exchange control, posts, railways, harbours and shipping and airlines administrations through independent regional corporations. East African Development Bank aims to invest 77 per cent of funds in Uganda and Tanzania.
6. Economic Community of West African States (ECOWAS)	Dahomey, The Gambia, Ghana, Guinea, Guinea-Bissau, Ivory Coast, Liberia, Mali, Mauritania, Niger, Nigeria, Senegal, Sierra Leone, Togo, Upper Volta	1975	Staged reduction to zero of internal customs duties and establishment of common external tariff by 1990. Free movement of labour and, ultimately, of capital. Harmonisation of agricultural, industrial, economic, and monetary policies and promotion of joint agricultural, marketing, research, and agro-industrial projects, together with schemes for joint development of infrastructure. Elimination of inter-state disparities in development: establishment of ECOWAS fund for co-operation, compensation, and development.
7. Union Douanière et Economique de l'Afrique Centrale (UDEAC)	Cameroon, Central African Republic, Congo (Brazzaville), Gabon	1966	Customs union with common external tariff, with preferences for EEC and 'French African' countries. Common investment code. Common central bank based in Paris. All countries members of the Franc Area.

Table 8.2. *(contd.)*

Organisation	Member States	Date of establishment	Main provisions of agreement
Africa *(contd.)*			
8. Communauté Economique de l'Afrique de l'Ouest (CEAO)	Ivory Coast, Mali Mauritania, Niger, Senegal, Upper Volta, (Observers: Benin, Togo)	1974 (formerly West African Customs Union – UDEAO)	Customs union with common external tariff. Joint policies to be developed on transport and communications, cattle and beef, industry, trade, tourism, etc. Intra-Community free trade in crude products: Regional Co-operation Tax on intra-trade in manufactures. Community Development Fund to be established. Common central bank based in Paris.
9. Maghreb Permanent Consultative Committee	Algeria, Morocco, Tunisia	1964-70	Permanent intergovernmental committee aiming at strengthening Maghreb co-operation. In abeyance since 1970.
Asia			
10. Association of South-East Asian Nations (ASEAN)	Indonesia, Malaysia, Philippines, Singapore, Thailand	1967	Not customs union. Gradual relaxation of barriers to regional trade. Joint negotiations with other countries (e.g. EEC) and within GATT. Private-sector consultation through Chambers of Commerce and Industry. Joint highway projects, tourist promotion. Consideration of Asian shipping line.
Middle East			
11. Regional Co-operation for Development (RCD)	Iran, Pakistan, Turkey	1964	Intergovernmental discussion and co-operation in fields of industrial co-operation (joint regional agreements on establishment of certain industries), transport (RCD shipping services on internal routes), joint public/private enterprises, trade expansion. No common tariff or free-trade area.

that intra-group trade within eight groups of developing countries aiming in some way at co-operation or integration had increased considerably faster than the same countries' total exports, or than the exports of all developing countries, at a rate of some 11 per cent a year, over the period 1960-71.[1]

The economic groups discussed in this paper vary enormously in their composition, number of countries, size and stage of development, as well as in their aims. Some (such as CARICOM) aim at complete economic integration eventually; others (e.g. RCD) are less ambitious.[2] Some (such as the RCD) are alliances of relatively rich countries with strong (potentially or actually) agricultural or industrial bases; others (e.g. UDEAC) comprise some of the poorest countries in the world. Some have a dominant partner (as in the East African Community), while in others political and economic power is more widely and evenly spread.

The majority of the groups have followed a pattern common among developed as well as developing countries; that of establishing a free trade area, or a fuller customs union or common market, over a predetermined period. In some cases, this framework was chosen (e.g. in the East African Community) because the member countries had previously been linked in a free-trade zone in which mutual preference was given to goods imported from the other members. The examples of the European Free-Trade Area (EFTA) and European Economic Community (EEC) also encouraged developing countries to try to reduce their own customs barriers for goods imported from other members of regional groups. The UN document referred to above suggests that the rigidity of GATT rules, prior to the adoption of Part IV in 1969, was the most important reason why ldcs generally undertook schemes of economic co-operation through arrangements intended to lead to customs unions or free-trade areas.[3] This is questionable: many of the countries (particularly those in Latin America) involved in economic co-operation agreements are not, or were not at the time, signatories to GATT and therefore should not have been too conscious of the need to adhere to its rules. A more likely influence was the generally accepted view that economic integration was a good thing, a view supported by a body of economic theory which favoured economic co-operation as a means of exploiting growth potential and furthering specialisation in areas where a particular group might be able to develop comparative advantages.[4]

REASONS FOR CO-OPERATION

In broad terms, there seem to be four main reasons why ldcs should get together. First, by doing so they achieve a larger total market for the goods which each of them produces. Second, they may be able to utilise complementary resources to build up national or regional specialisations. Third, these two possibilities may lead on to free some important bottlenecks on the road of economic development. Lastly, in creating a spirit of greater co-operation and freedom from old economic connections, there may be important political and psychological benefits.

Market Size

A principal rationale for economic integration or co-operation among ldcs is that larger markets may be able to use factors of production (land, labour, and capital), more efficiently than smaller ones. Most developing countries, considered individually, have small markets for goods produced and sold for cash, whether agricultural or industrial. Even where there is a large population, low levels of average income mean that total purchasing power is low.

Until recently, most developing countries (economies like Singapore and Hong Kong are the exception by force of circumstances) have regarded industrialisation with the aim of import substitution as the main route to development. In any economy, infant industries need to be protected against imports from established outsiders. However, without a wider market than the individual ldc can provide, many may never be able to emerge from behind their protective tariffs and quotas. With a wider, regional market, it is argued, unit costs of production could be reduced, and so the degree of protection needed.

Even where relatively thriving industries have already become established, the prospect of access to a regional market is, in principle, attractive. For example, a recent study of the ASEAN group points out that the market for consumer goods in the area, which in 1968 was already three times the size of any single member (the largest economies being Indonesia and the Philippines) was expected to double in size by 1980: 'Thus any manufacturer of such goods may hope, if access to other ASEAN markets becomes possible for his goods, to think in terms of an output some six times that which was available to him in 1968 within the market of his own country'.[5]

If economies of scale can result from access to a regional market, then in theory at least a net increase in welfare should result. But are economies of scale important, and might not enlarged access for major industries merely create regional monopolies?

It is well known that economies of scale vary greatly from industry to industry. No doubt in industries such as steel-making, artificial fertiliser production, and other chemical manufacturing processes – all heavily capital-intensive industries requiring a large initial investment and continuous process output for efficiency – there are considerable advantages to be gained from large-scale operation. But for many other industries – e.g. textiles (except the manufacture of artificial fibres themselves, really a branch of the chemical industry) or the type of export-orientated assembly industry in which many developing countries specialise – the absolute scale of operation may not be very important. Studies undertaken by the UN Economic Commission for Latin America estimated that in textiles, unit costs fell by only some 10 per cent as output doubled.[6] The OECD study of economic integration among developing countries points out that large size also has its disadvantages:

> Large-scale production generates certain countervailing tendencies that may compensate part or all of the economies of scale achieved in the productive process. For example, marketing and distribution costs may grow disproportionately with the size of output. Transport costs might exhibit the same tendencies, and in many developing countries, the existing transport system (which has been geared to exports to developed countries and to imports from them) may frustrate the economic forces which should normally determine the location of new plants. This would lead to unnecessarily high transport costs or might even prevent large-scale production.[7]

The study of the ASEAN group, quoted above, reinforces many of the reservations about the types of industry in which large scale is important. It points out that

> There has in general been rapid development in the region of those types of industry in which relatively small-scale production is efficient and in which considerable economies of transport costs can be made by meeting local demands from local production. On the other hand, the ASEAN countries have remained very heavily dependent on imports in those industries in which there are considerable economies from large-scale production.[8]

The list of industries suggested by the UN team as suitable candidates for joint industries to be planned for the whole ASEAN market is itself revealing: nitrogenous and phosphatic fertilisers, carbon black (for adding to rubber), caprolactam and ethylene glycol (raw materials for the manufacture of synthetic textiles), soda ash, sheet glass, newsprint, sealed compressors, small engines, typewriters, and steel itself. The general orientation of the plans outlined – as in most integration projects – is described as 'the opportunity for collective saving of imports from the outside world'.[9]

Probably the most general statement that can be made about economies of scale through ldc co-operation is that production of some types of goods for a larger market than the national one *can* be more efficient; even if it is not as efficient, in world market terms, as production in established industries in developed countries. However, a move to establish one industry to serve a complete region in a particular product-area may in the short run be unwelcome to countries previously importing at lower cost from outside the area; their balance of trade may actually be worsened by the new imports. Similarly, where one regional plant (even if theoretically more efficient) displaces a number of small, heavily protected national producers, the resulting disruption in individual countries may be difficult, politically and economically, to cope with. As is already shown in relations between developed and developing countries, in the reaction of established producers to new imports in the fields of textiles and footwear (for example) there may be real problems of adjustment. These are hard enough in developed countries with a highly diversified industrial structure; in poor, small countries with tiny industrial bases they may be almost insuperable.

The other advantage claimed for larger markets – that previously featherbedded producers may be exposed to competition, and that this will promote greater efficiency – runs counter to the 'economies of scale' case. If the aim is to develop new industries which require large-scale operation, then creating competition among existing small producers will not fulfil it. If there are at the outset no competing producers in the region, the larger market may just confirm the position of one dominant firm in an industry as a monopolist. The only case where competition might be expected to bring real benefits is where potentially competitive industries exist already and a choice of products in the same broad area would be desirable. If governments are prepared to accept competition from industries in other member countries of the group, with the risk that their own domestic producers may be driven out by that competition, this case can be made to work in practice. But it is often a big 'if'.

Use of Complementary Resources to Create Regional Specialisation

'Regional specialisation' can mean either of two things: specialisation *by* a given region in the production of particular goods, or the specialisation *within* a given region, under the impetus of a protected free-trade zone, by individual countries in the production of goods in which they have a comparative advantage. In the first category fall projects such as those aimed at using raw materials produced in one part of a region for processing in another; in the second, the attempts which many groups of developing countries have made to allocate different branches of production among themselves, with a view (in theory at least) both to their different factor endowments and to 'balance' within the region.

In any group of countries, some will be relatively rich in resources which others lack. One of the classic reasons for trade is the opportunity which it gives nations to take advantage of resources in which they are relatively abundant. The argument for regional co-operation builds on this basic case in suggesting that, through a division of labour among developing countries according to relative factor endowments, each one's resources can be better developed than would be the case separately. For example, investment by Gulf states in Pakistan's agriculture, combined with supplies of fertiliser at favourable prices in return for guaranteed supplies of wheat or maize, would be a reasonable division of labour between a group of countries which have large capital resources and reserves of raw material (oil) but which are short of productive land and labour to work it, and a country which has fertile land and a large population but little capital or raw materials. The special factor endowments of particular countries in a group may alternatively be exploited by the creation of a regionally integrated industry; e.g. the planned construction of a jointly owned Jamaican/Venezuelan aluminium smelter in Venezuela (near the source of energy for generating electricity used in smelting aluminium), taking its supplies from Jamaica.

For most ldcs, the change in thinking required in moving from planning their own industrial or agricultural development on a domestic basis to planning for regional co-operation is a big one. Many ldcs are still in the process of establishing their own national identity, without having the added complication of working out methods of regional co-operation. The problems may be exacerbated by the similarity of many countries' development programmes (often encouraged by aid and advice from developed countries). Most developing countries have begun by promoting import substituting industries of much the same kind: textiles, shoes, vehicle assembly (perhaps followed by the manufacture of vehicle parts and the development of metal working industries), and local 'manufacture' of paints, soaps, cosmetics, detergents – some of which may use local raw materials but which more often are vehicles for foreign investment in assembly-type production using imported materials and simply packaging them for the local market. Even those industries which use local resources productively, operate profitably, and are genuinely import saving (e.g. textiles, or soap using local oils, or vehicle-parts manufacture where value added may be high compared to raw material costs) may be more efficient in one country of a region than another. In this situation, simply opening national barriers to imports of a more competitive good from a neighbouring ldc may be traumatic enough. Deliberate regional planning, which involves giving up a domestic industry to buy the same goods from a new or larger enterprise in another part of the region, may be even harder to swallow.

For this reason, two main factors are generally taken into account in joint agricultural or industrial planning: the development of production in areas in which particular countries have an apparent advantage, and the need to have a certain regional 'balance'. Sometimes, as in the case of the development of a common agricultural policy in the Caribbean Community (CARICOM), both seem, happily, to coincide.

Regional Integration in Agriculture: CARIFTA/CARICOM

CARIFTA (now CARICOM) has gone some considerable way towards exploiting the different comparative advantages of West Indian states in agriculture. Three main agreements have been introduced over time among the member states: on rice, on oils and fats, and on trade and marketing of agricultural products in general.[10]

Within CARICOM, agreements on the supply and purchase of rice control trade between Guyana, the main producer, and firstly the Windward and Leeward Islands and Barbados, secondly, Jamaica, and thirdly, Trinidad and Tobago. Under the agreements Guyana undertakes to sell rice to the other parties, and they undertake to buy from Guyana as much of their consumption requirements as the country can supply. Estimates of imports required are submitted annually, but do not represent binding commitments; similarly, Guyana must provide production estimates and crop forecasts on request to other members but is not compelled to maintain stocks or to import to meet trade commitments if current production falls short of the forecast, although it must inform buying countries two months in advance if their requirements cannot be met. Prices are also fixed in advance annually, and are related to world market prices – a feature which keeps the agreement flexible, ensures that in times of surplus importers do not feel they are paying too high a price, and that in shortage periods Guyana is not required to sell at too low a price.

The Caribbean agreement on oils and fats which operated from 1959 to 1970, when it was incorporated into the general CARIFTA agreement on farm produce, insulates local output against foreign competition by setting import restrictions, regulating trade with countries outside the region, and dividing up both supply and demand among the countries of the area by means of export and import quotas. The agreement was mainly concerned with copra and coconut oil production and trade. Again, it set prices and quantities of oils and fats traded annually in advance, an arrangement which allowed processing industries to plan their inputs of raw materials and provided some measure of security for producers. There were restrictions on the volume of oils and fats other than coconut which might be imported into the participating countries (originally all West Indian territories, but latterly only Barbados, Dominica, Grenada, Guyana, St Lucia, St Vincent, and Trinidad and Tobago), and on the amount of copra which could be exported to countries outside the area, except in the case of a major surplus or of shipments intended specifically to promote the development of the oils and fats industry. Production of oils in the Caribbean area has increased, under the protection of the agreement, to approach self-sufficiency.

The wider agreement on the marketing of agricultural products signed by Caribbean countries in 1968 was modelled very largely on the oils and fats agreement. It covered a wide range of products in general consumption in the area, including carrots, peanuts, tomatoes, peppers, garlic, onions, potatoes and sweet potatoes, cloves, bananas, pork, poultry, eggs, oranges, and pineapples. Restrictions on imports, and prices at which trade should take place among the CARIFTA member states, were fixed every year. The overall aims were to promote import substitution in agricultural products in CARIFTA as a whole, and through the construction of a free-trade area within the group to develop farm resources in a way less dependent on the vagaries of world markets for principal tropical crops, and less traditional.

An early assessment of the CARIFTA marketing scheme suggested that in moving from the regulation of one group of products (copra and coconut oil) rather homogeneous in nature and produced under similar conditions throughout the area, to a large and varied group of products cultivated under very varying conditions, many of which were seasonal crops and most of which were perishable, the group might have gone too far too fast. The need for a new administrative process, the degree of supervision and of statistical information required, and the limited capacity of local administrations would make such an agreement difficult to apply. The author took the view that 'possibly the same results might be achieved by allowing unrestricted free trade in these products, by drawing up regional plans for agricultural development and by improving the marketing systems in order to regulate trade on a rational basis'.[11]

The CARICOM agricultural agreement, however, provides a good case of a scheme orientated towards exploiting comparative advantages within a region, and towards expanding the area in which import substitution takes place. In many ways it appears like the EEC's Common Agricultural Policy, a device to shield producers in the area from outside competition and to promote trade among the countries of the region: two aims which, as the CAP has shown, are quite compatible. Protection against outsiders allows internal trade to develop. The cost is generally higher (although possibly also more stable) prices than might prevail under generally free trade. The stability given to producers in the region by common marketing arrangements with stable, controlled prices may (as EEC experience has again shown) provide a framework within which farming and trade in farm products can develop much faster than without the safety net which such policies provide.

However, in any such arrangement, as in commodity agreements, the levels at which controlled prices are set relative to 'world' prices (if these can be reasonably accurately judged and if they are representative) are crucial to the operation. The CARICOM agreements appear to work reasonably well partly at least because annual or periodic price reviews have always been conducted – unlike EEC arrangements until recently – with one eye on the prices prevailing on world or other representative markets.

'Balance' and Regional Industrial Planning

As we have said, the problems which individual countries may see in changing from national to regional planning often make it necessary to build in some concept of 'balance' among the countries of a region in designing larger industrial projects. Projects in one country must be set off against those in another to ensure that all get a fair slice of the cake. But on what basis?

The UN team, in reporting on ways and means of developing regional co-operation in ASEAN, rightly stressed the importance of efficiency in planning the location of investment. But in creating a stronger regional unity it may be necessary to sacrifice strict economic efficiency in the interests of ensuring that all the members of a group can be seen to benefit. Some industries being set up in a particular region may only have one suitable location – e.g. those which are concerned in mining or which need easy access to sources of energy (aluminium) or water (papermaking). Others, however, particularly those in which a large labour input is required, such as assembly or packing industries, will be more 'foot-loose'. In these cases it may be necessary to encourage, or even to compel, if this is possible, investors to site their plants in a location which may not be the most attractive, simply to maintain the interest of the weaker partners in the group.

The problem is particularly acute when one country in a group appears to have all the advantages (Kenya is one such case within the East African Community, with good transport and communications, a government favourable to foreign investors, and a healthy industrial sector). Growth-points occur in any economy; and within a region, elimination of trade barriers without any 'regional policy' may simply ensure that the benefits all go to the strongest countries.

For projects in which location is not critical, a good deal of weight can be given to the political advantages of 'balance'. As one study of integration in Latin America has suggested, this need not increase costs prohibitively.[12] But there must be some compensatory mechanism to ensure that each new project not situated at the optimum location can sell its products competitively in the regional market. A wide range of means is used – often several methods jointly – to this end. Tariff preferences may be extended to less developed countries within a region by the richer partners. This has been done, for example, in the Andean common market where the three richer members (Chile, Peru, and Venezuela) freed all imports from the two poorer countries (Bolivia and Ecuador) by 1973, compared to a programme of trade-liberalisation among the three 'big' countries scheduled to be completed in 1980. The East African Community operates a system of 'transfer taxes', in many respects similar to internal import duties, which can be levied by countries whose intra-regional trade in particular products is in deficit (in practice by both Tanzania and Uganda on imports from Kenya). Development Banks or credit institutions may be required to give specially favourable terms to, or invest a certain proportion of funds in, projects in poorer countries. This is the case with the Caribbean Development Bank, the East African Development Bank, and the Andean Development Corporation. Industrial or agricultural co-operative planning may allow longer for projects to be put in hand and brought to the productive stage in poorer countries – again a method used by the Andean group in planning the allocation of industries to Bolivia and Ecuador.

One feature brought out by the UN team in its report on ASEAN is that it will almost certainly be easier to show benefits to all members of a co-operation arrangement if a large number of projects is envisaged. If only one or two big industries are planned for a region, there may be little locational choice, or big countries may be able to bid more successfully. If a regional plan contains many proposals, particularly if a fair number are for 'foot-loose' industries, it will be much more feasible, at least in principle, to divide the benefits among the participating countries.[13]

Easing Developmental Bottlenecks

Liberalisation of trade barriers among ldcs will not necessarily lead to a dramatic or immediate growth of trade, and even less to sudden great strides in development. Trade barriers in the form of tariffs, quotas, and so on, may be one bottleneck which constrains trade and investment; but others may need to be freed first before the effect of liberalising trade among groups of ldcs can be fully felt.

These bottlenecks can be physical, financial, psychological, or political. In so far as they can be solved by economic means, these means may relate more to investment in basic infrastructure, for example, the redirection of transport and communications facilities, than to the liberalisation of overt trade barriers.

The Brookings study of Latin American integration referred to above notes that:

> Historical and institutional forces have done much more to bias Latin American trade towards outside areas than have geographical barriers. Almost every country's production, transportation, and other trade mechanisms were developed by Europeans and North Americans interested primarily in purchasing Latin American raw materials and in turn using Latin America as an outlet for their

> manufactures. Transportation systems were therefore geared mainly to external trade, connecting ports with the centres of primary goods production and with the capital.
>
> Furthermore, the fear of neighbouring countries was so strong that transportation arteries along natural borders were purposely neglected. Not only are there few roads crossing from one country to another, but those that do exist are left in disrepair. Trans-shipment of cargo at frontier points on railroads and highways, still frequently required by national authorities (even when rail gauges do not differ) has imposed a heavy burden on intra-area trade.[14]

It is unlikely that reductions in trade barriers, even if a necessary condition for increasing intra-area trade, could ever be anything near sufficient. Transport, telecommunications and marketing networks, as well as adequate financial mechanisms, all need to be developed alongside.

Shipping development, for example, is a main requirement for the expansion of regional trade in both CARICOM and the ASEAN group, as well as to improve export possibilities in the rest of the world. In regional trade, projects which may create new products to be shipped within the group may not be able to be carried out unless adequate shipping and port facilities can be guaranteed. Similarly, unless port facilities can be developed, and the pattern of intra-regional shipping improved (e.g. using small local-trade vessels as collectors of goods for loading at some central point into bulk carriers jointly chartered), escalating transport costs may cut the competitive ability of efficient export industries.[15]

The development of new shipping facilities, moreover, requires large investment and skilful organisation. Finance for improving ports will usually have to be found outside most groups of ldcs. Like most infant industries, new shipping lines will almost certainly require considerable subsidies. And the training of people to operate new facilities will be as important as the finance for the developments themselves.

Again, the development of new banking and financial links for efficient inter-country payments among ldcs is also likely to be one of the preconditions for success in economic co-operation: this may involve, as a start, a move away from 'colonial' banking patterns linked to a metropolis, and may include the creation of new clearing houses and accounting units for inter-ldc trade. Within the Asian region, the UN

Economic Commission for Asia and the Far East (ECAFE – now ESCAP)[16] proposed in 1971 the establishment of an Asian clearing union, with a central clearing house and a unit of account based on the SDR, in which inter-Asian trading accounts could be settled and trade credit extended. And more ambitiously, two British economists have proposed that all ldcs as a group should set up a common accounting unit in which payments related to trade among them could be made.[17]

Greater integration among ldcs may also help to overcome the important developmental bottleneck which is represented by the need to import techniques and technologies, which may be badly suited to a developing country situation, from the developed world. Firms serving a regional market could, for example, gauge the needs of farmers throughout the area for particular machines adapted to their particular circumstances. Items developed in one ldc could be sold to others. In this way, it may be possible to develop indigenous technologies, or to adapt appropriate parts of imported techniques for use in ldcs.

Psychological Benefits from Co-operation: Less Dependence

One of the great drives to economic and political co-operation is the belief that unity is strength. Belief in continental political unity as a goal has in recent years been somewhat deflated – whether Nkrumah's Pan-Africanism or the Europeanism of the founders of the European Community. But on a smaller scale and with less grandiose aims, the simple idea that international co-operation can create greater strength and security still has many adherents among developing countries.

More common, now, is the belief that political unity in facing the outside world will bring economic benefits through, for example, increasing bargaining power: in confronting and negotiating with other governments, or in dealing with the activities of foreign investors. With this belief goes the idea that co-operation may, by increasing the internal strength of groups of developing countries, help to lessen ldcs' 'dependence' on their stronger trading partners, and in particular on the West. Examples of the first belief put into practice are the coherence of the forty-six Anglophone and Francophone African, Caribbean and Pacific (ACP) countries in negotiating the Lomé Convention, signed in 1975 with the enlarged European Community,[18] and the common policy towards foreign investors introduced by the Andean Group in 1971.[19]

SIDE-EFFECTS OF EUROPEAN LINKS: GREATER AFRICAN CO-OPERATION?

The solidarity shown by the Lomé Convention countries in dealing with the EEC may spill over into greater co-operation and new connections among themselves. There is some evidence of this happening among African countries already. Historically, there had been very little contact between British, French, and Belgian colonies in Africa. Even after independence, the structure of investment and trade, the existence of different currency areas based on the pound sterling and the French and Belgian francs, and the use of different languages, all imposed from outside, in trade and industry, have kept the different countries commercially separate.

Regional co-operation agreements among African countries have also, for many of the same reasons, been largely confined to those within the Anglophone and Francophone areas, with little contact between the two. This situation, however, is gradually changing, beginning with co-operation among small groups with a particular common problem, such as Senegal and the Gambia (trade and navigation along the Gambia river), and Liberia, Sierra Leone, and Guinea (the use of water resources). In 1975, however, a much larger co-operation agreement was signed among fifteen West African states including both Anglophone and Francophone states. The Economic Community of West African States (ECOWAS) aims at a customs union, free trade among the partners, and a common external tariff within fifteen years.

It is likely that at least part of the credit for the successful conclusion of this agreement should go to the contacts built up between Francophone and Anglophone countries during the negotiations for the Lomé Convention. The unity displayed by the developing countries in these negotiations was impressive: and that unity may persist, if only because it is necessary for all Lomé Convention countries to negotiate with the EEC as a group. In addition, countries can co-operate in seeking funds from the European Development Fund, 10 per cent of which is earmarked for regional projects.

OPEC AND CO-OPERATION WITH DEVELOPING COUNTRIES

Most developing countries have been very hard hit by the increase in oil prices since 1973. The countries most seriously affected by this and by inflation in the prices of their other imports include India, Pakistan,

Bangladesh and Sri Lanka, a considerable number of poor African countries, and some Caribbean states. Like developed countries, they have three main ways open to them to compensate for the damage to their economies: to try to cut down their fuel imports and exploit domestic resources, to improve their trade balances by increasing exports, particularly to oil producing countries, and to seek new aid and investment funds.

For a few countries, such as India, the first two are possibilities. Despite the poverty of the country as a whole, the Indian industrial and scientific structure is strong enough to exploit nuclear power and to explore new sources of energy, such as solar power, and India also has large reserves of coal. A country in its position, with a strong industrial base, can also envisage exporting capital, intermediate, and consumer goods to oil exporting countries. India has, in fact, concluded two such agreements with Iran and Iraq under which oil is supplied on favourable terms in exchange for exported manufactures.

Other countries which have an agricultural base or potential may be able to expand their exports of food products to oil producing countries, particularly to the Middle Eastern desert states which have no easy comparative advantage in agriculture, in exchange perhaps for fertilisers as well as oil itself. This may be the case, for example, for Pakistan.

Other countries have little option but to go in search of new aid. In 1974, OPEC members as a group increased their aid commitments very sharply to an estimated total for the year of some $11 billion, twenty-five times as high as the average of the previous three years. (This must, of course, be offset against additional revenue from oil in 1974 of $65 billion – almost as big as the total value of exports from developing countries *including* oil producers in 1972.)

To some extent at least, these aid commitments are geographically and culturally concentrated. Most of the commitments by the Arab oil producers have been to other predominantly Muslim countries such as Pakistan, the Sudan, Mauritania, Somalia, and the two Yemen republics: commitments by Venezuela and Trinidad and Tobago have included new contributions to the Inter-American and Caribbean Development Banks.

Is this pattern of assistance, linking oil producing states with the capital to invest in poorer neighbours with these neighbours, likely to persist? Is it likely to be beneficial in the long run to the non-oil producing countries? Or is it likely to evolve into another kind of dependence? At present, there is a clear indication of political solidarity between many of the oil producing developing countries and other ldcs. Both groups are underdeveloped, with the main significant difference being the new wealth of the oil producers. The latter's uncertainty about how long this new wealth may last, combined with a realisation that ways must be found to use it to promote development, and common attitudes towards ownership and control of natural resources in general have ensured, so far, a community of interest between OPEC members and other ldcs. However, there is no doubt that oil wealth gives the OPEC countries the possibility of growing faster, and of becoming more powerful, than other developing countries: and this, if it happens, may strain relationships which are now founded at least partly on the need for aid.

NON-REGIONAL CO-OPERATION: GATT CONCESSIONS

Trade among developing countries need not, of course, be confined wholly to regional trade. Various 'traditional' flows already exist (such as the export of cloves from Zanzibar to Indonesia, its biggest customer); other flows have grown up over time (such as that between India and East Africa); others persist despite their illegality in the importing country (such as the trade in gold, silver and other luxury goods between Arabian Gulf states and India which persists despite the Indian authorities' attempts to stamp it out).

Within GATT, a group of sixteen developing countries[20] signed in December 1971 a Protocol under which tariff preferences could be extended among members of the group. In principle the concessions are applicable to all countries in the group, as was necessary under GATT rules. However, any of the countries involved could refuse to grant concessions to any other: thus both Egypt and Israel could participate.

A wide range of agricultural, processed, and manufactured products is covered by concessions under the Protocol, but the lists vary considerably from country to country. Yugoslavia, Greece, Spain and India have the longest lists of goods on offer, but not necessarily the largest coverage of trade. In general, moreover, the depth of tariff cuts under the Protocol, which ranges from 12 to 50 per cent of mfn duty rates, many of which are extremely high, go much less far than even the concessions given by developed countries under the GSP. Many of them – covering products which are rarely, if ever, exported, by the countries to which concessions are given – may, moreover, be only of symbolic value. But the Protocol at least represents a start which may lead to further trade liberalisation among ldcs.

CONCLUSIONS

We have tried to show in this chapter why, and how, developing countries try to co-operate with one another and to increase their mutual trade. Progress in this field has indeed been patchy, but the spirit of co-operation is not dead, and the number and scope of co-operation agreements among ldcs has grown. The economic importance of the oil producing countries may increase the possibilities of such co-operation in future. In the last few years, too, developing countries have seen dramatically demonstrated that in unity lies strength, and it has become plain that in bargaining with developed countries co-operation among ldcs can give greater leverage than individual negotiations, even if not on the OPEC scale. The unity built up in such joint bargaining can also spill over into the construction of more harmonious relations among developing countries themselves. If these factors continue to combine, the next ten years will see developments in the fields of economic co-operation and integration among ldc economies far greater than the partial, though important, steps taken so far.

Notes

1. United Nations Economic and Social Council (ECOSOC) Document E.AC 54/L.54, 'Economic Co-operation Schemes in Developing Regions: an Appraisal of Mechanisms, Policies and Problems'. The groups studied were the Latin American Free Trade Area (LAFTA), the Central American Common Market (CACM), the Caribbean Free Trade Area (CARIFTA – now the Caribbean Common Market and Community, CARICOM), the East African Community (EAC), the Union Douanière et Economique de l' Afrique Centrale (UDEAC), the Union Douanière et Economique de l'Afrique de l'Ouest (UDEAO), Regional Co-operation for Development (RCD), and the Arab Common Market.
2. See, for example, Bela Balassa, 'Towards a Theory of Economic Integration', *Kyklos,* vol.14, Fasc.1, 1961; C.A. Cooper and B.F. Massell, 'Towards a General Theory of Customs Unions for Developing Countries', *Journal of Political Economy,* vol.LXXIII, October 1965.
3. Until then, the only justification which was allowed by GATT rules for discriminatory tariff treatment of one member by another was the creation of reciprocal free-trade areas (which GATT could regard as contributing to the world-wide reduction of barriers to trade).
4. See, for example, Bela Balassa; C.A. Cooper and B.F. Massell; R.F. Mikesell, 'The Theory of Common Markets as applied to Regional Arrangements among Developing Countries', in R. Harrod and D. Hague (eds.), *International Trade Theory in a Developing World* (London, Macmillan, 1963).
5. *Journal of Development Planning,* No.7, United Nations, 1974, p.18.

6. Quoted in K. Kahnert, P. Richards, E. Stoutesdijk and P. Thomopoulos, *Economic Integration among Developing Countries* (OECD DEvelopment Centre, Paris, 1969).
7. Ibid., p.22.
8. *Journal of Development Planning*, p.23
9. Ibid., p.93.
10. For a fuller discussion of these agreements, see United Nations, *Current Problems of Economic Integration: Agricultural and Industrial Co-operation among Developing Countries*, E.72.IID.6 (New York, 1971), pp.27-37.
11. UNCTAD, TD/B/374, p.37.
12. J. Grunwald, M.S. Wionczek, and M. Carnoy, *Latin American Integration and US Policy* (Washington, Brookings Institution, 1972), p.37. A study by Carnoy of fourteen products in six product groups (nitrogenous fertilisers, methanol and formaldehyde, pulp and paper. lathes, tractors, and powdered milk and cheese) showed that seven out of ten LAFTA countries (excluding Bolivia) would qualify as minimum-cost locations for one or more products, and that costs would be only little increased at a number of 'second-best' locations.
13. *Journal of Development Planning*, p.9.
14. Grunwald, Wionczek, and Carnoy, p.33.
15. Note that shipping costs on logs can represent up to 50 per cent of the cif value of European and US timber imports from ASEAN countries.
16. Economic and Social Commission for Asia and the Pacific.
17. Michael and Frances Stewart, 'Developing Countries' Trade and Liquidity: A New Approach', *The Banker*, March 1972.
18. See below.
19. See pp.236-7, Table 8.2.
20. India, Brazil, Chile, Egypt, Israel, South Korea, Mexico, Pakistan, Peru, Philippines, Tunisia, Turkey, Uruguay, Yugoslavia, Spain and Greece. (See GATT, *Basic Instruments and Selected Documents*, 18th Supplement, 1972.)

9 A NEW INTERNATIONAL ECONOMIC ORDER AND LDCS' TRADE

In recent years, there has been a growing emphasis on the need for structural changes in the organisation of the world economy – as witness the unprecedented series of international conferences on global economic issues between 1973 and 1976. This stems, in part, from the build-up of stresses and strains on the present system created by international monetary instability, global recession and inflation, the foodgrains crisis, and the sudden shock of the oil price rise. It also stems from the increasing pressure from ldcs for a radical change in international economic relations so as to redress the growing inequality between the developed and developing countries of the world, and to bring the needs of the poorest members to the fore. The various demands for structural change and reform in the interests of global equity and justice have been amalgamated into a single call for a 'New International Economic Order' (NIEO), adopted without a vote by the UN General Assembly.[1]

Most of the elements proposed for the NIEO[2] do not differ very much from those contained in earlier UN documents such as *The International Strategy for the Second Development Decade* (1970). This is hardly surprising given that the fundamental problems of trade and development have not changed and have even been intensified. But some of the proposals – particularly those concerned with commodity trade – were (or seemed) much more radical and more likely to shift power from the developed to developing countries. In this sector, the NIEO proposals reflected the principal concerns of non-oil producing ldcs, focusing on the need for a 'just and equitable' relationship – which has to be defined much more clearly – between ldcs' export and import prices, on their problems in relation to world food production and trade, and on improving access particularly to developed country markets for ldcs' exports of processed and manufactured goods.

When the call for an NIEO was first made, many ldcs, particularly commodity exporters, felt that perhaps at last they had an opportunity to change the balance of international power in their favour. Their reasons for thinking so were mixed, and to some extent paradoxical. On the one hand, commodity producers hoped that they might emulate the success of OPEC in bidding up prices for their traded raw materials, by banding together in producer associations which would serve as cartels. On the other, the many developing countries whose economies had been hard hit by the increase in oil prices – some of whom were at the same time suffering from grievous shortages of food – hoped that the very gravity of their problems would encourage both the Western countries and the 'new rich' oil producers to give them more help, both in financial aid and trading concessions, than before. There seemed to be a realisation on all sides that problems of development were a global concern, reflecting the interdependence of nation states and requiring international co-operation for their solution. And the rich countries initially seemed to be aware that it was in their own interests to help to reduce poverty in the Third World: if the poor countries were not to rock the global boat they must be allowed a greater share in piloting it.

Since the economic shocks of 1973-4, the situation seems to have changed a great deal. Non-oil producing ldcs still face very grave problems; many poor nations have become poorer, and it has become clear that the OPEC-conjured idea of 'commodity power' is an illusion as far as most commodities are concerned. Developed countries have, to a very great extent, been able to adjust to new levels of oil prices, in the short term; and the initial recession following the OPEC action may have been overcome. The recession itself depressed the prices of many commodities from the high levels of 1974, and stocks of many minerals in particular are now high. However, the prospect of another 'boom' in Western countries creates many uncertainties in commodity questions and some analysts feel that the next upsurge in prices which Western demand may cause may go even higher than before; particularly when demand in rapidly industrialising developing countries is taken into account. This would once again shift the balance of world economic power towards commodity exporting countries.

In the short term, then, the rhetoric of the NIEO seems rather high-flown. But uncertainty about the future has created divisions among the developed countries about the kinds of international policies to be adopted on commodity questions; divisions which created a major split for the first time in a major international gathering among the 'B Group' countries at the fourth UNCTAD conference in Nairobi in May 1976. Although the poor countries seem to have much less bargaining power to enforce their demands than it first appeared, the fact that Western countries still find it necessary to sit down at the conference table to try to satisfy, or find compromises for, ldcs' proposals is a sign that the latter are important. UN rhetoric may not be as empty on this occasion as it has often seemed in the past.

RAW MATERIALS

Raw materials, particularly minerals, were the key area pinpointed in the first declaration on the NIEO. Developing countries at that time had two main objectives: to increase their revenue from exports of raw materials and their own control over the extraction of mineral resources.

We have already noted in Chapter 3 that few countries are, or ever were, in as strong a monopoly supply position as the OPEC group. Even OPEC's monopoly, moreover, is not unassailable. The short-run effect of the 'oil crisis' in developed countries has been to cut petroleum consumption and increase investment in ways of saving energy, although the results are still only marginal. The longer-term effect will be – has already been – to push up investment in the search for alternative sources of fuel and energy. Some of these (e.g. North Sea oil extraction) may be available for only the relatively near future and at high, non-diminishing costs; to this extent the high price of OPEC oil may have encouraged a pattern of production which does not reflect real comparative advantage. Others are still at the very early stage of development, but hold a potential for diminishing costs in the long term; among these may be counted new uses of sun, wave and wind power and possibly nuclear fission.

Even in the short term, the combined effect of the recession of 1973-5 in developed countries and the energy saving measures undertaken has been to reduce industrial demand for petroleum by some 20-25 per cent. The same recession affected demand for other minerals, whose prices on international markets almost without exception began to decline markedly in the middle of 1974.

For the moment, then, the chances of commodity exporting countries forming effective cartels seem again to be small. But one effect of the OPEC action is that some governmental opinion in developed countries appears to have swung more heavily in favour of co-operation with ldc commodity exporters, as against simply letting 'free market forces' play on commodity prices and export revenues. Economic recovery in the West, by strengthening demand for raw materials, would once again increase 'world' prices and strengthen the bargaining position of producing countries.

There are now, therefore, two important factors which may balance the interests of consuming and producing countries. Consumers need to ensure access to supplies at 'fair' and relatively stable prices; producers need to ensure a market for their commodity exports at 'fair' and stable prices. Although there is a long way to go before the various proposals for regulating trade in primary commodities can be transformed into working agreements, this coincidence of interests does at least provide the basis for negotiation.

The past ten years have also seen a great increase in ldc ownership and control of their own mineral and plantation resources. Some countries have nationalised foreign-owned assets without compensation, and indeed have asked for compensation for the 'excess profits' expatriated by foreign companies. Others have nationalised and paid compensation on scales negotiated between their governments and the previous owners. Others, again, have either changed the basis of taxation in order to increase national revenue or have gone into joint ownership with the foreign entrepreneur. In insisting on greater control of national resources, particularly minerals, ldcs are merely following a path taken by developed countries long ago. But whatever measures are taken, the advantages of higher national revenue and a greater degree of control over one's 'own' national resources must be balanced against the risks of possible dislocation of production through the removal of skilled management and staff and reduced access to technology, and the costs of hiring replacements – both of which can be crucial.

PROCESSING OF RAW MATERIALS

Both the UN Special Sessions of 1974 and 1975 emphasised the desirability of increasing the degree of processing of raw materials in ldcs, thereby increasing the value added derived from raw material exports and creating new employment opportunities.

In recent years, ldcs have begun to develop a significant capability in the processing of raw materials for export. However, they still face two sorts of problem in diversifying into processing, the first on the supply side, the second in demand.

The ability of developing countries to process their own raw materials for export at an acceptable cost varies greatly. In some cases, for instance the processing of timber into plywood and wood laminates, processing in the country of origin appears to be just as viable as in the country of destination. In other cases – for example metal-refining – problems may arise because of the scale, technological complexity and capital intensity of the processing, although co-operation among ldcs can help. Costs of marketing the processed product may also inhibit the development of processing industries, as too may the costs and problems of transportation. Petroleum, for example, is more safely and economically transported over long distances in raw form and in bulk than when refined into a variety of products with different physical characteristics.

Meanwhile, on the demand side, developed countries' tariffs and other trade barriers are still a major obstacle to ldcs' processing of locally produced raw materials for export. A relatively low 'nominal' tariff on the total value of a product can give much higher 'effective' protection against ldc exporters of processed products. The GSP has helped ease the inhibiting effects of tariff (but not non-tariff) barriers, but its impact has as yet been somewhat limited in scope.

FOOD AND AGRICULTURE

The world food crisis of 1972-4 seemed to dash the earlier optimism for a 'Green Revolution' in ldcs' food production. Western developed countries as a group – the EEC as well as North America – consolidated their positions as the world's 'bread-basket', while many developing countries became even more dependent than before on imports. Thus a somewhat paradoxical situation has emerged. Western countries, the most highly industrialised parts of the world, struggle to cope with problems of meat, butter and milk powder 'mountains', not to speak of 'wine lakes', while a large number of developing countries, many of which have the physical capacity to grow a great deal more food, suffer apparently chronic shortages, and those ldcs which are capable of exploiting their comparative advantage in international food trade are inhibited by the protectionist policies pursued in developed country markets. Recent projections of food supply up to the year 1985, produced by OECD, suggest strongly that given likely continuing rates of growth of agricultural productivity and population in different regions of the world, this imbalance is likely to continue.[3]

Part of the reason for the imbalance in world food production lies simply in the relative degree of incentive that farmers in the developed and less developed worlds have received. There is no doubt that farmers in most, if not all, money economies, react 'correctly' to price incentives – they produce more in response to higher prices. The problem is to judge the level at which to set farm subsidies or price guarantees to bring forth sufficient output (assuming at least reasonable weather) at a price which consumers can pay.[4]

In the past decade, many European governments, at least, have opted for 'food security' and as great self-sufficiency as possible: a policy which, in its own terms, has been successful, although it has resulted both in high prices to the consumer – causing consumer resistance in some cases – and in a high governmental cost in surplus storage and export subsidies.[5] Developing country governments cannot, perhaps, afford the luxury of supporting farm prices to this extent. High farm prices mean a high cost of living for workers in town and an impossible cost for low-wage employees or unemployed people. And food subsidies are also a big strain on the national budget. It may often be cheaper, in cash terms, to take advantage of the subsidised surpluses of the developed world. Some have even suggested that such food surpluses should be deliberately planned and generated. But this would be to ignore both the production potential and the problems of access to food supplies in ldcs: food surpluses may co-exist with starvation (and have done so) through lack of purchasing power on the part of the poor.[6] The biggest task facing developing countries is to realise their production potential, while at the same time ensuring that food distribution and production are organised in such a way as to enable the poorest to benefit. This in turn implies more income earning opportunities for the poor and changes in land use, land tenure and employment which may in every sense be 'revolutionary'. It implies also a considerable increase in investment in food production, storage and marketing. All this cannot be achieved quickly and in the meantime Western farm output will continue as the major source for developing countries' growing food needs.

This is very discouraging. Although European farmers may be highly 'efficient' in purely production terms, in the main areas of food production they are not at all efficient in cash-cost terms. Exports are made at subsidised prices – except when world prices rise to disaster levels – and depress 'world' markets. Any developing country which can export, therefore, finds itself uncompetitive against subsidised exports from developed countries, and its efforts to increase its share of the market by raising its agricultural productivity are likely to be considerably hampered. For those countries which do not produce enough food and for which the burden of commercial imports would be unbearable, the flow of subsidised food aid may in turn be a serious disincentive to agricultural production.

There is no easy solution. To phase out the supply of developed country surpluses at a stroke would be, in the short run, a grave blow to many ldcs which have come to depend on food aid. And the uncertainty of year-to-year crop trends makes buffer stock of some kind highly necessary. Developed countries' 'food aid' in the years to come is likely to be needed in at least two forms: contributions (financial, technical, and in grain or other foods) to buffer stocks held, with international financing, in the major food-deficit countries – stockpiling which could mop up at least some of the food surpluses; and support in cash and technical assistance (where appropriate) to agricultural development programmes, including, where necessary and acceptable, food subsidy programmes.

Developing countries, of course, produce much more from the land than simply foodgrains, and can in many cases look to export other agricultural products, processed or unprocessed, in exchange for food and other imports. But the conditions under which these are imported into developed countries depend largely on the extent to which they compete with or complement the latter's own products. Thus a country which can fulfil a need for 'off-season' supplies or exploit a virtually 'luxury' demand – Cypriot new potatoes, or Kenyan strawberries by air freight, for example, or Egyptian green beans in the winter season – can do well out of the trade. But apart from these kinds of product, which are potentially significant exports – and 'tropical' raw products such as unprocessed coffee, tea, or cocoa, most agricultural products exported by ldcs remain heavily protected.

MANUFACTURES

We have noted that exports of manufactures have grown faster than those of any other group of products from ldcs in recent years. Although one group of relatively advanced ldcs is principally responsible, the number of countries involved in this trade has also increased significantly.

The development of manufactured exports from ldcs seems to be taking two forms. First there has been increasing investment in export-orientated ventures, frequently backed by multinational companies whose involvement ranges from complete ownership and control over production to the role of a contractual purchaser. In this sphere, the main growth area has been export processing, whereby one part of a multinational firm's production process is located in ldcs; inputs are imported from elsewhere in the firm, undergo some transformation, and are then exported often to another of the firm's subsidiaries. This sort of activity has been encouraged by developing countries through 'export processing zones' and by some developed countries through value-added tariffs. Secondly, there has been a marked shift in some countries towards exporting the output of industries originally established to provide import substitutes for the local market. These industries, often based on indigenous raw materials, tend to operate with less participation from multinationals than those in the specifically export-orientated sector.

The greatest scope for the expansion of ldcs' export earnings probably lies in the continued development of manufactures production for export. Developed countries currently offer the largest market for ldcs' exports although the oil producing countries are becoming increasingly important markets. But further development is beset by problems not only of access but of adapting local production in ldcs to the needs of overseas markets. The GSP has helped to ease the problems of access, although a large portion of ldcs' manufactures export still faces trade barriers. The problems of export supply are more complex since they relate not only to the general difficulties of industrialisation in underdeveloped countries but also to broader issues of development strategy, of employment creation and choice of technologies, of balancing the desire for self-reliance with the promotion of exports backed by multinational firms.

In the field of manufactures exports, the multinational firm has much to offer the ldc, especially if success is measured in terms of export growth. An established international corporation has the financial, trading and marketing connections and capacities which are likely to count for an enormous amount in developing new exports and it will usually be involved in producing for export goods for which there is an assured market, including goods to supply its own manufacturing operations world-wide. Against this must be set the possibility that the company may be solely interested in exploiting a particular advantage of the ldc concerned – e.g. cheap labour or easy access to minerals – without creating any connections with other sectors of the economy; that profits are unlikely to be reinvested in the exporting country and there will be no easy way of assessing whether the prices at which goods are traded are profitable to the national economy; and that the type of goods produced may have no relevance to local needs. By contrast, an indigenously developed product may show greater links with other sectors, but may be inefficiently produced, or badly adapted to export markets' standards and tastes, or not have adequate sales and marketing channels for export, or run up against developed countries' tariff or non-tariff barriers. The gains and losses from different modes and methods of operation come together in a very delicate balance of interests, which have yet to be fully reflected in the policies pursued by some ldcs on industrialisation and foreign participation.

TRADE WITH THE EASTERN BLOC AND OTHER DEVELOPING COUNTRIES

Not surprisingly, much of the discussion in this book and elsewhere on the subject of ldcs' trade problems focuses on those arising in the context of their trade with Western developed countries. These problems would seem far less pressing if alternative channels for international trade – and economic relations generally – could be developed. Ldcs' trading difficulties are the result not merely of the composition of their trade but also of its direction.

So long as the Eastern bloc retains its current, somewhat exclusive trading system and its preference for developing links with the Western developed countries rather than ldcs, it is unlikely to be a significant alternative to ldcs – except to the extent that individual ldcs become, like Cuba, virtually incorporated within the bloc's economic system. Moreover, ldcs' pattern of trade with COMECON countries is very similar to that of trade with developed countries *before* the recent growth in the relative share of manufactures exports. It is thus arguable that, while they might raise export earnings, attempts to foster such trade links would not radically improve ldcs' trading position. Whatever the case, ldcs in general have not looked to the Eastern bloc for alternative markets. Rather, increasingly, they have looked to each other.

The development of trade amongst ldcs still has a lot to overcome: poor infrastructure, including transport and marketing systems still geared to trade with Western countries and Japan; small markets even when ldcs band together; tariff structures and national plans which inhibit trade and encourage the development of rival industries; and competition from exports from established sources in developed countries. Nevertheless, the development of inter-ldc trade remains an important goal.

We have already noted that much of the trade which takes place among ldcs is organised on a regional basis, among neighbouring countries. Often such regional trade is undertaken within common markets, free trade areas, or other economic associations. Often, too, it builds on links – frequently ex-colonial – that already exist, or on complementarities among the various countries. In most ldcs there is a degree of informalised cross-border trade – some of which is officially categorised as smuggling – which might possibly be encouraged rather than discouraged, and most ldcs have some products which could be sold to their neighbours. However, the development of small-scale but possibly vigorous enterprise in these areas is often actively inhibited. Border trade is punished as smuggling, and government economic planners are often too concerned with creating large-scale regional projects (for which aid funds may be available) to consider 'grass-roots' trading possibilities.

A further inhibition to inter-ldc trade is the search for 'balance' among countries in regional trading arrangements. Both trade flows and investment projects must somehow be in balance for governments to be satisfied that their country is not somehow losing on the deal. Complex compensatory mechanisms are invoked against the growth of trade deficits, and one country's 'regional' cement works is traded off against another's 'regional' brewery. In this atmosphere it is not surprising that such projects often fail. Nevertheless, in regional co-operation programmes which include some richer and some poorer members, some measures must be taken to counteract the magnetic effect of the better-off or better-organised countries.

The OPEC countries, with their financial resources available for aid and investment, are seen as a new potential source of export revenue for some ldcs. It is well known that India and Pakistan, *inter alia,* have both concluded barter-type arrangements with Iran and Iraq in which manufactures, including many engineering products, are exchanged for oil. The development of joint aluminium smelting capacity between Jamaica and Venezuela, referred to in Chapter 8, is another example of the way in which such new links are being built up. And it is not unimaginable that Arab petroleum exporting countries, importing the vast majority of their food, may use aid and investment funds to promote the development of grain and livestock farming for export to themselves in friendly African countries – for example the Sudan – which have the capacity.

In reviewing ldcs' position in world trade, we have said relatively little on the role of international trade in economic development. This reflects our belief that, while external trade has historically played a strategic role in ldcs, it should be regarded as a variable element in development policy rather than as the key to economic development. Export-led growth may hasten the achievement of development objectives but it need not be the same as export-led development. The emphasis placed in development strategies on exploiting trade opportunities will clearly vary according to the resource-base and economic characteristics of the ldc concerned – Singapore will almost certainly have to give them more weight than India. At the same time, the case for participation in international trade must be judged according to the contribution of trade-orientated activities to development objectives as compared with alternatives.

The essential question of development policy, to which we referred at the beginning of this book, is how reasonable conditions of life can be created for the mass of the people in poor countries. There does not appear to be a good *a priori* case for supposing that withdrawal from international trade will enhance a country's development chances. But at the same time, participation in trade brings costs as well as benefits and trade-based projects and strategies should be evaluated accordingly. Benefits may be defined in terms of net increase in output and foreign exchange; equally significantly, in terms of their effects on investment, employment and output in other sectors, on income distribution in the country or region concerned, on opportunities for the development of local techniques and inventions and for the use of local physical, human and natural resources – among other things. Costs may be defined in terms of cash costs, of alternative costs (short- or longer-term) of importing the goods to be produced, or of the relative inefficiency of new industries as measured by the amount of protection needed to establish and maintain them. This is not to say that such costs or benefits will necessarily be easy to assess. Nonetheless, it is essential that international trade should be regarded neither as a panacea nor as an invention of 'foreign devils', but as an instrument of development.

Notes

1. *The Declaration and Programme of Action on the Establishment of a New International Economic Order,* UN General Assembly, Sixth Special Session, document A/9556 (Part II), May 1974.
2. See ibid., also R.H. Green and H.W. Singer, 'Towards a Rational and Equitable New International Economic Order: a Case for Negotiated Structural Changes', *World Development,* vol.3, no.6, June 1975.
3. OECD *Observer,* May-June, 1976.
4. See Peter Donaldson, *Worlds Apart* (Harmondsworth, Penguin, 1971), pp.114-15.
5. The EEC and Switzerland are among countries which have had to face this problem.
6. Note that in 1976 India has had record grain crops and faces problems of

storage and distribution, rather than of shortage and famine. Yet the basic problems of Indian rural poverty caused by lack of purchasing power and inegalitarian land tenure remain.

APPENDICES

1. Summary of Commodity Agreements and Arrangements in Force Since the Second World War

Commodity Agreements	Dates	Membership	Objectives	Methods	Present status
(a) CAs achieving 'global' status					
1. International Coffee Agreements	1959-62	Exporting countries (incl. France, Portugal, Britain for colonies)	Limitation or elimination of price fluctuations: promotion of consumption		
	1963-8 and 1968-72	Exporting and importing countries (41 exporting, 21 importing members)	'Equitable' prices and balance between supply and demand with adequate supplies for consumers and markets for producers. Elimination of excessive price fluctuations and surplus production. Promotion of coffee consumption.	Export quotas, no buffer stock (Brazil main stockholding country). Floor & ceiling prices govern cuts and increases in export quotas (quarterly). Relative size of quotas reviewed annually. 'New consumer' countries (ldcs) and E. European imports not counted against quotas. 1968-72 Agreement included Diversification Fund to encourage re-use of coffee land.	ICA put on 'standby' in September 1973 following US refusal to agree to world price increase to compensate for $ devaluation. Diversification Fund wound up. Negotiations continuing for new Agreement.
2. International Tin Agreement	1956-61 1961-6 1966-71 1971-6	Producers: – Malaysia, Bolivia, Thailand, Indonesia, Nigeria, Zaire, Australia. (90% of world production.) Importers: – Britain, Canada, India, Australia, Belgium/ Luxembourg, Denmark, France, W. Germany, Ireland, Italy, Japan, Netherlands, Spain, Turkey, S. Korea, Bulgaria, Czechoslovakia, Hungary, Poland, Romania, USSR, Yugoslavia. **Not** USA (23% of world consumption).	Prevention of 'excessive' price fluctuations: supplies at prices remunerative to producers and 'fair' to consumers: importance to producing countries of 'maintaining and expanding their import-purchasing power' recognised.	International buffer stock with floor and ceiling price levels. Export quotas reinforce 'floor' Maximum stock size 20,000 tons, contributed in kind or cash by producing countries (25,000 in First ITA). Buffer stock could be enlarged by credit purchases. In fact largest stock = 23,000 tons (1958) when world price £700/ton. Floor and ceiling have been continually raised to keep pace with rising trend in prices. US stocks crucial factor affecting prices.	Agreements still active. Prices high.
3. International Sugar Agreements	1954-9: 1959-62: 1963-8: 1969-73	All major sugar exporting and inporting countries **except** EEC, USA. Fourth Agreement applied to 13% of world output or 50% of trade. (Rest traded under preferential agreements).	Maintenance of stable prices, reasonably remunerative to producers: better balance between supply & demand; expansion of international trade, international co-operation on marketing.	Export quotas for main exporters (Cuba, Australia, Taiwan, S. Africa, Brazil, Poland, Czechoslovakia, India) are increased or reduced according to price levels. Importers should restrict own production of sugar.	Agreement abandoned since 1973 negotiations, when 'world' prices high and rising. No agreement on price levels, export quotas, or restriction of output (especially in EEC).

1. Summary of Commodity Agreements and Arrangements in Force Since the Second World War – Cont.

Commodity Agreements	Dates	Membership	Objectives	Methods	Present status
4. International Wheat Agreements (Wheat Trade Convention, Food Aid Convention).	1949-53: 1953-6: 1956-9: 1959-62: 1962-7: 1967-71 1971 –	Canada, US, Australia, Argentina, EEC, Sweden, Greece, Kenya, Mexico, Spain (exporting); UK, EEC, Japan, and 22 developing countries (importing). Commercial sales within Convention account for 60% of world trade: all transactions (incl. Government) for 85%.	Assurance of supplies of wheat and flour to importing, and markets for exporting, countries at equitable and stable prices: promotion of trade.	Floor and ceiling prices for commercial sales: mandatory proportions of purchases from members while world prices remain within limits.	Wheat Trade Convention purely consultative. Under Food Aid Convention Argentina, Australia, Canada, EEC, Finland, Japan, Sweden, Switzerland, USA contribute 4 million metric tons annually to food aid reserves.
5. International Cocoa Agreements	1973-6	43 countries: including Ghana, Nigeria, Ivory Coast, Brazil, Cameroon, Equatorial Guinea, Dominican Rep., Togo, Mexico (exporters); Australia, Bulgaria, Canada, Hungary, Romania, Sweden, Trinidad/Tobago, UK, USSR (importers). Not USA.	Price stabilisation within floor and ceiling levels.	Floor and ceiling prices maintained by export quotas & and buffer stock financed by levy on cocoa traded, by IMF buffer stock facility, or through credit.	Never operative, since cocoa price above ceiling since start. Buffer stock non-existent, but funds amassing.
	Oct. 1976-	Not fully ratified at time of writing. US not joining	As above, plus expansion of export earnings via increased consumption and production.	As above.	Active, but cocoa price above ceiling and some CPA members may leave if ceiling price not raised. Buffer stock non-existent.
6. International Olive Oil Agreement	1959-	EEC, Algeria, Argentina, Dominica, Greece, Israel, Libya, Morocco, Panama, Portugal, Spain, Syria, Tunisia, Turkey, Yugoslavia.	Olive Oil Council appraises annually overall supplies and needs. EEC participates as both exporter and importer.	Purely consultative.	In force with purely consultative status.
(b) Informal international arrangements (IIAs)					
7. IIA for the stabilisation of tea prices	1970-	17 exporting countries (Sri Lanka, India, Indonesia, Kenya, Uganda, Malawi, Mozambique, Argentina, Zaire, Turkey, Tanzania, Mauritius, Taiwan, Rwanda, Cameroon, S. Vietnam, Burundi) and 14 importing.	Increased export earnings in real terms from tea. Co-ordination and regulation of marketing policies. Export promotion.	Informal export quotas administered by Exporters' Subgroup. Proposals for minimum floor prices (December 1974).	Operative.
8. IIA for jute, kenaf and allied fibres	1965-	India, Bangladesh, Thailand, Indonesia (exporters); Belgium, France, W. Germany, Italy, UK, Japan, USA (importers).	Price maintenance and stabilisation	Indicative price range: intention of phased buying by importers. Possibility of buffer stock.	Not known.

1. Summary of Commodity Agreements and Arrangements in Force Since the Second World War – Cont.

Agreements	Dates	Membership	Objectives	Methods	Present status
9. IIA for sisal, henequen, and abaca	1967 (sisal & henequen) 1968 (abaca)	Brazil, Mexico, Tanzania, Angola, Mozambique, Kenya, Madagascar, Comoro Islands, Haiti, Indonesia, Taiwan (exporters); and 12 importing countries.	Market regulation and stabilisation.	Indicative price ranges. Global and national export quotas for sisal and henequen, and discussion of buffer stock.	Sisal/henequen arrangement operative: abaca arrangement inoperative since 1971.
(c) International Study Groups					
10. International Rubber Study Group	1944-	Most major trading countries including Malaysia, Nigeria, Singapore, Sri Lanka, Australia, Canada, India, EEC, USA, USSR, (30 in all).	Study of international action aimed at stabilising natural rubber prices.	Research, information, and consultation.	Active.
11. FAO Intergovernmental Group on Meat	1971-	54 members	Review of international meat trade and provision of statistics and information.	Discussion in context of FAO.	Active.
12. FAO IG on Oilseeds, oils and fats	1966-	All major countries except USSR which is not an FAO member	Review of trade.	Discussion.	Active.
13. FAO IG on Bananas		All interested FAO members.	Price stabilisation and general information.	Studies of trade.	Active.
14. International Lead and Zinc Study Group	1960-	All major countries incl. Australia, Canada, India, UK, USA, USSR & most EEC members. EEC has observer status. Financed by members.	Statistical information.		Active.
(d) Exporters' organisations					
15. Organisation of Petroleum Exporting Countries (OPEC)	1960-	Abu Dhabi, Algeria, Indonesia, Iran, Iraq, Kuwait, Libya Nigeria, Qatar, Saudi Arabia, Venezuela.	To unify members' petroleum policies and safeguard their interests generally.	Co-ordination of pricing policies and execution of oligopolistic power to raise prices.	Active.
16. Organisation of Arab Petroleum Exporting Countries (OAPEC)	1968-	Egypt, Kuwait, Algeria, Dubai, Libya, Abu Dhabi, Qatar, Saudi Arabia, United Arab Emirates, Bahrain, Iraq.	Co-ordination of members' activities in the oil industry.	As in OPEC	Active.
17. Intergovernmental Council of Copper Exporting Countries (CIPEC)	1968	Chile, Peru, Zaire, Zambia.	Co-ordination of measures to expand industry and copper exports, and increase in members' development resources. Attempts to stabilise and raise copper prices through joint action.	Sales cut of 10% from December 1974; increasing nationalisation of mining industries.	Active.

1. Summary of Commodity Agreements and Arrangements in Force Since the Second World War – Cont.

Agreements	Dates	Membership	Objectives	Methods	Present status
18. International Bauxite Association (IBA)	1974-	Australia, Guyana, Jamaica, Sierra Leone, Surinam, Yugoslavia.	Fair and remunerative returns for bauxite and alumina exports.	Co-ordination of taxation and local ownership policies.	Active.
19. Café Mondial	1973-	Exporting countries.	Price support.	Withholding of production. Heavily dependent on Brazilian finances.	Active.
20. Union of Banana Exporting Countries (UBEC)	1974	Mainly Latin America.	Price increase and stabilisation.	Co-ordination of export taxation policies.	Embryonic.
21. Cocoa Producers' Alliance (CPA)	1962-	Brazil, Cameroon, Ivory Coast, Ghana, Nigeria, Togo, Gabon, Ecuador	Price stabilisation: promotion of exports.	Export quotas: surplus stock control and disposal indicator prices.	'Economic' clauses are inactive. Production and sales promotion encouraged.
22. Association of Natural Rubber Producing Countries (ANRPC).	1975	India, Indonesia, Malaysia, Papua-New Guinea, Singapore, Sri Lanka, Thailand.	Stabilisation of natural rubber prices.	Buffer stock and supply control agreements.	First two-year agreement signed in December 1976 by Indonesia, Malaysia, Thailand, Sri Lanka, Singapore. Members to provide finance for buffer stock of up to 100,000 metric tonnes.

2. Statistics for Selected Commodities

Table A2.1 Exports of Raw Coffee from Selected Countries

	Exports 1971-3		Annual growth 1961-3 to 1971-3		Share of coffee exports in each country's total exports
	Q ('000 tonnes	V ($m)	Q	V	%
			%		
Developing countries					
Total	3,393	3,271	n.a.	n.a.	28.0 (1970-2)
Brazil	1,050	1,002	–0.1	+3.6	28.0 (1970-2)
Colombia	392	474	+0.6	+5.2	59.5 (1969-71)
Uganda	204	166	+4.6	+11.3	59.2 (1970-2)
Angola	192	165	+3.5	+10.6	30.7 (1970-2)
Ivory Coast	184	166	+1.3	+6.7	30.7 (1969-71)
Mexico	111	108	+1.4	+6.6	5.5 (1970-2)
Guatemala	104	111	+2.6	+5.1	33.6 (1969-71)
Indonesia	90	68	+3.0	+17.1	5.7 (1969-71)
Ethiopia	83	79	+2.9	+6.5	54.5 (1970-2)
Costa Rica	74	77	+3.1	+5.4	29.1 (1969-71)
Cameroon	68	70	+5.7	+12.0	23.0 (1969-71)
Zaire	67	55	+5.6	+18.2	4.4 (1968-70)
Kenya	60	65	+6.0	+8.0	28.3 (1970-2)
Madagascar	58	48	+2.2	+6.5	27.3 (1969-71)
Ecuador	54	47	+6.5	+10.3	17.5 (1967-9)
Peru	51	49	+3.1	+8.5	3.8 (1967-9)
Tanzania	50	52	+7.0	+10.7	16.9 (1970-2)
India	49	39	+6.6	+8.0	1.5 (1969-71)
Nicaragua	35	37	+4.7	+8.5	16.0 (1969-71)
Dominican Republic	32	33	n.a.	n.a.	10.3 (1970-2)
Honduras	31	31	+6.5	+10.6	13.0 (1969-71)
Papua/New Guinea	28	25	+23.7	+22.4	21.9 (1970-2)
Haiti	24	24	–	+3.0	38.9 (1969-71)
World total	3,489	3,407	+2.1	+6.0	
Ldcs as % of world total	97.2	96.0			

Source: FAO, *Yearbook of Agricultural Trade.*

Table A2.2. Exports of Tea From Selected Countries

	Exports 1971-3		Annual growth 1961-3 to 1971-3		Share of tea exports in each country's total exports
	Q ('000 tonnes)	V $m	Q	V %	(%)
Developed countries					
Total	60	86	n.a.	n.a.	n.a.
Netherlands[1]	28	24	n.a.	n.a.	n.a.
UK[1]	24	47	+3.7	+5.7	n.a.
Developing countries					
Total	629	580	n.a.	n.a.	n.a.
Sri Lanka	201	201	–	–1.9	57.3 (1969-71)
India	198	201	–0.6	–2.3	13.5 (1969-71)
Kenya	46	44	+11.6	+10.6	17.4 (1970-2)
Indonesia	43	29	+3.7	+2.5	1.8 (1969-71)
Malawi	19	15	+5.0	+4.9	20.2 (1970-2)
Uganda	18	16	+13.7	+11.5	6.0 (1970-2)
Mozambique	17	11	+6.5	+5.7	5.8 (1968-70)
Argentina	17	10	+10.4	+10.6	0.5 (1968-70)
Turkey	17	3	n.a.	n.a.	0.4 (1970-2)
Bangladesh	14	29	n.a.	n.a.	n.a.
Centrally planned					
Total	66	61	n.a.	n.a.	n.a.
China	52	48	n.a.	n.a.	n.a.
USSR	12	11	+6.0	+5.1	n.a.
World total	754	727	+2.4	+0.7	
Ldcs as % of world total	83.4	79.8			

[1] Mainly re-exports, or packaged.
Source: FAO, *Yearbook of Agricultural Trade.*

Table A2.3. Exports of Cocoa Beans and Cocoa Butter from Selected Countries

(a) *Cocoa beans*	Exports 1971-3		Annual growth rates 1961-3 to 1971-3		Share of cocoa exports in each country's total exports
	Q ('000 tonnes)	V ($m)	Q %	V %	%
Developing countries					
Total	1,192	797	n.a.	n.a.	n.a.
Ghana	382	246	–0.6	+2.5	69.7 (1970-2)
Nigeria	238	175	+2.4	+6.5	13.6 (1970-2)
Ivory Coast	150	104	+4.5	+9.3	20.1 (1969-71)
Brazil	101	70	+2.9	+7.4	2.1 (1970-2)
Cameroon	83	81	+1.6	+10.1	25.2 (1969-71)
Ecuador	42	25	+2.4	+3.6	22.1 (1967-9)
Dominican Republic	28	16	+4.5	+7.4	17.8 (1970-2)
Papua/New Guinea	27	14	+10.1	+11.1	43.1 (1970-2)
Togo	23	15	+7.6	+11.5	34.6 (1969-71)
Equatorial Guinea	21	15	–2.1	–2.3	n.a.
Dahomey	13	8	n.a.	n.a.	17.9 (1969-71)
Venezuela	11	7	—	–2.1	n.a.
Sao Tome/Principe	10	6	—	+4.1	n.a.
World total	1,202	805	+1.4	+5.0	n.a.
Ldcs as % of world total	99.2	99.0			
(b) Cocoa butter					
Developed countries					
Total	74	116	n.a.	n.a.	n.a.
Netherlands	54	85	n.a.	n.a.	0.6 (1970-2)
Developing countries					
Total	80	114	n.a.	n.a.	
Brazil	24	35	n.a.	n.a.	1.0 (1970-2)
Ghana	19	25	n.a.	n.a.	7.5 (1970-2)
Ivory Coast	11	16	n.a.	n.a.	4.2 (1969-71)
Cameroon	9	12	n.a.	n.a.	7.6 (1969-71)
Nigeria	9	15	n.a.	n.a.	n.a.
World total	154	231	n.a.	n.a.	
Ldcs as % of world total	51.9	29.4			

Source: FAO, *Yearbook of Agricultural Trade.*

Table A2.4. Exports of Pepper and Pimentofrom Selected Countries

	Exports 1971-3 annual average		Annual growth rates 1961-3 to 1971-3		Share of pepper exports in each country's total exports
	Q ('000 tonnes)	V ($m)	Q %	V	%
Developed countries					
Total	14	14	n.a.	n.a.	n.a.
Spain	10	9	+8.7	+9.4	0.4 (1971-3)[1]
Developing countries					
Total	165	139	n.a.	n.a.	n.a.
Singapore	38	31	(+2.1)	(+3.7)	1.2 (1971-3)
Indonesia	30	25	+3.0	+7.5	1.3 (1969-71)
Malaysia	30	25	(+9.6)	(+12.1)	8.2 (1969-71)[2]
India	22	22	−2.3	+1.5	0.9 (1969-71)
Brazil	15	15	+18.7	+20.5	n.a.
(Africa)	14	9	+5.7	+7.5	n.a.
Centrally planned					
Total	13	8	n.a.	n.a.	n.a.
China	11	7	n.a.	n.a.	n.a.
World total	192	160	+3.5	+6.4	
Ldcs as % of world total	85.9	86.9			

1 All spices.
2 % of exports from Sarawak only.
( ) estimated.
Source: FAO, *Yearbook of Agricultural Trade.*

Table A2.5. Exports of Rubber from Selected Countries

	Exports 1971-3 annual average		Annual growth rates 1961-3 to 1971-3		Share of rubber exports in each country's total exports
	Q ('000 tonnes	V ($m)	Q (%)	V	(%)
Developing countries					
Total	3,015	1,215	n.a.	n.a.	n.a.
Malaysia	1,465	653	+2.2	+0.1[1]	41.2 (1969-71)[1]
Indonesia	822	268	+2.5	–0.5	21.4 (1969-71)
Thailand	331	122	+5.8	+2.2	11.2 (1970-2)
Sri Lanka	140	62	+3.8	+1.3	20.3 (1969-71)
Liberia	80	41	+6.5	+4.9	14.4 (1970-2)
Nigeria	47	20	–2.0	–3.2	1.8 (1969-71)
Zaire	34	11	–1.0	–3.6	2.1 (1968-70)
South Vietnam	23	4	–5.4	–6.6	49.4 (1970-2)
Cameroon	16	6	+14.0	+6.0	2.1 (1969-71)
Ivory Coast	13	5	n.a.	n.a.	0.9 (1969-71)
Burma	10	4	–	–2.9	3.1 (1970-2)
World total	3,062	1,243	+1.5	–0.7	n.a.
Ldcs as % of world total	98.5	97.8			

[1] % and growth rates of exports from West Malaysia.
Source: FAO, *Yearbook of Agricultural Trade.*

Table A2.6. Exports of Industrial Fibres from Selected Countries

(a) *Jute, Kenaf, etc.*	Exports 1971-3 annual average		Annual growth rates 1961-3 to 1971-3		Share of fibres exports in each country's total exports
	Q ('000 tonnes)	V ($m)	Q	V (%)	(%)
Developing countries					
Total	918	223	n.a.	n.a.	n.a.
Bangladesh	689	152	—	(−0.9)	n.a.
Thailand	264	50	n.a.	n.a.	5.9 (1970-2)
India	35	11	+15.7	+18.7	0.7 (1969-71)
Burma	23	6	n.a.	n.a.	1.8 (1970-2)
Nepal	17	3	+18.1	+15.5	n.a.
World total	956	232	n.a.	n.a.	n.a.
Ldcs as % of world total	96.0	96.1			
(b) *Sisal*					
Developing countries					
Total	488	94	n.a.	n.a.	n.a.
Brazil	160	36	+2.0	+2.2	0.6 (1970-2)
Tanzania	145	23	−0.2	−4.3	8.4 (1970-2)
Angola	61	12	−0.3	−2.0	2.1 (1970-2)
Kenya	39	13	−3.5	−4.9	2.3 (1970-2)
Mexico	40	9	−0.9	—	0.3 (1970-2)
Madagascar	24	4	+2.5	—	2.2 (1969-71)
Mozambique	14	2	−4.4	−5.6	2.1 (1968-70)
World total	501	97	−2.1	−2.7	n.a.
Ldcs as % of world total	97.4	96.9			
(c) *Manila hemp*					
Developing countries					
Total	55	16	n.a.	n.a.	n.a.
Philippines	52	15	−3.9	−4.2	1.4 (1969-71)
World total	56	17	−3.9	−4.2	n.a.
Ldcs as % of world total	98.2	94.1			

Table A2.7. Exports of Minerals from Selected Countries

	Exports 1970-2 (annual average) Value $m	Share of minerals exports in each country's total exports (%)
(a) *Tin*		
Developing countries	638	1.1
Malaysia	318	17.9
Bolivia	102	52.5
Thailand	77	8.8
Indonesia	63	5.0
Nigeria	36	2.1
Zaire	20	3.0
World total	747	
Ldcs as % of world total	85.4	
(b) *Bauxite*		
Developing countries	202	0.4
Jamaica	89	25.5
Surinam	46	30.3
Guyana	19	13.3
Dominican Republic	15	5.7
Sierra Leone	7	6.5
Haiti	7	15.6
Indonesia	6	0.5
Malaysia	6	0.3
World total	278	
Ldcs as % of world total	72.7	
(c) *Manganese ore*		
Developing countries	109	0.2
Gabon	39	20.1
Brazil	32	1.0
India	15	0.7
Ghana	88	2.0
Zaire	6	0.9
Mauritius	5	6.7
Mexico	3	0.3
World total	194	
Ldcs as % of world total	56.2	

(d) *Copper*

Developing countries	2,431	4.2
Zambia	765	94.1
Chile	731	71.6
Zaire	449	68.3
Peru	208	21.7
Philippines	187	16.2
World total	4,495	n.a.
Ldcs as % of world total	54.1	

(e) *Phosphate rock*

Developing countries	229	0.4
Morocco	125	23.1
Gilbert & Ellice Islands (Banaba)	32	96.4
Tunisia	21	9.0
Togo	17	32.6
Senegal	14	8.5
Jordan	8	19.7
Israel	4	0
Algeria	4	0.4
World total	427	n.a.
Ldcs as % of world total	53.6	

(f) *Iron ore*

Developing countries	998	1.7
Brazil	226	7.0
Liberia	165	72.7
India	154	7.1
Venezuela	146	4.2
Mauritania	73	77.2
Peru	64	6.7
Chile	60	5.9
Swaziland	16	20.5
Malaysia	15	0.8
Sierra Leone	12	11.6
World total	2,649	n.a.
Ldcs as % of world total	37.7	

(g) *Zinc*

Developing countries	170	0.3
Peru	55	5.7
Mexico	50	3.2
Zaire	25	3.8
Bolivia	14	7.2
Zambia	13	1.6
World total	773	n.a.
Ldcs as % of world total	22.0	

(h) *Lead*

Developing countries	104	0.2
Peru	32	3.3
Mexico	21	1.3
Morocco	13	2.5
Namibia	13	25.9
Bolivia	7	3.7
Zambia	7	0.9
World total	494	n.a.
Ldcs as % of world total	20.2	

(i) *Silver*

Developing countries	110	0.2
Peru	58	6.0
Honduras	44	2.0
Mexico	30	1.9
Bolivia	15	7.5
Colombia	4	0.5
World total	578	n.a.
Ldcs as % of world total	19.0	

Source: World Bank.

FURTHER READING

The first section contains references to books and official publications selected respectively to give a broad coverage of the general issues of trade and development, and of the sources of current information on international trade and financial flows. The remaining sections include references for further reading on the main topics covered in Chapters 2–8. These reading lists are by no means exhaustive; further references will be found in the footnotes of each chapter.

GENERAL

Books

1. M. Barratt Brown, *The Economics of Imperialism,* Harmondsworth, Penguin, 1974.
2. P. Donaldson, *Worlds Apart: the Economic Gulf between Nations,* Harmondsworth, Penguin, 1971.
3. G. Helleiner, *International Trade and Economic Development,* Harmondsworth, Penguin, 1972.
4. H.G. Johnson, *Economic Policies towards Less Developed Countries,* London, Unwin University Books, 1967.
5. I. Livingstone (ed.), *Economic Policy for Development,* Harmondsworth, Penguin, 1971 (see Part II especially).
6. A.I. MacBean, *Export Instability and Economic Development,* London, Allen and Unwin, 1966.
7. H. Myint, *The Economics of Developing Countries,* London, Hutchinson University Library, 1967.
8. G. Myrdal, *Economic Theory and Underdeveloped Regions,* London, Duckworth, 1957.
9. S. Schiavo-Campo and H. Singer, *Perspectives of Economic Development,* New York, Houghton Mifflin, 1970.
10. D. Seers and L. Joy (ed.), *Development in a Divided World,* Harmondsworth, Penguin, 1971.
11. P. Streeten (ed.), *Trade Strategies for Development,* London, Macmillan, 1973.

Periodical Publications on International Trade and Financial Flows

12. Commonwealth Secretariat, *Tropical Products Quarterly.*

13. FAO, *Ceres* (monthly).
14. FAO, *Monthly Bulletin of Agricultural Economics and Statistics.*
15. FAO, *State of Food and Agriculture* (annual).
16. FAO, *World Production Yearbook.*
17. FAO, *World Trade Yearbook.*
18. GATT, *International Trade* (annual).
19. IMF, *Annual Report.*
20. IMF, *Balance of Payments Yearbook.*
21. IMF, *Direction of Trade* (monthly and annually).
22. IMF, *International Financial Statistics* (monthly).
23. OECD, *Development Cooperation: DAC Review* (annual).
24. UN, *Monthly Bulletin of Statistics.*
25. UNCTAD, *Handbook of International Trade and Development Statistics* (annual).
26. UNCTAD, *Trade in Manufactures of Developing Countries* (annual).

CHAPTER 2: THE INSTITUTIONAL BACKGROUND

27. *Beyond Diplomacy:* First Interim Report of the Special Committee of the Atlantic Council on Intergovernmental Organisations and Reorganisation, 1975.
28. D. Cordovez, *UNCTAD and Development Diplomacy: from confrontation to strategy,* special publication of *Journal of World Trade Law,* 1972.
29. G. Curzon, *Multilateral Commercial Diplomacy,* London, Michael Joseph, 1965.
30. K.W. Dam, *The GATT, Law and International Economic Organisation,* Chicago, 1970.
31. B. Gosović, *UNCTAD, Conflict and Compromise,* Leiden, Sijthoff, 1972.
32. H.W. Kramer, 'Changing Principles Governing International Trade', *Journal of World Trade Law,* May–June, 1974.
33. P. Tulloch, *The Politics of Preferences,* London, Croom Helm for ODI, 19
34. R.S. Walters, 'UNCTAD: Intervener between Rich and Poor States', *Journal of World Trade Law,* September–October, 1973.
35. S. Wells, 'The Developing Countries, GATT and UNCTAD', *International Affairs,* Vol. 45, No.1, 1969.

CHAPTER 3: COMMODITY TRADE AND ECONOMIC DEVELOPMENT

36. Brookings Institution, 'Trade in Primary Commodities: Conflict or Co-operation?' Washington, 1974.
37. P. Connelly and R. Perlman, *The Politics of Scarcity,* London, Oxford University Press for Royal Institute of International Affairs, 1975.
38. Commonwealth Secretariat, *Plantation Crops, Industrial Fibres,* and other periodic reviews of trade in specific commodity groups.
39. Commonwealth Secretariat, *Terms of Trade Policy for Primary Commodities,* Commonwealth Economic Papers, No.4, 1975.
40. S. Harris and T. Josling, 'Can World Commodity Prices be Explained?', *National Westminster Bank Quarterly Review,* August 1974.
41. T. Josling, 'The Commodities Revolution', Round Table, April 1974.
42. I. Litvak and C. Maule, 'Nationalisation in the Caribbean Bauxite Industry', *International Affairs,* January 1975.
43. C. Tugendhat and A. Hamilton, *Oil, the Biggest Business,* London, Eyre Methuen, 1975 (revised edition).
44. UNCTAD, *Problems of Raw Materials and Development,* TD/B/488, UN, New York, 1974.
45. UNCTAD, *An Integrated Programme for Commodities: Report by the Secretary-General of UNCTAD,* TD/B/488, Geneva, UN, 9 December 1974.
46. UNCTAD, *Commodities,* TD/184 (UNCTAD IV, Item 8, Main Policy Issues), Nairobi, May 1976.
47. UNCTAD, *Review of Recent Trends in World Commodity Markets,* TD/184/Supp.1.
48. UNCTAD, *Preservation of Purchasing Power of Developing Countries' Exports,* TD/184/Supp.2.
49. UNCTAD, *Relation between Prices of Commodity Exports from Developing Countries and Final Consumer Prices,* TD/184/Supp.3
50. UNCTAD, *Marketing and Distribution Systems for Primary Commodities,* TD/184/Supp.4. See also Nos. 6, 9, 12, 13-17, 93.

CHAPTER 4: COMPETING AGRICULTURAL GOODS: FOOD, FODDER AND FARM POLICIES

51. Commonwealth Secretariat, *Vegetable Oils and Oilseeds.*
52. S. Harris and G. Hagelberg, 'Effect of the Lomé Convention on the World's Sugar Producers', *ODI Review,* No.2, 1975.

53. International Sugar Organisation, *Annual Reports.*
54. International Sugar Organisation, *Statistical Bulletins.*
55. D. Gale Johnson, *World Agriculture in Disarray,* London, Fontana Books, 1973.
56. D.B. Jones, 'Food Interdependence and Europe', *ODI Review,* No.2, 1975.
57. Ministry of Overseas Development, Advisory Committee on Protein, *British Aid and the Relief of Malnutrition,* ODA, July, 1974 (and HMSO, 1975).
58. OECD, *Agricultural Policy in Japan,* Paris, 1974.
59. J.A. Schnittker, 'Grain Reserves – Now', *Foreign Policy,* 20, December, 1975.
60. U. Wasserman, 'Import Regulations for Meat into Europe', *Journal of World Trade Law,* March–April, 1974. See also Nos.13-17.

CHAPTER 5: LDCS AND THE EXPORT OF MANUFACTURES

61. G. Adams, 'New Trends in International Business, *Acta Oeconomica,* Vol.7, Nos. 3-4, 1971.
62. B. Balassa, *The Structure of Protection in Developing Countries,* Baltimore, Johns Hopkins Press, 1971.
63. G. Helleiner, 'Manufactured Exports from Less Developed Countries and Multinational Firms', *Economic Journal,* March 1973.
64. H. Hughes (ed.), *Prospects for Partnership,* Baltimore, Johns Hopkins Press, 1972.
65. M. Kidron, *Pakistan's Trade with Eastern Bloc Countries,* New York, Praeger, 1972.
66. I.M.D. Little, T. Scitovsky and M. Scott, *Industry and Trade in Some Developing Countries,* London, OECD and Oxford University Press, 1970.
67. D. Morawetz, 'Employment Implications of Industrialisation in Developing Countries: a Survey', *Economic Journal,* September, 1974.
68. C. Pestieau and J. Henry, *Non-Tariff Barriers as a Problem in International Development,* Private Planning Association of Canada, 1972.
69. UNCTAD, *Liberalisation of Tariff and Non-Tariff Barriers,* TD/B/C.2/R.1, 1969, and TD/B/C.2/83, 1969
70. UNCTAD, *Liberalisation of Non-Tariff Barriers,* TD/B/C.2/R.5, June 1973.
71. UNCTAD, *Review of the Schemes of Generalised Preferences,* TD/B/C.5/9, 1973, and TD/B/C.5/22, 1974.

72. UNCTAD, *The Kennedy Round: Estimated Effects on Trade Barriers*, TD/6, Rev.1, 1968.
73. J. Winpenny, Brazil: *Manufactured Exports and Government Policy*, London, Latin American Publications Fund, 1972.
See also: 26.

CHAPTER 6: DIRECT FOREIGN PRIVATE INVESTMENT AND LDCS' TRADE

74. J. Baranson, *Industrial Technologies for Developing Countries*, New York, Praeger, 1969.
75. J.H. Dunning (ed.), *International Investment*, Harmondsworth, Penguin, 1972.
76. J.H. Dunning (ed.), *The Multinational Enterprise*, London, Allen and Unwin, 1971.
77. S.G. Friedman and J.P. Béguin, *Joint International Business Ventures in Developing Countries*, New York, Columbia University Press, 1971.
78. S. Lall, 'Transfer Pricing by Multinational Manufacturing Firms', *Oxford Bulletin of Economics and Statistics*, Vol.35, No.3, August, 1973.
79. H. Radice, *International Firms and Modern Imperialism*, Harmondsworth, Penguin, 1975.
80. G.L. Reuber, *Private Foreign Investment in Development*, London, Oxford University Press, 1973.
81. C. Sebestyen, *The Outward Urge: Japanese Investment World-Wide*, London, Economist Intelligence Unit, 1972.
82. C.V. Vaitsos, *Policies in Foreign Direct Investment and Economic Development in Latin America*, Institute of Development Studies, University of Sussex, Communication 106.
83. R. Vernon, *Sovereignty at Bay*, Harmondsworth, Penguin, 1973.
84. UN, *Multinational Corporations in World Development*, ST/ETA/190, 1973.
85. UN, *Report of the Group of Eminent Persons to Study the Role of Multinational Corporations on Development and on International Relations*, E/5000/Add I (Part 1), May, 1974.
86. UNCTAD, *Channels and Mechanisms for the Transfer of Technology from Developed to Developing Countries*, TD/B/AC.11/5, 1971.
87. UNCTAD, *Restrictive Business Practices*, TD/B/C.2/104/Rev. 1, New York, 1971. See also Nos. 42, 43, 61, 63.

CHAPTER 7: FINANCE AND INTERNATIONAL TRADE

88. H. Aufricht, *The Fund Agreement,* Essays in International Finance, No. 23, Princeton, 1969.
89. T. Hayter, *Aid as Imperialism,* Harmondsworth, Penguin, 1971.
90. F. Hirsch, *Money International,* Harmondsworth, Penguin, 1969.
91. IBRD/IDA, *Annual Reports.*
92. K. Packenham and J. Gore-Booth, 'The Eurocurrency Market as a Source of Finance for the Developing World', ODI Review, No.2, 1974.
93. Y.S. Park, *The Link between SDRs and Development Finance,* Essays in International Finance, No.100, Princeton, 1973.
94. C. Payer, *The Debt Trap,* Harmondsworth, Penguin, 1974.
95. UNCTAD, *The Indexation of Prices,* TD/B/503, Supp. I, 1974. See also Nos. 19-20, 22, 23, 39, 100.

CHAPTER 8: ECONOMIC COOPERATION AMONG LDCS

96. B. Balassa, 'Towards a Theory of Economic Integration', *Kyklos,* Vol.14, Fasc. 1, 1961.
97. J. Grunwald, M.S. Wionczek and M. Carnoy, *Latin American Economic Integration and US Policy,* Brookings Institution, Washington, 1972.
98. K. Kahnert, P. Richards, E. Stoutesdijk and P. Thomopoulos, *Economic Integration among Developing Countries,* OECD Development Centre, Paris, 1969.
99. P. Robson (ed.), *International Economic Integration,* Harmondsworth, Penguin, 1972.
100. M. and F. Stewart, 'Developing Countries' Trade and Liquidity: a New Approach', *The Banker,* March 1972.
101. United Nations, *Current Problems of Economic Integration* (series).
102. United Nations, *Journal of Development Planning,* No. 7, 1974.
103. UN Economic and Social Council, *Economic Cooperation Schemes in Developing Regions: an Appraisal of Mechanisms, Policies and Problems,* E/AC.54/L.54, 1973. See also Nos. 10, 11, 82.

GLOSSARY OF TERMS*

Ad valorem duty: an *import duty* levied on the value of imports, generally expressed as a percentage rate to be applied to the declared value (usually *cif*) of the imported product. The absolute amount of duty levied thus varies with the declared value. Most import duties are of this kind.

Alternative duty: an import duty which consists of an *ad valorem duty* rate plus a *specific duty* rate, quoted together as alternatives. The duty applied will be the higher of the two. This form of duty tends to be used to prevent the absolute amount of duty falling below a given minimum when import prices fall – as when only *ad valorem* duties apply – and is found where the duty is levied for revenue as well as protective purposes.

Bound tariffs: tariffs which have been negotiated between contracting parties in GATT are said to be bound. Bound tariff rates are set out in schedules of concessions exchanged among contracting parties to the GATT. In general, contracting parties undertake not to change bound tariff rates except through a formal process of multilateral renegotiation, or in specified emergency situations such as short-term action to protect a country's balance of payments.

Brussels Tariff Nomenclature (BTN): see *Classification of trade.*

Cartel: central selling organisation of producers, who would otherwise compete with each other. The organisation assigns output quotas to members and fixes the price for the produce concerned, usually at a level above that which would prevail in a free market.

Classification of trade: internationally traded products are classified for statistical purposes and for the purpose of customs *tariffs.* The *Standard International Trade Classification, Revised, SITC (R),* or more usually just *SITC,* is chiefly used for statistical purposes and provides the basis for most trade statistics presented in this book. Customs tariff classification systems tend to vary but the *Customs Co-operation Council Nomenclature (CCCN)* – formerly the *Brussels Tariff Nomenclature, BTN* – used by the EEC among others – is the system most frequently encountered.

The *SITC* consists of ten main product sections numbered 0–9 Each of these contains divisions, subdivisions, and sub-subdivisions, the latter often being referred to as the four-digit-level of

*See Chapter 7 for definitions of terms used with reference to balance of payments.

classification. Thus, for instance, fresh apples are classified under section 0, food and live animals; division 05, fruit and vegetables; subdivision 051, fresh fruit and nuts; sub-division 051.4 giving the SITC, four-digit-level classification for fresh apples. The main SITC product sections together with the main products in each of them are listed below.

SITC (R) Code Code	SITC(R) product sections and main products	
	Title	Main products
0	Food and live animals	livestock; meat; dairy products; fish; cereals; fruit and vegetables; sugar; coffee; tea; cocoa; spices; animal fodder; including preparations of the above.
1	Beverages and tobacco	alcoholic and non-alcoholic beverages; tobacco and tobacco products.
2	Crude materials, inedible, excluding fuels	hides and skins; oil seeds, nuts and kernels; crude rubber; wood, pulp and paper; textile fibres; crude fertilisers and minerals; ores; scrap and waste.
3	Mineral fuels, lubricants and related materials	coal; petroleum and petroleum products; natural and manufactured gas; electric energy.
4	Animal and vegetable oils and fats	crude, refined and processed oils, fats and waxes.
5	Chemicals	chemical elements and compounds; mineral tar and petrochemicals; dyes and paints; medical and pharmaceutical products; essential oils and toilet products; fertilisers; explosives; plastics and resins, etc.
6	Manufactured goods, classified chiefly by material	basic manufactures of wood, leather, rubber, paper, textiles, cement, glass, ceramics, minerals, ferrous and non-ferrous metals, etc.

7	Machinery and transport equipment	electrical and non-electrical machinery, equipment for all modes of transport.
8	Miscellaneous manufactured articles, not specified elsewhere	plumbing, heating and lighting fixtures and fittings; furniture travel goods; clothing; footwear; precision instruments etc.
9	Miscellaneous transactions and commodities, not specified elsewhere	postal packages, pets, armanents, coins, gold.

It will be seen that the SITC sections 0–4 correspond roughly with what may be termed 'primary commodities' and SITC sections 5–8 with what may be termed 'manufactures', although this definition is far from adequate (see also Chapter 3, p.92, and Chapter 5, p.154).

The CCCN consists of 99 sections or chapters. Each chapter is subdivided, each subdivision having a four-digit code number: thus for instance, CCCN Chapter 09 consists of coffee, tea, maté, and spices; CCCN Ch.09.02 consists of tea. At the four-digit level, each CCCN heading or subdivision corresponds to a SITC four-digit code classification,e.g. the CCCN heading for tea, 09.02, corresponds with the SITC code for tea, 074.1. The ordering of products under the two systems is, however, different. Under CCCN, the first twenty-four chapters comprise processed and unprocessed agricultural goods and the remainder comprise industrial raw materials and products.

Commodity terms of trade (otherwise known as the *net barter terms of trade):* the ratio between the unit price of exports and the unit price of imports, measured over time, i.e. $\frac{\text{export price index}}{\text{import price index}}$ where the base year for each index is the same (= 100). This ratio measures the changes in the purchasing power of a unit of exports over a unit of imports. It is said to improve when the unit price of exports rises faster (or falls more slowly) than the unit import price and to deteriorate when the latter rises faster (or falls more slowly) than the unit export price.

Common external tariff: see *Customs union.*

Compound duty: import duty consisting of an *ad valoren* duty rate and a *specific duty rate,* both of which are applied to the imported product in question.

Customs union: a *free trade area,* involving the removal of internal import duties and the establishment of a *common external tariff* on trade with non-members.

Dumping: the practice of exporting goods at prices below those prevailing in the domestic market of the exporting country.

Economic union: a *customs union* which also provides for the free movement of capital and labour between member countries and for the harmonisation of various economic policies among member states.

Effective protection: a term applied to the protective effect of import duties on the *value-added* of the foreign supplier (see *nominal protection).* The notion of effective protection derives from the fact that *import duty* rates tend to be low on unprocessed goods and to be higher the greater the degree of processing – or value-added – the imported product has received. This phenomenon, known as *tariff escalation,* often has the effect of rendering the protection afforded to domestic producers of processed goods greater than is apparent from the nominal import duty rate. The measure of effective protection is the *effective tariff rate.* To give an example: suppose an importing country imposes a zero rate of duty on cocoa beans but a 10 per cent import duty on cocoa powder. Now, suppose the *cif* value of a ton of cocoa is £100 but if that ton of cocoa were processed, £150. The value-added in processing the beans into powder is thus £50. The import duty raises the cost of cocoa powder by £15 to £165. But since the duty is only levied on cocoa if it is turned into powder, it effectively falls on the £50 value-added. The effective tariff or duty rate is thus $\frac{15}{50}$ or 30 per cent. In other words, the deterrent effect of the import duty on the foreign cocoa supplier intending to increase his export earnings by further processing is considerably greater than the 10 per cent nominal duty rate would imply; and so too is the protection afforded the domestic cocoa powder producers.*

Fas (free alongside): see *Valuation of trade.*

Fob (free on board): see *Valuation of trade.*

---

*If cocoa beans carried a duty of more than zero, say 5 per cent, a similar calculation would follow. The extra duty levied is £15 minus the duty that would have been levied on the cocoa beans (£5), resulting in an effective tariff rate of $\frac{10}{50}$ or 20 per cent.

For (free on rail): see *Valuation of trade.*

Free trade area: a group of countries which grant each other preferential tariff treatment with a view to removing import duties on substantially all trade between members.

General rate of duty: the *tariff* applied by a given country to imports from countries with which it has no *mfn* or *preferential* trade agreement. It is above the *mfn* rate. With most countries being signatories of GATT, many countries no longer operate a general rate.

Import duty: a tax on imports levied for protective, revenue, or balance-of-payments reasons. See also *ad valorem, alternative, compound* and *specific duties.*

Import licensing: a system which may be applied to various imported products whereby importers are required to obtain a licence in order to import the products affected. It is used to supervise imports, e.g. to check that imports meet domestic health or safety standards, and to regulate imports. In the latter case, licensing may be discretionary, i.e. the issuing authority may withhold licences on an *ad hoc* basis; or it may be operated in the context of *import quotas,* in which case the issue of licences is stopped when the quota is filled.

Import quotas: a predetermined limit to the level of imports of a given product that may have access to the importing country's market during a specified period. Quotas may be defined in terms of volume or value and may be applied to imports from a specific country of origin, i.e. *bilateral quotas,* or to imports from all sources, i.e. *global quotas.*

Income elasticity of demand: the measure of the response of demand for a product to a change in income. Demand is generally expected to rise with an increase in income and vice-versa. If expenditure on a product increases or falls proportionately faster than income, demand for that product is said to be *income-elastic;* if proportionately slower, it is said to be *income-inelastic.* Income elasticity may vary at different income levels: for instance, at high income levels, demand for basic foodstuffs is likely to be more income-elastic than at low income levels.

Income terms of trade: measures the change in purchasing power of exports making allowance for changes in export volume, i.e. the

$$\frac{\text{export price index} \times \text{export volume index}}{\text{import price index}}$$

where the base year is the same for all indices. This measure thus gives an indication of the purchasing power of a country's export earnings over unit imports. Since a rise in export volume may more than offset a fall in export prices, a country's income terms of trade may show an improvement when its *commodity terms of trade* show a deterioration – or vice-versa.

Landed cost: see *Valuation of trade.*

Margin of preference: the absolute difference between the *preferential duty rate* on an imported product and the *mfn duty rate:* e.g. if the preferential duty rate were 10 per cent and the mfn duty rate 20 per cent, the imported product concerned would enjoy a margin of preference of 10 per cent.

Mfn (most-favoured-nation) rate of duty: the rate of *import duty* applied by a country to imports from countries with which it has an mfn agreement. An mfn agreement binds each party to treat imports from other parties at least as favourably as imports from countries which are not parties to the agreement. Most trading nations are parties to the mfn agreement under GATT. In certain circumstances, however, the latter allows signatories to treat imports from some countries *more* favourably than the *mfn* treatment, and, in practice, the mfn rates of duty tend to be the highest import duty rates: a country whose exports are subject to mfn treatment is arguably a 'least-favoured nation' (see Chapter 2, pp.55-6).

Monetary union: a group of countries with a common currency and monetary policy.

Net barter terms of trade: see *Commodity terms of trade.*

Nominal protection: the protective effect of import duties, measured in terms of the rise in price of the imported product resulting from the application of the import duty.* It is known as nominal protection because the rise in price is equivalent to the *nominal rate of import duty:* e.g. a 10 per cent duty will bring about a 10 per cent rise in price.

Non-tariff barrier (NTB): a trade restricting policy instrument other than an *import duty,* e.g. an import quota. (See also Chapters 2 and 5.)

---

*The initial imposition of an import duty, or any other sales tax, may lead the producer to cut his costs or profits so as to avoid increasing the price of his product to the consumer by the full amount of tax. The absorption of part or all of the tax by the producer does not alter the fact that his selling price will be increased by the amount of the tax.

Payments union: a group of countries with a common currency and monetary policy.

Preferential rate of duty: a rate of *import duty,* lower than the *mfn rate,* which is applied on a discriminatory basis to imports from certain countries. Thus, for instance, preferential rates of duty are applied by developed countries, including the EEC, to certain imports from ldcs under the Generalised System of Preferences (see Chapter 5), and by EEC member states to imports from each other under the Treaty of Rome. A preferential rate of duty or preference may entail complete or partial exemption from the mfn rate.

Price elasticity of demand: measure of the response of demand for a particular product, or products, to changes in its, or their, price. Generally demand is expected to increase when prices fall and to drop when they rise. If an increase or drop in price results in a proportionately greater decrease or increase in demand, the latter is said to be *elastic;* a rise in price reduces revenue (price × quantity) from sales of the product and a fall increases it. Conversely if the change in demand is proportionately smaller than the price change, demand is said to be *inelastic;* revenue thus increases with a price rise and falls when the price drops. *Unitary elasticity* is said to obtain when no change in revenue occurs: demand changes are in proportion with price changes. Price elasticity of demand may vary as tastes change and at different price levels.

Price elasticity of supply: the counterpart of *price elasticity of demand.* Supply is *inelastic* when a change in price brings little or no change in the quantity of goods offered for sale and *elastic* when a large change results. Generally, supply tends to be inelastic in the short-term and elastic in the longer term.

Specific duty: an *import duty,* fixed in money terms levied on imports by volume, e.g. per kg, cubic metre. The duty thus levied increases relative to import value as import prices fall and decreases as prices rise.

Standard International Trade Classification (SITC): see *Classification of trade.*

Tariff: a classified list of import duties, each item or rate of duty relating to a particular product in the classification (e.g. BTN). (The term is also frequently used as if it were synonomous with *import duty.*) Countries may vary the rates of duty applied according to the product's country of origin, as when *preferential* or *general rates of duty* are applied as well as mfn rates, and each set of duties applicable to imports from specific countries or groups of countries is referred to as a *tariff column.* Individual countries may thus have single column, two-column and more tariffs, e.g. a country operating a tariff with mfn rates and one set of preferential rates would have a two-column tariff.

Tariff escalation: see *Effective protection.*

Tariff quota: restriction by volume or, more usually, value on imports from a preferred source that can receive preferential tariff treatment, as, for instance, applied under the EEC's GSP (see Chapter 5). When a tariff quota is filled, the imports concerned from the preference-receiving country or countries are subject to the *mfn rate of duty,* instead of the preferential rate.

Terms of trade: measure of the terms and the changes in the terms on which goods are exchanged between countries or groups of countries, or on which one type of goods, e.g. primary commodities, is exchanged for another type of goods, e.g. manufactures. There are several terms of trade measures: see *Commodity terms of trade,* and *Income terms of trade.*

Valuation of trade: for statistical and customs purposes, goods traded internationally are valued at several points in transit. The two most common valuations are when goods notionally leave the country of origin *(fob)* and when the notionally enter the country of destination *(cif). Fob* or *free on board* is the value of the product plus the cost of delivering it to the quayside – or domestic point of departure – and of loading on to the ship – or other means of transport. *For* or *free on rail* is the specific term sometimes used when the goods leave the country of origin by rail. *Cif* or *cost, insurance and freight,* is the fob value plus the cost of transit, insurance and freight, but excluding unloading charges and customs duties, etc. Exports are normally valued fob, and imports cif in national accounts, but both may be valued fob in international trade statistics, and sometimes in national balance of payments accounts when additional, cif, costs are included as invisibles (see Chapter 7). Import duties are generally levied on the cif valuation. Two other valuations may be noted, namely *free alongside, fas,* which is fob minus the cost of loading; and *landed cost* which is *cif* plus the cost of unloading and clearance, but not customs duties.

Value-added: that part of the value of a product which is added during processing. See also *Effective protection.*

Variable levies: these are import duties which are not set as a percentage rate or, a specific amount, but are varied so as to ensure that import prices reach a certain minimum level, often so as to eliminate the possibility of price competition (unlike other import duties). For this reason, variable levies are often regarded as a *non-tariff barrier.* They are an important instrument in the EEC's Common Agricultural Policy.

Voluntary export restraints (VER): these are effectively bilateral quotas applied by the exporting rather than the importing country. They are 'voluntarily' imposed after pressure from the importing country, and are generally seen as a means for exporters to prevent the imposition of more restrictive measures by the importing country.

ABBREVIATIONS

ACP	African, Caribbean and Pacific EEC Associates under Lomé
ACM	Andean Common Market and Community
ASEAN	Association of South East Asian Nations
CACM	Central American Common Market
CAP	Common Agricultural Policy (of EEC)
CARICOM	Caribbean Common Market and Community (formerly CARIFTA)
CARIFTA	Caribbean Free Trade Area (now CARICOM)
CCCN	Customs Co-operation Council Nomenclature
CEAO	Communauté Economique de l'Afrique de l'Ouest (formerly UDEAO)
cif	cost, insurance and freight
CIPEC	Intergovernmental Council of Copper Exporting Countries
CMEA	Council for Mutual Economic Aid (or COMECON)
COMECON	see CMEA
CPA	Cocoa Producers Alliance
CSA	Commonwealth Sugar Agreement
DAC	Development and Assistance Committee (of OECD)
DOM	Départements d'Outremer
EAC	East African Community
ECAFE	UN Economic Commission for Asia and the Far East (now ESCAP)
ECLA	UN Economic Commission for Latin America
ECOSOC	UN Economic and Social Committee
ECOWAS	Economic Community of West African States
EEC	European Economic Community
EFTA	European Free Trade Area
ESCAP	UN Economic and Social Commission for Asia and the Pacific (formerly ECAFE)
FAO	Food and Agricultural Organisation
fas	free alongside
fob	free on board
for	free on rail
GATT	General Agreement on Tariffs and Trade
GDP	Gross Domestic Product

GNP	Gross National Product
GSP	Generalised System of Preferences
IBA	International Bauxite Association
IBRD	International Bank for Reconstruction and Development (World Bank)
ICA	International Coffee Agreement
ICO	International Coffee Organisation
IDA	International Development Association
ILO	International Labour Organisation
IMF	International Monetary Fund
ITA	International Tin Agreement
ITC	International Trade Centre (UNCTAD/GATT)
LAFTA	Latin American Free Trade Area
ldc	less developed country
MFA	Multifibre Textile Arrangement
mfn	most favoured nation
MNC	Multinational Corporation
NIEO	New International Economic Order
NTB	Non-Tariff Barrier (or NTM)
NTM	Non-Tariff Measure
OAPEC	Organisation of Arab Petroleum Exporting Countries
OECD	Organisation for Economic Co-operation and Development
OPEC	Organisation of Petroleum Exporting Countries
RCD	Regional Cooperation for Development
SDR	Special Drawing Right
SITC	Standard International Trade Classification
STABEX	EEC export earnings stabilisation scheme
UBEC	Union of Banana Exporting Countries (or UPEB)
UDEAC	Union Douanière et Economique de l'Afrique Centrale
UDEAO	Union Douanière et Economique de l'Afrique de l'Ouest (now CEAO)
UN	United Nations
UNCTAD	United Nations Conference on Trade and Development
UNDP	United Nations Development Programme
UPEB	Union de Paises Exportadores de Banana (or UBEC)
VER	Voluntary Export Restraint

INDEX

Further Reading, Glossary of Terms, Abbreviations, and individual countries and commodities only in Tables are not included in the Index.